PREHISTORIC LIFE

DAVID NORMAN

PREHISTORIC LIFE

THE RISE OF THE VERTEBRATES

with illustrations by John Sibbick

MACMILLAN USA

Dedication

This book was written as a sequel to my earlier book, *Dinosaur!*
and attempts to draw a broader picture of the evolution of life. First and
foremost it is for Emma and Andrew, who have had to bear with my
constant busy-ness over the past year. Room must also be made for a special
mention of the indefatigable "Nightingale Warblers". This book would
not have been possible but for the work of many palaeobiologists, some of
whose works appear in the bibliography. However, it is also offered
as a belated vote of thanks to Sir David Attenborough, who is, as he put it, a
"46-vintage" member of the Sedgwick club here at Cambridge,
who has been a source of support and inspiration over the last few years.

MACMILLAN
A Prentice Hall Macmillan Company
15 Columbus Circle
New York, NY 10023

Text © 1994 David Norman

Originated and simultaneously published in the UK by:
Boxtree Ltd
Broadwall House
21 Broadwall
London SE1 9PL

MACMILLAN is a registered trademark of Macmillan, Inc.

Library of Congress Cataloging-in-Publication Data

Norman, David, 1930-
   Prehistoric life: the rise of the vertebrates / David Norman.
      p.   cm.
   Includes bibliographical references and index.
   ISBN 0-671-79940-1
   1. Vertebrates, Fossil — Juvenile literature.   2. Evolutionary
paleobiology — Juvenile literature.   [1. Vertebrates. Fossil.
2. Prehistoric animals.   3. Evolution.]   I. Title.
QE842.N67   1994
566 — dc20   94-14091
                                                                    CIP
                                                                    AC

ISBN 0-671-79940-1

Edited by Esther Jagger
Designed by Kit Johnson
Colour Origination by Fotographics
Manufactured in Spain by Printer Industria Gráfica, S.A., Barcelona

10 9 8 7 6 5 4 3 2 1

Cover illustration by © John Sibbick

CONTENTS

INTRODUCTION

LIFE ON OUR PLANET probably began just over 3,500 million years ago. Rocks in Australia which date back to this time have yielded wafer-like traces of sediment called stromatolites, which were left behind by colonies of simple microscopic organisms. Tracing the history of life over such an immense period of time is no easy task. In fact it cannot be done comprehensively in a book of this size, so I am going to have to cheat a little. The subtitle, *The Rise of the Vertebrates*, gives the game away. While I intend to sketch out the origins of life and its early development until about 500 million years ago, after that time I shall devote myself largely to describing the evolution of vertebrates or backboned animals – the group to which humans belong. More specifically even than that, in later chapters I shall concentrate on land vertebrates.

There are two reasons for this emphasis. First, I want to focus in on the evolution of land vertebrates and tell at least part of their story as we understand it today, because I think it is particularly interesting. Second, I feel it is important that human beings, as a species of land vertebrate, should understand something of their position in the history of life. It is all too easy for us to subscribe, consciously or subconsciously, to the view that we are the most important creatures on Earth, and that all other species are here for our pleasure or amusement. It may pain readers to hear this, but I believe that the vast majority of humans suffer, albeit subconsciously, from these delusions of grandeur. It is revealed in the callous way in which we have exploited and polluted our planet and in the fact that we have been responsible for a minor mass-extinction of vertebrates over the past ten thousand years of our developing civilization. Saddest of all is that we do this inhuman thing through apathy and procrastination – we simply let it happen, metaphorically shrugging our shoulders and carrying on as usual. Yet we, as our species name rather arrogantly pronounces, are the "wise man," *Homo sapiens*; we have the most highly developed intellect, resourcefulness, and all-around ability of all species on the planet, and above all the technological sophistication to avoid many of the unpleasant side effects of our industrialization and staggering population growth.

We owe our Earth a little more than a shrug of the shoulders – we owe it endeavor and commitment. By unraveling a few of the trials and tribulations of the vertebrates during the 530 million years of their traceable history, I hope I can show you why. The culmination of this evolutionary story is, inevitably, the human race – but will life on Earth end at this point, or within a few hundred or thousand years, as a result of apathy or mismanagement? Let us hope not.

ABOVE *Some of the earliest clues concerning life on Earth come from layered masses of limestone known as stromatolites (literally "layered stones"), which are the petrified remains of blue-green algae. These are from South Africa.*

RIGHT *This beautiful illustration from Audubon's* Birds of America *depicts the passenger pigeon, a bird that was hunted to extinction in the nineteenth century – a tragic example of human inhumanity to other species.*

Passenger Pigeon. Male 1. F.2.
Columba Migratoria.

1

THE ORIGIN OF THE UNIVERSE

BIG BANG, PLANET EARTH, AND
THE PROCESS OF EVOLUTION

THE MOST PLAUSIBLE of all the explanations of the origin of the Universe has been popularized by the cosmologist Professor Stephen Hawking's *A Brief History of Time*. According to this theory the Universe was born (if that is the correct word) 15,000 million years ago. The entire contents of the known Universe originated from a point in Space known as a singularity – a point of infinitely small size and infinite density. If this seems impossible, it must be remembered that at this stage the laws of physics did not yet exist, and Time had not begun. This singularity then began to expand in an immense explosion, the so-called "Big Bang." As it did so, matter and the natural laws came into being. A very faint microwave "background radiation" has been detected in the far reaches of the Universe and is thought to be a remnant of the Big Bang.

*Our own galaxy, the Milky Way (LEFT),
and the celestial explosions of supernovae
(ABOVE) may look impressive, but they pale into
insignificance when compared to the immensity
of the Universe and to the "Big Bang"
which originated it.*

ABOVE *An artist's impression of the Milky Way, a spiral galaxy about 100,000 light years across and containing about 100,000 million stars. The red circle indicates the position of our own Solar System within it.*

RIGHT *If it were possible to obtain photographs from space telescopes looking back on our own Solar System, this is the kind of thing we might see. The Sun is at the center, with the planets orbiting elliptically. Planetary rings are also now known on Jupiter, Uranus, and Neptune. Between Mars and Jupiter lies the asteroid belt, composed of thousands of planet-like bodies up to 625 miles (1,000km) across.*

Today the Universe still appears to be expanding in all directions across space, because the color spectrum produced by distant stars shows a distinct "red shift" – a distortion of the wavelength of light produced by the stars as they move away from one another at sub-light (though still immense) speeds. This is a form of the familiar "Doppler effect" which causes the sound of a train whistle to change pitch, increasing as the train approaches and decreasing as it moves away from the observer. The background radiation is in fact a very short wavelength – gamma rays, X-rays, and light – but we detect it as comparatively long microwaves because it is moving away from us at a huge speed, and has therefore been shifted a great deal.

The matter created by the Big Bang was not spread evenly across space, and in some areas clumped together through gravitational attraction so that the matter condensed to form galaxies, swirling masses of dust and gas. Within the galaxies themselves this matter clumped further, so that some of it formed denser clouds. These continued to collapse under the influence of their own gravity. As this happened, collisions between their atoms produced such heat and pressure that the atoms began to fuse together in a nuclear reaction, giving out energy – in fact a star was created, which began to shine. As soon as the energy given out by the reaction balanced the gravitational energy of the collapsing matter, the young star would stabilize. Then the remaining dust and gas spinning around the star could begin to condense into planets and moons. Our own Solar System – the only planetary system we can observe in any detail – confirms this theory. All the planets move around the Sun in the same direction, and they are made of the same kind of matter as the Sun – though the inner planets have lost most of their lighter elements, blasted away by the intense radiation of the violent new star before it settled down.

The Earth is about 4,500 million years old, although the oldest known rocks date back only about 3,800 million years. The Moon and the planets seem to be the same age as the Earth; samples of Moon rock brought back by the various Russian and US space missions have been dated at between 4,600 and 3,100 million years

such as silicon, oxygen, and aluminium. But the separation is not complete. Throughout the mixture there are various radioactive elements including isotopes of uranium, thorium and potassium. These steadily decay, giving off heat. It is this heat which is responsible for the dynamic structure of the Earth.

Moving from the center outwards, the Earth consists of a partly molten metal core, surrounded by a "shell" of molten rock called the mantle, which in turn is enveloped by the crust. This crust – the surface of the Earth – is a relatively thin skin of cool rock, soil, and water. In the areas where the great continents lie, that skin may be up to 40 miles (60km) thick. On the floor of the oceans, however, only 3 miles (5km) separates the sea floor from the mantle.

Viewed without its covering of water, the Earth could be seen to be divided into a series of giant slabs, known as tectonic plates. Each plate consists of a piece of thick continental crust and thinner, low-relief ocean crust; the majority of plates include both kinds. Most of the boundaries between plates lie under the oceans; these may be either mid-oceanic ridges, forming underwater mountain ranges, or deep trenches, which frequently border the edges of continents. At the ridges molten rock bubbles up from the mantle, creating new oceanic crust and causing the plates to spread slowly apart. The trenches are places where two plates are moving together. One slides below the other and is forced down into the mantle, where it melts. This often causes violent activity, pushing up mountain ranges such as the Andes and creating volcanoes.

This remarkable arrangement means that the surface of the Earth is always in motion, no matter how permanent or fixed our own patch of the planet might seem. The tectonic plates act like huge conveyor belts carrying their cargoes of continents with them, and are "driven" by the heat rising from the Earth's core. Between the hot inner part of the mantle and the cooler layer just beneath the Earth's crust there are likely to be circulating currents of fluid mantle material – rising in some areas, spreading out beneath the crust, cooling and becoming more dense, and then falling back toward the core where it will become reheated and start the cycle going once again.

The effects of the moving continents

The way in which the plates move depends critically on the size of the Earth. There are just enough hot radioactive elements to allow the mantle to be molten but the outer crust to be solid. If the Earth were larger it would be so hot that the surface was molten, as on Jupiter. If it were smaller it would be "frozen" solid, like

old. The rock of the Moon is reminiscent of the basaltic rocks found on the floor of the oceans. However, Moon rocks may have been formed in a somewhat different way. The interior of the Moon has solidified, so its surface is not actively moving like that of the Earth (see below); nor is it eroded by the atmosphere. As a result the Moon presents us with a picture of the past virtually frozen in time.

STRUCTURE OF THE EARTH

As the Earth condensed, the heavier elements concentrated at its center. Our planet (like other planets) therefore has a dense core, consisting mostly of iron and nickel, surrounded by layers mostly of lighter elements the Moon. This has affected many aspects of the history of life on Earth. Moving continents act as rafts, carrying organisms from one part of the world to another over periods of millions of years. Moving continents change climates by altering meteorological conditions and patterns of ocean circulation. Continents may shift across climate zones. For example, southern Africa moved from Antarctic to tropical latitudes as the continent drifted northward between the end of the Carboniferous Period, 286 million years ago (mya), and the end of the Triassic Period, 210 million years ago. This shifting of land masses had a profound effect on the animals which were living there during this time.

MOVING ROCK, SEDIMENTS, AND FOSSILS

The huge forces which move the plates distort the rocks in them, causing layers of rock to rise, fall, and fold. In the heat and pressure below the surface, rocks can be bent as easily as a piece of white-hot iron. The rocks on the surface weather – they are worn away by water and wind, or cracked by frost. The pieces are carried away by rivers, forming sediments which settle to make layers of new rock. These sediments may fall on and cover the remains of animals and plants, which eventually become fossils enclosed in solid rock.

THE DYNAMIC EARTH

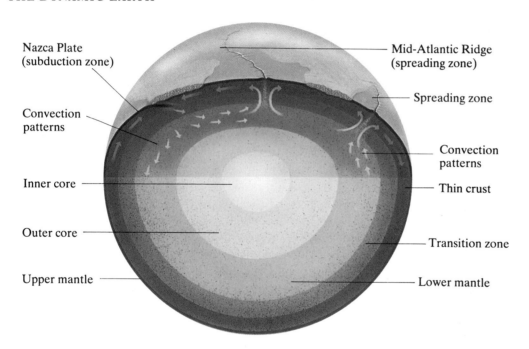

Nazca Plate (subduction zone)

Convection patterns

Inner core

Outer core

Upper mantle

Mid-Atlantic Ridge (spreading zone)

Spreading zone

Convection patterns

Thin crust

Transition zone

Lower mantle

Layering and its effects
LEFT *This cutaway picture shows how the Earth is layered, with an extremely hot molten core, a cooler mantle zone in which there are circulating (convection) currents of material, and a thin crust like the skin on a peach. The circulation of mantle fluids which rise and spread apart in places, and then cool and sink back toward the center, creates areas of tension (spreading ridges – pulling the crust apart) and compression (subduction zones – pushing crust areas together to form chains of volcanoes, mountains and earthquake zones).*

Trenches and plates
RIGHT *Removing the oceans shows the texture of the Earth's surface. The mid-oceanic spreading ridge (e.g. down the center of the Atlantic floor), shown in pale blue, marks the division between two great tectonic plates. The trench and plate boundaries running down the western Americas are responsible for the volcanic Andes and the earthquake zone of Mexico and California.*

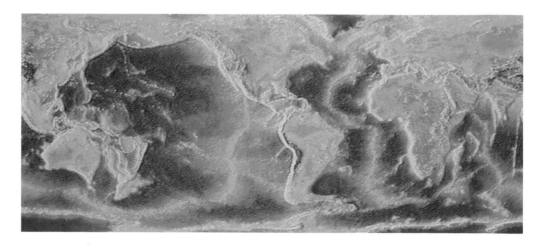

Tectonic movements and weathering are constantly exposing fresh tracts of rock on the surface. If these rocks contain fossils, those fossils can now be found.

Sediments build up in layers of rock, which can often be seen on an exposed rock surface, sometimes bent and buckled by tectonic forces. The age of these layers can be found by various methods, which allows any fossils in them to be dated too.

But for all the apparent dynamism of the Earth, these processes take place very slowly. The floor of the Atlantic is spreading apart at roughly the same speed at which your fingernails grow. Mountain ranges rise over tens of thousands of years, only to be weathered away over equally long periods. Some geological processes, such as volcanic eruptions, earthquakes, and even the deposition of mud and sand to silt up the mouths of rivers, are obvious today, and these will leave their traces in the geological record. But most geological events are imperceptible to short-lived humans.

MEASURING GEOLOGICAL TIME

One hundred years can seem like a long time – staggeringly long to children! One thousand years – say forty generations or the length of time since William the Conqueror invaded Britain – can just about be understood as a period of elapsed time; we can be helped to feel our way through such a time span by surviving historical documents and artefacts. But the mental shift needed to grasp the meaning of events occurring, say, one million years ago – when mammoths, saber-toothed cats and primitive humans walked the Earth – let alone 1,000 million years before that, which takes us back to the origins of the first complex forms of life in the seas, is very difficult indeed. It is equally hard to appreciate the interval between events in the history of the Earth, such as the 800 million years that elapsed between the condensation of cosmic dust to form our planet and the period of the first preserved traces of organic life. That timespan is 200 million years *longer* than the whole time taken for multicellular life to appear on Earth and reach the degree of complexity we see today.

How do we measure such lengths of time? Fortunately for us, time is locked away in the rocks of the Earth's crust as layers of mud, as fossilized organisms, even as crystalline granite; all of these represent part of the heritage of the Earth. Geologists have managed to unravel the history of the planet by measuring two forms of time: comparative time, which places events in a sequence one after the other; and absolute time, which gives a date measured in years.

Comparative and absolute time

In comparative dating the characteristic fossils of one rock sample are compared with those from another area. If they are broadly similar, it would be fair to suppose that they are of similar age. By drawing comparisons between rocks and their fossils from many different locations, the degree of similarity can be estimated. For example, fossil sequences from different areas may show overlapping ranges of form, so that a comparative sequence of ages can be arrived at. Some widely found fossils are of creatures which evolved very quickly, giving a clearly distinguishable sequence of forms which can be

The Atlantic Fault
ABOVE *The junction of the North American and European tectonic plates occurs in Iceland: rugged ravines and steep cliffs mark the line of the Atlantic Fault. To the left is the eastern edge of the American tectonic plate, to the right tectonic Europe. The two plates are gradually moving apart, which makes Iceland intensely volcanic. At the last major earthquake here, in 1789, part of the island dropped by 20 ins (50cm) in ten days.*

of considerable assistance. Graptolites, deep-sea animals with delicate but tough external skeletons, are classic examples of fossils that are both widespread in ocean sediments and evolved rapidly; they are therefore extremely useful for dating rocks by the comparative method. However, good though this method may be for creating sequences of rocks and their contained fossils, it does not measure time in years.

Timescale of Earth history. *The immense history of the Earth has been divided up by geologists into manageable time zones, the largest being the Eons (column 1). The Phanerozoic Eon is divided into three Eras (column 2), which are further subdivided into a set of smaller Periods (column 3). On this scale the time of appearance of the human species is equivalent to the thin black line at the top of the Quaternary Period!*

Absolute dating of rocks can be done by analyzing radioactive isotopes. Many naturally occurring elements have radioactive isotopes, which decay at a known rate. This rate is expressed as the time it takes for half of the amount of radioactive isotope to break down into a more stable isotope, and is therefore known as the "half-life." Therefore, if an estimate can be made of the proportions in which the radioactive isotope and the stable one were first formed, and if their proportions in the present-day sample can be analyzed, it becomes possible to calculate how long it must have taken the isotopes to reach their present proportions.

Unfortunately not all rocks contain the requisite radioactive isotopes, so it is not possible to date all rocks equally accurately. Nevertheless, isotope dating of rocks provides geologists with standard time markers, between

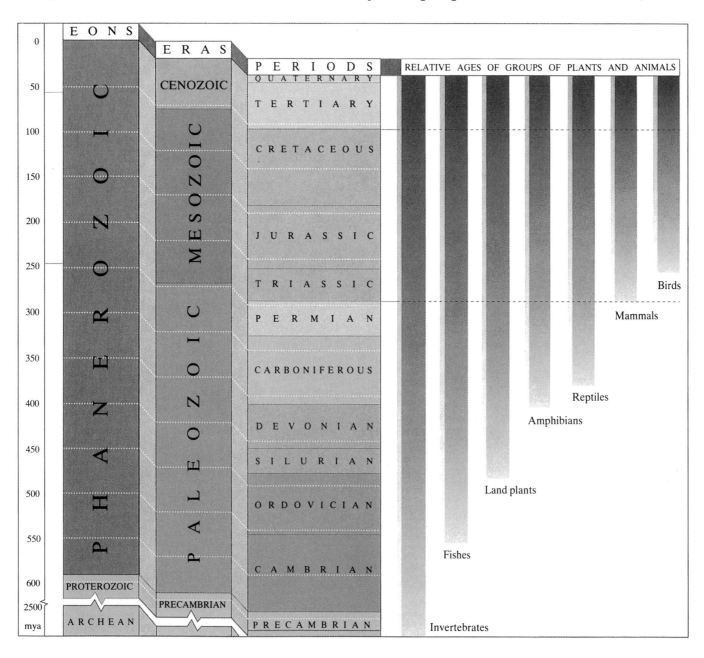

which comparative dating can be used to estimate intermediate times. The result is a fairly reliable geological timescale for the history of the Earth.

Eons, Eras, and Periods

The timescale is broken up into blocks of time of decreasing size, the largest of which are the three Eons. The first, known as the Archean Eon (literally "ancient"), ranges from the earliest known rocks (3,800 million years ago) to about 2,500 mya, and was once considered to be essentially barren of life – though this is now known not to be true. After the Archean comes the Proterozoic Eon ("early life"), which continued until about 540mya, its end being marked by the appearance of the first complex forms of life. This in turn is followed by the Phanerozoic Eon ("visible life"), the time during which complex forms of life are present in the fossil record, and which continues right up to the times in which we now live.

The Phanerozoic is further subdivided into three Eras: the Paleozoic Era ("ancient life," 540–245 mya), the Mesozoic Era ("middle life," 245–66mya), and the Cenozoic Era ("recent life," 66mya to the present).

The Eras are split into Periods, and for the most part I shall be referring to the fossil record and the animals that lived in the past within the framework of these geological Periods. The Periods themselves are further subdivided by geologists into Stages, but to save confusion – except in Chapters 9 and 10, which are a special case – I shall only refer to times within Periods as being Early, Middle or Late. (Early and Late are sometimes also referred to as Lower and Upper respectively.)

FOSSILS AND FOSSILIZATION

Fossils are one of the keys to the past. Even before it was appreciated how old the Earth was in real terms, ancient philosophers began to unlock some of the mysteries of time by the use of fossils discovered in quarries or sea cliffs. "Fossil" was once used to describe anything dug out of the earth – the term comes from the Latin for "dug up." But today "fossil" has a much more precise meaning: it refers to the remains of organisms preserved in rock, which can range from parts of their bodies (bones or shells, for example) to evidence of their activities (footprints, bite marks, or even droppings).

Fossils form as a result of the accidental burial of a dead plant or creature in sediment – sand, grit, clay or mud. If burial does not occur, the normal processes of decay or scavenging by other organisms return the dead creature's bodily chemicals to the environment in which

Upended by unimaginably powerful tectonic forces, the sea bed from the Mesozoic in the foothills of the French Alps has been tilted at a steep angle. Erosion has removed the overlying sediments so that the animals whose carcasses lay on the sea bed after they had died are once again exposed. Numerous ammonite shells, such as the ones here, can be seen. They may have all been killed simultaneously because many sizes, in other words both young and old, lie on the same layer of rock: perhaps the sea became starved of oxygen by a growth or bloom of algae.

it once lived. The various forms of sediment are the natural products of the process of rock weathering, and are carried by rivers down to lakes or the sea where they are deposited on the bottom in muddy layers. Organisms living on the lake or sea floor, or washed there after death, are constantly being showered with a fine rain of sediment which will eventually bury anything that does not move.

Clearly, if the animal lived in water, or even better on the sea floor, there would be a good chance of its remains being buried. Land-living creatures are far more poorly represented in the fossil record: after it had died, the animal would need to be rapidly washed into a river and then down to a lake or the sea before being buried. But the vast majority would have rotted or been scavenged before anything of this kind could have happened. The fossil record is therefore strongly biased in favor of sea creatures.

The history of a carcass between death and final burial can vary enormously. Careful excavation of fossils and study of the distribution of the remains can, in some instances, allow paleontologists to investigate the circumstances of death and burial in surprising detail. This special branch of the science of paleontology is called taphonomy – literally "the laws of burial."

Once burial under sediment is complete, the organism is no longer at any great risk from disturbance. The rain of sediment continues and the remains of the organism become entombed ever deeper and more heavily. Any soft tissues would continue to rot and eventually disappear; though in some instances an imprint of the soft parts or of their carbonized remnants may be preserved on the layers of sediment immediately surrounding the carcass. The increasing weight of sediment gradually crushes the body flat, with the exception of the heavier and stronger skeletal parts such as shells, teeth, and some of the bones.

At the same time the particles of sediment too become compressed, so that what was originally a soft, loose layer becomes compacted to form sedimentary rock. In many cases, for instance limestones, sandstones, and mudstones, the sedimentary rock may be quite hard, but in others it may retain a degree of softness, as with clays and shales.

Once fully entombed within the rock, the skeleton becomes a fossil. The kind of fossil it becomes depends on the later history of the rocks in which it is buried.

Simple preservation

When the skeletal parts are unaltered chemically, despite having been buried for perhaps millions of years, the result is an example of simple preservation. For instance, many bones of extinct creatures such as mammoths, dinosaurs, and fish may be preserved with exactly the same chemical make-up that they had when they were first buried.

Mineralized fossils

These are composite materials. They contain the original chemicals which formed the skeleton of the animal, but in addition the minute spaces which were originally filled with collagen or other soft tissues may become filled with another mineral, carried into the hard part of the skeleton by water. These extra minerals give the skeleton a stone-like feel, and are the reason for some fossils being called petrifactions or petrified (literally "turned to stone").

Natural casts and molds

The original skeletal parts may be dissolved by the ground waters, particularly if they are acidic. The dissolved skeleton leaves hollows in the sedimentary rock, forming a natural mold of the original fossil. Alternatively, the hollow space may subsequently become filled with another mineral which solidifies to form a perfect cast of the original skeleton, with all the original information.

Mummification and trace fossils

In very rare cases, for example creatures dying in deserts, their bodies might dry out and become buried in shifting sand. The toughened, dried tissues of the body tend to mold the sand grains, which then harden into sandstone, leaving a vivid picture of the soft parts of the creature. Usually the original tissues disappear, leaving a mold – but in this case of the creature's skin rather than its bones. This has sometimes happened to dinosaurs, preserving the texture of their scaly skin, about which we would otherwise know nothing.

Other traces of animals' existence may be revealed in trackways preserved in dried sediments, which record the evidence of the movement of animals, or in feeding traces such as bite marks or nibbled leaves. There may even be evidence of reproductive behavior – burrows, eggs, or nesting sites – but such remains are extremely uncommon.

Exposure and discovery

Once sealed in the sedimentary rock, the organism is destined to become a fossil and has every chance of lasting for many millions of years without deterioration. But will it ever be discovered? This depends, first, on the rock being exposed on the surface by tectonic movement and weathering (see pages 12-13) and, second, on someone finding it. Obviously the chances of this happening are tiny. Once the fossil is exposed on the surface it may weather away and be destroyed in a relatively short time, particularly if the cliff is by the sea and pounded by waves. This will have been the fate of countless millions of fossils in the past. But nowadays there is more chance that a keen-eyed fossil collector, or a trained paleontologist, may spot this evidence of prehistoric times before it is lost once again to the Earth's remorseless geological processes.

EVOLUTION

Preserved fossils show clearly that plants and animals of the past were not the same as those living today. They have evolved: the ancient organisms varied slightly from generation to generation and, over millions of years, one kind or species gradually changed into a new one. This process of evolution is still going on today.

The ideas on which our modern understanding of evolution is based did not develop until the middle of the nineteenth century. Previously it had generally been thought that our planet and the species living on it had been created in their present form and could not

HOW FOSSILS ARE CREATED

Burial in sediment

This is one of the commonest ways of fossil formation. Here an Archaeopteryx has died and fallen into a lake. Once waterlogged, the body sinks to the bottom. If not scavenged by other animals it will gradually be covered with layers of muddy sediment brought down by streams flowing into the lake. The flesh rots away, leaving the hard skeleton encased in limy mud. Over many, many years the sediments build up, compressing the mud into limestone. Later tectonic movements lift the lake bottom above ground, where erosion begins. Chance, or human intervention in the form of quarrying, may re-expose the fossilized remains of the ancient bird.

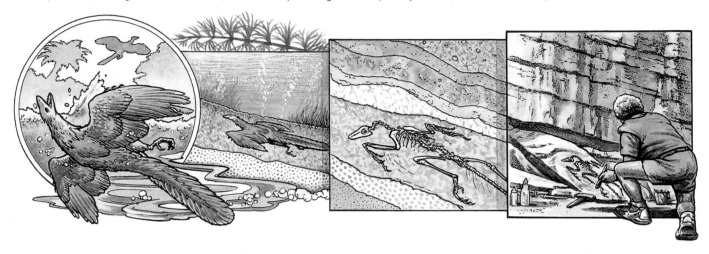

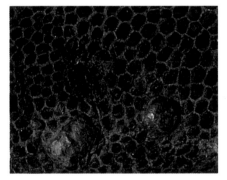

Skin impressions

Soft part preservation is relatively rare: this skin impression of a dinosaur was left on the sediment surrounding its carcass. Skin pigments tend not to survive, so at present no dinosaur colors are known.

Trace fossils

Fossil footprints offer different insights from body fossils: the length of the creature's stride, how fast it was moving, and, in cases of multiple trackways, whether they were sociable animals.

Soft tissue preservation

Very infrequently remains of the soft tissues of an animal, including the musculature, have been found preserved in fossils. Quite how this happens has been a major puzzle to paleontologists for a long time. But now some remarkable experiments have been carried out by Dr Derek Briggs at the University of Bristol. By mimicking in the laboratory the probable environment of preservation, he has shown that the mineral calcium phosphate may become deposited in the muscle tissue of the bodies of shrimps (Crangon) in such a way that individual muscle fibres are still visible. Mineralization of this kind provides the potential for "ghosts" of the original soft tissues to become fossilized.

Mummification

Here some baby armored dinosaurs (Pinacosaurus) have been buried in a sandstorm. In such situations skeleton and skin impressions are usually very well preserved.

change. This belief in what was called Special or Divine Creation, as the result of the actions of a Creator or God, was accepted by many famous scientist-philosophers of the late eighteenth and early nineteenth centuries.

However, there were some dissenters from this view. Through closely comparing fossils with the anatomy of living animals, the Frenchman Baron Georges Cuvier (1769–1832) established that they were different. To explain this finding he invented a catastrophe theory: floods and earthquakes must have periodically devastated parts of the world, and subsequently new forms from elsewhere in the world moved in to repopulate these regions.

One of Cuvier's colleagues in Paris, Jean-Baptiste de Lamarck (1744–1829), had a fervent belief in evolution. In the early nineteenth century he proposed that organisms had an internal urge to improve themselves, and that they would develop new features in order to cope with new conditions. These newly acquired characteristics, he contended, would then be passed on to their offspring.

There is an obvious parallel between Lamarckism and our own experience of life – we tend to learn things during our lifetime and pass them on to our children as part of their own learning process. But unfortunately for Lamarck it has been impossible to demonstrate either an internal urge for self-improvement in nature (I exclude humans and their culture from this argument because I think they are a special case), or that characteristics acquired during the lifetime of an organism can be passed on to its offspring.

Darwin and Natural Selection

Many people other than Lamarck believed that organisms had evolved over time; this seemed to be one of the logical reasons why the earliest known fossils appeared to be relatively simple forms of life, and later ones more complex. But no one could explain how this might have happened. Then came Charles Darwin (1809–82), who will always be regarded as one of the most famous biologists in history because it was he who provided the most logical mechanism for the way evolution works. His theory was called Natural Selection, and it can be explained through two observations which he made.

First, all the members of a single species tend to vary a little; no two individuals are absolutely identical. Darwin noted that breeders of pigeons, for example, exploited these variations when mating individuals and in so doing were able to create some exotic forms which do not appear in the wild. Darwin concluded that these variable characteristics could be inherited by their offspring.

Charles Darwin, who in the mid-nineteenth century transformed the framework within which biologists worked. After 140 years the main principles of his theory of evolution remain intact.

Second, it had been noted that parents are capable of producing far more offspring than are needed to maintain their populations in nature, but that the Earth is not knee-deep in mice, worms, or any other particular species. Population growth must therefore be limited by shortage of food, disease, and predators. Darwin concluded that the individuals most likely to survive and breed would be those best able to find food, resist disease, and avoid being caught and eaten – these he termed the "fittest" organisms. His theory was that only the fittest members of a species tend to survive.

Combining these two observations, he amassed a great deal of evidence which he presented in *The Origin of Species* published in 1859. In this book he argued that, since species varied and only the fittest individuals survived, there was some mechanism which allowed nature to select particular types of organism for particular ways of life. This notion provided a very dynamic view of life – one that allowed organisms to appear and change with time – and for there to be an active relationship between the Earth and its inhabitants.

Darwin's concept flew in the face of the general consensus at the time – which centered on a belief in the creation of all forms of life by God. His theory was regarded as abhorrent by many people simply because it was so mechanical: it suggested that life just grew and responded to changes around it in the physical world, rather than being directed by the wisdom of an omnipotent being. It is difficult for us today to imagine how upsetting this theory must have been to the great majority of God-fearing people in the mid-nineteenth century.

Mendel and Neo-Darwinism

Darwinism has proved to be an extremely robust theory – that is to say, it has been subjected to extensive criticism from time to time, but has always emerged more or less unscathed, and in some instances greatly strengthened. In the twentieth century it has been modified somewhat in the light of experiments carried out by the Austrian monk Gregor Mendel. Although Mendel published his findings in 1866, not long after Darwin's controversial work, this was in an obscure journal and it was overlooked by contemporary scientists, Darwin included. It was not until 1900, long after both men were dead, that Mendel's work was rediscovered.

For many years Darwin had tried, unsuccessfully, to understand how characteristics (or characters, as they are often called) were passed on from one generation to the next; he supposed that parental characters were in some way blended or shared among their offspring. But Mendel's experiments on garden peas (*Pisum sativum*), using the simple characters of seed shape and color, showed that they acted more like particles and divided up in a predictable way in the offspring. These characters have since been named genes, and Mendel's work has formed the foundation of the science of genetics.

The subsequently modified version of Darwin's theory, which incorporates the idea of the genetic basis of inheritance, is called Neo-Darwinism – literally, New Darwinism. The discovery of the structure of DNA in the 1950s by James Watson and Francis Crick has allowed scientists to investigate the structure of genes at the molecular level, and this has further strengthened our understanding of heredity and the process of evolution in ways that would have astounded Darwin.

Paleontologists have tinkered with Darwin's theory a little by looking at the process of evolution as it is demonstrated in the fossil record. In the early 1970s Professors Niles Eldredge and Stephen Jay Gould proposed that fossils of marine creatures indicated that evolution may not have occurred, as Darwin and others believed, as an almost imperceptible series of changes over millions of years, but in a much more jerky fashion. They called their proposal "punctuated equilibrium." By this they meant that evolution does not proceed by slow, smooth changes, but rather by a continuing sequence in which periods of equilibrium, when everything appears to be stable and species vary only a little, are punctuated, or interrupted, by short periods of rapid change. The geological succession appeared to show just that – a set of similar fossils in one section of rock, followed by an abrupt change so that a different but related fossil organism appears in the rock lying immediately above.

This challenge to the general framework of Neo-Darwinism has created controversy among modern evolutionary biologists and paleontologists, some of whom favor the idea while others do not. For the moment, evolutionary theory is being enriched by the perspective that paleontologists can add to the work of modern biologists – and that must be a good thing.

In 1871 Darwin speculated on the origins of life in a letter: "[In] some warm little pond, with all sorts of ammonia and phosphoric salts, light, heat, electricity, etc. present . . . a protein compound was chemically formed ready to undergo still more complex changes . . ." The next chapter will explore the origins of life and consider how far we have progressed in the century and a quarter since Darwin had those provocative and inspired thoughts.

Study of the dark and light forms of the peppered moth, Biston betularia, *has provided a remarkable demonstration of Darwin's theory of evolution in practise. At the height of industrialization in Britain soot blackened the bark of trees, leaving this normally light-colored moth clearly visible to predatory birds. By contrast the rarer dark form was not so easily spotted, and as a result greatly increased in number. Later, when pollution decreased, the bark of trees became lighter and favored the by now rarer light form.*

2

BEGINNINGS
OF LIFE

FROM SIMPLE CHEMICALS TO
LIVING ORGANISMS

THE SMALL AND deceptively stable-seeming planet on which we live is young in comparison to the age of the Universe. The puzzle is: how did the earliest forms of life arise?

It is now generally accepted that life arose very early in the history of the Earth. As proposed by Darwin, events seem to have started with the creation of simple carbon-based molecules. These chemicals reacted with one another to form longer, more complex compounds known as polymers, which in turn reacted with one another to form more and more complicated chemical structures until one was formed that could be called living. However, this explanation is incomplete: it does not say where, or when, the spark of life arose and turned the aggregation of chemicals into a living organism. To put it simply, how do we distinguish between living and non-living things?

ABOVE *How helically coiled DNA – the blueprint of life – replicates itself. The double strand unwinds and new daughter strands are copied onto each of the original strands.*

RIGHT *Electron micrograph of the bacterium* Pseudomonas aeruginosa, *magnified about 50,000 times and artificially colored for clarity. It is common in the human gut, in the air, and in swimming pools.*

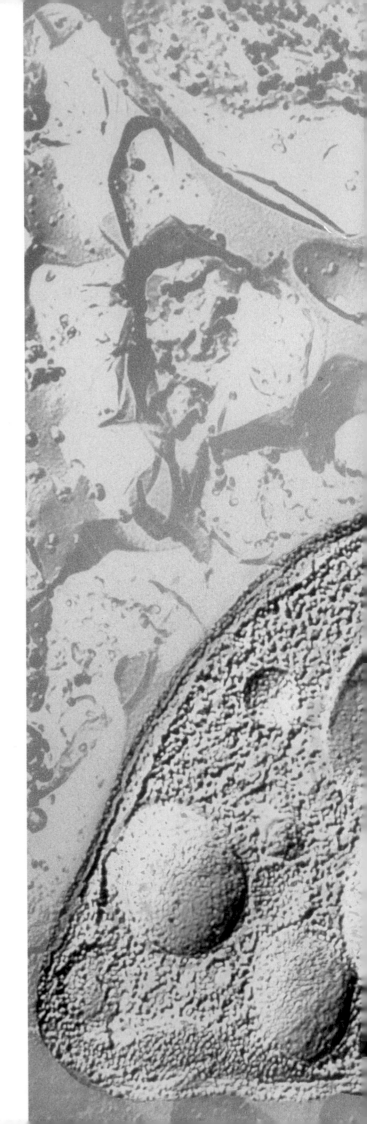

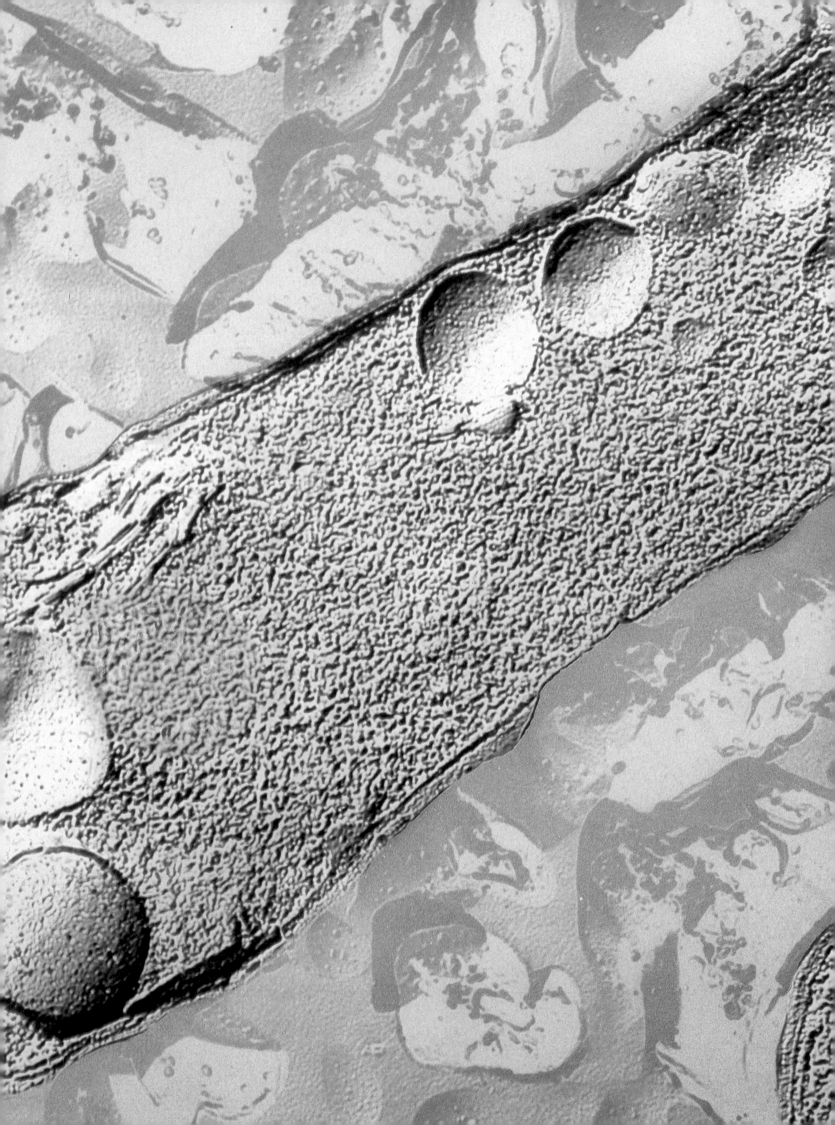

WHAT IS LIFE?

There is a classic definition of what it means to be alive. Living things must be able to do seven things: breathe, eat, excrete, move (if only in a very restricted way), respond to stimuli (at least to some extent), grow, and reproduce themselves. The last two are particularly important, and I shall concentrate on these. Living creatures must be able to take in chemicals and convert some of them into energy and others into materials that can be used for growth. They must also be able to produce offspring – new individuals similar to their parents.

Bacteria as "simple" life forms

To get an idea of what early forms of life were like, let's turn to some of the smallest life forms found today: to the microscopic world of prokaryotes, better known as bacteria. Bacteria measure just a few microns (thousandths of a millimeter) across and can be seen only under a microscope. Most are encased inside a rigid cell

Escherischia coli, a bacterium of the human gut used as an indicator of water pollution, in the act of mating. In this false color transmission electron micrograph a "male" is shown linked by narrow tubular bridges to two "females" as DNA passes between them. Features such as drug resistance and the ability to digest certain foods are transferred in this way, enabling changes to take place in the population and giving rise to new strains of bacteria.

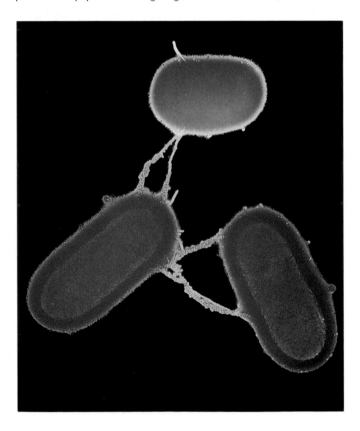

wall, within which lies a soft cell membrane composed of proteins and lipids (fatty substances); this contains the cell fluid or cytoplasm, a mixture of water, simple sugars, fats, proteins, and other chemicals. There are also some larger molecules anchored to the cell membrane. These are involved in the production of energy, of the proteins which are the bacterium's building materials, and of the long strands of nucleic acid which are the "program" that keeps the bacterium functioning. Nucleic acids exist in two forms: DNA (deoxyribonucleic acid), which is like a library of information for the design and working of the bacterium; and RNA (ribonucleic acid), which transfers sections of that information to wherever it is needed so that new proteins can be assembled.

The bacterium, like all living things, breaks down food to produce sugar, which it breaks down in turn to release energy. This energy is stored in a chemical called ATP (adenosine triphosphate), which provides the power for the chemical reactions which keep the cell running. All these chemical reactions are controlled by enzymes, which are special types of proteins. There are enzymes to digest food, to copy DNA onto RNA so that this can go to make proteins, to gather the pieces that make up the protein, and much more – all the myriad processes which sustain life.

The so-called "simple" form of life, the bacterium, has turned out to be incredibly complicated. It lives only because a tremendous amount of chemical cooperation takes place within the confines of the cell membrane. The enclosed space created by the membrane is vitally important because it provides a haven within which all the chemical interactions can take place without interference from the outside world. But at the same time the contents of the cell need to interact with the outside world so that chemicals may pass into and out of the bacterium. Food, in the form of simple chemicals, can enter, while waste – the by-product of the chemical reactions happening within – can pass out.

Viruses

Some readers may be wondering why I did not choose a virus as an example of the simplest form of life. Viruses are indeed considerably simpler than bacteria in their chemical make-up; most viruses consist of a layer of tough "coat" proteins around a strand of nucleic acid. However, an isolated virus could not be called a living organism. It shares many features with genuinely living things, but it cannot grow or reproduce by itself. A virus can grow and reproduce only when it is inside another living organism – it is no more than a parasite. In fact it is less than one: most parasitic animals can do some

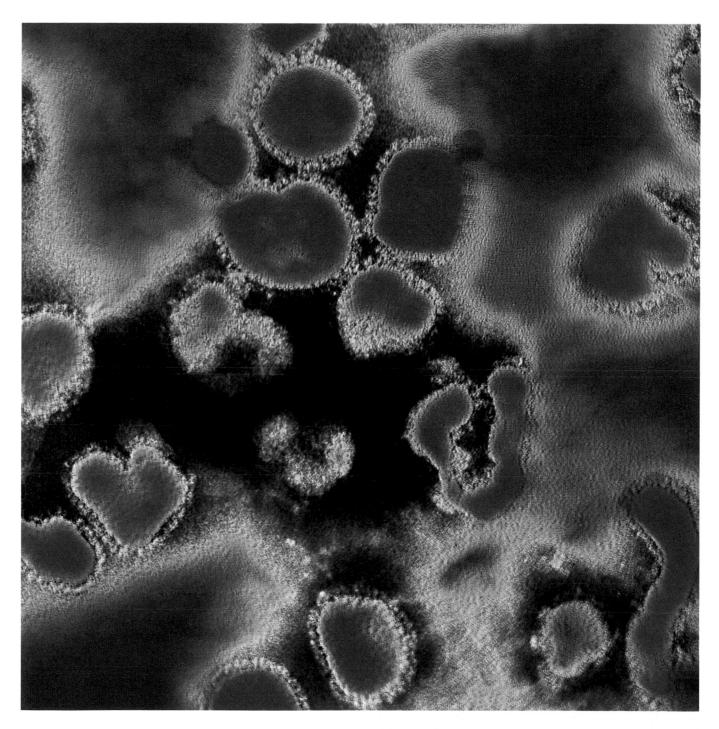

things without their hosts, but when a virus is outside a living cell it is completely inert. When the virus encounters a cell it releases its own nucleic acid, which takes over control of the host cell. It then uses the cell's own machinery to make thousands of copies of itself until the host cell bursts and dies, releasing thousands of new viruses.

So in some ways viruses straddle the boundary between living and non-living. Life could clearly not have evolved from such specialized parasites, because in the earliest phases of the Earth's history there would have been nothing to parasitize. It seems most likely

Beijing flu virus. Each virus has a core of ribonucleic acid (orange), surrounded by spike-shaped proteins (green dots) which stick to cells in the human nose and throat and replicate inside them. Although the immune system attacks these invaders, flu viruses can change their chemical structure to create new strains which the immune system does not recognize.

that viruses evolved from earlier, more complex, organisms – perhaps from strains of parasitic bacteria – that gradually shed everything except the protein coat which protected their nucleic acid strand, and came to depend entirely on their host cell to sustain their existence.

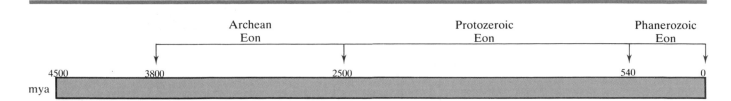

| | Archean
Eon | | Protozeroic
Eon | | Phanerozoic
Eon |

4500   3800   2500   540   0

mya

Timescale of Earth history. *Since its formation 4,500 million years ago the Earth has undergone a series of changes. At first our planet was molten-hot and bombarded by huge meteorites. Then about 3,500 million years ago chemical evolution began, culminating in the appearance of the first living organisms during the Proterozoic Eon. The Phanerozoic Eon saw the rise of complex forms of life.*

THE EARLIEST LIFE FORMS AND THEIR ENVIRONMENT

It is probable – perhaps inevitable given the complexity of the chemical interactions that take place – that the earliest organisms were a good deal simpler than a modern bacterium. Even so, it still requires an enormous leap of the imagination to take us from an early Earth of simple chemicals to one inhabited by simple living cells with all the features needed to keep them alive. This early Earth may well have been like that envisaged by Darwin, in which the waters were enriched by chemicals reacting with one another. This liquid is often referred to as the "primordial soup."

To place early life in its proper perspective we need to understand certain things. They concern the age of the Earth, the time when the organisms that became the first known fossils appeared, and the nature of the Earth and its atmosphere during this time.

Dates and timespans

As explained earlier, the Earth is 4,500 million years old, while the oldest known rocks – the Isua rocks of western Greenland – have been dated at 3,800 million years. The oldest known fossils are the stromatolites, and a few other remains of micro-organisms, which have been found at Warrawoona in Australia and have been dated at 3,500 million years. This would allow about 1,000 million years for life to arise; but, for reasons which are outlined below, it seems very probable that the time available was considerably shorter.

How fast did the Earth condense?

There are many theories to explain how the Earth was formed from cosmic dust and debris. At one extreme it is thought that the Earth condensed very quickly in cosmic terms – in about 100,000 years. The gravitational energy of the collapsing matter would have been released as a great deal of heat, causing the entire Earth to melt. At the other extreme the condensation of the Earth is seen as a very slow process, in which the gravitational energy was released much more gradually. In these circumstances only the inner parts of the Earth would have melted under the compressive forces and the heat generated by radioactive decay, while the surface remained solid. Obviously, if the whole Earth did melt, then any chemicals likely to have been involved in the origins of life but brought in on cosmic dust, or by meteorites, would have been destroyed.

The effects of meteorite bombardment

A further complication has arisen after examination of the surface of the Moon and other planets in our Solar System. Until about 3,800 million years ago most planets, including the Earth, were being heavily bombarded by huge meteorites. A fall of one or more 7 mile (10km) wide meteorites has been suggested as one of the causes

This 100 ft (30 m) wide crater was made by a modest-sized meteorite striking the surface of the Moon. The impact may have occurred during the meteorite storms that raged between 4,600 and 3,800 million years ago.

of the extinction of the dinosaurs. This would certainly have had an enormous environmental effect. Even larger meteorites, of 40 miles (about 60km) in diameter and more, would have supplied enough energy to boil the oceans. So it seems likely that any living systems that appeared on Earth very early on would have been regularly destroyed.

This leaves a relatively short period, around 200 million years, available for the development of life on Earth. Some scientists have stressed that the origin of life is fraught with so many improbable events that a period of at least 1,000 million years would have been necessary to see it through. However, as Professor Stanley Miller, at the forefront of practical experimentation on the chemical evolution of life, has pointed out, we are here talking about staggeringly long periods of time. In the violent conditions of the young Earth, with chemical reactions going on at a tremendous rate, it is hard to envisage such a slow, steady development. It seems much more likely that a chance reaction formed the first vital molecule, after which things happened quite quickly on a geological timescale – in perhaps tens of millions of years.

Was the early Earth hot or cold?

Ever since Darwin imagined his "warm little pond" it has been widely assumed that life emerged in just such conditions. But such ideas are probably incorrect, for a very simple reason. The higher the temperature, the greater the speed at which chemicals tend to decompose, particularly some of those vital to the origins of life processes, such as proteins, nucleic acid strands, and sugars. But if much of the water of the oceans was tied up as ice, leaving equatorial areas of chemically rich cold "soup," the important chemicals would have lasted longer and conditions would have been more favorable for the construction of some of the larger and more complex molecules.

The primitive atmosphere

Although there is no way to discover the composition of the atmosphere shortly after the formation of the Earth, it seems likely that this was very different from that of the present-day atmosphere. There would have been considerable outgassing from the mantle of the Earth, so that the atmosphere would have contained large quantities of water vapor, hydrogen, nitrogen, methane, ammonia, hydrogen sulphide, and carbon monoxide; these are the gases released by volcanoes today. The crucial point is that it is unlikely that free, uncombined oxygen would have been present.

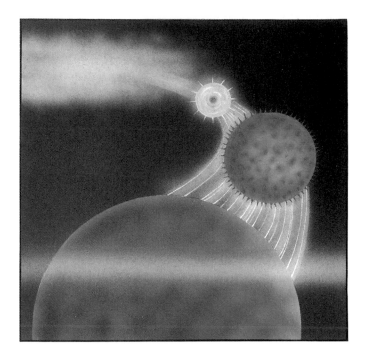

It is likely that the Earth formed in one of two ways. The first possibility (ABOVE) *is that it condensed relatively rapidly and an enormous amount of gravitational energy was given out. The planet started out as a molten globe, which cooled over time so that its surface eventually solidified.*

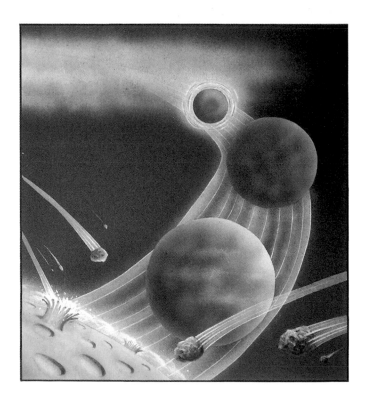

In the alternative scenario the cosmic matter condensed at a much slower rate, so that the core of the Earth gradually heated up as the gravitational force increased. The Earth's layered structure with a molten core, a fluid mantle, and a hard crust would have developed as the matter built up.

LEFT *As a young researcher in the 1950s Stanley Miller took Darwin's notion of "some warm little pond" at its face value, and constructed an apparatus to re-create the early atmosphere of the Earth. Into this mixture of gases he discharged electrical sparks, and then analyzed the products of the chemical reaction that resulted.*

RIGHT *While most meteorites burn up and form "shooting stars," larger ones can hit the Earth like a massive bomb. This one was found in 1871 in Mexico. Recent theories on the extinction of dinosaurs have focused on Mexico's Yucatan peninsula, where a meteorite up to 12 miles (20km) in diameter may once have caused an environmental catastrophe.*

EXPERIMENTS: THE SEEDS OF THE ORIGINS OF LIFE

In the 1920s two scientists, Alexander Oparin and J.B.S. Haldane, independently arrived at a theory for the origin of life. They deduced that the Earth had a reducing atmosphere – one that lacked free oxygen – and was composed of the gases listed above. Energy sources such as ultraviolet light from the Sun (which is mostly shielded out today by the ozone layer), electrical discharges, radioactivity, volcanic heat, and so on would have promoted chemical reactions between the gases, leading to the formation of chemicals necessary for life.

In 1953 this theory was tested by Stanley Miller, who discharged a stream of electric sparks into a mixture of the gases thought to be present on the Earth at the time life emerged. After a while he was able to collect measurable quantities of a number of biologically important molecules, including amino acids – the building blocks of proteins, and therefore of life. The experiment has been repeated using slightly differing conditions, and it has proved possible to produce 17 of the 20 vital amino acids and a huge number of other biologically active chemicals.

It seems that the early conditions on Earth were appropriate for the formation of the chemicals on which life later came to depend. The crucial questions are: how did these chemical precursors become larger and more complicated, and how did they then become part of a system that was recognizably alive?

Attempts to convert the simple chemicals created in Miller's experiments into larger and more complex ones have not met with much success. This is mainly because a great deal of energy is needed to make the reactions occur, and water needs to be removed. Since these reactions tend to be reversible, and they are supposed to have occurred in the sea where there is no shortage of water, this stage in the origin and manufacture of such chemicals is rather puzzling. However, such problems have not stopped work on the general subject. Sidney Fox of the University of Florida used heat to make amino acids react together to form proteinoids – small protein-like molecules which have some of the properties of enzymes.

EVIDENCE FROM METEORITES

Another source of molecules of this type has been identified in outer space. It has long been known that there are some quite complex chemicals in the cosmos. It is thought that these may have formed on dust particles thrown out from stellar explosions, so that these particles might have become coated in organic molecules. No one has captured an interstellar dust particle to establish whether this is true, but there is interesting evidence from much larger interstellar particles – familiar to us as meteorites.

The Orgueil meteorite, which fell in southern France in 1864, was of a type referred to as a carbonaceous

chondrite. On first examination it appeared to contain biological molecules and microfossils, confirming the observation that organic molecules may indeed be present in outer space. Later studies, however, suggested that the biological molecules may well have been contaminants from Earth, and that the "microfossils" were in fact pollen grains.

In 1969 samples were taken from a freshly fallen meteorite – the Murchison meteorite from Australia – which was of a similar type to the Orgueil one. It contained a significant quantity of biologically active chemicals, including a wide range of amino acids.

The importance of this discovery is its confirmation that biologically active molecules are being formed throughout the galaxy; they seem to be a natural product of chemical evolution on a cosmic scale. The ease with which such chemicals seem to form suggests that such reactions did take place on primitive Earth – and by implication could have taken place on other planets in the galaxy.

THE GREAT LEAP FROM CHEMICALS TO CELLS?

If life arose as a by-product of widespread chemical evolution, then quite complex chemical reactions must have been taking place before the appearance of the first simple organisms. It seems unlikely that all the chemicals necessary for life would parcel themselves up inside a cell wall unless there was some obvious advantage, and unless circumstances allowed for the creation of such membrane-enclosed structures.

The work of Sidney Fox has helped to explain how groups of chemicals may have come to be "packaged" inside membranes. After producing proteinoids, he attempted to redissolve them in warm water, which he then left to cool. He discovered that he had created tiny spherical structures with a very uniform diameter of about 2 microns. These "microspheres" proved to be very stable indeed, and bear a remarkable resemblance to cells.

Microspheres and mini-environments

Like cells, these spheres have a double membrane; it actually behaves rather like a true cell membrane in that it allows small molecules to pass through much more readily than large ones, and reseals itself if punctured. In the real conditions of the early Earth, it seems unlikely that the very first cells ("protocells") would have been able to manufacture their own chemical needs. In these circumstances a leaky membrane may have been ideal, allowing the protocell to absorb chemicals from the surrounding water. Curiously, Fox's microspheres appear capable of assisting some chemical reactions and even, on some rare occasions, of swelling and dividing almost as though they are reproducing.

If membranes did originate as microspheres, they would have contained a "mini-environment," an enclosed system within which chemical activity could proceed in stable and favorable conditions. This implies that chemical evolution would begin to take a multiplicity of different routes: those occurring in the sea being different in type and quality from those occurring inside microspheres, and many of the microspheres evolving in directions determined by the chemicals that they happened to contain.

Microspheres and their contained systems of chemicals would break down and re-form, greatly enriching the mixture of chemicals, and the possibilities for chemical reaction, in the early waters. Evolutionary pressures of selection might have begun to exert themselves on these minute chemical systems. Clearly those microspheres that contained, by sheer chance, chemicals capable of sustaining their systems for longer would survive in preference to their less favored companions, and might even divide or replicate themselves on occasion.

This scenario for converting a microsphere into something approaching a protocell still leaves a huge gulf between the latter and what we would today regard as a simple living cell. Changes would be necessary which would make the membrane selectively permeable rather than simply leaky; complex proteins would need to be assembled on nucleic acid templates; division would need to be coordinated by the nucleic acids; complex chemical pathways would need to be established for the manufacture and breakdown of products; and a system for generating and absorbing energy would need to be developed in order to power the chemical machinery of the cell. That is quite a step. Division in such protocells, for example, would presumably be simply a consequence of swelling or growth, and there would be no guarantee that the daughter cells would contain the same chemical systems as their parent, or that they would even survive the process of division.

Distant ancestors?

Are microspheres, as the distant ancestors of the earliest living cells, a realistic possibility? Conditions on Earth may well have been right for their formation. Free amino acids would very likely have been present in lakes or the sea. Provided that they could have been concentrated so that they melted together, perhaps in the heat of the sun or possibly through the action of hot volcanic lava, the circumstances for the formation of proteinoids would have been met. Exposure of such proteinoids to warm water would have yielded microspheres. None of this is inherently improbable, given the apparent widespread formation of biologically active molecules throughout the Universe.

Some fossils from the Archean Eon look remarkably similar to microspheres. Experiments have been conducted in an attempt to mimic the conditions of their fossilization, using modern algae, fungal spores, and proteinoid microspheres. All three have ended up in much the same form, closely resembling the actual fossils. Further tests on very early microfossils with a similar appearance seem to rule out algae and fungi – leaving the intriguing possibility that some early fossil structures were indeed microspheres.

THE ORIGINS OF MULTICELLULAR LIFE

Fossils dated at between 3,000 million and 1,000 million years old are mostly 1 or 2 microns in diameter. The size of these so-called "body fossils" is consistent with their

---

THE WORKINGS OF A CELL

Cell structure
Eukaryotic cells are far more complex than bacterial (prokaryotic) cells. The cell is surrounded by a membrane enclosing the cell sap (cytoplasm), which contains all the chemicals of the cell's machinery. Within the cytoplasm of eukaryotic cells are special mini-organs called organelles. These organelles include the nucleus (which contains the DNA), chloroplasts (which trap the Sun's energy), mitochondria (energy generators), chemical "factories" and communication channels. Surprising though it may seem, mitochondria contain their own DNA, are capable of dividing on their own, and are the same size as bacteria. So were bacteria the precursors of mitochondria?

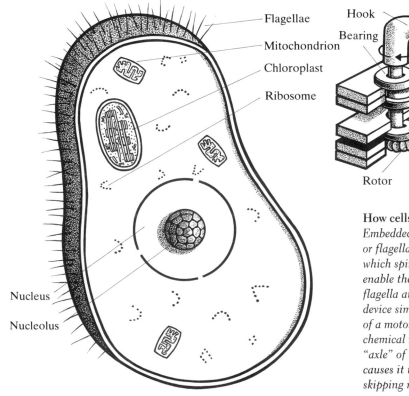

Flagellae
Mitochondrion
Chloroplast
Ribosome
Nucleus
Nucleolus

Hook
Bearing
Flagellar filament
Rotor
Stator

How cells move
Embedded in the walls are cilia or flagella, whip-like structures which spin like wheels and so enable the cell to move. These flagella are powered by a rotary device similar to the drive-shaft of a motor-car: the cell's chemical machinery drives the "axle" of the flagellum and causes it to whip like a skipping rope.

being prokaryotic (bacteria-like) forms of life possessing a simple strand of nucleic acid, and with the chemical machinery of the cell either distributed within the cell fluid or attached to the cell membrane. But about 1,000 million years ago larger microfossils begin to appear, 5 to 15 microns in diameter. These fossils, found in chert rocks, look suspiciously like the remains of eukaryotes – that is, the cells seem to have some of their working parts collected in a central nucleus, which can be seen in the fossil as a darker area.

Eukaryotic cells are more complex in structure than those of bacteria (the classic prokaryotes) for two reasons. One is the nucleus, in which their nucleic acids are stored. The other is a collection of smaller bodies, scattered throughout the cell fluid, known as organelles (literally "little organs"). These house other parts of the chemical machinery of the cell, including the energy-producing mitochondria; ribosomes, which translate nucleic acid into proteins; and chloroplasts (found only in plant cells), which contain layers of pigment which trap and use the energy of light. Some cells are fringed with whip-like flagellae, which propel these cells through the water in which they live.

Endosymbiosis and cooperation

The origin of the first eukaryotes is an intriguing problem that has generated a fascinating theory, suggested by Professor Lynn Margulis. It is suspected that eukaryotes evolved from prokaryotes living together cooperatively within a single membrane – the so-called endosymbiotic theory. The term comes from "endo-," meaning within, and "symbiosis," meaning cooperation for mutual benefit. For example, lichens which encrust rocks are not a single organism but a symbiotic partnership between algae and fungi. And the tiny *Paramecium*, a protist (a creature of the same kind as an amoeba), contains many small green inclusions which are in fact algae named *Chlorella*. These two organisms live quite happily one inside the other; the protist protects and nourishes the algae, which in return use sunlight to produce sugars which can be consumed by the protist.

The endosymbiotic theory supposes that early prokaryotes formed an association within a larger "mother cell." The "mother cell" engulfed various bacteria, and these evolved into many of the organelles that are now found inside eukaryotes. As partial proof of this theory it has been shown that both chloroplasts and mitochondria contain their very own ribosomes and nucleic acids, which are strikingly similar to those of living prokaryotes.

This suggestion, though not accepted by everyone, is by far the most convincing theory of the origin of eukaryotic

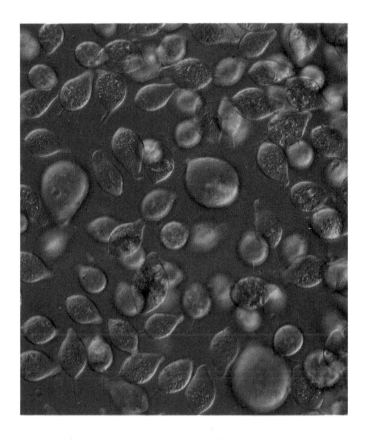

Micrograph of a colony of microbes found in the gut of a termite. Termites eat wood, but no animal is capable of digesting the cellulose from which wood is made. However, microbes living in termite guts are able to produce the enzymes needed for this process. Microbes and termite are said to live symbiotically (living together to their mutual benefit) – the microbes acquire a safe home in return for their services as digesters of cellulose, which they convert into usable sugars. Similar relationships exist between protistans (single-celled eukaryotes) and termite gut bacteria. Such observations considerably strengthen Professor Lynn Margulis's endosymbiotic theory for the origin of eukaryotes.

cells. If it is correct, it accounts for the abrupt leap in biological evolution that was made by the appearance of the first eukaryotes. It is from these eukaryotic cells that all later multicellular life – including the organisms that I shall describe in later chapters – are descended.

One thousand million years ago the complexity of life forms began to increase dramatically. Colonies of eukaryotic organisms may well have begun to aggregate and live cooperatively – though as yet there is no firm fossil evidence to confirm this. Many algae live in crude aggregations today – as strand-like filaments or mats, or floating globular structures – and it must be supposed that similar organisms were abundant during the period between the origin of the early eukaryotes and the appearance of the first truly organized organisms about 600 million years ago. Fossils of these latter creatures were first discovered in the Flinders Mountains of southern Australia, and will be described in Chapter 3.

3

THE STRANGE
CAMBRIAN
WORLD

A WINDOW ONTO THE PAST:
THE BURGESS SHALE

THE FOSSIL RECORD suggests that, for 3,000 million years, life on Earth can be traced through a variety of single-celled organisms known as cyanobacteria or blue-green algae. Not only were these single-celled organisms the ancestors of today's living things, they also had a profound influence on the planet as a whole, because they changed its atmosphere. They used their chemical machinery to trap the energy of sunlight and generate free oxygen, and it was this free oxygen which allowed the growth and development of much more complex and active forms of life.

Dominated by a large cruising predator with wicked hooked claws, Anomalocaris (LEFT), the sea floor in Cambrian times was a hive of activity, so far as we can tell from the fossils. Top left is the small, shimmering, eel-like image of perhaps the most important and intriguing of all Burgess Shale creatures, Pikaia – probably the earliest chordate, and possibly our earliest ancestor. The worm-like Aysheaia (ABOVE) was smaller than Anomalocaris but no less fearsome to its favored diet, sponges, whose soft bodies it tore into with its sharp spines.

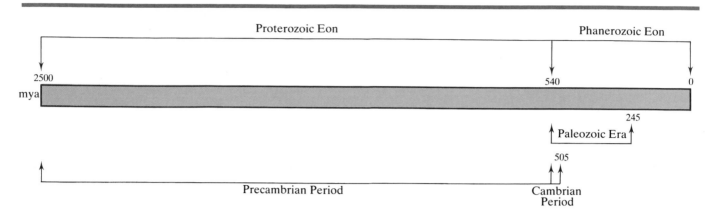

Timescale of Earth history. *The first four-fifths of our planet's history charts the rise of biological chemicals and simple organisms. But in the Phanerozoic complex animals appear: first the enigmatic*

Ediacara fauna, some of which resemble inflatable mattresses, and then a bewildering variety of creatures preserved in wondrous detail in the Mid-Cambrian Burgess Shale.

Multicellular forms of life seem to appear on the scene in Late Precambrian times as a variety of rather unusual fossils which have proved extremely difficult to interpret. Quite what came before them is uncertain; there may well have been a long period of the earlier Precambrian during which extremely small, soft-bodied, but relatively complex organisms lived on, or perhaps between, the grains of sand and mud on the sea floor; but if they did, they left no trace that has yet been found in the fossil record.

AN EXPLOSION OF LIFE FORMS

Beyond the latest Precambrian there occurred what has appropriately been called an explosion of life forms, many of which seem to be extraordinary experiments in animal design. For a long time it was supposed that the idea of a sudden rise of complex forms of life in the Cambrian Period (on the Proterozoic–Phanerozoic border) was in fact a fallacy created by the nature of the fossil record, and that it simply represented the time when the first shelled creatures began to appear. Since shells are hard objects, they are much more capable of being preserved than soft-bodied creatures. However, from recent research it really does look as though the Earth presented these early organisms with a "clean sheet" upon which to develop all manner of designs.

In terms of the variety and diversity of marine organisms on Earth, it seems clear that there was rapid growth across the Precambrian–Cambrian boundary, which continued to rise until the middle of the Ordovician Period. From that time right up to the present day, the level of diversity has remained relatively constant, although

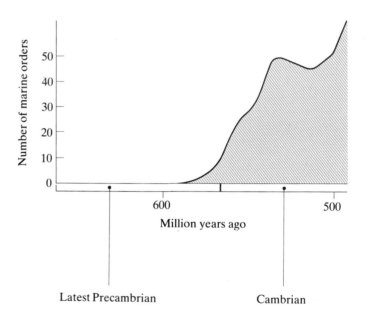

ABOVE *Charting the rise of complex forms of life reveals a dramatic increase in the Early and Middle Cambrian. Does this simply reflect the appearance of hard skeletal parts and therefore of more fossilizable material? Or does it represent the first real surge of life, made possible once complex multicellular forms of life had appeared on Earth? The Burgess Shale favors the latter view.*

during this immense span of time the individual species have changed very significantly.

If we look first at the various types of early multicellular organisms, what emerges is largely unexpected and unfamiliar, and indicates a world far removed from our own. Yet, despite the overwhelmingly different nature of the Cambrian Period, it is just possible to trace fragile threads of our own ancestry – or at least the ancestry of the major group of animals to which we belong.

THE VENDIAN FAUNA

The known fossil record of animals and plants – creatures more complex than the simple single-celled organisms described in Chapter 2 – begins in rocks that are between 550 and 600 million years old. This is the last section of the Precambrian Period, known as the Vendian. In the earliest Cambrian, within a relatively short space of time, animals with mineralized (shelly or bony) skeletons begin to appear. This is the dawn of the Phanerozoic – the Eon of "visible life" – in which we can see with the naked eye the fossilized remains of early life on Earth.

The time of origin of the first complex forms of animal life is a little uncertain, for two reasons. First, the earliest animals are relatively rare as fossils because they are soft-bodied. Second, and more fundamentally, because sediments are laid down so slowly, those in which fossils are preserved rarely contain minerals that formed at the same time that the sediments were deposited, nor do they possess the radioactive isotopes that can be used to determine age. The techniques used are therefore less precise than those that have been applied to metamorphic and igneous rocks, which changed or formed rapidly. Recent estimations have been made by measuring the ratios of lead and uranium in crystals of zircon collected from volcanic ash beds. Uranium decays to lead very slowly, with a half-life of many millions of years. This means that by measuring the proportions of the two elements it is possible to get a reasonably accurate figure even for such an immense age. As a result, the Precambrian–Cambrian boundary is now being brought forward to between 550 and 530 million years ago – most older textbooks preferred a date of around 600 million years ago. The Cambrian Period seems to have lasted until about 510–500 million years ago, and into that timespan was compressed an enormous burst of evolutionary activity – it is known as the "Cambrian Explosion."

One would expect that the earliest complex (multicellular) organisms would have been insubstantial – that is to say, soft-bodied creatures. Their bodies can be regarded as a loose amalgam of cells which cooperated with one another and gained mutual sustenance and support. At this stage in the evolution of life it seems unlikely that there would have been significant subdivision of labor – in the sense that some cells, for instance, could be entirely devoted to the building of skeletal tissues (shells or internal hard parts) for the benefit of the remainder of the "crew."

The problem with this scenario is that the chances of fossil remains of such organisms being preserved, and then surviving virtually unaltered in the rocks for the

ABOVE *The purple stinger* (Pelagia noctiluga), *an Australian jellyfish, typifies the delicacy and softness of many sea creatures. Amazingly, some of the earliest complex fossils known from southern Australia resemble jellyfish.*

next 600 million years, seems unimaginably remote. If we choose an example from today – a jellyfish has the right degree of cellular organization and "soft-bodiedness" – it is extremely difficult to imagine anything as floppy and gelatinous leaving any fossilizable impression whatsoever. And yet paradoxically that is exactly what seems to have happened, for some of the earliest soft-bodied creatures have been discovered in rocks that date back to the Precambrian–Cambrian boundary. The first of these discoveries was made half a century ago in southern Australia.

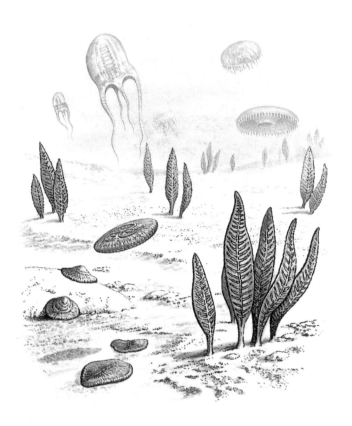

Following the discoveries by Reg Sprigg, and the early interpretation of scientists, the common reconstruction of the Ediacaran world was as shown here, with large sea pens (relatives of living forms) and jellyfish in abundance. Such apparently "simple" forms of life seemed appropriate for these ancient oceans – but are these views correct? Others later challenged them and offered quite different interpretations.

The Ediacara discovery

In 1946 a keen young amateur geologist named Reg Sprigg discovered some unusual saucer-shaped fossil impressions while walking near Ediacara in the Flinders Mountains of southern Australia. He immediately identified the fossil as the impression of a jellyfish and named it *Ediacara flindersi*. Over the next year or so a variety of disk-shaped fossils of this general type were discovered in the area. All of these were thought to be jellyfish impressions and fitted quite neatly with the idea that such creatures, which today have a relatively simple body organization and are consequently often described as "primitive," would have been among the earliest to have populated the oceans.

In 1957 a schoolboy, Roger Mason, came across some peculiar fossil impressions that looked a little like the fronds of ferns. He made this find in rocks of Late Precambrian age in Leicestershire in the English Midlands, near Charnwood Forest, and they were therefore named *Charnia*. At first they were thought to be

algae, but this idea was rapidly dismissed when similar fossils were described from Ediacara as sea pens (pennatulate cnidarians, looking rather like a bunch of anemones on a stick). Since the late 1950s other Ediacaran faunas (now referred to as Vendian faunas or vendozoans) have been discovered around the world, notably in Namibia, Newfoundland, and Byelorussia (White Russia). The majority of these fossils have been studied and almost all have been compared with modern groups of animals – notably jellyfish, soft corals, or sea pens, and segmented worms of various kinds.

Some of the Ediacaran types of fossils do indeed seem to show relationships, even if a little distant, to modern forms. One of the most characteristic groups is one of simple disk-shaped fossils with three radiating canals inside (*Tribrachidium, Anabarites, Skinnera*). These have been called "trilobozoans" (three-lobed animals) and are thought to be close relatives of modern jellyfish (medusans); they certainly look similar, except that modern forms have four body lobes. Also quite frequently found are ribbon-like traces. These seem to represent the tracks left by actively moving organisms crawling across the sea floor, perhaps grazing on the film of blue-green algae that would have covered any reasonably well-lit surface under the water.

Problems of interpretation

In the 1970s this view of Vendian animals as an assortment of creatures that were a little strange, but with a little ingenuity quite comparable to modern forms, began to be challenged. First, the Namibian fossils – most of which were obscure, spindle-shaped objects – could not readily be fitted into living groups. At first they were referred to as a completely new and independent group known as petalonamids. This provoked the idea that perhaps all Vendian creatures were unique and have since become extinct. A development of this concept was the suggestion that the Vendian creatures were simply the end product of an as yet unknown sequence of evolution of multicellular organisms during the Late Precambrian Period.

Vendian quilted mattresses

It was in the early 1980s that Professor Dolf Seilacher of Tübingen in Germany came up with an entirely novel suggestion to explain the Vendian fauna. To start with, he confirmed the difficulties encountered when trying to make these creatures fit into modern groups. For example, although some of the fossils indeed seemed to resemble soft corals, when their detailed structures were examined the comparison collapsed. Soft corals consist

QUILTED ANIMALS

Tribrachidium.

Shown (BELOW) *resting on the sea floor, and* (RIGHT) *in fossil form,* Tribrachidium *is thought to belong to an extinct group of jellyfish (Medusae) relatives, named "trilobozoans" because their bodies had three curved lobes. Those of modern jellyfish are divided into multiples of four. These trilobozoans may have swum freely like Medusae, or have crept along the sea floor.*

Dickinsonia

This curious fossil (BELOW LEFT), *abundant in Ediacara and elsewhere, has been the subject of much speculation by paleontologists. For a long time it was thought to be an early segmented worm, and then to be a stiff, "air-mattress"*

creature. But careful study of fossil impressions has revealed them to have a front and back end, and to exist as expanded or contracted forms (suggesting a flexible body wall). Also, many of the impressions show a smooth rim indicating where the body has contracted just before it became buried in sediment. It is shown (BELOW RIGHT) *as a mobile, worm-like creature ploughing over the sea bed.*

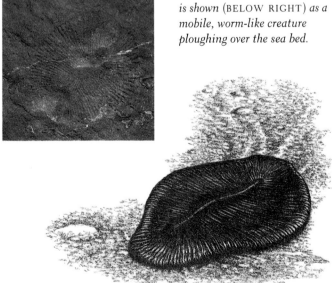

of branching colonies of tiny polyps with spaces around each to permit water to circulate and bring in microscopic particles of food. However, examination of the Vendian fossils shows that their branches are not separated in the same way, but consist instead of flattened lobes of apparently connected tissues.

Seilacher also noticed that many of the Vendian creatures seemed to be "quilted" – they had flattened strips, looking as if they had been stitched down, at regular intervals along or across the body. This gave rise to the possibility that these creatures were built rather like inflatable mattresses. Seilacher suggested that they were immobile (quite a number had identifiable stalks for attachment to the sea bed), tough-skinned organisms, completely unique and unrelated to the worms and jellyfish that constituted the standard forms for comparison at this time.

This is not a design seen in any animals living today – earthworms do have something basically similar in terms of a compartmented body, but they are not flattened. The Vendian fauna may represent an entirely novel, and ultimately unsuccessful, experiment in early life-form design. But there are hints, noticeably from the tracks and trails preserved with these creatures, that there were also other more conventional worm-like creatures whose remains have not been preserved since their bodies were far less substantial.

Though this view of vendozoans is quite beguiling in many ways, it is still only a suggestion. Some of the supposedly quilted animals such as *Spriggina* and *Dickinsonia* have for a long time been thought to be relatives of modern animal groups – they are bilaterally symmetrical and seem to have a front and rear end. Such features make them appear very much like mobile creatures, rather than stiff, quilted organisms that were permanently anchored to the sea bed. In particular *Dickinsonia*, despite the opinions expressed by Seilacher, does not seem to have been a rigid "air mattress" type of organism, as far as can be seen from the preserved remains that have been uncovered.

The paleontologist Dr Mary Wade has shown that individuals with the same number of segments (presumably therefore of the same "age," since they seem to have grown by adding segments at the rear end) can be of different sizes. One beautifully preserved slab bears two *Dickinsonia* with the same number of segments, but of widely differing sizes. In addition, the edges of the preserved area of the fossils have a distinct "halo," which seems to show that the body contracted immediately before it became buried. Neither of these observations fits comfortably with the idea of the rigid, quilted organism, but both accord well with the notion of a flexible, mobile animal.

THE *SPRIGGINA* DEBATE

An early worm . . . ?
Spriggina *has a head at one end, a segmented body, and a tapering tail end. When the fossil was first discovered, these features led Glaessner and many of his fellow paleontologists to view it as an early, but relatively conventional, segmented worm* (BELOW).

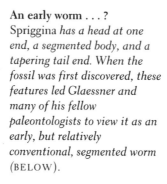

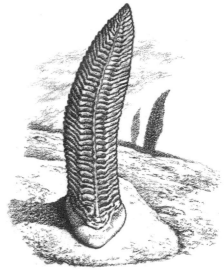

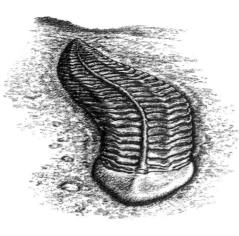

The fossil evidence
(ABOVE) *This well-known fossil from Ediacara has been given two interpretations. Both are illustrated on the right – but at present paleontologists do not know which of these versions, if either, is correct.*

. . . or a stationary creature?
Seilacher's recent, more radical alternative opinion is that Spriggina *may not, as some believe, be an ancestor of the later arthropods. The "head" could be the holdfast of a creature which was more like the leaf or frond of a fern and stood stationary in the water* (ABOVE).

Spriggina is less easily resolved. Seilacher's view suggests that the curved, shield-shaped end of the organism was a "holdfast" – its area of attachment to the sea bed – while the long, segmented part of the body was a "frond." The more traditional view of Glaessner and many others interprets the segmented body as just that, and the shield-shaped area as a genuine head. Another favored notion is that *Spriggina* is one of the earliest arthropods (jointed-legged creatures), perhaps a forerunner of the trilobites. The fossil evidence is frustratingly equivocal at present, but it does seem that not all of the curious Vendian organisms should be regarded as immobile quilted mattresses.

It is conceivable that the genuinely quilted creatures were grappling with the problems of increasing size. Many are quite large – 4ins (10cm) or more in diameter – while others are long and ribbon-like, such as the spindle-shaped organisms from Newfoundland. Increasing the size of an organism can have a potentially disastrous effect on its functions. Doubling the length and width

of a surface quadruples its area. Doubling the length, width, and height of a solid makes its volume eight times bigger. If the quilted organisms were indeed relatively simple (as their structure seems to indicate), and did not have complex internal systems for transporting food, waste, and respiratory gases, they could not have become much larger while remaining the same shape. This problem is evident in modern insects, which breathe by taking in air through holes in the side of the body. If an insect is too large, air simply cannot diffuse through to the middle of the body. Large dragonflies solve the problem by being extremely long and thin. It is possible that the quilted creatures, faced with a similar situation, coped in a different way – by evolving extremely flat bodies.

It is very difficult to imagine what kind of lives these quilted vendozoans led. One possibility is that, as with giant clams (*Tridacna*) today, their tissues housed photosynthetic bacteria so that sunlight provided the nutrients for their tissues. Such an interpretation is very tempting if these organisms lived in relatively shallow water, and their wide, flat shape would present the maximum area to the light. Unfortunately at least some of the quilted fossils – notably those from Newfoundland – lived something like 330 ft (100m) below the surface, at which depth light levels are really too low for this sort of lifestyle to be sustainable.

Alternative suggestions include the notion that these organisms lived at the junction between the oxygen-rich waters above the surface of the sea bed and the oxygen-poor mud beneath, and acted as chemical factories which bridged the two environments. Perhaps, like *Dickinsonia*, they lay prostrate on the sea bed, covered with a mat of blue-green algae, right on the boundary layer. Even the free-standing frond-like creatures such as *Charnia* may have rooted their anchors in the mud and extended their frond into the oxygen-richer water above in order to bridge the two environments. Yet even here there are exceptions: *Pteridinium* was a frond-like organism that lived in deep water and had virtually no roots; perhaps it simply absorbed organic material through its body wall.

The mystery of preservation

The incredible fossils at Ediacara are generally preserved on the underside of quartz-rich sandstones. The grains of the original quartz sand are well rounded, and between them the spaces are filled with secondary quartz that has been laid down like a kind of mineral cement. The layers of sandstone are usually only a hand's breadth thick, and are often marked on their upper and lower layers by ripples which represent the original surface of the sea bed (either as a natural surface on top, or on the lower surface as a cast of the layer below). Successive beds are indicated by a very fine layer of sediment, which probably marks the position of a thin mat of cyanobacteria (blue-green algae) that would have covered all well-lit exposed sediment surfaces at the time.

Although it was thought for a long time that the sea bed was relatively shallow and perhaps the area was intertidal (uncovered at high tide), it is now believed that the water was considerably deeper. So the geological setting shows sandstones derived from weathered sands (the reason why they are well rounded, rather than sharp and angular) that have been stirred up by short-lived storms and later dumped in deeper waters – burying and preserving a "snapshot" of the sea bed at the time when it was deposited.

One extraordinary feature of the preservation of the fossil impressions at Ediacara is that the underside of the sandstone beds bears concave impressions of these fossils. This implies that the sand on the sea bed flowed

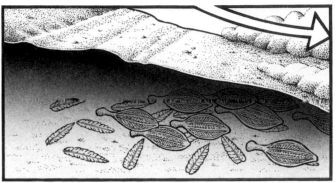

Free-standing Charniodiscus *are shown attached by a holdfast to the sea floor* (TOP). *Lying in front of them are spindle-shaped organisms whose random arrangement ensures that none overlaps the next. Does this mean that they could move apart and thus avoid one another?* ABOVE *After a disastrous volcanic eruption the* Charniodiscus *have been knocked flat in the same direction as the rush of water and sediment which has buried them, while the spindle-shaped organisms are arranged as they were in life.*

upward, as the sediments were compacted, into the hollows left by the quilted organisms. This process seems inconceivable unless the roof of sand above the creature was already strong enough to resist the force of gravity. Whether this strength derived from the early cementing of the sand grains, or from the strength of the tissues of the quilted creature, is impossible to decide.

Ediacara-type material found in Newfoundland consists mainly of characteristic spindle-shaped fossils and frond-like organisms with circular holdfasts. All appear to be buried under a thin layer of volcanic ash. Curiously, the spindle-shaped fossils tend to be scattered randomly on the surface, lying in all directions, while the frond-like organisms are found lying all in the same direction. From this it has been suggested that the frond-like organisms (*Charniodiscus*) stood upright in the water and were knocked over in the same direction by the sudden pulse of volcanic sediment, while the spindle-shaped fossils grew prostrate on the sea bed and in no particular orientation.

Thus the preservation of these Late Precambrian fossils is a matter of good fortune – in the first instance as a result of periodic storms causing rapid burial of sea-floor creatures beneath layers of sand, in the other a consequence of periodic falls of volcanic ash. The Namibian deposits also suggest that the organisms were buried rapidly beneath moving masses of sand.

The difficulties encountered in deciding how closely the Vendian creatures are related to living organisms is only one sign of the sheer strangeness of the world in these early times.

The end of the quilted creatures?

Quilted creatures do not seem to have survived very long beyond the Precambrian–Cambrian boundary; but, even though at present this is only deduced from trace fossils (traces of tracks and trails left behind by organisms), more normal "worms" may well have shared the world with them. The meandering paths made by these organisms suggest that they were mobile and bilaterally symmetrical, with an anterior and posterior end, a relatively simple nervous system, and sense organs of sufficient sophistication to allow them to "graze" the microbial mat which must have covered the sea floor in any shallow, well-lit area. Curiously, there is no convincing evidence of the presence of burrowing creatures among Vendian communities; these only begin to appear in the Early Cambrian Period.

By the very end of the Precambrian the curious Vendozoans had become extinct. Why the quilted creatures in particular died out is a mystery – one of a series of extinction events that have punctuated the history of life (more obscure perhaps, but no less dramatic, than the loss of the dinosaurs 540 million years later). Fortunately the extinction was not total: some forms did manage to survive, presumably relatives of the organisms that left the tracks and trails with the vendozoans. The problem faced by paleontologists is trying to explain why selected groups of organisms survive such extinctions, while others perish. Was there something peculiar about the biology or design of the non-survivors, or were they simply the victims of chance?

It is also at about this time that a range of burrowing organisms – including cnidarians, nematodes, annelids, and arthropods – begin to make their appearance in the fossil record. It has been suggested that this widespread development was associated with the appearance of predators, since burrowing is one of the first means of escape. If this is the case, the immobile erect or prostrate quilted creatures may have provided rich pickings to begin with – and their demise may indeed be related to such an event.

SMALL SHELLY FAUNAS OF THE TOMMOTIAN

During the Tommotian or earliest Cambrian – immediately following the major extinction event which marks the disappearance of the distinctive Vendian faunas around the world – there appear what are termed "small shelly faunas." Among the most frequently found fossils in these Early Cambrian times are archaeocyathids – curious champagne glass-shaped organisms. Their body construction is basically that of two cups, one inside the other, each of which has sieve-like walls; the two cups are held apart by narrow radial walls. The lower, pointed end of archaeocyathids has what appear to be "roots," which presumably secured the whole organism to the sea bed, while the upper, open end of the cup probably housed the creature's main organs. Among living creatures today it is the sponges and corals that seem closest to these in general organization, since both sorts of organism can live in cup-like structures. The sieve-like body wall is perhaps more reminiscent of sponges in general, but the more these archaeocyathids are investigated the more bizarre they seem.

Other traces of organisms from the Early Cambrian include curious tubes and horn-like structures which presumably housed small living creatures (*Tommotia, Hyolithellus, Lenargyrion*). Some of these shells look like curved, pointed hats (*Latouchella, Anabarella*) or snail shells (*Aldanella*). It has been suggested that they were inhabited by molluscs, or were the valves of brachiopods, but nobody really has any clear idea what lived in, or produced, these enigmatic little fossils.

The reconstructions opposite show speculative lifestyles for the organisms that lived in these shells – lifestyles consistent with their structure. The shells are rather narrow from side to side, which suggests that the animal, if it was a mollusc, would have had a narrow foot with its gills hunched up inside the shell just above the foot. These animals may have ploughed through the layer of sediment on the sea floor, eating from the mat of blue-green algae on the surface. Quite where the gill might have been located and which way round the shell went (whether it was hooked forward, or curled backward) is the source of some debate. One possible solution may be provided by the small, similarly shaped shell of a creature named *Yochelcionella*, which has a little tube like the exhaust pipe of an automobile projecting from the area just beneath the curled tip of the shell. It has been suggested that this device may have allowed the current of water to pass out from the gill area behind the shell. This means that the shell probably curled backward at the tip, rather than forward, and that the gills were lodged up on the sides of the shell near the back edge.

Latouchella

Latouchella

This creature is often found as shell casts (the preserved infilling of the original shell). It is likely that early molluscs with a creeping foot lived inside.

Yochelcionella

The extraordinary "snorkel" beneath the curled tip was probably the "exhaust pipe" for water passing over the gills, which lay under the mantle and shell.

Yochelcionella

Microdictyon

This creature remained a puzzle while only its circular sieve plates were known. When whole animals were discovered they resembled modern velvet worms, the sieve plates forming a kind of armor plating.

Tommotia

These large, angular shells with regular (possibly growth) bands may have been occupied by a cephalopod ancestor – one that combined a simple foot-like structure with long grasping and sensory tentacles.

Hyolithellus

These tiny fossils are another of the many enigmas of the Tommotian. It is very tempting to place a slender-tentacled mollusc in them, as shown here – but in truth the inhabitant of the shell is at present entirely unknown.

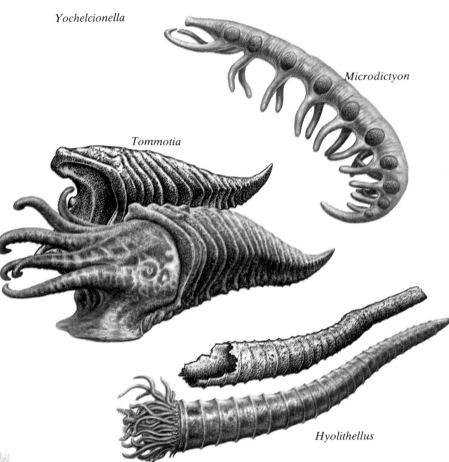

Microdictyon

Tommotia

Hyolithellus

Lenargyrion

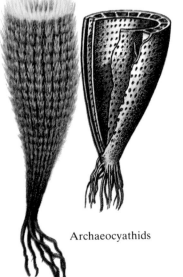

Archaeocyathids

Lenargyrion

Another mystery, it is so far known only from these curious disk-shaped structures, which may well be the armor plating of some larger creature as yet undiscovered. The similarity between these and the early remains of Microdictyon is quite striking.

Archaeocyathids

The structure of these fossils is well known – two sieve-like containers one inside the other and separated by thin struts. The animal was probably vaguely sponge-like and anchored to the sea floor.

In addition to these, large numbers of sharp, angular plates (scales, spicules, or sclerites) have also been recovered; they were supposed to represent the body armor of creatures named halkieriids. Some animals bearing scaly armored coats have been identified in Canada in what are known as the Burgess Shale deposits, of the Middle Cambrian (see below), and it was assumed that these earlier forms would be rather similar to these generally heavily armored, perhaps vaguely slug-like, creatures. Eventually a complete halkieriid was discovered in 1990 in northern Greenland – and proved the theory wrong. *Halkieria* turned out to be a long, tubular, worm-like creature, covered in tiny, overlapping sclerites, but capped on either end by a limpet-like shell.

In China another extraordinary form was found. Previously this had been known only from curious rounded sclerites with a criss-crossing net-like pattern, on account of which it was named *Microdictyon* ("tiny net"). It now proved to be an animal with a cylindrical body, along the flanks of which were arranged ten pairs of the curious sclerites, and beneath which were ten pairs of leg-like appendages. The discovery of *Microdictyon* was to have a dramatic and amusing effect on the interpretation of one of the later Burgess Shale creatures, *Hallucigenia*.

Fossil fragments from Canada led early researchers to speculate that halkieriids looked like armored slugs. But recently better-preserved halkieriid fossils have been discovered in Greenland, and reveal a sausage-shaped body covered in small scales or sclerites, with a limpet shell-shaped cap at each end of the animal. Halkieria *does, however, seem to have been slug-like in habit, crawling along on a foot.*

One of the more recent observations concerning animal life in the Early Cambrian raises the question of general body form and possible biological interactions. The organisms of the Late Precambrian were notably unarmored. *Dickinsonia* and *Spriggina* may well have represented mobile, segmented creatures which developed a flattened form in order to increase their contact with the surface beneath them, which would have made movement easier.

However, this kind of body form would have become extremely vulnerable once worms with barbed probosces began to appear – the soft, flattened body would have been easily torn apart by these predators. One solution would have been to develop some form of armored covering – either a hard carapace (the trilobite solution) or a chain mail-like covering of sclerites (the halkieriid solution). The other option would seem to have been avoidance: cnidarians, nematodes, annelids, and arthropods all burrowed into the sea floor.

The animals of the Early and Middle Cambrian seem to be increasingly segmented and armored in various ways – with long spines, with thin sclerites, or with denser, almost chain mail-like, covering. In most cases this would seem to be an appropriate defense against predatory worms which would probably have tried to swallow their prey whole, rather than a means of thwarting hunters with jaws and teeth. The disappearance in Middle Cambrian times of the "cataphract-armored" forms (those covered in small plates rather than big shells) may well coincide with the appearance of the latter kind of predator, at which point continuous shells rather than sclerites would have become much more effective as defensive armor. *Anomalocaris*, a predator with a functional biting mouth, is one of the most dramatic animals of the Middle Cambrian Burgess Shale.

THE BURGESS SHALE

A remarkable window on life during the Cambrian Period came to light in 1909 with the discovery of an unusually abundant deposit of fossils in some Canadian rocks known as the Burgess Shale. Charles Doolittle Walcott, who was at that time head of the Smithsonian Institution in Washington, DC, discovered the site during his explorations in the Rockies. The site lies in what is now the Yoho National Park in eastern British Columbia. The extraordinary richness of this discovery can be appreciated when it is realized that over 70,000 fossils have been collected from the Burgess Shale alone.

The state of preservation of these fossils is exquisite. Soft-bodied creatures, for instance, are revealed in remarkable detail, even to the extent of fine filamentous

hairs on the limbs of tiny shrimp-like creatures. The out-line of the intestines and even the gut contents – the evidence perhaps of last meals – can be seen in a variety of creatures. They are all preserved as imprints on very fine-grained muds that have turned to shale.

The animals of the Burgess Shale probably lived on mud banks built up along the base of a massive, nearly vertical wall called the Cathedral Escarpment, a reef constructed primarily of calcareous algae (today's reef-building organisms, such as corals, had not yet evolved). Such habitats, in moderately shallow water, adequately lit and well aerated, generally house a wide and typical range of marine creatures. From that point of view the Burgess Shale holds an ordinary fauna from habitats well represented in the fossil record.

The extraordinary variety of anatomical designs found among its members cannot be attributed to any pecu-liarity of its ecology. Sunlit conditions and well-aerated waters do not favor fossilization because they encourage scavengers to feast on any dead animals, and microbial activity will ensure rapid decay of whatever remains. To

In the finely layered rocks which have been buckled up and twisted to form the Rocky Mountains of western North America are the Burgess Shale localities of British Columbia. This is a view of Raymond's Quarry, not far above the original site so laboriously excavated by Charles Doolittle Wallcott. The animals are found by carefully and painstakingly cutting, splitting, and then examining the chunks broken from the rock face. The beautiful mountainous backdrop, added to the sheer scientific excitement associated with any discovery in the Burgess Shale, must make this one of the most exhilarating places in the world to hunt for fossils. Such collecting is, however, strictly controlled by the Canadian Federal Authorities: the site lies inside the Yoho National Park, and it is unlawful to collect here without a permit.

be preserved as fossils, these animals needed to be buried elsewhere. Perhaps the mud banks near the foot of these towering escarpments became thick and unsta-ble from time to time, so that slight earth tremors might have caused the mud to slide into deeper waters devoid of oxygen. Rapid burial in mud here would preserve soft-bodied creatures, because there would be no scavengers and very little microbial activity.

The fact that the Burgess Shale animals are found only in a relatively confined band of shale supports the notion that they were preserved in a series of very local mudslides. The lack of decay which we have presumed to be associated with oxygen-free conditions is also neatly linked to the absence from the Burgess Shale of any tracks and trails – so prominent in the Ediacara – and supports the notion of rapid inundation and burial in a life-inhibiting environment. It is this remarkable set of circumstances that has provided us with a unique snapshot of Cambrian sea-floor life.

Unclassifiable enigmas

The pattern of Walcott's work is reminiscent of that done on the Ediacara fauna, where scientists attempted to shoehorn fossil forms into recognizable groups of later animals. Early illustrations reconstruct the Burgess Shale as a reasonably familiar sea-floor community of creatures, an interpretation that remained unchallenged until the early 1970s.

A detailed review of the Burgess Shale fauna began after survey work and new collecting under the auspices of the Geological Survey of Canada. Professor Harry Whittington – an authority on trilobites, the primitive arthropods found as abundant fossils in Cambrian and younger rocks – was assigned to the project, since the fauna were thought to consist primarily of arthropods. Thanks to the efforts of Professor Whittington and his colleagues, first at Harvard and then at Cambridge, England, very many forms from the Burgess Shale have now been described.

Marrella was one of the first arthropods to be thoroughly studied at this time. It is a tiny creature no more than ¾ inch (2cm) in length. The animal has two long antennae which project from the sides of the head shield; these served as sensors or feelers. The head area shows no evidence of eyes, and is composed of a block-shaped shield with two pairs of very prominent, swept-back spines. Behind the head shield the body tapers gradually as a series of jointed segments, from each of

One of the most abundant of the Burgess Shale fossils, and the most splendid-looking, is this tiny but remarkable arthropod. It seems likely that "shoals" of these beautiful little creatures swam in the Cambrian seas, and presumably formed the staple diet of many of the contemporary predators. They seem to be the ecological equivalent of present-day krill, the shrimps which are hunted by the giant baleen (or whalebone) whales. Fortunately for Marrella *there was nothing like these whales in Cambrian times. The only predator was* Anomalocaris, *which probably chased individual specimens rather than gulping down great shoals.* Marrella's *long, elegant spines may well have served as protective devices.*

which projects a jointed leg for scuttling over the sea bed; above each leg is a fragile, feathery gill.

Detailed study of the shape and arrangement of the head, feeding limbs, and walking limbs finally proved conclusively that this animal was not a trilobite ancestor, as Walcott had supposed, but an arthropod that could not readily be classified with any known group of arthropods. Admittedly it was a little like crustaceans and a little like trilobites, but not enough like either to draw firm conclusions about relationships. *Marrella* was to become the first of a long line of frustratingly awkward creatures that did not fit neatly into the types of organisms known at that time.

The fact that it is the most abundant of all the Burgess Shale animals – thousands of specimens have been discovered – suggests that it was a very successful life form. How *Marrella* lived is uncertain. It seems most likely that it scuttled across the sea bed, feeding on minute organisms – perhaps blue-green algae. Its long and rather elegant paired spines most probably served as defenses, making *Marrella* unpalatable to the numerous predatory worms and primitive arthropods found in the same deposits.

Opabinia was another strange and this time extremely rare creature described by Harry Whittington. This 3 ins (8cm) long animal had been considered very important by Walcott, who thought that the elongated, segmented body must be that of an animal midway, in an evolutionary sense, between annelids (segmented worms such as earthworms and ragworms) and arthropods. *Opabinia* had an extraordinary long "nozzle" at the front and a segmented body behind; it was also assumed to have had jointed legs tucked underneath.

However, yet again detailed study showed that this animal was genuinely unusual. For a start, it had five eyes. The curious tubular and presumably flexible "nozzle" beneath the head extended forward and ended in a pair of spiny jaws. The mouth lay behind the base of the "nozzle" and pointed backwards – it seems likely that the "nozzle" with its jaws could be bent back to fill the mouth with items of food caught in the jaws. The segmented body had paddle-shaped gills attached on either side of its undersurface, and near the tail end were three pairs of more fin-like lobes directed upward and outward. All the characters of this animal made it impossible to classify as either arthropod or annelid – so it was another enigma.

It is clear that *Opabinia* was a predator. With its many paddles and tail fins it would have been able to cruise above the bottom sediments, using its all-around vision to search for prey. The long "nozzle" could be used to impale and immobilize a victim without risking injury to the more delicate parts of its own body.

HALLUCIGENIA — WHICH WAY UP?

Stilts and tentacles . . .
The first restoration of this bizarre creature shows a tubular body on seven pairs of stilts. The tentacles were thought to be used for catching food particles and passing them into the gut. The globular "head" is a mysteriously crushed object with no identifiable characteristics.

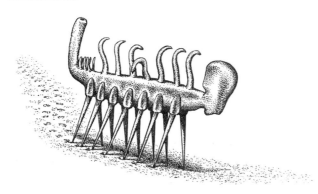

. . . or fleshy legs and spines?
Following the discovery of well-preserved lobopods ("fleshy-legged creatures") in China, Hallucigenia has been flipped over. The stilt-like "legs" are now thought to be defensive spines along its back, and the "tentacles" have been converted into fleshy (lobopod) legs. Despite the new discovery, it is still far from certain how many pairs of legs there are, and which is the front and which the back end!

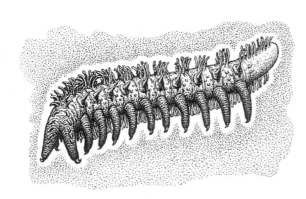

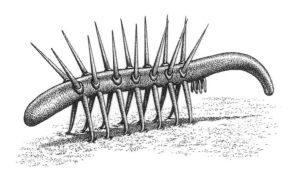

Hallucigenia was a particularly puzzling animal from the Burgess Shale. It was named because of its fantastically bizarre shape. About 1¼ins (3cm) long, the animal appears to have had a tubular body, with a round but very ill defined "head" at one end and a long, curved, tubular tail at the other. Along the main part of the trunk were seven pairs of sharp spines, above which there appeared to be a row of seven soft, tubular tentacles, with a cluster of smaller tentacles situated at the base of the tail.

The first reconstruction of this remarkable animal showed that it stood on its spines, as if on stilts. It was thought to move rather inefficiently along the mud of the sea bed, and the tentacles along its back were believed to be individual mouths capable of passing food into a communal gut. But in recent years new investigations have shown that the whole animal needs to be flipped onto its back. The "tentacles" were actually paired fleshy legs, while the stilt-like "legs" of the original reconstruction are in fact defensive spines which project from the animal's back.

Aysheaia is yet another Burgess Shale creature shaped like a worm with legs. The legs are fleshy and barbed, and at the front of the head there is a mouth with a pair of tentacles on either side. One rather peculiar feature of its fossils is that they are frequently found with remains of sponges. It has been suggested that *Aysheaia*'s spiky legs and clawed feet would have been perfect for crawling around on sponges; the creature may even have used its barbs to tear the bodies of the sponges and thus make feeding easier.

In most of their details *Hallucigenia* and *Aysheaia* resemble the relatively rare living onychophorans or velvet worms of southern Africa, Southeast Asia, the Caribbean and South America; these creatures tend to live in moist areas, particularly under the bark of rotting trees. They have a curious method of defense, which is to squirt over any attacker sticky fluids produced in large glands on the sides of the head. All the known living velvet worms are exclusively land-living. However, it would seem that during Burgess Shale times they were not only abundant and varied – quite a range has been found in the Lower and Middle Cambrian deposits – but that they were also probably marine creatures.

Alalcomenaeus is a shrimp-like animal with a relatively large head shield, on the edges of which are two eyes set on short stalks. Behind this is a set of 12 tapering segments, ending in a flattened paddle. Beneath the segments are paired legs for moving over the bottom and for swimming above it. On the inside of the legs are long, sharp spines that in side view can be seen hanging below the body. Whittington suggests that the spines were a part of its feeding apparatus and that the animals

Found in the Caribbean, this velvet worm (Maroperipatus torquatus) *has an elongate body and curious paired, fleshy legs. These features have led many to suspect that animals such as* Hallucigenia *and* Aysheaia *are distant relatives of velvet worms. Here a female is giving birth to a pair of young.*

may have been scavengers of dead or dying creatures on the sea bed. The long spines would have been capable of gripping and perhaps shredding the flesh of creatures such as the large soft-bodied trilobite *Tegopelte*. The torn flesh would have been passed up a groove at the base of the legs which carries food to the mouth – a common feature in these kinds of arthropods.

Leanchoilia is another curious little arthropod, shaped like a sea slater or gribble. The head is a triangular shield with a strange horn-like upturned prong, behind which is a compact, segmented body and a short, spiky tail. The "legs" are quite short, while the gills, which lie just outside the legs on either side, consist of large fleshy lobes which extend below the general level of the body and undoubtedly served as paddles, so that *Leanchoilia* would have been an adept swimmer.

While the body in general terms is not startling, it does have one peculiarity – the pair of so-called "great appendages." Just beneath the head are a pair of very large jointed structures, each of which bends at first downward and then sharply forward, branching into three long, whip-like extensions (presumably acting as antennae or feelers – useful for an animal that appears to be blind) and a small cluster of three sharp claws. From the way that some of the fossil specimens are preserved it seems that these "great appendages" could either be projected forward, perhaps for sensing and grappling with prey (as with *Opabinia*, page 46), or lie tucked beneath the body so that they did not get in the way when the creature was swimming.

CREATURES OF THE BURGESS SHALE

Opabinia captures **Amiskwia**
LEFT *One of the larger predatory, "worms" of the Burgess Shale,* Opabinia *had five eyes which would have given it excellent vision. Its slowness at swimming would have been compensated for by the long mobile jaw. The defenseless, gelatinous little* Amiskwia *would have been easy prey for Mid-Cambrian predators.*

Sanctacaris pursues *Leanchoilia*
RIGHT *The flattened tail and paired limbs of* Sanctacaris (TOP) *were used for propulsion, while the sharp-spined limbs round the head could tear at prey. The resting* Leanchoilia *is well protected by is plated body. If flipped onto its back, the slow-moving* Wiwaxia (FAR RIGHT) *is potentially more vulnerable.*

The scale of life in the Burgess Shale

Aysheaia
¾–1 inch (2–3cm)

Sanctacaris
4 ins (10cm)

Alalcomenaeus
1½ ins (4cm)

Wiwaxia
1–2 ins (3–5cm)

Amiskwia
1 inch (3cm)

Leanchoilia
2–3 ins (5–8cm)

Opabinia
3 ins (8cm)

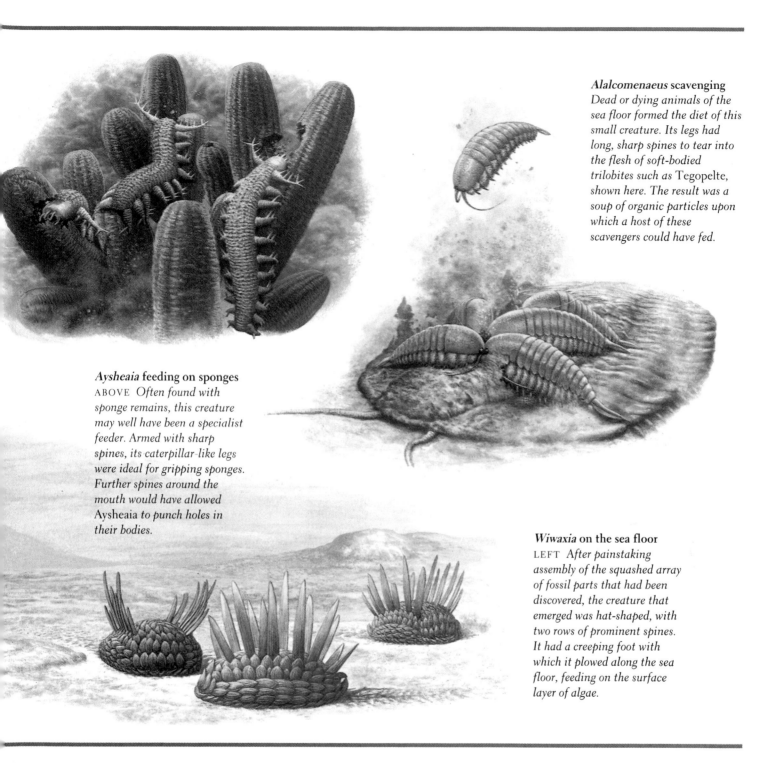

Alalcomenaeus scavenging
Dead or dying animals of the sea floor formed the diet of this small creature. Its legs had long, sharp spines to tear into the flesh of soft-bodied trilobites such as Tegopelte, shown here. The result was a soup of organic particles upon which a host of these scavengers could have fed.

Aysheaia feeding on sponges
ABOVE *Often found with sponge remains, this creature may well have been a specialist feeder. Armed with sharp spines, its caterpillar-like legs were ideal for gripping sponges. Further spines around the mouth would have allowed Aysheaia to punch holes in their bodies.*

Wiwaxia on the sea floor
LEFT *After painstaking assembly of the squashed array of fossil parts that had been discovered, the creature that emerged was hat-shaped, with two rows of prominent spines. It had a creeping foot with which it plowed along the sea floor, feeding on the surface layer of algae.*

Hallucigenia
1 inch (3 cm)

Pikaia
2 ins (5 cm)

Anomalocaris
24 ins (60 cm)

Marrella
$\frac{3}{4}$ inch (2 cm)

THREE CREATURES IN ONE

One of the most amazing detective stories of all, Anomalocaris has been assembled from what were once thought to be other Burgess Shale animals.

Original *Anomalocaris*
BELOW LEFT *The original material of Anomalocaris ("unusual shrimp") was thought to be a tail to which was added a rather shrimp-like body. In fact the "tail" was one of the large feeding arms of Anomalocaris.*

Laggania
This rather nondescript large fossil, which was once thought to be some form of sponge, has turned out to be the body of Anomalocaris.

Peytoia
RIGHT *Once believed to be a bizarre, jellyfish-like creature with a curious pineapple ring structure, Peytoia is now known to be the mouth part of Anomalocaris.*

The real *Anomalocaris*
ABOVE LEFT *Between them, Harry Whittington in Cambridge and Derek Briggs in Bristol finally solved the mystery. They joined these various "animals" together to produce the largest predator of the Burgess Shale. At 2 ft (60 cm) long or more, the real Anomalocaris was a gracefully built, slow-moving carnivore, one of the first with real jaws.*

Anomalocaris is the largest and evidently the fiercest of all Cambrian creatures. It remained unrecognized for an inordinately long time. The name means "odd shrimp," which turned out to be most appropriate. Parts of this creature were found in the 1880s on Mount Stephen in the Canadian Rockies, not far from the site of the Burgess Shale – whose existence was at that time unknown. It was named on the basis of what appeared to be the tail and trunk of a shrimp-like creature – no head was found at that time.

When the Burgess Shale was discovered several decades later, and its fauna studied, various odds and ends were described. As well as the mysterious *Anomalocaris*, these included a creature named *Peytoia*, which was supposed to be a ring-shaped jellyfish; another named *Laggania*, believed to be a sponge; and something that appeared to be the feeding limb of a giant arthropod. After a great deal of detective work by Dr Derek Briggs and Professor Harry Whittington, it was finally realized that the *Laggania* was the body of *Anomalocaris* and *Peytoia* its mouth, while the original specimens named *Anomalocaris* and the feeding arm were just that – the feeding arm of a giant predator nearly 2 ft (60cm) in length.

As now reconstructed, *Anomalocaris* was a remarkable animal. Its soft, segmented body was provided with a series of muscular flaps running down the sides; these, it is presumed, could be moved in a coordinated wave passing backwards, rather like the waves passing down the fins of cuttlefish. *Anomalocaris* would have been a large cruising predator of midwater and bottom-dwelling creatures. The powerful grasping arms would have first disabled prey and would then be twisted inwards towards the mouth, where the jaws would operate like pairs of sharp guillotines, slicing the prey into pieces that could be passed back down the gut for digestion.

Sanctacaris was discovered a short distance from the classic Burgess Shale site, and in very slightly earlier rocks, among many of the familiar animals of the Burgess Shale. Des Collins, a paleontologist from Ontario, found the remains of a remarkable arthropod 4 ins (10cm) long. It has a broad, flattened head with prominent eyes, plus a broad segmented body which ends in a flat tail flap and beneath which are a set of broad, paddle-like gills. This was clearly an active swimmer and a predator of other swimming creatures. Beneath the head is a battery of large, clawed feeding arms, which would have been used to grasp and tear apart its prey. Detailed study of this animal suggests that it is close to the ancestry of all later chelicerates – that is to say, of arthropods such as eurypterids, horseshoe crabs, scorpions, spiders, and mites. It lacks the large claws (chelicerae) which give the group its name, but that may be simply because that feature had not yet evolved. Unlike so many other Burgess Shale creatures, *Sanctacaris* relates in a direct way to living groups today.

Wiwaxia is very puzzling. About 2 ins (5cm) in length, the fossil remains tended to appear as an irregular mass of sclerites or scales where the animal had been compressed under the mud which formed its tomb. Gradually, through painstaking work by Dr Simon Conway Morris it became possible to piece together a pattern. The animal consisted of a naked sole, with which it crept along the sea floor. The domed upper surface was covered by an array of tidily organized overlapping scales, and along the upper surface were two rows of longer spines. On the underside, near the front end, was a pair of curved jaws which were presumably used to scrape algae from the sea floor. There was evidence that the sclerites had been damaged by predators but had then healed, that scales seemed to be shed from time to time, and that on occasions the whole animal was capable of molting or shedding its outer skin and growing a new one.

Comparisons had been drawn with halkieriids (see page 40) because both had similar sclerites, and attempts have been made – though without much success – to tie forms such as *Wiwaxia* to the origin of molluscs. These animals were clearly surface "grazers" which crept along on a muscular foot – hence the comparison to molluscs. This meant that they were slow-moving and potentially vulnerable; their defensive armor enabled them to survive the rise of many of the jawed carnivores in mid-Cambrian times, but this body design was rapidly superseded by shells.

Messages from the rocks?

Two things in particular emerge from a consideration of the Cambrian Period. First, and most obviously, this Period, as evidenced by the Burgess Shale, definitely seems to mark a spectacular rise in the range and variety of organisms. In the space of a few million years the pace of evolution of animal life appears to have increased enormously. Many attempts have been made to explain this phenomenon – linking it with rising oxygen levels, the first appearance of predators, and changes in ocean chemistry – but none is entirely convincing. The rapid emergence of complex forms of life still remains one of the Earth's great mysteries.

The other, slightly less obvious, fact is that, although there was a wide range of animal types in the Middle Cambrian, there was also very high mortality. It seems as if only a few lucky survivors persisted through into the Late Cambrian and Early Ordovician Periods; they seem to have suffered the fate that befell the vendozoans in the Late Precambrian and Early Cambrian. Why some body plans survived periods of major extinction, while others perished, is another evolutionary conundrum. One argument is that some possessed features that enabled them to survive in the prevailing conditions, such as adequate defenses against predators, while others did not. An alternative view puts it all down to contingency – some were simply lucky survivors. Into that group of lucky (or plucky) organisms fell one small but evolutionarily important creature, *Pikaia*.

Links to human ancestry

Among the amazing and unexpected animals of the Burgess Shale there are a small number that possess some kinship with the fauna of today – genuine arthropods related to scorpions and trilobites, as well as shrimp-like crustaceans and some recognizable worms.

Pikaia is a peculiar little worm-like creature no more than 2 ins (5cm) long. It was recognized by Walcott and named in honor of nearby Mount Pika.

Walcott claimed that it was a polychaete worm, a relative of modern ragworms, but he was wrong. The segmentation of the body is dissimilar, and in fact shows

Named after Mount Pika in the Rockies, this small, worm-like creature of the Burgess Shale may be our earliest ancestor. The fossils seem to possess a suite of potential chordate characteristics, including a notochord (precursor of the vertebral column) and segmented muscles (myotomes) to power the tail, and can be presumed to have had a nerve cord and a pharynx with gill slits.

the regular series of muscle blocks called myotomes which are very characteristic of early chordates – the group to which the human species belongs. In addition to the muscle blocks *Pikaia* has a stiffening rod or notochord (from which the name "chordate" comes) running more or less the length of its body; this served as an anticompression device against which the muscles could work, and as a "coat hanger" for the body organs. At the front of the body there is also an enlarged internal gill area – or pharynx, as it is called in chordates. *Pikaia* has yet to be described in detail, so it is not known whether other parts of the anatomy associated with chordates are all there.

This little animal is surprisingly similar to modern-day *Branchiostoma* (better known by its old name, *Amphioxus*). This creature spends most of its adult life sitting in sand and gravel, with just its mouth and tentacles sticking out of the surface, drawing in food currents (microscopic organisms are filtered out on its gills) and water for respiration. When disturbed, it is a rapid darting swimmer, using its tail fin to great effect. It is possible that *Pikaia* had a similar lifestyle, but it is also possible that the creature was an active swimmer. *Pikaia* is known from only about 30 specimens, so it was evidently not particularly abundant and therefore may not have been exclusively burrowing in habit – otherwise many more examples are likely to have been preserved.

What are chordates?

Members of this group are recognized by various characteristics, of which some have been described above for *Pikaia*. Another important feature is a spinal nerve cord running along the top of the notochord, enlarged at the animal's front end to accommodate the sense organs – in fact, some kind of brain. Chordates also have a tubular blood system including kidneys in pairs.

Modern chordates comprise three important, but by no means equally abundant, groups. The vertebrates, animals with a backbone or vertebral column – including fishes, amphibians, reptiles, birds, and mammals such as ourselves – are very abundant throughout the world. The tunicates are moderately abundant marine animals that live inside a gelatinous tunic – hence the name. They include sea squirts, which live attached to rocks and seaweed and are occasionally found washed up on the seashore (if you squeeze them they squirt water – hence the name), as well as seagoing salps. The third group consists of the acraniates. These relatively rare marine animals lack a cranium or braincase, and comprise just a few species of small, soft-bodied, spindle-shaped animals including *Branchiostoma*, which was described above.

Although the chordates include attached, almost plant-like creatures such as tunicates, all three groups possess, at some stage in their life cycle, the typical features described above. So before it turns into an adult sea squirt the tunicate goes through a youthful stage, known as a larva, when it exhibits almost all the chordate characteristics. Its larva, called the "tadpole larva" (this merely refers to the general shape, and has nothing to do with the typical tadpoles of frogs), has a long tail with muscles, a notochord, a nerve cord and a well-developed pharynx. Much of this is reorganized when the "tadpole" metamorphoses into an adult tunicate – the tail and most of the nervous system are lost, and the animal becomes simply an enlarged, stationary pharynx. The relatively simple, swimming way of life seen in *Branchiostoma* and larval tunicates may well have been how all prehistoric chordates lived.

The origin of chordates

But how did chordates arise in the first place? A great deal of attention has been paid by paleontologists to a variety of apparent near relatives of the chordates, in order to try to understand human ancestry in the context of the history of life on Earth. There are two principal groups to which chordates show some affinity, and both seem at first sight singularly unlikely. The hemichordates, which consist of acorn worms and some minute tentacled creatures known as pterobranchs, are

WHAT ARE CHORDATES?

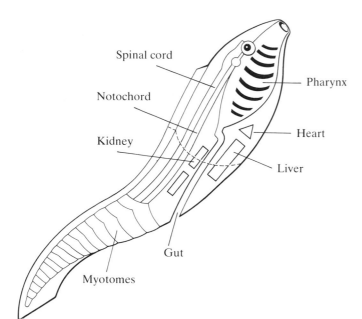

Spinal cord

Notochord

Kidney

Myotomes

Gut

Pharynx

Heart

Liver

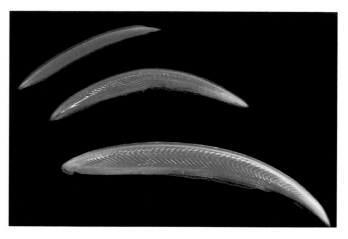

Branchiostoma
ABOVE *These tiny, filter-feeding, Pikaia-like modern creatures of the sea bed exhibit all the classic chordate features.*

Chordate characteristics
ABOVE *All the modern chordates display this suite of anatomical characteristics at some stage during their lives – humans, for instance, exhibit many of them during their embryonic growth in the womb. These features provide us with a useful checklist for identifying members of this important group.*

Sea squirts (tunicates)
The chordate group is vast and extremely wide-ranging. At first sight it may seem surprising that sea squirts belong to it. However, while the adult (RIGHT) is specialized for filter feeding, the larval form (ABOVE), which is known as the "tadpole larva," exhibits a full set of chordate characteristics.

WHY ZOOLOGISTS LINK CHORDATES WITH HEMICHORDATES AND ECHINODERMS

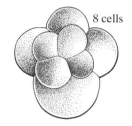

Indeterminate cleavage

2 4 cells
8 16

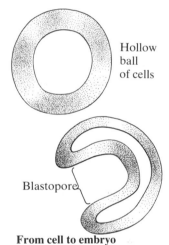

Determinate cleavage

8 cells

Hollow ball of cells

Blastopore

From cell to embryo

Cell division and development

LEFT *Once a chordate egg* (TOP) *has been fertilized it begins to divide into two, four, eight, sixteen daughter cells, and so on. The cells divide at rightangles to one another at first, to make neatly stacked rings. This is known as indeterminate cleavage, which means that the cells have not yet "decided" what they are going to be: splitting here can produce "twins". The only other animal groups whose cells divide in this way are hemichordates and echinoderms. Other groups of animals such as invertebrates show a more tightly packed spiral arrangement of cells* (CENTER). *This is called determinate cleavage – each cell "knows" where it is. The subsequent development of the cell mass into an embryo* (BOTTOM) *also differs. The first opening or blastopore becomes the anus in chordates, hemichordates, and echinoderms, whereas in invertebrates it becomes the mouth.*

either soft-bodied creatures which burrow in the sediment using a front end that looks rather like an acorn, or small, globular-bodied animals with a little group of tentacles on top which fan the water to catch minute particles of food; the extinct graptolites also appear to belong to this group. The second group, the echinoderms, comprises sea urchins, sea cucumbers, starfish and other related forms including crinoids, all of which have a curious fivefold symmetry (like a five-pointed star), calcite skeletons, and unique structures known as tube feet.

The reason for zoologists trying to link chordates with hemichordates and echinoderms is that, in all three groups, the cells of a fertilized egg develop into an embryo in the same way. Cleavage or cell division is radial, so that at first the cells settle into rings; cell division is also inde-

terminate rather than determinate, which means that the early embryo can be divided into two and each will still develop into a complete animal. In other creatures – for example, worms, molluscs, and insects – development is different. At first the cells form a spiral pattern rather than rings; and cell division is determinate.

In invertebrates the first opening that develops in the embryonic mass of cells (the blastopore) becomes the mouth, which is why worms, molluscs, and insects are called protostomes (literally, "first mouth"). In chordates, hemichordates, and echinoderms, however, the blastopore becomes the anus and a mouth develops at the other end of the embryo. For this reason they are known as deuterostomes ("other mouth"). This unifying set of characteristics has given rise to a number of ideas

Hemichordates: acorn worms
OPPOSITE ABOVE *These curiously shaped seashore worms, with their very acorn-like front ends, seem improbable chordate relatives. Yet they appear to have several features in common, including gill slits.*

Early echinoderms: sea cucumbers
OPPOSITE BELOW *Members of the same group of animals as the more familiar starfish and sea urchins, sea cucumbers such as* Thelenota *creep along the sea floor using hundreds of tiny tube feet. When disturbed, they have an alarming tendency to spew out their intestines to scare off predators.*

Later echinoderms: starfish
LEFT *Despite their hard calcitic skeletons, fivefold symmetry, and extraordinary tube-foot system (none of which are seen in any other group of animals), echinoderms share their pattern of cell division and development with that of acorn worms and chordates, which seems to link these groups genealogically.*

about how and when chordates first appeared. All the unspecialized chordates, echinoderms, and hemichordates have similar larval stages. It has therefore been supposed that changes in the form of the larva in early ancestral forms could have resulted in the patterns seen in these three groups today, even though as adults there is very little resemblance between them.

In the late 1960s Dr Dick Jefferies of the Natural History Museum in London made a radical suggestion – though this was built on ideas first put forward in the 1930s. He worked on early, irregular echinoderms – ones that were not shaped like a five-pointed star – of the Ordovician and Silurian Periods. Jefferies proposed that chordates were closely related to an unusual group of early echinoderms known as stylophoran echinoderms.

He singled out two particular groups, the cornute (boot-shaped) stylophorans and mitrate (more globular-bodied) stylophorans, and investigated them in great detail.

Cornutes were small, peculiarly shaped echinoderms. They had a skeleton of calcite, which enables their fossils to be identified as echinoderms, but these do not look like any creature living today. The body consists of a rim of hard calcite which in shape resembles an ankle boot. The central portion of the body is composed of small grains of calcite, which were evidently held together by a layer of soft tissue. A row of valve-covered holes is found down the left side of the body, and on the ankle of the "boot" are two movable projecting plates that enclose a small, pyramid-shaped mouth. Attached to the edge of the boot is a long, segmented arm or tail.

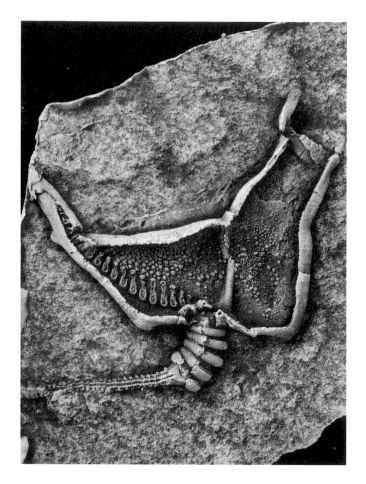

The cornute Cothurnocystis elizae *(ABOVE) is 440 mya. Note the small openings (gills?) on the left-hand side. The tail may have been used to drag it backwards through the sediment.* Mitrocystites mitra *(LEFT), a typical mitrate, is dated at 470 mya. The mosaic of calcite plates which make up the globular part of the body is well shown, as is the tail.*

It is supposed that *Cothurnocystis*, a typical example of a cornute, lived prostrate on the sea bed and fed by stirring up the mud with its arms, so that muddy particles were released. The soft, central part of the body is thought to have acted like a bellows, drawing water and food into the mouth and then pumping the water out through the valved holes. Just behind the valves there appears to be an anus, and behind this a tail or arm which is thought to have been used to help the creature to move.

The hypothesis is that it was swung to one side and hooked into the sea bed and then flexed, so that the whole body was moved diagonally backwards in a series of jerks.

So what provoked Jefferies to implicate such strange creatures in the origin of chordates? It can be seen that this creature has "head" and "tail" ends. The head consists of the boot-shaped part of the animal, inside which are a mouth, gills, and gill slits for the water to leave the body. This part is therefore a pharynx. Just behind the anus is a tail, which Jefferies reconstructed with a notochord running down the middle, myotomes, and a dorsal nerve cord. Basically this animal was built like a tadpole larva, but with a calcite (echinoderm-like) external covering.

The fact that the gill openings are clustered together on the left-hand side of the body is curious. But even that can be linked to chordate ancestry, because early stages of the development of living chordates and echinoderms show this sort of left-handed asymmetry.

Mitrates are a later group thought to have evolved from cornutes. A typical representative would be *Mitrocystites* which, like all mitrates, is symmetrical in shape. The body is again encased in calcite plates, but they seem to form a rigid casing rather than the flexible, bellows-like arrangement of the cornute. The mouth is a narrow slit at one end, while the other end has attached to it a large, curved, segmented tail which hooks downwards from the body. Again the anatomy is unusual. The upper surface of the body is more or less flat, while the undersurface is convex and marked with tiny undulating ridges. The tail is curved downwards, and on its upper and outer edge is a series of prominent curved plates.

Careful analysis of the shape and arrangement of the body and tail led Jefferies to suggest that mitrates lay at the surface of the sediment layer on the sea bed. In order to move, the creature used its tail to drag its body backwards through the surface layer. Large curved spines on the tail provided good thrusting surfaces to grip the mud.

The mitrates show a shift away from ancestral asymmetry to symmetry, which is thought to parallel the shift in the origin of the more symmetrical deuterostomes (chordates). Again, one needs to stretch the imagination in order to understand why it can be considered close to chordate ancestry. Once more the main, globular part of the animal is considered to be equivalent to a head, which contains the mouth and a pharynx for filtering food and for respiration. This is followed by a muscular tail containing the other chordate components – notochord, segmented muscles, and a dorsal nerve cord.

The leap of faith

If this anatomical hypothesis can be accepted – and a number of paleontologists, especially ones who work on echinoderms, do not accept it – irregular echinoderms seem to share a number of chordate features. What is needed at this point is an assumption, a leap of faith. At some stage

The axolotl (Ambystoma mexicanum) *is a curious type of salamander found only in Lake Xochimilco in Mexico. Unlike other species of salamander, in some ways it never grows up – it is a kind of amphibian Peter Pan! Although it retains the feathery external gills which are normally lost at metamorphosis, it is able to breed in this juvenile state. This situation is an example of what is known as pedomorphosis (retention of juvenile conditions into adulthood). The axolotl in this photograph is a laboratory-bred albino – in the wild state they are normally dark brown.*

in the evolution of this group of echinoderms, did some lineages lose the characteristic calcitic skeleton and become naked, soft-bodied creatures, though retaining the other chordate characteristics?

Since all echinoderms seem to have a larval phase which lacks a calcite skeleton, it is certainly possible that, if these larval stages could have delayed the moment at which they developed calcite, and thus became effectively adult while still mobile, they might have been chordate ancestors. Cases of larvae failing to metamorphose into adults, and becoming sexually mature as larvae, are known in the present day. It is known as pedomorphosis – literally "child form." Some varieties of *Branchiostoma* do it, as do some salps (tunicates). So do some more complex creatures, such as salamanders – the Mexican axolotl is a famous example of a larval salamander that can reproduce. So the proposal is not completely without precedent.

Jefferies supposes that mitrates lost their calcite skeletons and became the ancestors of *Branchiostoma* and its relatives.

What to believe?

The ancestry of mobile, soft-bodied, free-swimming creatures such as chordates is likely to remain in doubt. Such organisms are unlikely to be preserved as fossils. There are clearly some fundamental affinities between echinoderms and chordates which are revealed in their common patterns of development. Whether stylophoran echinoderms reveal the details of chordate ancestry as proposed by Jefferies is fascinating, but open to debate.

Not only are the evolutionary stages disputed, but so are the actual details of their anatomy. For example, the organ described as a "tail" by Jefferies is regarded as a "feeding arm" by some echinoderm biologists; consequently they completely reject the idea that its internal anatomy includes a notochord, muscle segments, or a dorsal nerve cord. Equally, there are doubts about the function of the gill valves and the identity of parts of the supposed pharynx. And, from a purely practical point of view, how do you rapidly convert an animal with a nervous system and muscles that move it backward through the sediment by flexing its tail downwards (a mitrate) into an animal that moves forward through the water by flexing its tail from side to side (a chordate)?

The fossil record provides little help. At one time the stylophorans were believed to pre-date the chordates, and therefore gave some support to Jefferies' ideas. Things have changed, however, because now the earliest known cornute stylophorans come from the Middle Cambrian of North America, while *Pikaia* is found in the similarly aged Burgess Shale; the two groups therefore seem to have been quite distinct by Mid-Cambrian times.

So at present the origin of chordates – our own lineage – remains a mystery. There are undoubted links between chordates, echinoderms, and hemichordates – but as to which group was the ancestor of which (if any), paleontologists still have little clear idea. Jefferies' ideas are certainly challenging, but require acceptance of an interpretation that has no fossil evidence to back it up.

Pikaia is the one solid link to the Cambrian, and even this species is rather frustratingly similar to modern *Branchiostoma*. How such relatively insignificant little fossils survived the extinctions that affected so many creatures in the Late Cambrian is uncertain, but survive they certainly did, and ultimately spawned groups that would dominate first the seas, then the land, and finally the skies.

4

THE TEEMING SEAS

AN EXTRAORDINARY VARIETY OF MARINE LIFE

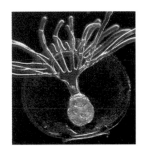

AFTER THE STEEP rise in life in the seas during the Early and Middle Cambrian Period, there was a temporary lull before another rapid rise in diversity with the onset of the Ordovician Period. The increase in number and variety of animal groups simply reflects the openness of the environment, and the readiness with which organisms can colonize and exploit a whole range of ecological niches. But this state of affairs could not be maintained forever. As more and more species arose the ecological opportunities would have declined, and each new species would have been less and less likely to produce new ones. The follow-on effect would have been a steady decline in the rate of appearance of new forms and a gradual leveling off of diversity.

ABOVE *The planktonic larva of a living brachiopod* (Lingula). *Such tiny organisms lie near the bottom of the food chain which still supports all marine life today.*

LEFT *Among the largest and most aggressive early predators of the seas were the eurypterids. Armed with large claws and paddles, some of these distant relatives of living scorpions reached lengths of 6 ft (2m). Many early vertebrates, such as the jawless fish* Pteraspis *shown here, were heavily armored in defense.*

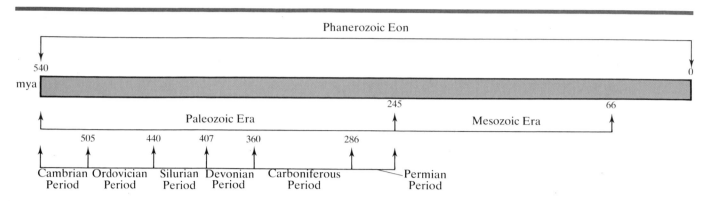

Phanerozoic Eon

540

mya

0

245

66

Paleozoic Era

Mesozoic Era

505   440   407   360   286

Cambrian Ordovician Silurian Devonian Carboniferous   Permian
Period   Period   Period   Period   Period   Period

Timescale of Earth history. *The timespan of this chapter runs from the Late Cambrian to the Permian Period, and is dominated by events occurring in the seas. The overall picture is a succession of* *rises and falls of groups of creatures. While everything in the Cambrian may have seemed strange, by the end of the Permian the groups that survived are much more familiar to us.*

TWO EVOLUTIONARY PHASES

The disappearance of distinctive Cambrian forms, and their replacement by "newer" Ordovician species, show a definite pattern. What appears to have happened, according to the fossil record, was a two-phase rise in the complexity of life: the "ancient" Cambrian fauna (the first phase) was replaced by the diversification of a range of creatures that originated at the end of the Cambrian or in the Early Ordovician (the second phase).

Some paleontologists have noted a change in the type and variety of animals in the seas between the Cambrian and Ordovician Periods. In the Cambrian they seemed to be relatively slow-moving "generalist" feeders, but in the Ordovician they were apparently more specialized for swimming and feeding. This "new breed" of animals suggests a more dynamic, up-tempo pitch to life.

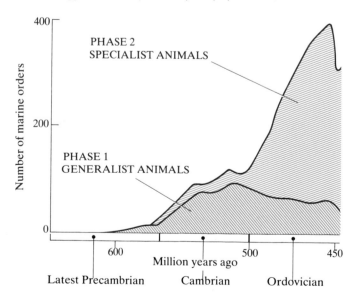

The animals of the second phase included molluscs (bivalves, gastropods, cephalopods), articulate brachiopods (see page 63), echinoderm groups (crinoids, asterozoans), ostracods, corals, and graptolites. This is not to say that all the Cambrian animals became extinct – several groups, such as the trilobites, lived alongside newer ones through succeeding periods. Indeed, in some cases the remnants of the Cambrian Phase persisted until the Permian extinction (see page 145).

Why the evolution of marine creatures took place in two stages is a mystery. It has been suggested that the animals of the second phase exhibit a range of specializations not attained by those of the earlier phase. For example, a considerable range of active predatory animals, such as swimming cephalopods, asterozoans (starfish), eurypterids, and fish, appear; there also emerged a profusion of bottom-dwelling sediment "grazers" and suspension feeders – articulate brachiopods, crinoids, bivalve molluscs, and corals – together with various animals that bored into hard substrates.

The notion of a specialized creature is rather a tenuous one, but good examples of both specialization and generalization can be found among the arthropods. Trilobites, which arose in the Cambrian Period, are not specialized. They had a series of jointed legs on which they could scuttle across the sea bed; the legs were used for both feeding and locomotion, and with minor modification could be equally well used for swimming or burrowing.

In contrast the eurypterids, an arthropod group which appeared later, in the Ordovician, are specifically adapted for a predatory way of life. Their legs are at the front end, some modified as large paddles for swimming, others for moving about on the sea bed, and others still for catching and dismembering prey.

Improved climatic conditions

The paleontologist J.W. Valentine suggested that the principal cause of the change in animal life across the Cambrian–Ordovician threshold was an improved and more stable climate worldwide. This was linked to the pattern of continental break-up (see page 12) and the spread of maritime climatic conditions as seaways intermingled with large land masses. In general, the larger a land area, the greater the temperature changes it experiences. For instance, the Sahara and Gobi deserts today can be subjected to searing daytime temperatures followed by freezing nights; while in a coastal area or on a fairly small island (such as California or Britain) the nearness of the sea keeps the temperature at a fairly constant level.

More stable climatic conditions may have allowed animals to become greater specialists. Perhaps this is the reason for the marked decline in certain sorts of detritus feeders and scavengers, and the rise of specialist predators and suspension feeders. It might indeed account for the changes in the fossil record, but that is not proven. Research carried out by J.J. Sepkoski at the University of Chicago suggests that the population changes would have taken place whatever the environmental conditions – they were just a product of the biological system once it had started in the Early Cambrian.

Let us take a look at the creatures of the Paleozoic Era. They reflect on the one hand the quickening pace of evolution following the Cambrian Explosion of complex forms of life, and on the other the consolidation of certain types of lifestyle.

MOLLUSCS

Of living marine animals, molluscs are the most varied; several types have spread to fresh water and some, such as slugs and snails, have even invaded the land. Their fossil record can be taken back to the Early Cambrian. It is often helpful to make a mental construct of a probable ancestral form, or "archetype," of a group of creatures, as a means of explaining how its features evolved.

The archetypal mollusc is thought to have had a large, flat muscular foot by which the animal crept along the sea bed. At the front of the foot was a head with some sort of sense organs (tentacles) and a mouth housing a peculiar feeding device known as a radula. This was a strip of tissue with a mat of tiny teeth on the surface, which could be pushed out through the mouth and scraped over the sea bed. Above the foot, the body was hunched up to form a cavity for the main body organs, covered by a sheet of tissue known as the mantle. The

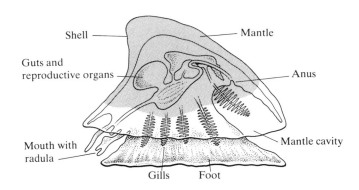

Detailed study of living and fossil molluscs has led biologists and paleobiologists to hypothesize about the earliest mollusc ancestor. This archetypal mollusc was thought to have lived under a cup-shaped shell, to have crept about on a flat foot, and to have had a repeated series of gills running down the side of its body.

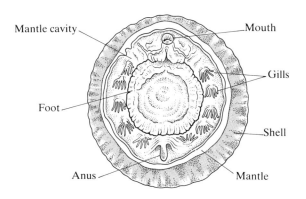

After this theoretical animal had been constructed, some strange examples of real molluscs were dredged up from the depths of the oceans. Neopilina is a living marine mollusc which looks uncannily like an archetypal mollusc – note in particular the large muscular foot, the regular series of gills along either side, and the simple conical shell.

mantle was important because the shell of the mollusc grew from it. The shell and mantle overlapped the sides of the foot and enclosed a narrow cavity along the sides of the body into which hung a series of leaf-shaped gills. The foot was anchored to the shell by several pairs of large, powerful muscles which often left distinctive marks on the inside of the shell.

In 1957 some animals that conformed surprisingly closely to this archetype were dredged out of deep-sea sediments. The first example, named *Neopilina*, has a simple conical shell, a broad foot with a mouth at one end and an anus at the other, and a set of paired gills along either side within the mantle cavity. Internally there are paired muscles which run down into the foot. Since that time several other species of these rather simple molluscs, called monoplacophorans, have been collected – all from water more than 650 ft (200 m) deep.

It seems that in the Cambrian a number of different body designs appeared, based on the molluscan archetype. They allowed creatures to exploit surface and subsurface environments as deposit feeders, suspension feeders, and predators. Although the start was relatively slow, by Ordovician times they had evolved into the recognizable groups of today. But before we look at prehistoric molluscs, it makes sense to distinguish between the various kinds with reference to familiar living examples.

Gastropods

This group includes the slugs, snails, and limpets. The name "gastropod" means "stomach foot," a rough description of the creature's layout. The shell is often spirally coiled, though it can be modified as in limpets, or lost altogether as in slugs. As a group the gastropods are linked, regardless of their external appearance, by a process known as torsion (twisting) which occurs during larval development.

What happens is that the shell and viscera (guts) are twisted back against the front end (the head and foot). As a result the shell tends to grow in a coil above the body. Torsion brings the mantle cavity around from the rear of the animal so that it is directly above the head. The head itself is more elaborate than in primitive molluscs such as monoplacophorans, having sense organs – eyes, touch-sensitive tentacles, and an olfactory (smelling) organ. The arrangement of the head and foot, with its retractor muscle (a single strand which runs up the spire of the shell), is such that, if the creature is disturbed, the head and sense organs are withdrawn first and protected by the sole of the foot, which is drawn in afterwards.

The feeding apparatus in gastropods is also more sophisticated than in primitive molluscs. The simple radula with its rows of teeth, ideal for scraping up algae, shows a range of modifications associated with predators: devices for drilling into other creatures' shells, and venomous darts for killing prey.

Bivalves

Next to the gastropods in terms of abundance are the bivalves, which include clams, oysters, mussels, and cockles. The body is enclosed within two shells or "valves," usually of equal size, which are linked together along the top of the animal by a hinge and ligament. The hinge is often quite complex, with sets of matching ridges and grooves forming a joint which prevents the valves from becoming dislocated. The valves are drawn together by adductor muscles running between the valves, which act against the elastic ligament which

under normal circumstances tends to pull them apart. Thus in the "relaxed" state the valves gape and the animal inside is in contact with its environment.

The foot is not large and flat as in the molluscs described above, but is quite often long and thin. It can be protruded between the valves and used for movement, and the combination of movable valves and foot can be employed for burrowing in soft sediments on the sea floor where most bivalves live. In some species, however, the valves have specially hardened edges which allow them to burrow into wood – a mollusc called *Teredo* was the scourge of wooden sailing ships – or even rocks near the seashore. Some bivalves, for instance mussels, have become stationary, attaching themselves by a bundle of threads called a byssus to rocks and algae; while others, such as scallops, can actually swim quite fast by clapping their valves together like castanets.

The majority of bivalves are suspension feeders. The body cavity within the valves is filled with a very fine, almost gauze-like curtain called the gill. A current of water, set up by movable cilia (fine hairs), passes in at one end of the cavity and out at the other. In between, the fine mesh of the gill forms a net on which minute particles are caught and transferred by the cilia to the mouth. Waste products are carried away from the animal with the departing flow.

Cephalopods

This remarkable group of molluscs, very different from those described above, includes octopuses, squids, and cuttlefish. The name "cephalopod" means "head foot," a fair description of the creatures' curious folded-up anatomy. Cephalopods are quite rare today, but this was not the case in previous eras; ammonites in particular were extremely abundant. Most living forms, except *Nautilus*, have a much reduced shell. Formerly (and to this day in *Nautilus*) the shell consisted of a coiled set of chambers, the body occupying the largest one adjacent to the aperture. The body is connected to the chambers by a thin tube called the siphuncle, which can be used to replace the water in the empty chambers with gas so that the animal maintains its buoyancy as it grows.

Unlike a bivalve, whose body runs in a straight line beneath the hinge, the body of a cephalopod is curved back on itself, so that the anus is quite close to and beneath the head. The head has a very prominent pair of eyes, indicating that these are intensely visual creatures – indeed, many are swift and dangerous predators. Part of the foot is reduced to a sort of mobile nozzle beneath the head. The enormous mantle cavity can be used as a bellows to pump water through the nozzle, which enables these creatures to move by a form of jet

RIGHT *The internal layout of an ammonite, based loosely on the structure of its nearest living relative, the nautilus. The coiled and chambered part of the shell contains gas and acts as a flotation tank to aid buoyancy. Ammonites lived as predators or scavengers. To assist this lifestyle they were endowed with excellent vision, long grasping tentacles, and a formidable mouth which combined a sharp beak and venom glands with a rasping, tooth-covered tongue.*

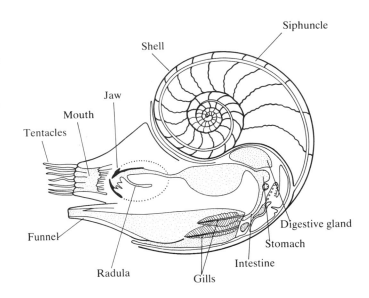

BELOW *Ammonite fossils display the multiple-chambered shell of the animal, but of course the important soft parts do not survive the fossilization process and are therefore lacking. This is a pyritized fossil of the ammonite* Echinoceras raricostatum, *in which the original material of the shell has been replaced by iron pyrites, popularly known as fool's gold. The piece of fossilized sea bed behind can be seen to contain a variety of ammonites and worm casts.*

propulsion – the combination of jet propulsion and neutral buoyancy makes cephalopods very adept swimmers. Another part of the foot is developed into a fan of suckered tentacles. These tentacles enable octopuses to move about on firm surfaces, but most cephalopods use them for catching prey and pulling it into the mouth. The mouth itself is armed with a very powerful, parrot-like beak which can also inject venom into its prey. The beak first slices the prey, after which the pieces are minced by the radula.

The earliest molluscs

Some of the earliest mollusc shells date from the Tommotian (Early Cambrian) and are extremely small – about the size of a pinhead. Examples with simple, laterally flattened, or curled shells include *Latouchella*, *Aldanella*, *Anabarella*, and *Yochelcionella*, variously found in Siberia, the US, Australia, and Greenland. The general consensus is that these are related to living monoplacophorans.

It is of interest that the shells of *Yochelcionella*, *Anabarella* and *Latouchella* are narrower than those of their descendants, show less trace of the "scars" where the muscles were attached to the shell, and do not seem to be designed to have pairs of gills along the sides of the body. The large vent in *Anabarella*, and the peculiar nozzle in *Yochelcionella*, suggest that this part of the shell lay at the rear of the animal and enabled it to exhale from the gill cavity as it moved forward through the mud.

The narrowness of the shell has been interpreted as a step on the evolutionary line toward the bivalves. It is supposed that forms such as *Anabarella* tended to plough through the surface sediments and set up feeding and respiratory currents along the sides of the shell, and that they were succeeded by forms with progressively deeper valves which sat on the sediment. Some forms from the Middle and Upper Cambrian, known as rostroconchs, apparently show this intermediate status and even the beginnings of a bivalved shell. The shell does not seem truly valved, but rather to have fractured regularly in life – perhaps because of the wedging effect of the narrow foot as it pushed between the valves – and then to have healed with growth. Later rostroconchs were two-valved, but never developed special valve-closing (adductor) muscles and so cannot be called bivalves.

Genuine bivalves appear just after the Tommotian with *Fordilla*, but they appear to have had poor hinges and small gills compared to modern forms. On this account they may well have been neither effective burrowers nor suspension feeders, and possibly fed on the soupy sea-floor layer of algae. Large gills and stable valve hinges appeared in the Early Ordovician Period.

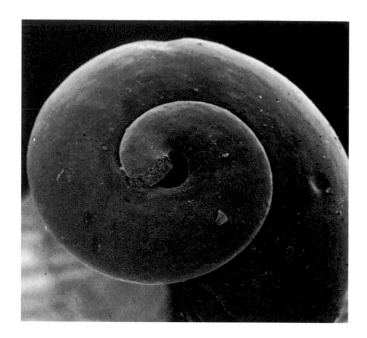

Aldanella, with its beautifully coiled shell, seems very close to what might be expected of an early gastropod, and may perhaps have evolved from a relatively unmodified type like *Latouchella*. Following the rise of more elaborate predatory types in the Early Cambrian, the coiling may have developed as a means of defensively retreating into the shell and protecting the sense organs with the foot.

Late in the Cambrian, the first cephalopods appear. *Plectronoceras* consists of a horn-shaped shell divided

Similar to the ammonite illustrated on page 61, some living and many fossil cephalopods are able to control their buoyancy by using gas-filled chambers inside their shells. This Late Cambrian fossil, Plectronoceras, *has chambers near its tip, which suggests that it was an early member of the group.*

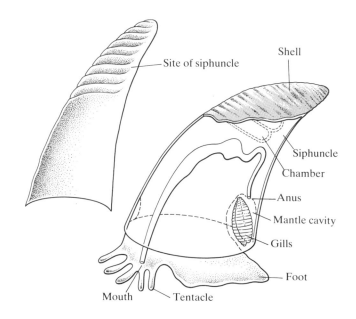

LEFT *The distinctive coiling of* Aldanella *from the Early Cambrian implies that its body had already become twisted – the process known as "torsion", common to the very successful gastropod group of molluscs. Is* Aldanella *an early relative of modern gastropod molluscs?*

RIGHT *Living brachiopods such as* Lingula *are much rarer than their fossil ancestor. The simple shell contains a curled lophophore, used to catch and filter tiny particles of food. Unlike bivalve molluscs, these animals have a muscular stalk by which they attach themselves to the sea bed.*

into chambers; in the fossil the remains of the siphuncle running through the chambers is visible. The animal may well have evolved from a relatively conservative *Latouchella* type of mollusc in the Cambrian. This creature may have had a tendency not to twist the body, as in the case of gastropods, but to hunch it deeply into a tall, narrow shell, combined with a reduction of the large creeping foot. As the animal grew it drew away from the tip of the shell and blanked off a chamber, leaving a thread of tissue in contact – the siphuncle.

These animals were probably not adept swimmers to start with, but may have been relatively fast-moving predatory surface dwellers, using part of the foot as elongated sensory tentacles and perhaps for grasping prey. Buoyancy, and more adept swimming using jet propulsion, were a long way off.

Brachiopods

With origins in the Early Cambrian, brachiopods are relatively rare in the present day. They have a stalk by which they anchor themselves to the sediment, and a two-valved body. The name, which means "arm foot," refers to this anchor. Brachiopods are also called "lamp shells" because the shell of some kinds resembles a primitive stone oil lamp. These creatures are sometimes confused with bivalve molluscs, but are in fact not at all closely related. For example, the valves covering the body are at top and bottom, rather than left and right as in the case of bivalves; also the valves are different in shape. *Lingula* ("tongue," because of its shape) is a well-known living example, and the majority of early fossil forms seem remarkably similar to it, which has led to the animal being described as a living fossil.

The brachiopod lives in the sediment, anchored in place by a long muscular stalk which projects out of the narrow end of the valves. The valves themselves do not have a proper hinge as in bivalve molluscs, and this group of brachiopods (the most ancient) is said for this reason to be "inarticulate"; later brachiopods, which appear in great abundance from the Ordovician onwards, have a proper hinge and are said to be "articulate." When the animal is feeding the valves gape at the sediment surface, and its cilia waft particles of matter into a complex folded gill-like structure known as a lophophore, which serves the same purpose as the gills of bivalve molluscs. When it is not feeding, the valves are closed and the animal can withdraw into the sediment by using its contractile stalk.

Modern forms are relatively rare, though they are widespread around the world. During the later Paleozoic, however, brachiopods were extremely abundant, playing a leading role in the sea-floor community as sediment and suspension feeders.

GRAPTOLITES

These curious creatures are now thought to be extinct relatives of the living hemichordates. Their remains are confined to Ordovician and Silurian rocks. They were evidently sea-floor creatures, though some may well have formed floating colonies. The fossil evidence consists of curious, shiny, saw-edged lines on the surface of rocks; these are the skeletal remains of the string-like colonies in which these tiny animals lived, and account for their name, which means "written stones," because the lines resemble handwriting. The animal appears to have been

FOSSIL GRAFFITI

Graptolites
These small, globular animals lived as organized colonies on or just above the Paleozoic sea bed. Each animal sat in a small cup of horny tissue, from which projected a frilly head of tentacles which filtered tiny organisms out of the water. Members of the genus illustrated here, Didymograptus, *are often known as "tuning fork" graptolites because of their shape. This specimen, from the Ordovician Period, was discovered in Wales.*

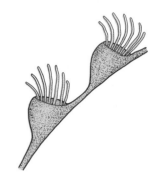

Linked hollowed cups
The compressed strands of tissue actually consist of stacks of hollowed cups, linked along a common strand.

small and globular-bodied, with a whorl of tentacles at the top which acted as a device for sieving particles of food from sea water or from just above the sediment layers on the sea floor. The soft body of the animal was protected by a small, hard casing, and the casings were connected by strips of tissue.

Graptolites have proved very useful to paleontologists. First, they are extremely abundant in ocean-floor sediments and seem to have been very widely distri-buted around the world. Coupled with this, the patterns in which their colonies built up are very distinctive, as indeed were the chambers in which they lived – even though precious little is known about the soft-bodied creatures that lived inside those chambers. This means that it is relatively easy to identify different species of graptolite. Finally, individual species seem to have lived for relatively short periods of time, only to be succeeded by new species of distinctively different appearance.

Add these characteristics together and it may be appreciated that graptolites – though perhaps not the most exciting of fossils – can be extremely useful to paleontologists. Paleozoic rocks can be dated on a comparative scale by the species of graptolite they contain.

ARTHROPODS

The Paleozoic was also a time when arthropods – creatures with jointed limbs and a hard external skeleton (exoskeleton), like today's insects, spiders, and crustaceans – increased in number and variety.

Trilobites

These arthropods appeared in the Early Cambrian and persisted stubbornly through succeeding periods. There are not many Early Cambrian types, but they rapidly radiated in the Early Ordovician to become a varied and numerous group of animals living on or in the sea floor, while a few species may have been swimmers.

Their general anatomy and way of life are typified by the species *Olenoides* from the Mid-Cambrian, which has been described in great detail by Professor Harry Whittington on the basis of beautifully preserved specimens from the Burgess Shale. The body is covered by a hard, jointed carapace, very distinctively divided into three lengthwise strips (the three lobes from which the name "trilobite" comes) by a pair of grooves running along either side of the midline. At the front is a large head shield or cephalon, from beneath which project two jointed antennae. Over much of the body are scattered small mounds, tubercles, and sensory hair pits, which allowed the creatures to sense their surroundings.

On either side of the cephalon are multifaceted eyes, perched on small mounds and similar to the compound eyes of modern king crabs. Just beneath the eye and curving forward and backward across the cephalon is a fine line which is believed to be a weak point at which the carapace split apart when the animal molted (see page 66). The edges of the cephalon and segments of the carapace are marked by backward-pointing spines – probably protective since they shroud the delicate gills which lie just above the walking legs.

The construction of the carapace enabled the animal to flex vertically but not laterally. This allowed some trilobites to roll themselves tightly into a ball like a woodlouse – most likely a defensive posture against predators, but possibly a reaction to sudden burial in mud, changes in salinity, or any other type of disturbance.

The body cavity lay beneath the central ridge of the carapace, but relatively little is known about the arrangement of the internal organs apart from the gut tube which ran down the middle. The most curious aspect of the trilobite was its method of feeding. There were no special mouth parts, such as jaws or modified legs surrounding the mouth, which would enable it to catch and manipulate or shred food items. All the food processing, if that is the right word, took place on the bases of its many legs.

The walking legs were long, slender, and jointed like those of a woodlouse or sea slater, and would have allowed trilobites to hurry along the sea floor or plough through the sediment with considerable power. The stance of the legs was wide, giving them the stability to withstand water currents which might otherwise have buffeted the creatures or flipped them over as they scurried about. The legs would have been moved in rhythmic waves along the body, as in modern centipedes. Attached to the upper surfaces of each jointed leg,

under the canopy formed by the sides of the carapace, were the gills, delicate feathery surfaces where respiration took place. At the rear end of the animal was another pair of delicate, jointed, sensory tentacles called cerci.

Seen from in front or behind, the legs had sets of internal spines. Further out on the limbs these were used for gaining a grip on the sea floor, but nearer the middle of the body they had a different purpose. Here the spines were clustered together and pointed inward. The bases of each pair of legs projected downward from the body of the animal, enclosing a narrow channel lined with small, sharp spines; this is known as the "food groove." Sediment, including organisms stirred up from the sea floor, would have been trapped by the curtain of legs and the internal spikes would then have acted like the teeth of many jaws, catching items of food and moving them into the groove. After that the normal action of the legs, swinging to and fro as the creature walked along, would have made the food move forward along the groove by a sort of ratchet effect until it was pushed in at the mouth, which faced backwards down the length of the groove.

Legs, then, were very important to trilobites. They were not only for walking and swimming; they also supported the gills for breathing, snared food on their insides, and conveyed it to the mouth.

Trilobites were one of the dominant life forms on the bed of the Paleozoic oceans. Within a fairly conservative body form characterized by the three-lobed carapace and serially repeated legs they seem to have led surprisingly varied lifestyles. They ranged in size from a few millimetres to 16 ins (40 cm) in length. Some burrowed through the sediment on the sea bed, while others ploughed across the sea floor or swam in midwater. Animals such as the "ramshorn" type of trilobite, shown here, had extravagant "horns" which probably served a defensive function similar to that of the spines of the Cambrian arthropod Marella. Some of the smaller trilobites with very long spines making a fringe down the sides of their body are thought to have been swimming forms which used the spines to slow down their rate of sinking.

HOW TRILOBITES LIVED

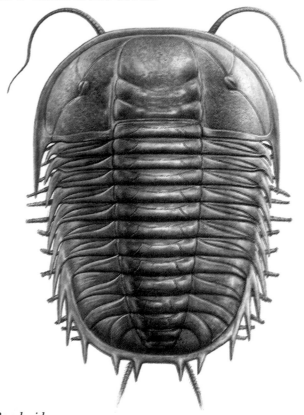

Paradoxides
One of the best known – and one of the largest – of all the trilobites is the genus Paradoxides, *whose body length ranges up to 14¹/₂ ins (37 cm).*

Swimming
Conocoryphe, *a small (³/₄ inch/2 cm long), blind Cambrian trilobite, beats its legs rhythmically as it swims.*

Molting
Paradoxides *hunches up its body so that the cephalon (head shield) can split and the fresh animal can emerge.*

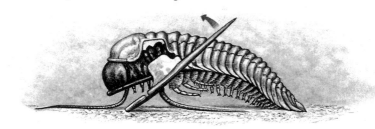

Molting

One of the major problems confronting trilobites, and indeed all animals with an exoskeleton, was the problem of growing larger. It is the same problem that would have confronted a young medieval knight. Make him a suit of armor when he is 15 years of age and it would be impossible for him to get into it a year or two later. Arthropods solved this problem by periodically molting, and trilobites were no exception. Indeed, the majority of trilobite fossils known are of shed skins rather than of entire animals.

One or two remarkable clues tell us how trilobites shed their skins. In some fossils the cephalon seems to have folded back on the rest of the body, almost as if someone had put the trilobite's head on back to front. This was eventually interpreted as a recently shed skin.

The furrow running across either side of the head in the region of the eye, as mentioned earlier, is found very consistently on all trilobites with eyes (a few of them were blind). It is confidently believed that these lines mark preset breaking points so that the trilobite could emerge from its old shell as a vulnerable, soft-bodied creature. During this stage it could inflate its body before its cuticle hardened to form a protective covering.

Trilobites persisted through the Paleozoic as a whole, although their forms vary. At the Cambro–Ordovician boundary the specifically Cambrian trilobites became extinct and were replaced by a considerable variety of new families. Beyond the Ordovician Period, trilobites maintained their range and variety well into the Silurian and Devonian, although hardly any new families emerged; but at the end of the Devonian they underwent a rapid decline. This has been linked to the rise in predatory jawed fish during the Devonian. Nevertheless, one lineage managed to survive until the end of the Permian, at which time this, along with a very wide range of marine creatures, died out in one of the most dramatic extinction events in the entire history of the planet Earth.

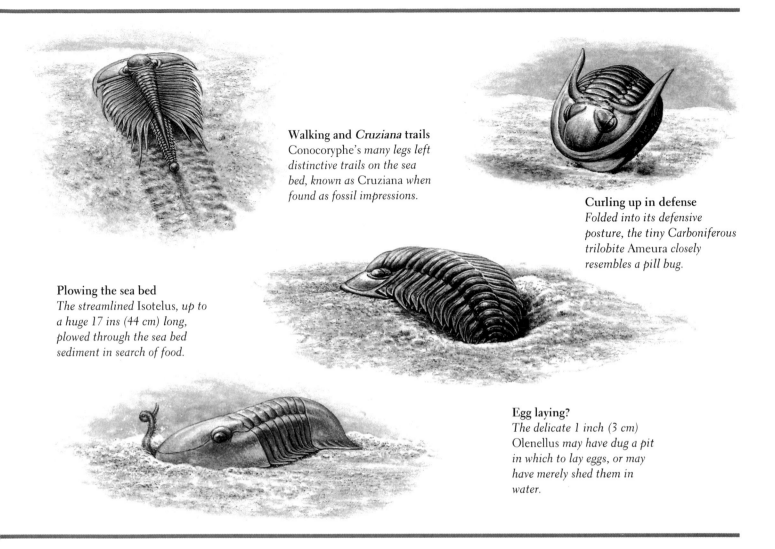

Walking and *Cruziana* trails
Conocoryphe's *many legs left distinctive trails on the sea bed, known as* Cruziana *when found as fossil impressions.*

Curling up in defense
Folded into its defensive posture, the tiny Carboniferous trilobite Ameura *closely resembles a pill bug.*

Plowing the sea bed
The streamlined Isotelus, *up to a huge 17 ins (44 cm) long, plowed through the sea bed sediment in search of food.*

Egg laying?
The delicate 1 inch (3 cm) Olenellus *may have dug a pit in which to lay eggs, or may have merely shed them in water.*

Eurypterids

Also rising to prominence in the Early Paleozoic were the eurypterids or water scorpions, which belonged to the group of arthropods known as chelicerates (meaning "biting claws") that includes living spiders, scorpions, and horseshoe crabs. Eurypterids persist in the fossil record from the Ordovician through to the Permian, and ranged from relatively small creatures 4 ins (10cm) or so in length to monsters of 3 to 6 ft (1 to 2m).

The body of a chelicerate is quite distinctive when compared to that of something like a trilobite, because it is divided into a head end (prosoma) and a tail portion (opisthosoma). The prosoma carries the paired limbs, the eyes, and the mouth, while the opisthosoma has no legs and can be variously modified into a simple tapering tail, a stinging weapon (as in the case of true scorpions), or a paddle to aid swimming (as in eurypterids which, despite their popular name, are not strictly scorpions). The first limbs on the head are the biting chelicerae which lie just in front of the mouth. These are followed by pedipalps, which are often used as feelers, rather like the antennae of trilobites. Finally, the chelicerates have four pairs of legs.

Pterygotus, one of the largest of the eurypterids, is found in Silurian rocks. Growing to lengths of over 5 ft (1.7m), this was a formidable creature. All eurypterids seem to have been aquatic and many were aggressive predators. Indeed the large prosoma of *Pterygotus* has a pair of large eyes embedded on its upper surface, which shows it was a hunter. The chelicerae are very long, jointed structures ending in formidable, spine-encrusted jaws, used for catching and crushing prey before passing it to the mouth. Behind the chelicerae are four roughly equal-sized limbs (including the pedipalps) which may well have been used for scuttling across the sea floor in pursuit of bottom-dwelling prey, or perhaps for disturbing the sea floor to uncover or disturb potential prey lying buried just beneath the surface. Behind the four conventional legs are a pair of much longer, paddle-

CHORDATE/VERTEBRATE RELATIONSHIPS

ECHINODERMS
(SEA URCHINS
AND STARFISH)

HEMICHORDATES
(CEPHALODISCUS)

TUNICATES
(SEA SQUIRTS)

SHARKS
AND RAYS   ACANTHODIANS

LOBE-FINNED
FISH

MAMMAL-
LIKE
REPTILES   LIZARDS
AND SNAKES

— MAMMALS

TURTLES   DINOSAURS

BACKBONE
(FIRST
VERTEBRATES)   JAWS   BONE

LEGS   SHELLED
EGG   SYNAPSIS   DIAPSIDS   BIRDS

CROCODILES

STYLOPHORANS ACRANIATES
(MITRATES   (BRANCHIOSTOMA)
AND
CORNUTES =   AGNATHANS
POSSIBLE   (LAMPREYS)
CHORDATES)

PLACODERMS RAY-
FINNED
FISH

— MODERN
AMPHIBIANS

PLESIOSAURS
AND
ICHTHYOSAURS

EARLY
TETRAPODS

Key

LIVING REPRESENTATIVES

EXTINCT REPRESENTATIVES

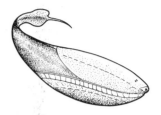

ABOVE *Sacambambaspis
from Bolivia is a well-preserved
Upper Ordovician vertebrate.
The large head shield covered
the gill chamber, with further
armor plating over the gill
openings and flexible tail.*

LEFT *All vertebrates have a
backbone, segmented muscles,
a spinal cord, and a pharynx.
Relationships between living
groups as shown here imply a
historical "family tree".*

ended limbs, which must have been used for swimming. The opisthosoma of *Pterygotus* was long and segmented, ending in a flattened paddle, and it seems very likely that the tail also beat up and down rather like that of a dolphin to aid swimming. The tail may in fact have been used specifically to provide a rapid burst of speed to catch swimming prey, while the paddle-like legs were capable of a steady cruising pace.

The huge *Pterygotus* must have been one of the top predators of the Silurian seas, and the combination of sharp vision, powerful claws and good swimming abilities would have meant that few animals could have withstood its attacks. Very heavily armored jawless fish or ostracoderms ("bony skins"), as they used to be called, were particularly prominent in the Silurian. It is likely that the armor plating of these fish, which were mostly slow-moving and bottom-dwelling, was at least partly due to the presence of large, aggressive eurypterids.

Smaller eurypterids included *Eurypterus* (after whom the group is named) and range down to 4 ins (10cm) or less in length. In many of these the elongate grasping chelicerae seen in *Pterygotus* were replaced by claws perched on the head, just in front of the mouth. In these forms the four pairs of walking legs were used much more for grasping smaller prey and drawing them close to the mouth so that they could be shredded by the chelicerae. The paddle was well developed, but the tail ended in a long spine rather than in a similar flattened paddle. It seems likely, therefore, that these animals were cruising predators and scavengers rather than strictly pursuit predators like *Pterygotus*.

THE RISE AND RISE OF THE CHORDATES

The chordates, as explained earlier, comprise at least two types of creature: the acraniates (*Branchiostoma*) and the tunicates (sea squirts), neither of which were or are very abundant. However, there is a third group of chordates which have been singularly successful. These creatures are usually termed vertebrates (animals possessing backbones).

Although the vertebrate group comprises less than 5 per cent of all known species today, these animals are important because they include the majority of the largest, most active and most intelligent animals on Earth. Fossils of vertebrates are rarely as numerous as those of invertebrates, but many are very well preserved, which allows details of the animal's internal structure to be worked out so that anatomical changes can be traced through the fossil record. This makes the group very rewarding to study from an evolutionary perspective.

In Mid-Cambrian times the first hint of chordate organization was revealed with the discovery of *Pikaia* (see pages 49-50). But this little creature lacks any trace of the more familiar and recognizable features: a bony skeleton, a vertebral column or backbone, ribs, and paired fins or jaws. Indeed, after the Mid-Cambrian Period the fossil record once again goes silent as far as the chordates are concerned.

Until quite recently, the earliest fossil remains of vertebrates consisted of some bone-like fragments suspected of belonging to armored fish from Upper Ordovician rocks in the US. Beyond that the earliest definite indications of fish were full skeletons from the Early Silurian.

However, new discoveries have extended the history of this group of chordates back to the Lower Ordovician Period in Australia, with the discovery of *Arandaspis*; others, equally well preserved, have come from the Upper Ordovician in Bolivia (*Sacambambaspis*).

Agnathans – the jawless fish

One characteristic that all these chordates share is a hard, phosphatic bony armor – one made of calcium phosphate, rather than the calcium carbonate of most invertebrates. This armor forms a solid casing around the head and body of the animal. Another feature, though less immediately obvious, is that they have mouths, but no jaws with which to open and close them – hence the name "agnathan," meaning "jawless." It seems almost as though a *Pikaia*-like creature had simply been encased in bone.

Hemicyclaspis is a typical creature of this kind. Although some of the simplest agnathans had a mouth which was merely a slit-like opening near the front of the head, sometimes surrounded by bony plates, in *Hemicyclaspis* and some others the mouth was apparently surrounded by soft lips. Behind the mouth was a solid head casing which enclosed and protected the sensory organs and the front part of the dorsal nerve cord – a "brain" which was expanded to accommodate the inputs from the three primary sense organs (taste/smell, sight, and hearing/balance). Near the front of the head was a single nostril (paired in some forms) for "tasting" the water. On the top were two prominent eyes, and between them, in a number of these early fish, a median or third eye.

In the side wall of the braincase was a system of narrow tubes containing hair cells which provided information about the movement of the body and gave the creature its sense of balance. Another set of hair cells located in grooves on the surface of the head and body provided

the brain with information from pressure waves in the water and nearby water movement – a form of hearing.

One rather mysterious feature of these agnathans is the presence of two finely plated curved areas on the upper edges of the head shield, and another on the top of the head. These areas are connected to the brain by channels inside the head shield, and it has been suggested that they may have been either special electrical sensors, or else electric organs for giving shocks to predators. But at present there is no evidence to support either theory.

The brain in its protective casing integrated the sensory inputs, and controlled the activity of the animal through the dorsal nerve cord. This cord sent information from the brain to control body movements and general activity, and also received sensory input about what was happening elsewhere in the body.

Beneath the braincase lies the pharynx, which in these early vertebrates comprised the entire area behind the mouth and beneath the upper head shield. Water drawn in through the mouth by raising and lowering the floor of the pharynx with muscles (or rammed in by the fish swimming forwards with its mouth open, a method known as ram ventilation) passed through the gill filaments and then out via rows of gill openings on the lower sides of the head shield. Food particles were sieved out on the surface of the gills and passed back into the gut, so that feeding and breathing were a single combined operation.

Behind the head was the body, approximately triangular in cross section and tapering in a streamlined manner; it was covered in jointed bony armor plating. There were ridges or fleshy fins on the sides of the body, presumably to add stability and some degree of control while swimming. The body ended in an asymmetrical tail fin, with a large upper lobe into which ran the end of the vertebral column or the notochord (it is not known

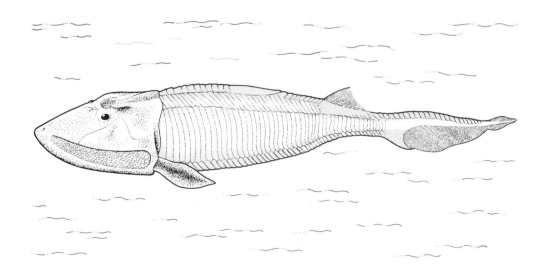

Silurian jawless fish are common in freshwater lake deposits. Many, like Hemicyclaspis *shown here, were flattened from top to bottom, with a very broad head shield and a long, "fishy" tail. The tail was upturned, and provided some lift as these animals swam. They probably ploughed along the bottom scooping up sediment and filtering it over the gills. The eyes perched on the top of the head allowed these animals to keep watch for predators.*

which of these the creatures had). This type of upturned (heterocercal) tail is common to most early fish, and is still seen in sharks today.

The flattened head shield and combination of eyes and nostrils on top of the head and mouth underneath that were seen in *Hemicyclaspis* suggest that this was a bottom-dwelling animal. Certainly the design would seem to be suited to such a lifestyle. The flattened form would tend to reduce "lift" when water flowed over these fish while they were lying on the bottom. The rather stiff armor plating of the body makes it unlikely that the creature would have been a very adept swimmer. It probably wriggled along in the mud of the sea floor, sucking up detritus and straining it through its gills.

Later, Upper Ordovician agnathans seem to have been more active, with a long, flexible tail, and a head surrounded by an upper and lower shield of bone separated along the sides by a row of gill cover plates. The eyes were right at the front, rather than on the top of the head shield, and the whole body was deeper and more streamlined than that of *Hemicyclaspis*; these were very probably midwater swimming forms. There was a mouth beneath the eyes, and it seems possible that these agnathans breathed by ram ventilation, at the same time sieving out planktonic organisms on their gills for food, rather like a modern paddle-fish or basking shark would do.

Other midwater swimming forms include *Pteraspis*, *Pharyngolepis*, and *Thelodus*. The latter, a member of a rather mysterious group known as thelodonts, is only known from fossil impressions of what seems to be a fine layer of small scales, rather than large plates of bone. These remains tend to be very ghostly and indistinct in appearance.

Of the bottom dwellers, the most impressive must have been *Drepanaspis*. These very large fish were 3 ft (1m) across in some cases, very flat, and equipped with a broad mouth for scooping up sediment.

The more this group is studied, the more bizarre it appears. Recent discoveries in eastern Asia include a completely new group of agnathans, the galeaspids, which have solid head shields sculpted into rather outlandish shapes. An example is *Sanchaspis*. These fishes have a long "rostrum" or nose spine, which may have been used to probe or stir up the mud of the sea floor; alternatively, the combination of this spine and long, curved shoulder spines may have been a defense against predators. *Pituriaspis* from the Devonian of Australia is yet another recently described form which has a solid and very elaborate head shield dominated by elongated rostral and side spines.

The absence of jaws and teeth severely limited the range and variety of foods that could have been eaten by these early vertebrates. As with *Pikaia*, it seems likely that the earliest vertebrates may have swum through the surface water layers, sieving plankton and using ram ventilation, rather than relying on cilia to sweep water over the gills. A simple mouth opening is all that is required for this way of life, and a number of fusiform (spindle-shaped) agnathans do indeed seem to have lived like that. However, the algae-covered muddy bottom of the shallow seas also offered a rich supply of organic material, and a significant number of these early forms seem to have adapted to a bottom-dwelling lifestyle in order to exploit it. This rather more sedate way of life brought with it a need to alter their shape and develop more heavy defensive armor to fend off the large, aggressive eurypterids of this time. Again, the absence of jaws and teeth did not present a particular problem, since such food would mainly have consisted of fine particles.

The great mobility of these early vertebrates, provided by the muscular, laterally flattened tail, meant that they were able to seek out new feeding areas; this gave them a distinct advantage over the more or less stationary deposit-feeding invertebrate groups and suspension feeders. Their relative abundance as fossils in rocks of the Silurian and Early Devonian suggests that their lifestyle was quite successful. Towards the close of the Devonian Period the agnathans dwindled as a group and finally disappeared from the fossil record. However, there are living representatives of this group – they bear little resemblance to the agnathans of the Paleozoic seas, but share with them the absence of jaws and teeth.

Living agnathans

River and sea lampreys and deep-water hagfish are soft-bodied, eel-like creatures and possess no trace of jaws. Sea lampreys are parasites which attach themselves to the outsides of fish and even marine mammals with the aid of their round, sucker-shaped mouths. They feed on their host's skin, flesh, and blood by punching holes into the sides of the body with their rasping tongue – a structure similar in function to that of a gastropod mollusc. Hagfish are scavengers which burrow into and feed on the flesh of dead or dying animals; like lampreys, hagfish have a large, tooth-covered tongue which scrapes away at the flesh of their prey.

The fossil records of these two groups can be traced back to the Carboniferous Period. However, there is a tantalizing gap between the first known fossils of either group and the last known fossils of the armored agnathans, which became extinct before the close of the Devonian Period.

In neither case are these animals very much like the Paleozoic agnathans, yet their lack of jaws marks them

Otherwise known as cyclostomes ("round mouths"), lampreys such as the Pacific lamprey (ABOVE) lack true jaws. They attach their sucker-like mouths to their prey and use their tooth-covered tongue to lacerate its flesh. The river lamprey (RIGHT) shows the row of gills forming the pharynx.

out as truly agnathan. For a long time it has been assumed that living agnathans evolved from distinctive groups of Paleozoic agnathans – the lampreys from creatures similar to *Hemicyclaspis* and the hagfishes from creatures closer to *Pteraspis*.

However, the new discoveries made from the Lower Ordovician seem to have changed all that. One of the most recent interpretations is that the hagfishes have no obvious relatives among the Paleozoic groups, and may date back to the earliest radiation of vertebrates in the Late Cambrian. Lampreys are proposed as descendants of midwater swimming forms such as *Pharyngolepis*, while forms similar to *Hemicyclaspis* seem to be a little closer to the first creatures to have jaws – the line of vertebrates that ultimately produced the human species.

It is very interesting that agnathans should still exist today, but both of the living groups are highly specialized in their habits. As a result they provide relatively little evidence to elucidate either the way of life or the relationships of the early agnathans.

The first jaws

The earliest true jawed fish (acanthodians or spiny sharks) are found in the Upper Silurian, during the time of the agnathan radiations. The evolution of jaws and teeth was an enormously important innovation for vertebrates, for it meant that they could gain access to a much greater variety of food than that available to the agnathans. Jaws also provided possibilities for defense and manipulation of food which did not exist before.

From embryological studies and through comparing anatomy it would appear that the jaws evolved from the anterior gill arches in the pharynx. Each of the gill openings in a typical vertebrate is surrounded by a gill arch skeleton, a series of jointed bony rods and muscles which provide a muscular pumping action to ventilate the gills. It would appear that the front gill arches were converted into a pair of jaws. The gill arch immediately behind the new jaws shifted forwards to connect with the jaw hinge, so that it could be stabilized, and the normal gill opening was shifted upwards to lie in the space between the gill arch, upper jaw, and braincase. This reduced gill pouch, known as the spiracle, is still present in sharks and rays today. The lower part of the gill arch which supports the jaw hinge also helps to support the floor of the mouth. In later vertebrates, including ourselves, it provides anchorage for the tongue and its associated muscles.

This wholesale reorganization of the front end of the pharynx was extremely important because it allowed specialization to occur in those parts of the pharynx associated with feeding and respiration. Previously, these two functions had been combined, which demanded a compromise in their design. Breaking that connection provided the opportunity for novelty in respiration and feeding, and considerably spurred the evolution of vertebrate design. The gills could now become highly specialized respiratory surfaces with fine, delicate filaments to improve the exchange of gases, which had been difficult while grit and other particles were constantly washing over them. The jaws for their part now allowed all manner of food to be captured, and some force to be used in

THE EVOLUTION OF JAWS FROM GILL ARCHES

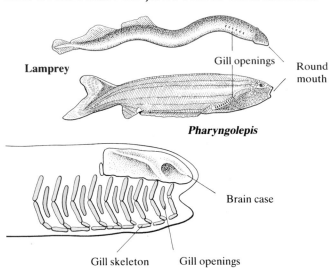

Jawless fish

ABOVE *Living* (TOP) *and fossil* (CENTER) *jawless fish have round mouths and a full set of gill openings. The schematic diagram shows their general skeletal layout, with a row of gill arch bones supporting the flesh around each of the gill openings.*

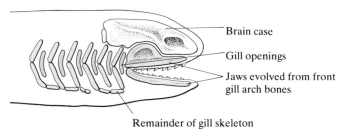

Early vertebrates

In the early vertebrates, the front gill arch bones of jawless fish were probably converted into jaws and lined by tooth-shaped scales. The first gill opening lies just behind the jaw joint, which at this stage would therefore not be very stable.

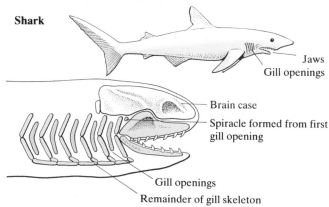

Modern sharks

The well-developed jaws of sharks are partly linked to the braincase. The gill arch just behind them has swung forward to form a connection that stabilizes the jaw joint, so the gill opening (now called a spiracle) has been "squeezed" up above it.

crushing the food – though this depended on the strength of the jaw-closing muscles and the degree of firmness with which the jaws were attached to the rest of the head skeleton.

Linked to the appearance of jaws was the development of teeth. In their simplest form, teeth are mineralized conical structures lining the jaws. They are composed of a bony base covered by a layer of dentine and a hard outer coating of enamel-like material. Even in early fish the shape and arrangement of teeth varied enormously, from sharp spikes for grasping and puncturing, through blades for cutting, to flattened plates for crushing.

There have been four major groups of jawed fish (collectively known as gnathostomes, "jaw mouths"): acanthodians and placoderms, both of which are now extinct; the still living cartilaginous fish (sharks, rays, skates, and chimeras) and the bony fish (the familiar carp, minnows, tuna, piranhas, and so on). In addition to jaws, these groups possess a number of other unifying characters: paired nostrils (these were extraordinarily variable in agnathans – the majority had single nostrils as far as we can tell), body muscles divided into upper and lower portions, a system of paired fins, and in all early members of each group an upturned (heterocercal) tail.

The first fins

The development of jaws in vertebrates allowed them to become predators, for which they needed good vision, speed, and maneuverability. Vision was always well developed in vertebrates. Speed requires streamlining and powerful body musculature – again basic attributes of chordates as a whole. Maneuverability demands control surfaces which allow for subtle movements and changes of direction in response to the evasive action of prey. It is fins that provide this ability in fish, and their pattern and arrangement reflect the conflicting requirements of moving in water.

Vertebrates are composed of bone and muscle, both of which are denser than water. Without some form of compensating mechanism fish will sink to the sea bed. This so-called negative buoyancy was characteristic of all early vertebrates – hence their tendency to be bottom dwellers – and created constant instability when they moved about.

In addition to the downward gravitational force acting on the center of gravity of the fish, there is an opposing lifting force caused by its body displacing water. This acts on the fish's center of buoyancy, which may not be in the same place as its center of gravity. Vertebrates are not evenly constructed: there tends to be more bone near the front of the animal around the head, gills, and jaws. This means that the center of buoyancy is further

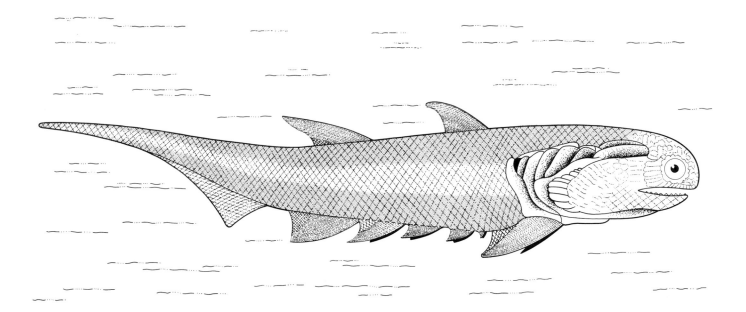

back than the center of gravity. As a result, fish tend not only to sink because they are negatively buoyant, but also to pitch downward at the front, like a submarine diving, because the tail is less dense than the head end.

To counter this, fish have fins at the front end (pectoral or shoulder fins), which they can use to keep themselves level. The dorsal fin (on the back), and the pelvic and anal fins at the rear, stop the fish rolling over. Many of the fish that are described in the following pages experimented with the distribution of fins in order to modify stability, control, and overall maneuverability. What they achieved was a fine balance between stability and instability.

Acanthodians

These creatures of the Upper Silurian, also known as spiny sharks, were the first vertebrates to possess both jaws with teeth and fins. The vast majority of them were small (4 to 6ins/10 to 15cm long), with very streamlined, laterally flattened bodies. As a group they persisted into the Permian, but the main thrust of their evolutionary radiation appears to have been in the Middle and Upper Devonian Periods.

Most were covered with a layer of small, diamond-shaped scales very different from the heavy armor plating of the agnathans. Their eyes were very large and placed well forward – exactly what you would expect of a hunter. The jaws were long and lined with sharply pointed teeth. Behind the jaws there were five gills on either side, each covered with a valve-like flap – though in a few (such as *Climatius*) a single large flap called the operculum covered the entire gill area.

The fins appear to have been triangular webs of skin stretched behind curved spines. The general pattern of

Acanthodians were the first jawed fish and represent a great spur to the evolution of swimming vertebrates. Fins of various kinds developed to assist maneuverability in water. Jaws also allowed many carnivores to appear, which in turn pressured their prey to increase their ability to take avoiding action. This concept of an "arms race" between the species is just as true today as it was in the Silurian.

fins and spines is as follows. There are two fins in the midline along the back (dorsals), another single fin beneath the tail (anal), and a variable array of lateral paired fins along the lower sides of the body. In some acanthodians the number of paired lateral fins is reduced, but these fish were clearly experimenting with the general layout of their paired fins. Some acanthodians had extremely long spines, and it seems likely that these were a defensive adaptation to prevent them from being swallowed by larger predators.

Placoderms

The next major group of jawed fishes are again bony – hence their name, which means "plated skins." They first appear, as very scrappy fossils, in the Late Silurian, and rise to dominance in the Devonian Period; however, they barely survive that Period and only a few poor fossils are known from the Early Carboniferous.

Most placoderms were larger than acanthodians, ranging from 1 to 2ft (30 to 60cm) in length. The front half of their body was covered in large curved plates of bone, forming a rigid shield, with a joint between the head and the shoulder region. The remainder of the body was either covered with fine bony scales or had none at all. The best-known placoderms belong to one of two subgroups, the arthrodires and the antiarchs.

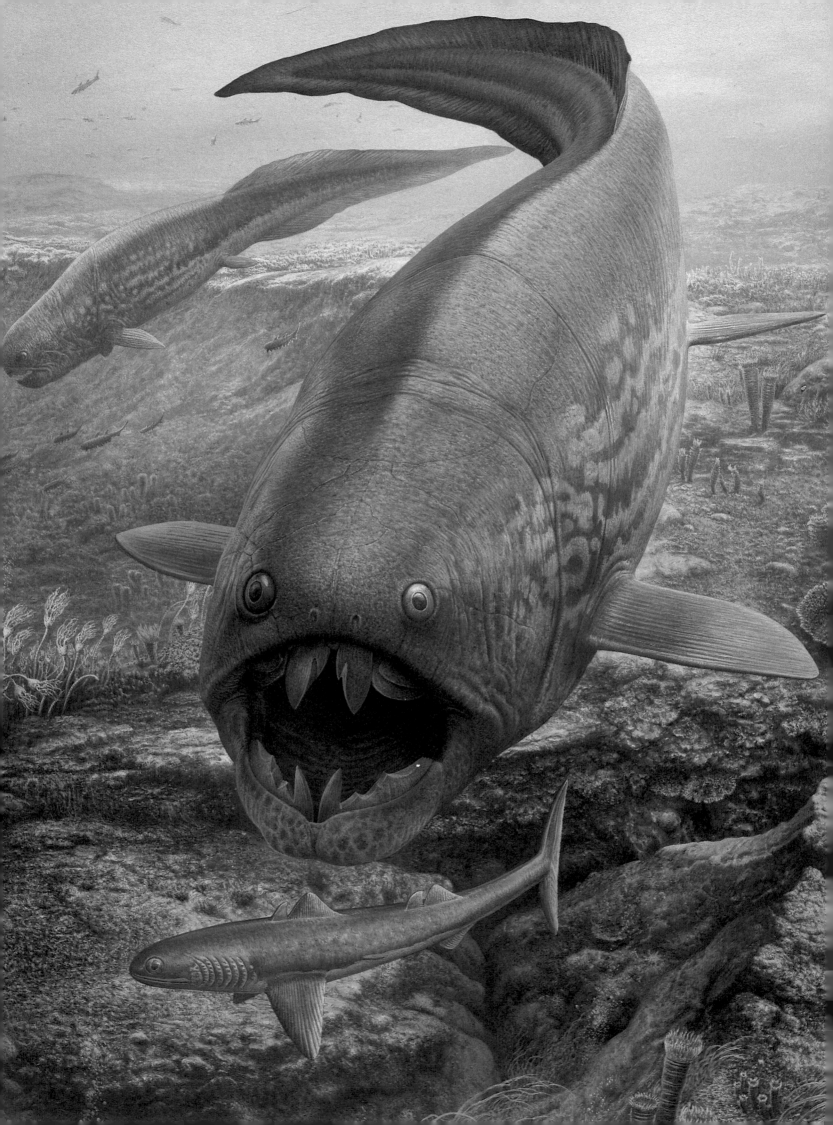

"Arthrodire" means "jointed neck." *Coccosteus* (a relatively modest 1ft/30cm in length) and the gigantic *Dunkleosteus* (about 30ft/10m long) are well-preserved examples of this group that were undoubtedly fierce predators. Most arthrodires were equipped with large eyes, and powerful jaws lined with sharp-edged plates of bone which resembled jagged guillotine blades. The curious ball-and-socket joint between the shoulder and head allowed the head to be rotated back against the body, presumably to provide that fearsome mouth with a wider gape in order to grab larger prey; or it may perhaps have allowed them to plough up bottom-dwelling prey more easily.

The remainder of the body was virtually scaleless, which implies that arthrodires were extremely flexible, and there are traces of bony supports forming a distinct vertebral column, as well as bony rays supporting the median fins. The structure of the paired pectoral fins is uncertain, but fossils show that arthrodires did have large sockets on the side of the shoulder shield, so these fins were probably extremely mobile. All these factors suggest that arthrodires were fast-moving, highly maneuverable fish.

The antiarchs, like the arthrodires, were mostly confined to the Devonian Period. Most do not exceed 1ft (30cm) in length, and again the front of the body is encased in heavy bony plates. Some have a thin covering of scales, but many have a virtually naked tail. There is evidence of two dorsal fins, a heterocercal tail, and fleshy pelvic fins. The most unusual feature, however, is the remarkably crab-like pectoral fin. Jointed to the side of the head shield, this was presumably used as a leg and may well have assisted antiarchs to move slowly just above the sea bed. The eyes of *Bothriolepis*, a typical example, are placed on the upper part of the head, and the mouth is lined by a set of cutting plates rather smaller than those of the arthrodires. The mouth is also relatively small, and slung under the head rather than opening to the front.

This combination of features suggests that antiarchs may well have filled a similar niche to the earlier agnathans – that of bottom-dwelling sediment feeders.

The rise of jawed fish resulted in the rapid appearance of a classic pyramid of predators and prey. At the very top of the pyramid in the Devonian was the giant arthrodire Dunklosteus (LEFT), *often erroneously called* Dinichthys. *Reaching lengths of perhaps 30 ft (9m) and with a skull over 6 ft (2m) long, these were mighty fish. Their jaws were lined not with pointed teeth, but with huge curved plates of bone which acted like guillotine blades. Large (over 6 ft/2m long) early sharks such as* Cladoselache (bottom of picture), *although fearsome in their own right, were dwarfed by, and undoubtedly prey to, these gigantic arthrodires.*

However, the presence of cutting teeth implies a more active feeding strategy. It is possible that they spent much of the time cruising just above the sea bed, or slowly walking across the sea floor on their pectoral fins, feeding on small invertebrates and suspension feeders – they would have found rich pickings in the shallow parts of the sea floor.

Neither the specialist predatory arthrodires nor the bottom-feeding antiarchs survived for long into the Carboniferous Period. Their roles seem to have been taken over in succeeding Periods by the next two groups: the cartilaginous and bony fish.

Cartilaginous fish

This group, scientifically known as chondrichthyans, includes today's sharks and rays. It is the last major group of fish to appear in the fossil record; none is known from earlier than the latest part of the Lower Devonian. Their fossil record is poor because, as their name suggests, their skeletons are made of cartilage, which does not preserve as well as bone. In the past it was supposed that this was a primitive characteristic, but it has now been demonstrated that this development is a specific adaptation to assist in maintaining buoyancy (see page 76). Chondrichthyans do have true bone, though not in their skeletons but in their skins, which are covered in tiny sharp spines known as dermal denticles; and in their teeth, which are similar structures on a larger scale.

The chondrichthyans are divided into two subgroups. The holocephali (rat fish) are curious creatures, relatively scarce in the fossil record. They are represented today by the chimeras, which live in deep waters. Much more numerous and interesting are the elasmobranchs (sharks, rays, and skates).

True sharks date from the Upper Devonian. A typical example from this time is *Cladoselache*, which is illustrated opposite in the unwelcome company of the terrifying predator *Dunkleosteus*. *Cladoselache* reached a length of 6ft (2m) or more, and was recognizably shark-shaped. Its body was streamlined and there were two dorsal fins, each with a blunt spine immediately in front. The pectoral fins were very large and triangular, and appear to have been relatively stiff – rather like the wings of an airplane. There was a pair of small pelvic fins and a deep, symmetrical tail that formed a very effective paddle. The jaws were long and the eyes, unlike those of modern sharks which tend to be quite small and some way back on the head, were fairly large and located near the tip of the snout. Unusually for a fish, the head and gill skeleton was entirely separate from the shoulder girdle, which meant that the head was relatively mobile.

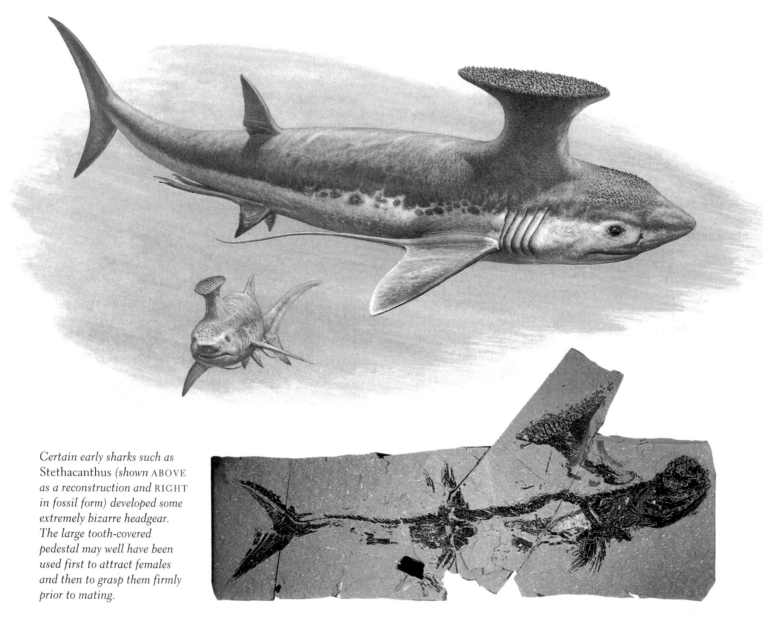

Certain early sharks such as Stethacanthus (shown ABOVE *as a reconstruction and* RIGHT *in fossil form) developed some extremely bizarre headgear. The large tooth-covered pedestal may well have been used first to attract females and then to grasp them firmly prior to mating.*

While the majority of sharks conformed to a general pattern, the occasional discovery comes as a shock. The appearance of the Carboniferous shark *Stethacanthus* from Bearsden in Scotland was quite unexpected. When an entire skeleton of this shark was discovered it was revealed to have a bizarre tooth-covered projection above its head. This is thought to have been a special clasper, enabling males to latch onto females while mating. Because shark fossils are so rare, for reasons explained above, paleontologists are probably quite unaware of an enormous amount of biological and evolutionary diversity in sharks.

Sharks have solved the problem of buoyancy by two adaptations. Cartilage is less dense than bone, so the skeletons of sharks are more buoyant than those of all bony fish. But cartilage alone does not solve the problem of moving effectively in the sea – sharks are still slightly denser than their environment. Unlike the bony fish (see page 79), sharks have never possessed a lung which could serve as an onboard buoyancy tank. They manage to maintain their position in the water by a combination of hydrodynamic lift and hydrostatic lift.

The hydrodynamic solution is found in the shape of the relatively stiff pectoral fins and the snout, with its arched upper and flattened under surface. These provide a lift force when sharks swim – they are in effect operating like underwater aircraft. But there are two distinct disadvantages to this method: first, the animals have to swim continuously, and second they are unable to swim backwards.

The hydrostatic solution involves the accumulation of low-density oils in the liver. If enough can be stored, the density of the shark will approach that of sea water and it can float indefinitely. This is what happens in the case of the giant whale sharks and basking sharks. A drawback to this solution is that the liver, and thus the whole body, need to be large, so that swimming at any speed consumes a lot of energy.

The great majority of sharks are medium-sized and streamlined, with well-developed pectoral fins and quite large oily livers. As a result they tend to use a combination of these two methods to maintain their position in the water and therefore swim more or less continuously. Such sharks do not pump water through their gills to respire, but rely on ram ventilation – they swim with their mouths open. Indeed, if not allowed to swim continuously they risk suffocation.

RIGHT ABOVE *Being heavier than water creates problems. Most sharks use their fins and flattened snout to create upward forces which counteract their tendency to sink, but it also means they have to swim continuously. An alternative strategy (RIGHT BELOW) is to store huge quantities of low-density oil (squalene) in the liver, which evens up the pressure and makes animals such as the whale shark (BELOW) neutrally buoyant. The drawback is that such creatures have to be very large to store enough oil.*

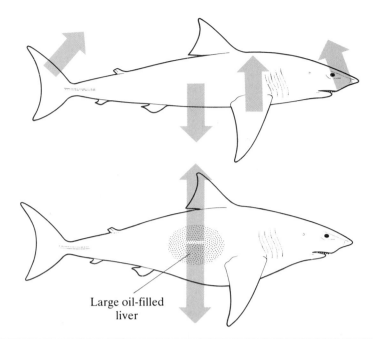

Large oil-filled liver

LEFT *The grey nurse shark* (Eugomphodus taurus) *shows features typical of modern sharks: streamlined in form, it has a curved mouth lined with wickedly sharp teeth. The jaws are normally slung up against the snout, but can be swung forward and protruded in order to improve their bite when prey is near.*

RIGHT *The manta ray (*Manta alfredi) *is a most impressive member of the shark family. Unlike typical sharks it does not use its long tail for locomotion. Instead it makes use of its greatly enlarged pectoral fins, which act like the wings of a bird for underwater "flight". These animals slowly cruise tropical and subtropical waters and feed on plankton. Note the hitch-hiking remoras* (Echeneis naucrates).

The jaws of early sharks were long and fixed to the sides of the skull. However, in modern forms the jaws are rather different. They tend to hang free beneath the braincase, suspended by ligaments and the anchorage provided by the hyomandibular (the upper bone of the next gill arch). This might seem a flimsy arrangement, but it proves extremely valuable for sharks when feeding. When approaching prey sharks swim rapidly and open their mouths; at the same time the hyomandibular is swung forward so that the jaws and teeth are pushed into the prey. The jaws are closed as the hyomandibular retracts, pulling the jaws inward and tearing off a chunk of flesh, which is then swallowed.

All the power of the feeding action is derived from the swimming speed of the fish, which drives the jaws onto the prey – the jaw muscles themselves are rather weak. But this ability to use the jaw muscles to exert a powerful bite is a late development which probably did not rise to prominence until the Devonian.

Most rays and skates have in a sense given up the battle to stay afloat, and taken to a bottom-dwelling life. They are dorsoventrally flattened – that is, from top to bottom – and the tail is much reduced. In some forms it has become a long, whip-like structure. They propel themselves with greatly expanded pectoral fins, which act rather like the wings of a bird. The majority are scavengers and predators of invertebrates; however, one major exception are the huge manta rays, which have reverted to a filter-feeding way of life.

The bony fishes

More than half of the living groups of vertebrates are bony fish, known as osteichthyans. This is the longest-surviving group of jawed vertebrates. They first appeared in the Lower Devonian, and since the decline of the acanthodians and placoderms at the close of the Devonian Period they have gradually evolved to become the dominant fish in the world's waters. The internal skeleton and external scales, then as now, are made of bone. The skull is heavily armored, and the teeth are fixed very firmly to the jaw bones. The gills, immediately behind the jaws, are not visible as in sharks but are covered by a plate of bone, the operculum; they are ventilated in most cases by raising and lowering the floor of the mouth (using the lower part of the gill skeleton), and by using the operculum as a simple valve to prevent water from flowing back into the gills.

The pattern of fins seen in chondrichthyans, placoderms, and some of the later acanthodians is repeated here. There are paired pectoral fins, paired pelvic fins, a row of dorsal fins (usually either two or one), and an anal fin just in front of and beneath the tail.

Most primitive bony fish seem to have possessed a pair of air-filled pouches. These served as crude lungs, or buoyancy tanks, or both. Many modern bony fish that inhabit stagnant ponds come to the surface and gulp air to help them breathe, and it seems likely that their remote ancestors had the same ability.

There are two major types of bony fish, distinguished by the form of their fins: they are the actinopterygians ("ray fins") and the sarcopterygians ("fleshy fins"). The ray-finned fish have been the most important and abundant group of fish consistently throughout their history. Of their fleshy-finned relatives only a very few are alive today – several species of lungfish and the coelacanth. They are, however, an important group because it is from them that the remaining classes of vertebrates (amphibians, reptiles, mammals, and birds) evolved.

Actinopterygians are first found, as rather scrappy remains, in the Late Silurian Period; they are first known in detail from the Lower Devonian. The earliest well-preserved examples appear in freshwater deposits; but by the time of the Middle Devonian, when they were abundant, their remains are found in both marine and freshwater deposits.

In general terms the actinopterygians were small fish (2 to 8 ins/5 to 20cm in length) with a single dorsal fin, a strongly heterocercal (but noticeably forked) tail, paired fins supported by a fan-like arrangement of long, thin, bony rays, large eyes, and a short snout. As in the case of the sharks and their relatives, the two dominant themes in the ray-finned fish are their methods of moving and feeding. Evolutionary change in these two areas was largely responsible for the huge variety of bony fish alive today.

The early actinopterygians (often referred to as palaeoniscids, "ancient swimmers") had relatively thick armored scales, but this does not seem to have unduly compromised their swimming ability. Most probably this was because lungs or an air bladder provided extra buoyancy. The fins were not stiff as in the early sharks, but thin and somewhat flexible, which enabled them to enjoy an increased range of movement, and therefore hydrodynamic control, while swimming.

The jaws of these small predators were adapted for snapping. The bones of the upper jaw were rigidly attached to the rest of the skull, and the lower jaw would be opened and sharply shut against the upper one, driving the small, sharp teeth into the prey. The jaw-closing muscles lay in a cavity under the cheek region of the skull. From the start the feeding techniques of bony fish relied much more on a muscular biting action than did those of chondrichthyan fish such as sharks.

Among the bony fish of the Paleozoic Chirodus *is unusual in having a very deep body, together with teeth modified for crushing rather than biting and cutting.*

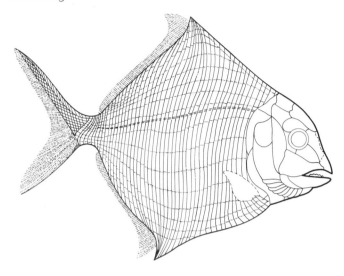

The Carboniferous palaeoniscid Rhadinichthys *was a streamlined, aggressive predator with diamond-shaped hard scales as body armor, and prominently rayed fins.*

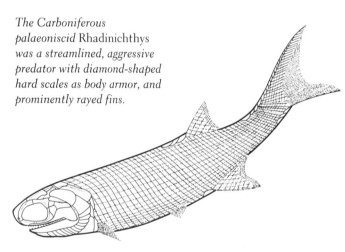

Cheirolepis, *a predator from the Devonian, belongs to a family all of its own. Though otherwise similar to* Rhadinichthys, *it has relatively small, square scales.*

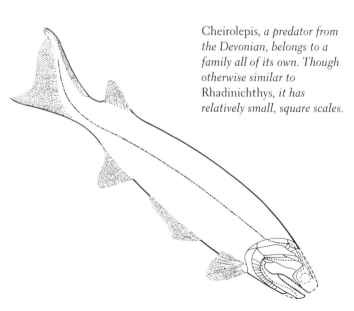

Bony fish such as *Chirodus, Cheirolepis, Moythomasia, Rhadinichthys,* and *Dorypterus* were abundant and successful during much of the remaining Paleozoic Era, before declining in the Triassic. By the end of the Paleozoic a number of subtle changes had begun to take place. The upper and lower lobes of the caudal (tail) fin were becoming outwardly symmetrical; as a consequence the tail produced less lift. The fins were losing their role as stiff "wings," and had fewer rays so that they were much more flexible and able to control movement more finely. Probably linked to the symmetry of the tail was the fact that the scales were now considerably less heavily armored.

All these factors seem to be functionally linked in a progression. The buoyancy provided by the lung or air bladder allowed the tail to generate more forward thrust and less lift; the fins no longer needed to provide just lift and became control devices; the resulting greater speed and agility allowed these fish to avoid predators more easily; and in consequence they could have less heavily armored scales.

During the Late Permian a number of distinctive changes occurred in the evolution of the palaeoniscids, in particular in the way the jaws worked. The bones of the upper jaw became loose at the back end near the jaw hinge, so that when the lower jaw opened the rear end of the upper jaw was able to swing downward and forward. As a result the mouth became more circular than the long, grinning jaw seen in earlier forms. The new mouth had two advantages – it permitted a limited sucking action so that prey could be drawn into the mouth before it was bitten; and, more importantly, the loosening of the upper jaw bones allowed the jaw muscles to become larger, so that the bite became much more powerful as well.

A variety of palaeoniscids began to elaborate these changes in the action of their jaws, in combination with the lightening of the body armor and the changing shape of the caudal fin and paired fins. What evolved was in effect a new and improved type of bony fish, the holosteans, which appeared in the Permian and dominated the seas during the Early Mesozoic (Triassic and Jurassic).

Several types of fish living today reflect the general anatomy of holosteans. These include the bowfin (*Amia*) of the Mississippi, an aggressive predator. Its skull is surprisingly heavily armored, but its jaws can be moved flexibly to produce a rounded, sucker-like mouth. This enables *Amia* to feed on smaller fish, which can be drawn in by enlarging the mouth and simultaneously taking in water (normally part of the breathing cycle).

The holosteans were ultimately replaced by yet another wave of evolutionary development within their

AIR-BREATHING FISH

Cocoons for survival

ABOVE *Lungfish from Africa live in ponds and lakes which occasionally dry out. In these circumstances most fish would* *asphyxiate, but lungfish are able to survive periods of drought by burrowing down into the mud and forming a cocoon.*

Lungfish on land

BELOW *Although* Protopterus annectens *is at home in the water like any other fish, its well-developed lung enables it to survive just as well on land where it must breathe air. The lungfish's fins, however, are rather long and fragile and clearly unsuited for the task of supporting its body on land – some of the ancient air-breathing fish, which are known to us today only from fossilized skeletons, were considerably better equipped in this respect.*

own ranks. These fish, which began to appear in the Jurassic Period, are referred to as teleosts. Since that time they have dominated the seas and rivers of the world. The final changes that took place in this group involved complete external symmetry of the tail and even thinner scales. They were to develop complete control over their buoyancy by converting the original lungs used for gulping air, as found in the earliest palaeoniscids, into a refined buoyancy tank, whose volume can be adjusted so that the fish is able to move up and down in the water as required.

Once again there is a follow-on effect from this development. Because they are neutrally buoyant the fins, no longer constrained to act as hydrofoils, can be used in all sorts of ways: for fine adjustments to body position while "hovering," for moving the fish backwards as well as up or down, and for all manner of other potential uses – flying, making sounds, walking, and courtship displays.

The sarcopterygians, or lobe-finned fish, appeared in the Early Devonian. They were on average considerably larger than actinopterygians (10 to 40 ins/25 to 100cm in length) and were all marine, which indicates a clear distinction between the two groups right from the beginning. They are instantly distinguished by the presence of two dorsal fins and the shape of their paired fins; these have a fringe of fine fin rays, but the central portion of the fin has a scale-covered, muscular, bone-reinforced central portion (the "lobe" of the name).

As with the early actinopterygians, it seems likely that these were aggressive predators in their Devonian heyday. The majority of lungfish had heavy crushing and cutting teeth, distantly similar to the tooth plates of some placoderms, which they would have used to feed on molluscs and other prey.

One group of lobe-finned fish was the dipnoans ("double breathers") or lungfish, of which some are still living today in Africa, South America, and Australia. They provide unequivocal evidence that these fish possessed lungs, because the living forms use them to complement their gills when the ponds in which they live grow stagnant and breathing becomes difficult. The African lungfish is able to burrow into the mud at the bottom of lakes or ponds that are drying out, and produce a cocoon in which to rest and breathe air until the waters return. Lungfish burrows have been found from the Devonian, so this trait is extremely long-lived. Presumably it was a considerable aid to survival in conditions that would otherwise have killed all fish.

The group of lobe-finned fishes to which the coelacanth belongs goes back to the Devonian Period. It is an intriguing exercise to compare the anatomical details of the fossilized specimen (ABOVE) with that of modern examples such as (LEFT) Latimeria chalumnae from the Comoro Islands of the Indian Ocean. This, the only living coelacanth species, is an aggressive predator that lives at great depths in the ocean, and is surprisingly similar in most respects to fossil coelacanths. Until the unexpected discovery of living specimens in the 1930s it was thought that the coelacanths had died out with the dinosaurs in Cretaceous times.

Another group whose ancestry can be traced back to the Devonian Period includes the living coelacanth, a large marine fish 3 ft (1m) or more in length, which lives at great depths off the Comoro Islands in the Indian Ocean. It was not discovered until the early twentieth century, which caused a sensation because until then the last coelacanths were thought to have died out in the Cretaceous Period – during the reign of the dinosaurs.

These large fish again seem to be aggressive predators, with powerful teeth and jaws. They beautifully display the fleshy-lobed fins so characteristic of the group.

From the point of view of vertebrate evolution, and the origin of all subsequent groups, the most important lobe-finned fish are those of the Devonian. The anatomy and way of life of these early fish have been investigated in detail, because through them it may be possible to trace the origins of the first land vertebrates.

One particularly well-studied lobe-finned fish is *Eusthenopteron*. When it was thoroughly examined by the paleontologists Mahala Andrews and Stanley Westoll, it revealed many of the attributes which seem to be crucial to the eventual land-living vertebrates. It is

quite certain that these early fish possessed lungs – an essential characteristic for any vertebrate that is going to survive on land. But what of the future legs – how might they have evolved? The answer to this question seems to be linked to the lobed fins.

The covering of fine scales on the fins was painstakingly picked away with delicate needles, to reveal the internal skeleton of the fin. Although not precisely what one might expect from the leg or arm of a walking animal, the skeleton exhibits all the essential components. It has an upper bone which attached to the shoulder bones (equivalent to the humerus or upper arm bone), and beneath this a pair of bones (similar to the forearm bones, the radius, and ulna). Beyond that, the pattern of bones becomes indistinct and more closely related to the support of the fin rays. However, the essence of a future vertebrate land limb was present. This combination of lungs and potential limbs set in motion the possibility of life on land.

EUSTHENOPTERON – FINS TO LEGS?

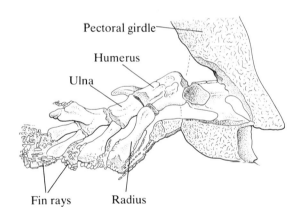

Pectoral girdle

Humerus

Ulna

Fin rays

Radius

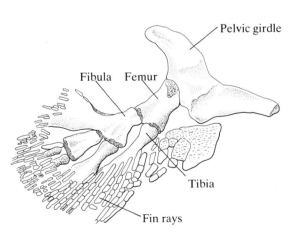

Pelvic girdle

Fibula Femur

Tibia

Fin rays

Revealing the evidence

LEFT *Painstaking work, which has involved picking away the surface layers of sediment, and then the scales covering the outer surface of the fins of* Eusthenopteron, *has enabled scientists to illustrate in amazing detail the precise organization in the bones of the pectoral or front fin* (ABOVE) *and the pelvic or rear fin* (BELOW). *All the essential elements of a walking creature were present – an upper arm bone, equivalent to the modern humerus, which attached to a shoulder bone, and below it a pair of bones which were the counterpart of the radius and ulna in the forearm of man and other limbed vertebrates. In effect* Eusthenopteron *has primitive arms and legs. Careful study of the way in which these bones are jointed together has made it possible to reconstruct the likely range of movements achievable by these early fin/limbs.*

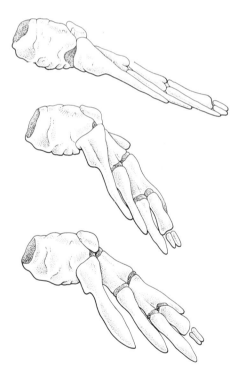

Primitive legs

ABOVE *The fins could be "trimmed" (TOP), as might be expected of a fin gliding through water, but they could also be moved sharply down and rotated backward* (CENTER AND BOTTOM) *to produce movements close to those of a primitive leg.*

5

GAINING THE LAND

THE ESTABLISHMENT OF A BEACHHEAD

THE EMERGENCE of life from the water and onto the land was not a concerted effort over a short period by some heroic early forms of life, but took place in fits and starts over a vast timespan – probably in excess of 3,000 million years. This view is based on the discovery of stromatolites which are thought to have resembled the domes of blue-green algae seen in isolated parts of the world such as Hamelin Pool at Shark Bay in Australia. These domes are exposed at low water, and therefore could be considered, at least temporarily, land organisms. But the blue-green algae can hardly be said to exploit life on land: they simply tolerate exposure to air and sunlight for a few hours during the tidal cycle.

ABOVE *This underwater view of modern stromatolites at Shark Bay in Australia provides an almost perfect snapshot of the shallow seas of the Early Precambrian. When the tide goes out the tops of these dome-shaped structures are exposed, requiring cyanobacteria to cope with life on land – no matter how temporary*

LEFT *Bridging the gap. Acanthostega (LEFT) is in most respects a fish, despite its four stout legs. Ichthyostega (RIGHT) looks like a much sturdier land-living tetrapod, but its fishy tail indicates a preference for water.*

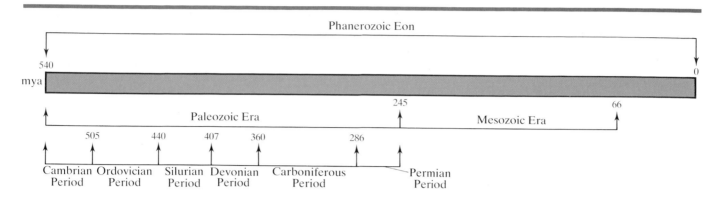

Timescale of Earth history. *Gradually life ceased to be confined to the water and its margins. From the Silurian onward genuine land plants established a bridgehead, creating rich, water-retaining soil and the beginnings of an ecosystem which was exploited first by invertebrates, and then in the Devonian by the first land-dwelling vertebrates, the tetrapods.*

The blue-greens also made another vital contribution to the beginnings of land-based life. Water, chemically H_2O, is a mixture of hydrogen and oxygen. By removing the hydrogen the blue-greens made oxygen available – and oxygen is essential for the production of energy, which many land animals need in large quantities.

Life in water provides a number of advantages which need to be compensated for if life is to succeed on land. Water is a supporting, protective medium that contains nutrients and gases. It is much less subject to extremes of temperature than air. And finally, it is a medium for transferring the sexual elements of the life cycle.

In contrast, life on land is subject to water loss, the effects of gravity, and greater ranges of temperature (both day and night, and seasonal); in addition, ultraviolet (UV) radiation from the Sun can damage the chemical bonds along the strands of DNA: abnormalities in growth or development, or in the creature's offspring, may result. Any organisms evolving on land have to develop strategies for coping with these factors. For example, the blue-green algae at Shark Bay have special UV-damage repair mechanisms for their DNA. More complex organisms require mechanisms to prevent desiccation (drying out) and to cope with temperature fluctuations. The fossil record is very patchy in relation to the colonization of the land; however, there are a number of features associated with land life that provide at least part of the story.

PLANTS, THE FIRST LAND PIONEERS

A considerable number of structural features needed to be developed by plants if they were going to be able to survive on land:

o A thickened waxy covering (cuticle) to reduce water loss, and possibly also to protect the tissues from damage by ultra-violet light.

o A system of skin pores that will open and close (stomata) so that gas exchange can occur for photosynthesis to take place. Photosynthesis is the process by which pigments such as chlorophyll, which are contained within the plant, can trap the energy of sunlight for the plant's own use.

o A supportive skeleton to prevent the plant from collapsing under its own weight.

o Water- and nutrient-conducting systems which will enable these vital substances to reach the aerial parts of the plant.

o Water-absorbing organs (roots).

o Small, resistant spores (seeds), which can be blown about on air currents: essential if plants are to colonize the land.

Many modern liverworts and mosses have a very short life cycle, which allows them to survive less favorable conditions and take advantage of short periods of warmer weather. The development of tough, resistant spores meant that these parts of the life cycle could not only survive harsh conditions such as extremes of drought, heat, and cold, but could also be widely distributed. Drought resistance can alternatively be achieved by the whole plant – some mosses have tissues that can dry and then rehydrate without loss of function. Chemicals known as flavonoids are able to protect plant tissues from UV damage. These are found both in complex plants and in mosses and other early plants.

Much of the evidence suggests that complex land plants – in other words, not just simple forms such as algae and perhaps lichens living on exposed surfaces –

began to appear in moist land areas in the Late Ordovician, in a part of the world which was to become the North Atlantic continents. But at that time much of this continental block lay in the tropics, and its climate seems to have ranged between wet tropical and marginal desert. It would have been a challenging environment for any plant. It appears that following a Late Ordovician Ice Age, the areas where many Early Devonian fossils are found would have experienced wet variable-to-tropical conditions. In more recent times, the Ice Ages which affected the Northern Hemisphere repeatedly within the last million years were followed by rapid colonization by liverworts and mosses and other plants that had adopted strategies for thriving on moist land. Was this the way plants first colonized the land?

Fossil evidence

The earliest fossils come from the Late Ordovician and Early Silurian, and consist largely of isolated spores, spore clusters, and fragments of cuticle and tubular structures. These appear to show a strong resemblance to parts of modern liverworts. Indeed, liverworts have characteristics that may well have suited them to early land colonization. Some live on algal crusts on land in shallow, temporary pools, and in soils together with blue-green algae; some also live symbiotically with nitrogen-fixing blue-green algae.

Nitrogen is essential for the formation of proteins, yet plants can neither manufacture it nor trap it from the air. But some bacteria, for example the blue-green algae, can extract it from the air – for this reason they are known as nitrogen fixers. Early land pioneers that inhabited marginal habitats covered by a blue-green algal mat may have found it distinctly advantageous to harbor nitrogen-fixing organisms in order to help them grow their body tissues, thus forming an essential link in the process of colonizing the land. So some of the earliest land plants are likely to have been ancient relatives of the modern liverworts and mosses.

By Early to Middle Silurian times the fossil remains include more body parts of plants that were potentially land-living. These include portions of branching stems, and what appear to be water-conducting tubes. Branching stems are today associated with plants that stand tall, with strong tubular walls for carrying water and nutrients and for supporting spore capsules. The higher up on a plant the spores are, the more widely dispersed they will be. This is a distinct advance over the mosses and liverworts, which tend to have tangled, ground-hugging forms.

Lichens are fungi living cooperatively with photosynthetic algae – an incredibly tough amalgam which allows them to inhabit places as inhospitable as Antarctica. Organisms such as this may have colonized the land in the late Precambrian.

RHYNIE, SCOTLAND – 400 MILLION YEARS AGO

Marginal plant life
Beneath the fields just outside the village of Rhynie in Scotland are some flinty rocks known as the Rhynie Chert. When cut into thin slices and then polished and examined under the microscope the cherts reveal fragments of some of the earliest land plants. From this evidence, and our understanding of the geological setting in which the cherts were deposited, it has been possible to piece together a detailed picture of the landscape and scenery in this part of the world. Against a backdrop of volcanic activity and erupting geysers, shallow ponds are seen here surrounded by dense stands of early vascular plants. Plants seem limited to areas adjacent to water, but were soon to spread further inland.

Between the Middle Silurian and the Early Devonian, the first reasonably well-preserved plants with identifiable cuticles, water-conducting vessels, and strengthened branching stems and spore capsules are found in South Wales, Ireland, and Bohemia. These include small plants only about 1in (2.5cm) tall such as *Cooksonia*, which has a simple, branching form; and *Steganotheca*, a slightly larger, more bush-like plant about 2ins (5cm) tall. Overlapping these is a much more substantial group of plants from deposits of Early Devonian age under farmland at Rhynie in Scotland. This site has proved very important, because the plants preserved here are frequently found as three-dimensional structures, rather than as squashed films.

It appears that the plants at Rhynie lived on the sandy banks of shallow pools which frequently dried out. The area surrounding these pools was one of geysers, hot springs, and volcanic cones, some of which may have been active. As a result of flooding by hot spring water rich in minerals such as silica, these early plants became entombed with very little distortion – the silica solution hardened and turned to a rock form known as chert (the Rhynie Chert), and in some cases they were literally preserved as they stood.

Aglaophyton has been carefully reconstructed by paleontologists from the detailed fossil evidence. Its underground root system, supportive stem tissues, water-conducting vessels, and pores permeable by gases and water all indicate that this plant possessed the basic requirements for life on land.

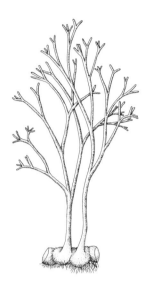

Horneophyton
ABOVE *This plant had water-conducting tissues and formed bush-like growths. The spores were borne in barrel-shaped chambers at the branch tips.*

Asteroxylon
BELOW *The 20 inch (50cm) stems of this plant were covered in spirally arranged scaly leaves. It resembles living clubmosses such as Lycopodium.*

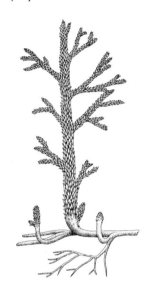

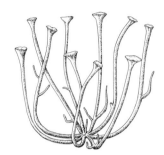

Sciadophyton
ABOVE *Radiating upward and outward from a central disk were photosynthetic branches; the cup-shaped upper ends of these branches contained the male and female parts.*

Rhynia
BELOW *Up to 8ins (20cm) tall, Rhynia had tough strands of vascular tissue to enable it to stand upright on land, and pores to control water loss.*

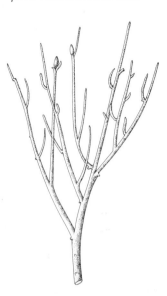

This marvelous state of preservation has enabled paleontologists to reconstruct the dominant types of plant, such as *Aglaophyton*, *Rhynia*, *Horneophyton*, and *Asteroxylon*. *Aglaophyton* is large, in the region of 1 ft 6 ins (45cm) tall. It has a horizontal underground root rather like a rhizome (root stem) from which short, hair-like roots sprout at intervals, and simple upright stems which branch at intervals and end in conical spore capsules. The tissues of the plant, which can be seen clearly in cross sections of pieces of rock, show that there was an outer cuticle, inner supporting tissues to strengthen the plant stem (parenchyma), and specialized water-conducting vessels (xylem and phloem). In addition, the aerial portions of the stems bear small pores (stomata) which are guarded by special cells capable of regulating the size of these pores, so that respiratory gases and water can pass through. It seems that these plants had developed all the essential equipment for life on land: roots to anchor the plant to the earth and absorb water and nutrients, a cuticle to prevent water loss and damage, strengthening and conducting tissues, and means to control gas and water loss.

Psilotum is a living plant which shows strong similarities to these Devonian examples. It has a simple branching form with terminal spore sacs. Its underground rhizome and lack of leaves and true roots are all characteristics of the Rhynie plants. Some have suggested that these plants are indeed living descendants of the Rhynie plants. Their most puzzling aspect, if they are indeed descendants of the Devonian forms, is their fossil record; there is not a trace of Rhynie-like plants since the Devonian.

Living alongside the simple, branched plants described above are others known as lycopods because they bear a strong resemblance to living clubmosses (*Lycopodium*). *Asteroxylon*, a typical example, grows over 1 ft 6 ins (45cm) tall. Lycopods are upright plants which grow from an underground root system. Their surface is covered by tiny, scale-like leaves arranged in spirals around the stems, and their spores are shed from small, purse-shaped (or, in larger forms, club-shaped) structures near the upper ends of the stems.

There appears to have been quite a wide variety of clubmosses of this type – *Drepanophycus*, *Protolepidodendron*, *Baragwanathia*, *Sawdonia*, and *Zosterophylum*. All spread by the growth of the underground stem, and would presumably have been very quick to colonize suitable moist ground wherever their spores germinated.

These lycopods would probably have formed dense, bushy ground cover for marginal areas of land from the Devonian onwards. Later in the Devonian the lycopods underwent a dramatic radiation, producing giant forms such as *Lepidodendron*, the first genuinely tree-sized plants, so that forests came into being.

STABILIZING THE LAND

The absence of any form of land ecosystem during the Cambro–Ordovician Period meant that the land was barren except for algal films near the shore and on river banks; there may have been some early lichens, an extraordinarily hardy amalgam of algae and fungi that can still live in the most harsh environments today. The land would have been almost as bleak as the surface of the Moon, without any real soil that would have been capable of retaining water. Unlike the Moon, however, weathering of upland areas by rain, wind, heat, and cold created large, perpetually shifting deposits of sediments in lakes and near the seashore.

The value of substantial ground-cover plants cannot be overemphasized. Plants form a protective layer above the sediment, and so slow down the erosion caused by wind and water. The plant roots also bind and stabilize the sediment. Even more important than this, the plants add an essential ingredient in the form of organic material (humus) as a consequence of the constant cycle of germination, growth, and death. Organic plant material becomes incorporated into the structure of the sediments and creates soil. Because of this organic content the soil tends to absorb water like a sponge and retain it as a moist layer available for use by plants – the whole system is self-reinforcing.

So the early colonization of the land began to take place as a result of the critical development and spread of plants that were capable of holding themselves upright and creating a form of ground cover. After this, the progress of animals onto land was guaranteed.

It seems likely, therefore, that during the Silurian the land surface would have undergone a quiet revolution – possibly quite a rapid one in geological terms. Areas around watercourses would have begun to support substantial amounts of vegetation, genuine soil would have built up, and water would have begun to be trapped in increasingly moist, organically rich areas surrounding the watercourses. Relatively sheltered and rich in nutrients, locations of this kind would have been ideal for exploitation by any organisms that could cope with the difficulties posed by living on land. Success in this endeavor was achieved by different groups of animals in different ways.

HOW ANIMALS LEARNED TO LIVE ON LAND

Life on land presents animals with problems similar to those faced by plants. Most obviously they need some form of body support which will hold them up against the force of gravity; they need a system that will allow them to move around; they need a waterproof skin to prevent excessive water loss; and they need to be able to survive much more rapid temperature changes than are experienced in water.

Animals appear to have coped with such adaptations with varying degrees of success. For example, two very successful marine groups, the coelenterates (jellyfish, anemones, and corals) and echinoderms (starfish, sea urchins, etc.), have been unable to colonize the land at all. Coelenterates failed to develop an effective skeleton for body support or movement on land, and their way of life relies upon currents of water carrying food particles to them. The echinoderms, although possessing a skeleton of calcite plates which is rigid and potentially capable of supporting them on land, are inextricably tied to the water. They move by means of a hydraulic system which draws sea water into a series of tubes which operate hundreds of tiny, fleshy tube feet – clearly this system has no prospect of working on land.

Molluscs

Other animal groups have been able to make the transition – or at least some of their members have managed it. Molluscs are extremely successful in the sea, and certain of them have achieved some success on land. Cephalopods, among the most active and intelligent of carnivores and scavengers in the sea, are adapted to open-water marine habitats and have never penetrated the intertidal zone or lived near the land. Bivalves are extremely abundant in and on the sea floor, and a few have successfully invaded the intertidal zone. Mussels are familiar on the seashore, and are able to survive periods of exposure to the air during the tidal cycle. Similarly, cockles in the sand of the intertidal zone are frequently left in drying sand, and can cope with these conditions by expelling water from between their valves and breathing through their lining to the mantle cavity until the return of sea water on the next tide. But though they can survive temporary exposure to land conditions, they can by no means exploit them. Only one group of molluscs has been able to do that: the gastropods – snails and slugs.

Gastropods can be traced back to the Early Cambrian, and may well have been among the earliest animals to colonize the land. Their potential to move onto land can

Creatures such as these gastropod molluscs on a Scottish beach live in seawater when the tide is in, but have to deal with the dehydrating effects of sun and wind when the tide goes out. Animals that can cope with these conditions have to be very hardy and seem potentially pre-adapted for life on land.

be seen today in the many species found in the intertidal zone – limpets, periwinkles, and whelks – where they live as predators, general scavengers and algal "grazers." Because they are relatively slow-moving they are unable to move with the tides, and have to employ various strategies to survive in the open air. Limpets clamp themselves to the rocks of the seashore and await the incoming tide. Others, such as periwinkles, tend to inhabit damp crevices between the rocks, temporary rock pools, or the moist areas beneath mats of seaweed. Such short-term habitats cut down water loss through the skin, but require them to be able to breathe air through the skin or via a simple bellows like a lung. They also need to be able to survive more hostile temperatures, since they are at the mercy of wind, rain, and direct sunshine on the exposed shore.

The gastropod body plan seems tolerably well suited to conditions on the shore and ultimately on dry land. They move by means of their muscular foot, which limits both the size to which they can grow and their speed on

land. The shell, however, is an extremely valuable asset: it offers protection from predators and a waterproof covering into which its owner can retreat in dry conditions. But it is a double-edged benefit, for a shell is an unwieldy and inflexible structure to carry around on land. It limits the gastropod's ability to pass through narrow gaps or into crevices – its otherwise extremely fluid body would be able to do so with ease. The shell is also relatively heavy, and this tends to limit the maximum size to which these creatures can grow on land. Slugs are basically snails that have abandoned their shell (some still show it as a remnant on the back), and as a consequence are much more mobile than snails; however, they are more vulnerable both to desiccation and to predators. The other main drawback with gastropod design is the moist body surface – while this is essential for the operation of the muscular creeping foot, and contributes to their ability to breathe air, it does mean that the body is always at risk from desiccation.

As a result, the exploitation of land by molluscs – contrary to the belief of many gardeners – is rather limited. They tend to inhabit relatively moist, well-watered areas on land, and do not cope particularly well with dry conditions, which they avoid either by burrowing (in the case of slugs) or by retreating into their shells until moisture returns.

Arthropods

Toughness and adaptability, then, are essential for dealing with life on land. These features are particularly well demonstrated by the arthropods. This is the group which has exploited the land most successfully – today it is the insects which dominate life on land and in the air, both in number and in variety.

The reasons are fairly simple. The tubular, jointed skeleton with its impervious cuticle is an ideal device for reducing water loss, and the jointed limbs are well suited to scuttling over uneven terrain; insects also seem to have been capable of inventing a variety of ways of breathing on land. However, it is not the insects that provide clues about the origins of terrestrial arthropods, but groups that are today relatively less numerous – crustaceans, arachnids (including spiders and scorpions), and myriapods (millipedes and centipedes).

The crustaceans – a group dominated by sea creatures such as crabs, lobsters, and shrimps – provide a very useful illustration of how arthropods may have begun to invade the land. The group known as isopods ("similar legs") seem to cross the divide between sea and land almost imperceptibly. Isopods include sea slaters or gribbles, and woodlice.

Sea slaters (*Ligia*) feed on decaying vegetable matter, including rotting wood. In form they are reminiscent of trilobites – though they are not at all closely related. They have a simple, jointed carapace covering the upper part of the body, a pair of antennae at the front, and numerous similar-shaped legs projecting from beneath the carapace. Fast and agile runners, they are able to survive as scavengers of the intertidal zone and have all the virtues of hardiness associated with life in this area. Like gastropods, they prefer moist habitats, but are much faster-moving, more responsive and better able to seek out moist areas and so avoid desiccation.

Woodlice (*Oniscus*) and the very similar pill bugs (*Armadillidium*) are common inhabitants of the leaf litter in woodland and grassland. They are extremely like sea slaters in form, but completely terrestrial. They like to live in the damp layer just beneath the forest floor, beneath the bark of rotting trees or in the leaf litter, but have also spread into semi-arid areas such as deserts where they can survive beneath stones. Their habit of living on rotting vegetation has led to them being very abundant in some areas, and they are an important element in the forest ecosystem.

Isopods demonstrate how easy it may be for some organisms to begin to invade the land if they start in the right place, in this case the seashore. Provided that the anatomy is not restrictive (the problem faced by jellyfish, for example), and that they are sufficiently adaptable to survive in such a hostile environment, they are in a sense preadapted to life on land. Viewed from this perspective, the conquest of the land was perhaps not such a dramatic leap into the unknown after all. It would appear that animals of various sorts had the potential to invade the land from very early on. What they lacked was the opportunity.

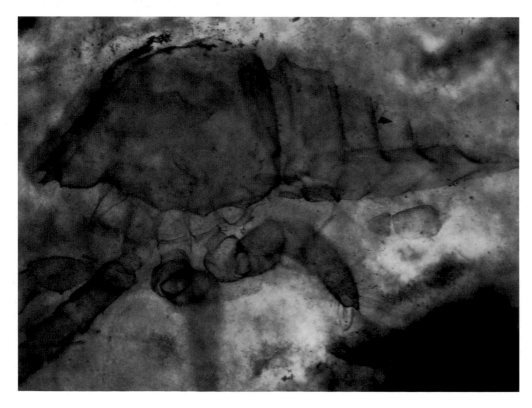

Ludlow-age animals (about 400 million years old) are being found in increasing numbers at various localities. This thin, finely polished slice of Rhynie Chert (also of Ludlow age) can be seen to contain a beautifully preserved land animal – Palaeocharinus, a spider-like trigonotarbid about one-fiftieth of an inch (0.5mm) long. It lived among plant stems which were also preserved in the hot-spring deposits in Scotland where this fossil was discovered. Spiders and scorpion-like creatures, along with millipedes, seem to have been among the earliest colonizers of the land at this time. Until recent discoveries, this tiny trigonotarbid was the earliest land animal known to paleontologists.

The rise of land plants on the margins of watercourses during the Late Ordovician or Early Silurian Period created the potential for sediments to form stable soil, and for a water-retentive land-based ecosystem to develop – one into which scavenging animals would be able to move relatively freely and easily. If this is indeed what happened, then the development of land plants should coincide very closely with the appearance of the first land animals.

THE EARLIEST LAND ANIMALS

On the outskirts of the English town of Ludlow in Shropshire lie geological deposits which date back to the Upper Silurian and contain the remains of early agnathan fish and acanthodians. More recently, collecting from these rocks has revealed the earliest remains of land animals, including two types of centipede and an early spider-like arachnid. They have been found close to fragmented remains of plants such as *Cooksonia* and parts of *Rhynia*-like plants, as well as the remains of undoubtedly aquatic eurypterids and shrimps.

The unusual aspect of this discovery is that all three of these early land animals are predators rather than scavengers. This suggests that the scavenging and herbivorous part of the land community is yet to be discovered – an encouragement to further collecting in this area. It also indicates that the history of land invasion by invertebrates must substantially predate the Upper Silurian, because by that time the terrestrial ecosystem had evolved far enough to have set up a food chain in which undoubted predatory forms were feeding on the more generalized herbivores and scavengers.

Fish to amphibians

It can be safely assumed that the first land animals were invertebrates, and that they had invaded the land by the Early Silurian, if not before. The story of vertebrates gaining a foothold on land begins substantially later in the fossil record – during the Upper Devonian. The earliest known fossil vertebrates with legs suitable for life on land, creatures called tetrapods ("four-footed"), which were some 20 to 25 ins (50 to 60cm) long, have been found in very late Devonian rocks in Greenland. There are indications in Australia of earlier footprints that may have been made by a tetrapod; these have been dated at Middle Devonian. However, no skeletal remains have yet been discovered; and since footprints alone do not necessarily indicate the presence of a genuine tetrapod, for the moment most attention is focused on the Greenland remains.

The battle against gravity

All the vertebrates discussed so far have been aquatic, and have therefore been designed with a view to minimizing the energy required to swim through water (making the body smooth and spindle-shaped with a fin at the rear), improving buoyancy (with the aid of oily livers or swim bladders and reduced scales), and increasing maneuverability (with the assistance of strategically placed fins). Given this combination of features it is difficult for us to envisage fish as suitable ancestors for the earliest tetrapods. Yet, paradoxically, this is the path that evolution appears to have taken.

As with other forms of life on land, the problems of support against gravity, water loss, and temperature change have to be overcome by vertebrates too. Of all these factors, gravity is by far the most important because vertebrates are on the whole much larger and heavier than invertebrates.

In water the weight of a fish is largely irrelevant – water provides buoyancy, and flotation devices can provide whatever other compensation is required. So fishes can be as large as they want to be. The only limiting factor would appear to be friction when the fish is swimming – the larger the fish, the greater the viscous drag that needs to be overcome, and therefore the slower it tends to swim.

On land, however, body weight is critical – without support the organs would collapse or be crushed under the weight of the rest of the body. Legs are therefore essential if any vertebrate is to survive on land – they provide a system for levering the body clear of the ground, so that the organs are not compressed and can function normally. However, legs in themselves are insufficient: they need to be anchored to a supporting framework within the body. So the internal skeleton must be connected to the legs, which would otherwise be pressed into the sides of the body and cause severe damage to the internal organs.

In fish the front fins (potential legs, as will be shown later) are connected to the shoulders and head skeleton, so there is at least a modicum of contact with the rest of the skeleton. But this is of limited use on land because, if the front legs are forced to bear much weight, the stresses passing through the shoulders and the rear of the skull to the vertebral column, while holding the body clear of the ground, would tend to pull the skull apart. Separating the skull from the shoulder girdle was an important early development which allowed the shoulders and underlying ribs to form a framework to support the front legs independently of the skull. Perhaps more importantly, when the head was separated from the shoulders it became movable on a distinct neck. This new characteristic made the head more mobile and so facilitated feeding on land.

The rear fins of typical fish are merely attached to plates in the body wall, and are of little use in supporting weight. Clearly, if these rear appendages are to work as legs, a bony connection needs to be established between the fin plates and the vertebral column above them. In the earliest tetrapods this development is achieved by the growth of the fin plates up toward the posterior ribs and vertebral column until they combine to form a bony pelvis.

The combination of pillar-like legs linked to the vertebral column, rather like a bridge consisting of a span and two piers, forms the essential framework for support of the body organs on land. Bridges are, however, static, while animals move. Movement requires overall flexibility

BUILDING LAND VERTEBRATES FROM FISH

Major structural changes
A number of adaptations are required to convert a fish into a land-living vertebrate. Strong legs and feet, which in turn need strong points of attachment onto the skeleton, are essential. At the rear the pelvic bones expand and connect with the backbone to give firm support. But the front legs are less well attached: they connect to the shoulder bones which hug the ribs, and to strengthen the backbone and support the shoulder bones the ribs become much enlarged. In addition, the shoulder bones need to disconnect from the head, and a neck must develop. Land animals also acquired an eardrum (FAR RIGHT) – a very different hearing arrangement from the sensory system of fish.

Strengthening the backbone for walking
LEFT *Fish backbones are not strong enough to support a body on land. The spines enlarge for the attachment of supporting muscles, while the vertebrae also enlarge and link together more rigidly. And to prevent excessive twisting of the backbone, interlocking prongs develop on the spines.*

of the body: limbs have to have joints and muscles so that they can be moved and act as levers, and toes are needed to grip the ground. Movement also requires the support of the body to change as each limb is raised off the ground in walking. This results in substantial twisting forces, which need to be counteracted. The vertebral column therefore needs to be strengthened.

Fossil evidence for the first tetrapods

Three tetrapods from Greenland have been described to date: *Ichthyostega*, *Acanthostega*, and *Ichthyostegopsis*; only the first two are known in detail. *Ichthyostega* is a large animal of nearly 3 ft (1m) in length, with a broad, flat head, large jaws and teeth, and a long snout. The neck is short and the body barrel-shaped and supported by short, powerful legs. There is some evidence that parts of the body were covered in scales; and, most remarkable of all, it possessed a fish-like tail.

It seems clear that at least one of the earliest tetrapods was a swimming predator capable of pursuing fish and other large prey, using its legs as paddles and its fish-like tail for sculling through the water. Therefore, rather than showing a suite of adaptations for living solely on land, one of the earliest tetrapods would appear to have been more at home in water, even though it was capable (as its legs seem to show) of moving on land. Perhaps the best comparison that can be drawn is with modern crocodiles, which are most at home as predators in water but spend an appreciable amount of time resting on land.

Following new discoveries in Greenland, *Acanthostega* has been studied in great detail in recent years by Drs Jenny Clack and Mike Coates at Cambridge, England. Another remarkably fish-like creature, it is similar in many respects to *Ichthyostega* rather than a pioneering tetrapod. The body (in the region of 2 ft/60cm long) is long and flattened and the tail is very large and diamond-shaped – far too deep to have been convenient for movement on land. The legs are well developed and possess a large number of digits – eight on the front and seven on the hind limbs. This discovery caused some surprise, because it had long been supposed that all tetrapods had at most five digits. *Acanthostega* also had internal gills for breathing water in a very fish-like manner.

So the general image of the very earliest known fossil tetrapods is one of rather large animals with legs, and therefore capable of moving on land to some extent. But their way of life was essentially water-based – they were predators of the many bony fish living in the Late Devonian, rather than pursuers of the hosts of small- to medium-sized invertebrates inhabiting the plant-filled moist lowlands adjacent to lakes and rivers.

Origins of the first tetrapods

As described on pages 82-83, some of the bony fish living in the Devonian Period possessed a suite of anatomical features that were potentially very well suited for the evolution of early tetrapods. These lobe-finned fish, of which *Eusthenopteron* is perhaps the best-known example, were large predators 3 ft (1m) or more in length, and many of them appear to have lived in freshwater rivers and lakes. What were the circumstances which may have led perfectly well-adjusted fish to pursue a much more difficult and hazardous life on land? Several theories have been proposed over the years.

Early in the twentieth century it was recognized that the rocks of the Late Devonian were frequently stained red, and that this coloring was caused by rust from the iron ore that they contained. The conditions that might have led to the formation of rust were thought to be seasonal wetness, and a hot, semi-desert environment. A very tempting scenario was built up. If the ancestors of early tetrapods were fish living in small lakes or ponds that periodically dried up, evolution might have selectively favored the ones that possessed both lungs to breathe air in the stagnant shallows, and rudimentary limbs to enable them to walk in search of fresh sources of water.

A completely different theory considers that the move to land could only have occurred under conditions that would have favored animals vulnerable to desiccation. Creatures which live today in warm, tropical streams and ponds do not experience drying of their environment so much as stagnation of the water and overcrowding. In some circumstances this leads to migration from areas of water when it is sufficiently humid on land. For example, under such conditions the catfish *Clarias* is able to cross land in search of new habitats. Some have linked partial drying of the environment and population pressure in small lakes with a tendency to migrate from these bodies of water when conditions are humid enough.

Finally, there is the notion, put forward by Theodore Eaton in 1960, that the earliest tetrapods originated in water and that their initial adaptations were to special aquatic circumstances. He related the modifications of limbs, hearing, air breathing, and feeding to life in warm, shallow waters low in oxygen. If his hypothesis is correct, the radiation of true land-living tetrapods is a much later occurrence stemming from various lines of aquatic tetrapod.

Most popular discussions of the origin of tetrapods are centered on the first two ideas presented above. It is curious that the last theory has attracted the least attention, yet it accords increasingly with the evidence from the fossil record.

In recent years a number of extremely important discoveries have been made in Greenland by a team of paleontologists from Cambridge. This photograph shows the skull, with a slightly distorted snout tip, of the early tetrapod Acanthostga. *It has been nicknamed "Grace" after the pop singer Grace Jones.*

What do the rocks and fossils tell us?

The rust-stained "red beds" of the Devonian Period do suggest at least periodic dry seasons at this time in the Earth's history, and Devonian vertebrates are well represented in red bed rocks. However, the vast majority of these fossils are fish rather than early tetrapods. There are also vast areas of the world at this time that are effectively unknown from a geological point of view, and it seems extremely unlikely that a climate with periodic aridity would have been worldwide.

The fossils so far indicate aquatic predatory animals which exhibit a variety of tetrapod characteristics, notably limb and girdle skeletons, necks, and ears. How did these features benefit fish?

It is generally agreed that early tetrapods inhabited freshwater lakes and river systems; also that these waters were warm, relatively shallow, rich in plant life, and, as

with comparable present-day systems, subject to periods of oxygen shortage. In such conditions the ability to breathe air would have been valuable. Large-bodied fish in shallow water may have been able to prop themselves up to breathe by using their pectoral fins, especially if they were supported by a lobed-fin skeleton. This has two advantages: not only can the head be raised clear of the water so that air can be gulped, but at the same time the body weight does not compress the abdomen and lungs and thus force air out. Disconnection of the head from the shoulder girdle at this stage may have allowed the head to be moved more freely to facilitate the gulping of air.

The front legs, therefore, may have taken on an occasional role as body props to facilitate breathing, but they may also have been used for walking, or levering the body over the bottom, when these fish were moving about in very shallow water. Clearly the ability to grip the bottom with toes rather than with fins would have been useful, but the number and arrangement of the toes would have been of minor significance – possibly the more the better, if grip was the sole criterion.

Limbs may have had yet another purpose in connection with the predatory habit of these fish. *Acanthostega* has the general appearance of a predatory fish similar to a modern pike. Characteristically, these fish have all their main fins clustered at the rear of the body so that they can propel themselves forward in a fast, darting movement – they are essentially lurking predators which use a burst of speed to overcome their victim. If this was the lifestyle of *Acanthostega*, its legs and toes may well have been used for creeping slowly through the dense aquatic vegetation in pursuit of potential prey, and then thrusting against the bottom as part of the final lunge.

LEFT *Like a freshwater bandit, a pike* (Esox lucius) *lies in wait for its prey beneath a jetty. The deep, paddle-like tail enables it to make very fast, darting runs to overwhelm its victim. This lifestyle may be similar to that of early tetrapods such as* Acanthostega.

RIGHT *"Boris" is the best articulated* Acanthostega gunnari *skeleton in the Cambridge collection. This specimen has revealed some fascinating information about these earliest-known tetrapods. One of the most remarkable discoveries is the fact that the hand has eight digits.*

So tetrapod adaptations seem to be emerging as features to cope not so much with the rigors of life on land, as they have so often been viewed in the past, but with a lifestyle associated with swampy conditions in the Devonian Period. Land-living seems to have been a strategy that became available simply as a by-product of the evolution of life in the waters – and one that was taken to rather reluctantly at first, or so it seems from the fossil record.

The evidence in recent years from *Acanthostega* has been very important in reassessing tetrapod origins, but it also demonstrates the role of chance. New discoveries may yet be made in earlier rocks which lead to a complete re-evaluation of this theory. For example, the creatures we see in the Late Devonian may turn out to be descendants of a set of fully terrestrial Middle Devonian tetrapods that have reinvaded the waters in order to take advantage of abundant prey – a strategy followed in more recent times by whales and seals.

Carboniferous environments

Although there is little doubt that plants of various types were well established during the Devonian, it is not until the succeeding Period, the Carboniferous, that evidence for tree-dominated forests emerges in the swampy lowland areas; they are known to geologists as Carboniferous coal swamps. Gigantic lycopods from this time have been discovered; these are huge woody trees with trunks reaching diameters of 6ft (2m) or more, and attaining heights of 150ft (50m). *Lepidodendron* is a well-known tree-sized lycopod whose trunks and root systems have been found; another large lycopod, *Sigillaria*, reached heights of 90ft (30m) or more. Slightly more familiar are the tree-sized *Calamites*; these are related to modern horsetails, which are common in marshy environments. They grew from underground stems and had a curious segmented arrangement to their trunk and branches, which is characteristic of the

A magnificently realistic recreation of the luxuriant plant and animal life of the Carboniferous swamp forest environment. In the past, museums have often tried to portray life in ancient environments by the use of dioramas. Unfortunately these frequently look amateurish and fail to convey effectively what the scientists have learned. But in the Field Museum in Chicago this most remarkable and beautiful diorama has been created, which summarizes all the essential elements of a Carboniferous coal swamp. Fourth from the left is the base of a large lycopod or clubmoss, Sigillaria rugosa, on which a primitive cockroach (Archaeoblattina beecheri) is resting. Two species of the large lycopod Lepidendron *can be seen on the extreme left; while second from the right is the tree-sized horsetail* Calamites annularis stellata, *with its whorls of fronds. Various primitive amphibians and insects, including an example of the early dragonfly* Meganeura monyi, *can be seen on the plants and in the undergrowth.*

group as a whole. Nearer the ground were a variety of ferns and tree ferns (such as *Psaronius*) which grew to 9 ft (3 m) or so, together with other seed-bearing trees vaguely resembling conifers (for example, *Archaeopteris*).

Huge and very dense forests of these early plants developed in the extensive lowland swamps around rivers and lakes and near the sea. The continual cycle of growth and death of these plant communities allowed the gradual build-up of huge mats of rotting vegetation, which formed thick layers of peat. Periodic flooding of these low-lying areas by the sea cut short the life of the forests for a while, and the peat layers were capped with layers of sand which hardened to form sandstone. When the seas retreated the dense forested areas grew up once again, and the cycle of deposition repeated itself over tens of millions of years. The thick bands of peat gradually became compressed to form lignite and eventually coal – the huge coal deposits that have been mined so intensively for the last two centuries.

Before coal mining became heavily mechanized, miners regularly used to uncover the fossilized remains of animals and plants in the coal deposits. Their finds provided a regular supply of new fossils to paleontologists in the late nineteenth and early twentieth centuries, and in this way a picture of the coal swamps was built up.

Amphibians of the coal swamp

Some of the earliest amphibians have been discovered in the oil shales – organically rich silty clays – of the Lower Carboniferous of Scotland. At first these records were puzzling. It seemed that the earliest tetrapods – apart from the celebrated creatures from the Upper Devonian of Greenland – were, paradoxically, legless animals known as aistopods. However, in recent years new work at an old quarry at East Kirkton, between Edinburgh and Glasgow, has unearthed a fauna which includes land-living amphibians, a creature close to the origin of reptiles, and various invertebrates including the earliest harvestman spider, the earliest scorpion, and giant eurypterids, as well as abundant plants.

During the Carboniferous Period there was a great range and variety of amphibian tetrapods (described more fully in Chapter 6). At one extreme were very large, crocodile-sized creatures such as *Eogyrinus* which undoubtedly hunted in the deeper waters of the swamp environment; forms such as *Gerrothorax* lay in wait on the bottom; *Diplocaulus* swam in the streams. There were also various smaller, generally newt-like forms (nectrideans), and a range of medium and small forms which were compact and quite strongly built land predators; the larger ones included anthracosaurs, while other, smaller types such as gephyrostegids and microsaurs were probably insect eaters. Although amphibians were adept at consuming prey, they never came to terms with the difficulties of eating plants, and therefore never evolved as a series of herbivores. That was to be the province of the early reptiles.

Like modern forms, the amphibians found in the coal swamp deposits appear to have laid jelly-covered eggs in water; from these emerged tadpoles or larvae, which fed and grew in this form for an appreciable time before undergoing metamorphosis into the adult animal. This style of reproduction was fine in the well-watered coal swamp areas, but not in the drier upland areas. While the amphibians retained a water-based method of reproduction, and have never really broken their links with water, another group of early tetrapods did break that link by inventing a way of reproducing on land which did not require them to lay eggs in water. They invented a shelled egg; we call them reptiles, and they were the real conquerors of the land.

6

CONQUERING THE LAND

FROM TETRAPODS TO THE EARLIEST REPTILES

MANY OF THE classic features of land-living tetrapods – a neck, lungs, a strong skeleton, legs, and toes – have turned out to be features that were developed among a group of fish in order to cope with life in shallow, potentially stagnant water. Viewed from this perspective, exploiting the land seems to represent very much a sideline for fish rather than a pioneering event for early tetrapods. Perhaps this is the right way to look at things. After all, it is hardly likely that the earliest tetrapods would have been endowed with an overwhelming urge to become land dwellers; they were simply vertebrates making the best of a lifestyle made possible by their combination of anatomical and physiological characteristics.

ABOVE Dimetrodon *is one of the very early carnivorous mammal-like reptiles. Even at this stage they could control their body temperature – in this case by using a large, skin-covered "sail".*

RIGHT *One of the earliest-known reptiles is* Hylonomus, *whose remains have been discovered in sediment formed from the rotted centers of ancient lycopods. These invertebrate-eating creatures may have fallen into such natural pitfall traps and been buried.*

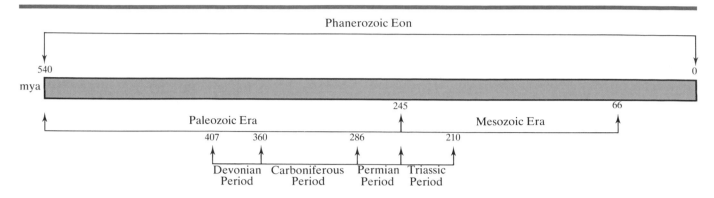

Phanerozoic Eon

540

mya

0

245

66

Paleozoic Era

Mesozoic Era

407   360   286   210

Devonian Carboniferous Permian Triassic
Period   Period   Period   Period

Timescale of Earth history. *From the Carboniferous Period onward the land began to be dominated by reptiles. At first they were small, lizard-like animals, but during the Permian some very large* *mammal-like reptiles such as Dimetrodon and Edaphosaurus appeared. Such creatures reigned on land throughout most of the Permian and Triassic Periods.*

COMPARING LIVING AMPHIBIANS WITH EARLY TETRAPODS

The early tetrapods from the coal swamps are called amphibians. We naturally tend to associate them with modern amphibians such as newts, salamanders, and frogs, which live a life between water and land (hence the name, which means "life on both sides"). We saw at the end of Chapter 5 that they reproduce in a similar way. But when looked at in greater detail, early tetrapods and modern amphibians are very different.

Living amphibians

Today's amphibians have a soft, moist skin through which they are able to breathe. This supplements their lungs, which are relatively inefficient – amphibians do not have a rib cage to help pump air in and out of the lungs. Dependence on the skin for breathing has one extremely important consequence: nearly all modern amphibians are less than 4ins (10cm) in length. They have to be small in order to maintain a high ratio of surface area to body volume, so that there is enough skin to allow adequate respiration.

The skeletons of amphibians are relatively feeble – although, admittedly, the frogs are highly specialized for jumping. All tend to live in moist areas because otherwise their porous skins would be likely to dry out quickly. They also prefer generally cold environments, which make it easier to breathe through the skin – at low temperatures, oxygen dissolves better in the moisture on the surface of the skin.

This extraordinary combination of characteristics allows modern amphibians to live in cold, damp places on land, and to exploit them extremely effectively. Their

Today's amphibians (salamanders, frogs, and apodans) are remarkable creatures. The skin through which they breathe has to be kept moist and so they tend to inhabit wet areas, where they live on small parcels of nutritious food – invertebrates. Amphibians are very successful at occupying a kind of habitat that mammals, birds, and reptiles would find intolerable.

cold bodies require little fuel because their body chemistry works quite slowly. Most of their breathing is "passive" – that is, they simply absorb oxygen through the skin on the surface of the body or inside the mouth. They do not have rib cages, so they have to make quite an effort to inflate their lungs. Inflation of the lungs is mostly linked to sound production – for instance, the croaking of frogs – which in turn is linked to attracting mates and reproduction. All of today's amphibians are carnivores, feeding on a wide range of invertebrates and small vertebrates – as food, animals are highly nutritious and do not call for a complex digestive system.

Eating plants is in comparison much harder work; it needs good jaw muscles and teeth, as well as complicated stomachs, and would therefore be quite costly in energy terms for amphibians.

Despite all these limitations their generally low-energy lifestyle makes them admirably suited to this particular ecological niche today. Certainly no other group of vertebrates can manage to live better in cold, damp environments – not even the highly sophisticated and adaptable mammals.

Early tetrapods

Like living amphibians, no early tetrapods seem to show any sign of having been plant eaters – but there the similarities end. In comparison to today's amphibians, these were large animals – from about 1 ft (30cm) long up to 6 ft (2m) or more. They had heavy, bony skeletons (including a heavy rib cage) and strong limbs. In a number of cases there is clear evidence of some form of tough body covering, consisting of either bony armor or thinner scales.

From these differences alone it is obvious that early tetrapods had a very different way of life from modern amphibians. Their large size and large rib cage indicate that they were dependent for breathing on lungs rather than on the skin; this is confirmed by the evidence that some had a scaly and presumably not very porous skin. The heavy skeleton also indicates that they were capable of moving on land and were generally powerful animals – presumably they were aggressive predators. These were not tiny animals living in moist areas under rocks, but heavy, bold creatures which ranged freely around the swampy landscape.

EARLY TETRAPODS DIVERSIFY

The spread of tetrapods onto land, begun almost accidentally by the lobe-fins, does not appear to have been a one-way activity. Many of the early tetrapods seem to have returned to the water rather promptly in order to take advantage of the abundance of fish which teemed in the lakes and rivers. They adopted the sort of lifestyle that we associate today with crocodiles and alligators; the earliest forms were creatures such as *Ichthyostega* and *Acanthostega*, but in the Carboniferous Period these were superseded by a bewildering variety ranging from tiny, newt-sized creatures, generally known as lepospondyls, to the larger forms, known as temnospondyls.

LEPOSPONDYLS

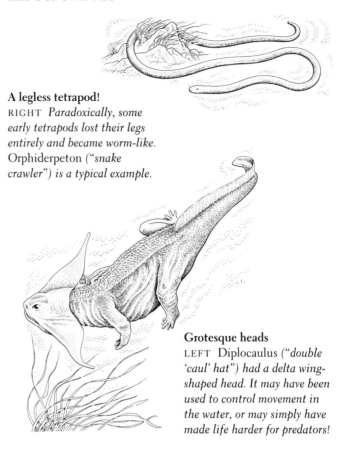

A legless tetrapod!
RIGHT *Paradoxically, some early tetrapods lost their legs entirely and became worm-like. Orphiderpeton ("snake crawler") is a typical example.*

Grotesque heads
LEFT Diplocaulus ("*double 'caul' hat*") *had a delta wing-shaped head. It may have been used to control movement in the water, or may simply have made life harder for predators!*

Lepospondyls

Some of these creatures such as *Ophiderpeton*, were very eel-like, while others were very much like modern newts – at least in body form. The most dramatic members of this group, however, were animals such as *Diplocaulus* and *Diploceraspis*, which appeared in the Early Permian and reached lengths of 2 ft (60cm) or more.

The bodies of these creatures were relatively normal, but their heads were quite bizarrely shaped: the back corners were spread out into long, tapering "wings," whose purpose has puzzled paleontologists for a long time.

It may have been that they were simply a means of defense – it would have been extremely difficult to swallow something with a head shaped like that. Alternatively, it is possible that these projections had a function in swimming. It has been suggested that the wings of bone on the head acted like a submarine's rudder and diving planes to steer the animal and allow it to dive and surface, either to avoid predators or in pursuit of prey.

Temnospondyls

Pholidogaster had a long body and tail and short limbs, and was one of the earliest temnospondyls from the Carboniferous. Its long body would have made it an excellent swimmer, while its large head and teeth show it to have been a predator. Others, such as *Cyclotosaurus* and *Paracyclotosaurus*, developed larger, flatter heads and looked even more alligator-like, but perhaps the most bizarre development shown by this line of early tetrapods is displayed by *Gerrothorax*.

Growing to a length of 3 ft (1m) or more, *Gerrothorax* had a markedly flattened body, but it did not have an alligator-like head. Instead, its head was very broad, with the eyes perched on top and frilly external gills in the neck area – to all intents and purposes it was a flattened, overgrown tadpole.

The flat body of *Gerrothorax* was armored at top and bottom. It probably spent its time lying motionless on the bottom of lakes or large rivers, waiting for prey to swim past before lunging at them and engulfing them in its very broad mouth – a strategy reminiscent of modern angler fish. The majority of these rather ungainly creatures would undoubtedly have been at home in a swampy environment rather than on dry land.

By contrast, other temnospondyls became much more thoroughgoing land animals, with stocky bodies, powerful legs, and large heads. Some later types from the Early Permian, such as *Eryops*, which grew to 6 ft (2m) long, must have been formidable on land or in the water. The similarly built *Cacops* was only about 16 ins (40cm) long, but had even sturdier limbs, heavy bony scales on its back and, in relation to its body length, a huge head for taking large prey.

SMALL IS BEAUTIFUL

Although these heavy land predators must have been the top carnivores of the time and in their own way successful, they were destined for extinction. The fossil record shows that they died without leaving descendants that were better able to exploit the land. Why this was so is uncertain, but it is often suggested that such specialist predators are less adaptable to changing circumstances – perhaps an example of the dangers of becoming too much of a specialist.

Curiously, it is to smaller and relatively insignificant early tetrapods that we have to look to trace the history of the groups of vertebrate animals that were ultimately

At one extreme, early tetrapods such as Pholidogaster *returned to the water as large, crocodile-shaped creatures. Clearly these were powerful swimmers and savage predators.*

BELOW *Some aquatic tetrapods were perpetual larvae. The large predator* Gerrothorax, *which kept its larval gills, probably lay in wait for prey on lake bottoms.*

Flattened early tetrapods such as Paracyclotosaurus *also lived in ponds and lakes. Growing up to 9 ft (3m) long, they probably caught their prey with a rapid snap of their jaws.*

The small but sturdily built Cacops *(foreground) was one of a variety of land-living Early Permian creatures. Its large head and tough, scaly skin suggest a highly aggressive predator. In the background is* Casea, *a larger early (synapsid) mammal-like reptile which fed on plants such as the* Equisetum *shown nearby.*

to dominate the land. This theme of major groups originating with small animals is one that recurs in the history of the vertebrates: the first reptiles were all small, and so were the first mammals and first birds.

This actually raises a question about the origin of the first tetrapods. The earliest ones so far known, *Acanthostega* and *Ichthyostega*, were quite large animals, 3 ft (1m) or so in length. Were there earlier, smaller forms, living in drier areas on land, that have yet to be found? Small size would certainly have been an advantage to the first land animals, simply because supporting the body weight on primitive legs would have been much easier if the body was smaller.

SAURIOMORPHS

So far we have looked at the swamp-loving tetrapods and some of the large carnivores. There was also a third, and rather popular, lifestyle pursued by some early tetrapods – one that was only to be expected, given that the land was populated with invertebrates at quite an early stage.

This third category consisted of small, lightly built predators with sharp, spiky teeth, capable of capturing and eating the various invertebrates that populated the upland areas in and around the Carboniferous swamps. Many of these little creatures are similar, which has led to some confusion over their relatedness. I shall call them sauriomorphs (meaning "lizard-form"), because to the untrained eye they all resemble little lizards. The similarities arise through evolutionary convergence; most small, scampering vertebrates tend to look the same because their bodies are subjected to similar physical pressures.

One group of upland early tetrapods are called microsaurs, a name which means "little lizards" but is a misnomer because they are most definitely not lizards. Microsaurs are found in Carboniferous rocks and are mostly small, with compact bodies, long legs for running, and box-shaped heads, their jaws lined with small, sharp teeth. This style of body is ideally suited to scampering among plants and in the litter of the forest floor in search of small prey.

From the arrangement of the bones in the head, and the backbone and legs, they still appear to be closer to amphibians than to living reptiles, and may well have laid jelly-enveloped eggs in water. But what they do demonstrate very clearly is that some early tetrapods may have been able to survive away from water for considerable periods – perhaps only returning to water briefly, to spawn during the mating season.

Another group of sturdy tetrapods which included small, lizard-like creatures was the anthracosaurs ("coal lizards"). *Gephyrostegus*, for example, was alive in the Late Carboniferous Period. Again it was a sturdy little creature with long legs, a compact body, and a long tail. The head was long and pointed, and the jaws were lined with sharp, pointed teeth – ideal for cracking open the cuticles or shells of invertebrates. Again, it seems probable that these creatures reproduced themselves in a similar style to amphibians.

Finally, there is another group, roughly contemporary with the other two groups: the reptiles. Again they were small, scampering, lizard-like creatures, of which a good example is *Paleothyris*. Its characteristics are practically identical to those of the previous two groups, and yet we call it a reptile – why? And what do we mean by the distinction between amphibian and reptile, especially when it is applied to such early fossil types?

HOW TO TELL AMPHIBIANS AND REPTILES APART

There are many differences between living amphibians and reptiles. Amphibians have moist skins, while those of reptiles are scaly; amphibians have a simpler heart than reptiles; amphibians have poor kidneys, but reptiles have very efficient kidneys; amphibians do not have a rib cage, while reptiles do. The most important difference of all, however, is that amphibians lay jelly-covered eggs in water (frogspawn, for instance), while reptiles lay shelled eggs on land. The invention of the shelled egg broke the final link between the vertebrates and water, and at long last cleared the way for them to exploit the drier upland areas.

Using these criteria, it is quite easy to distinguish between the two groups today. But the differences are not so clear if all the evidence has to come from fossils. Nearly all the differences noted above concern soft tissues – the ones that do not preserve during fossilization. The only hard evidence concerns the shelled eggs and the ribs. But the chances of finding fossilized eggs from a small creature of that age are virtually nil, and we have seen that all early tetrapods have well-developed rib cages – it is only the modern amphibians which have lost their ribs.

The problems become apparent when comparing the skeletons of *Paleothyris* and *Gephyrostegus*, which look very similar. How do we tell them apart? Why do we think that *Paleothyris* is the early reptile? The argument is long and complex, but can be simplified by looking at the back edge of the skull in each animal. In *Paleothyris*

TOWARD TRUE REPTILES

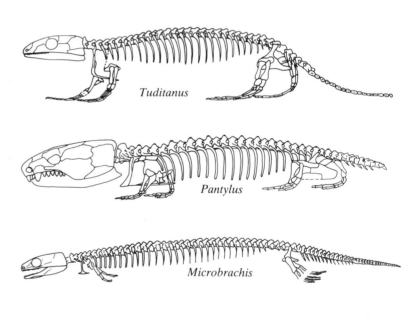

Tuditanus

Pantylus

Microbrachis

Rhynchonkos

Sauriomorphs
Some early tetrapods, known as microsaurs, seem to have remained small, developed sturdy skeletons, and appeared lizard-like in general shape. They probably represent one of several lines of tetrapod that began to exploit drier upland areas in pursuit of arthropod prey. The microsaur skeletons shown here are sturdy, while their skulls are box-shaped and their teeth sharply pointed for cracking open the bodies of arthropods.

it is smoothly curved, whereas in *Gephyrostegus* it has a deep notch cut into it. Called the otic notch, it is where the edge of the eardrum was attached.

So the answer is simple. Early reptiles have no otic notch, but amphibians do. This suggests that the earliest reptiles were deaf – perhaps if they had no otic notch they did not have an eardrum. The questions we want to investigate now are the obvious ones. Where did reptiles come from? And how did they evolve? To answer them I would like to use an argument developed by Professor Robert Carroll of McGill University in Montreal. It centers on the most important feature of reptiles, their ability to lay a shelled egg on land, and on a general observation from the fossil record – that all the earliest fossil reptiles are small.

Since the only vertebrate animals that existed before reptiles were early tetrapods that reproduced by laying jelly-covered eggs, it seems reasonable that among those living in upland areas, feasting on the abundant invertebrates, there may have been some which preferred to lay their eggs on land rather than to return to the water for this purpose. Being able to hide eggs on land may be an advantage, because it reduces losses – many predators enjoy the easy pickings at spawning time and feast on amphibian eggs. Reproducing on land may also be safer for the adults, which are exposed to a wide range of predators when they congregate during the mating season. If it were possible to lay jelly-covered eggs on land, that may have been the first step on the path to laying shelled eggs on land.

The habits of amphibians today tell us that the first step was indeed possible, because a number of them do just that. Many tropical frogs, as well as some salamanders, hide their eggs on land. Adult mountain

Early tetrapods versus reptiles

BELOW *The differences between genuine reptiles and the wide range of similar early tetrapods are subtle. The skeletons of* Gephyrostegus *and* Paleothyris *appear very similar – indeed not unlike those of the microsaurs alongside them. Yet* Paleothyris *is regarded as a reptile, while* Gephyrostegus *is one of a variety of non-reptile early tetrapods. One particular difference lies at the back of the head – that of* Paleothyris *is smoothly curved, while that of* Gephyrostegus *has a notch cut into it.*

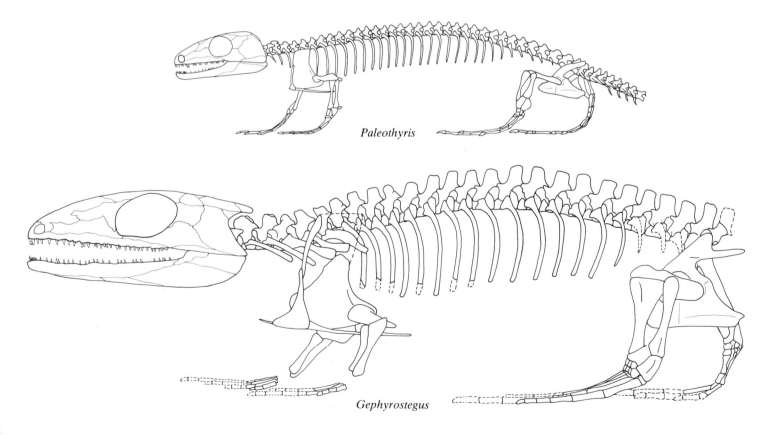

Paleothyris

Gephyrostegus

EGGS MAKE A DIFFERENCE TOO

Reptile eggs

Like birds' eggs, those of reptiles are covered by a protective shell. Beneath that shell lie a series of membranes which enclose the growing embryo and ensure that it will survive on land. One membrane enables the embryo to breathe, another acts as a food store for it, yet another is a waste storage area, while the amnion provides a cushioning pool of liquid. All phases of growth are completed within the egg, and when the young reptile hatches it will emerge from the egg as a perfect miniature of the adult.

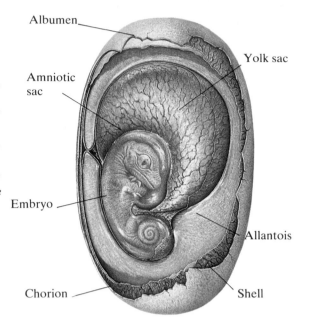

Albumen

Yolk sac

Amniotic sac

Embryo

Chorion

Allantois

Shell

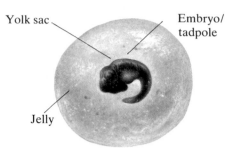

Yolk sac

Embryo/ tadpole

Jelly

Amphibian eggs

ABOVE *Modern amphibians, like the early tetrapods, lay jelly-coated eggs which are relatively safe if laid in water. The embryo grows, nourished by its yolk, until it emerges as a tiny swimming "tadpole" larva. It then continues to feed and grow, sometimes changing radically in appearance, until it develops into an adult.*

salamanders that lay eggs on land are smaller than those that lay in water. It appears that laying eggs on land penalizes the adults, because they have to grow directly from the tiny hatchlings that emerge from the egg, rather than via a large larval stage, and thus never have an opportunity to grow big.

The central idea that seems to emerge is that the ancestors of reptiles may well have laid jelly-covered eggs on land, and may well have been kept to a small body size. This accords with the earliest fossil reptiles being very small creatures.

The next point, which makes sense of the otic notch to accommodate the eardrum, also relates to size in these ancestral reptiles. When the head is extremely small, as it must have been in these early forms which were no larger than about 4ins (10cm) long, the part of the braincase which encases the balancing organs of the ear has to be so large that it fills the space on the side of the head where the otic notch would normally be. The eardrum is therefore "squeezed" backward behind the head, rather than being lodged in a notch as it was in earlier amphibians.

CONCLUSIONS

If we now put all this together, a coherent story begins to emerge. Early tetrapods moved from shallow water on to land. Some of them adopted a lifestyle as small, agile

hunters of invertebrates in drier upland areas. Some of these sauriomorphs developed the habit of laying jelly-covered eggs on land, rather than returning to water to spawn, and became very small. Limitations on the size of the adults that developed from these eggs led to a change at the back of the skull in which the otic notch and the original eardrum were lost. The gradual evolution of additional membranes and a shell around the egg improved the ability of the embryo to survive on land and allowed the egg to increase in size. This stage marked the beginning of the true reptiles.

Animals such as *Gephyrostegus* and *Paleothyris* seem to be fairly close to the amphibian–reptile transition in terms of both size and appearance, but they cannot be both ancestor and descendant. *Gephyrostegus* lived in Late Carboniferous times, after the date of the earliest known reptiles.

THE EARLIEST REPTILE

Until quite recently the earliest known reptile was a creature named *Hylonomus* ("forest mouse"), which has the unusual distinction of having been found inside rotting tree stumps. An area in Nova Scotia called Joggins is known for its ancient *Lepidodendron*-like lycopods. The lower parts of these trees are preserved, and it appears that they formed dense stands which were occasionally killed by saltwater floods.

After the trees died they rotted and collapsed, leaving a broken stump sticking out of the ground. Sediment deposited around the rotting base eventually encased the trunk, leaving the inside to rot and collapse. Deadly pitfall traps were thus created, into which unwary animals fell to their deaths. Eventually the hollow stumps filled with more sediment and this hardened, leaving a cast of the original tree stump. Careful examination of these ancient casts has revealed the skeletons of the little scampering animals that lived on the land in the Middle Carboniferous – including that of *Hylonomus*.

The remains of Westlothiana lizziae *("Lizzie"), a reptile-like early tetrapod discovered in Scotland in the 1980s, were originally offered for sale to the highest bidder on the international market. But, rightly, they are now in the collections of the Royal Scottish Museum in Edinburgh.*

LIZZIE: TETRAPOD OR REPTILE?

Very recently, an animal extremely close to the early tetrapod–reptile transition was discovered by the intrepid fossil collector Stanley Wood at East Kirkton in Scotland. Given the popular name of "Lizzie" in recognition of the fact that it may be an early lizard, this animal is scientifically known as *Westlothiana lizziae* because it was found in the West Lothian region. When first discovered it was hailed as the earliest known reptile – it comes from the latest part of the Lower Carboniferous Period and therefore predates *Hylonomus* – but since the find was announced the specimen has been studied in depth and its status as a true early reptile is the subject of hot debate. In many ways the difficulty of deciding the affinity of *Westlothiana* emphasizes the difficulties that were explained above.

JAWS, TEETH, AND MUSCLES

Apart from the soft anatomy of these early tetrapods – a topic about which paleontologists can argue incessantly – some of the clearest differences between primitive amphibians and reptiles can be seen in the bones of the head. In ancient tetrapods such as *Ichthyostega*, the jaws were little more than snapping devices. The creature's head was low and flat, while the jaw muscles were arranged like a fan underneath the bones of the skull roof and attached to the back of the lower jaw. This arrangement was ideal for "throwing" the lower jaw at the upper jaw, so that the teeth snapped together, but the teeth could not be pressed together tightly in a "hard" bite. As a result of this, many of the early tetrapods had large stabbing fangs on the roof of the mouth to help them impale prey.

The heads of sauriomorphs, however, were deeper, shorter, and much more compact. This shape had a number of advantages. First, the jaws could be closed more powerfully because they were shorter and the muscles exerted greater leverage. Second, at the back of the head the jaw muscles could be rearranged into two parts – one to snap the jaws together quickly, the other to press them firmly shut to give these animals a hard bite. And finally, the short, compact skull was also better able to withstand all the extra stresses associated with biting very hard.

Ichthyostega

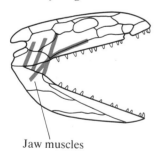

Jaw muscles

Paleothyris

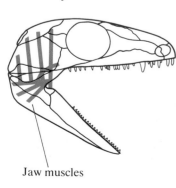

Jaw muscles

In an early tetrapod such as Ichthyostega (LEFT ABOVE) the head is long and low. The jaw muscles form a fan shape where they spread out beneath the skull roof and behind the eye and attach to the back end of the lower jaw. This means that the jaws can be quickly snapped shut, but the teeth cannot be clamped together in a "hard" bite. However, reptiles such as Paleothyris (LEFT BELOW) the main jaw muscles have been modified into two portions: one runs directly downward onto the jaw, while the other runs backward from the back of the palate. This combination of muscles allowed reptiles not only to snap their jaws shut, but also to bite when their jaws were closed. This gave them two advantages: their abilities as carnivores were improved, and some of them could also eat plants.

SKULL WINDOWS REVEAL REPTILIAN ORIGINS

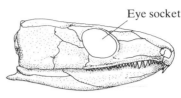
Eye socket
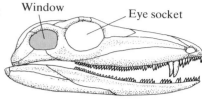
Window   Eye socket

Anapsids
The skulls of members of this group have no fenestrae or windows – openings to give extra space for the attachment of jaw muscles. Anapsids are represented by the earliest fossil reptiles, and today by tortoises and turtles.

Synapsids
In this group there is a single opening low down on the side of the skull. In the fossil record synapsids are represented by the creatures known as mammal-like reptiles, whose line leads through to mammals such as ourselves.

Being able both to snap their jaws shut like a trap and to bite hard may very well have allowed these animals to accommodate in their diet new foods, such as tough insect bodies and shells. The creatures may also have turned for the first time to plants, which represented a huge untapped food resource for land-living vertebrates, and one that had apparently been exploited very quickly by the early land invertebrates – molluscs, woodlice, millipedes, and cockroaches.

The early sauriomorphs had solid little skulls. But in the Late Carboniferous the back part of the skull – the area immediately behind the eye socket – began to be punctured by arched openings known as windows or fenestrae (the Latin word for windows). These openings appear to allow extra space on the side of the head for the attachment of the jaw muscles – muscles seem to be much better at attaching themselves firmly to edges than to flat surfaces. There are four main forms of skull – anapsid, synapsid, diapsid, and euryapsid ("-apse" means "arch", and the names refer to the number and disposition of the arched openings). Each style gives its name to a group of reptiles whose ancestry can be clearly traced through the fossil record.

All the reptiles, birds, and mammals of today can be traced back through the first three of these groups to origins in the Carboniferous Period. The synapsids and diapsids are clearly more important than the other two groups, since they were the antecedents of mammals and birds. I shall therefore concentrate on these as the history of the vertebrates unfolds. But the anapsids and euryapsids are also interesting, and will feature from time to time in the story.

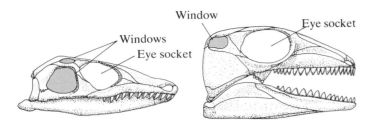

Diapsids
With two openings at the back of the skull, the diapsid group includes a wide range of lizard-like creatures among its members. It also encompasses crocodiles, dinosaurs, flying reptiles (pterosaurs), and birds.

Euryapsids
These, with a single opening high on the side of the skull, are the only completely extinct group. They are represented in the fossil record by the swimming reptiles: ichythyosaurs, plesiosaurs, nothosaurs, and placodonts.

REPTILES, PLANTS, AND ECOSYSTEMS

From the Late Carboniferous onward the reptiles spread rapidly on land. Their strong legs and tough skin allowed them to explore dry upland areas, and their ability to lay durable eggs meant that they did not need to return to water to breed. The improvements to their teeth and jaws enabled them to develop as bigger and better carnivores, putting a strong evolutionary pressure on their prey either to develop strong defenses or to run faster.

Better jaws also allowed reptiles to eat plants. The rise of reptile herbivores in the Late Carboniferous and Early Permian Periods undoubtedly provided a major spur to the evolution of land ecosystems in many complex ways. Plants were forced to develop defenses. Tough cuticles, waxy leaves, sharp spines, and plant poisons probably made their appearance at this time.

But herbivores had the potential to aid plants as well. Seeds with tough coats could be eaten, pass undamaged through the animal's gut, and be deposited in a pile of dung which made a perfect fertilizer for the plant that grew from the seed. In this way, too, the seeds could be dispersed over a large area.

In turn a variety of herbivores evolved to cope with the different sorts of plants available at the time, and an equal variety of carnivores evolved to prey on the herbivores. An immensely complex web of evolutionary interactions on land developed.

The earliest known communities of reptiles have been reconstructed from the tree-stump fossils found at Joggins. They include both early anapsids such as the small insectivorous *Hylonomus* and very early synapsids (*Archaeothyris*); and in slightly younger rocks in Texas there is the first diapsid, *Petrolacosaurus*. All look virtually the same, apart from the openings at the back of the head. However, there are some subtle distinctions that were to become significant in time. *Archaeothyris* was considerably larger than *Hylonomus*, and large size features early in the synapsid line. *Petrolacosaurus* had long legs, suggesting that it was a fast runner – speed is a constant theme in the evolution of the diapsids.

ANAPSIDS

The fossil record of the anapsids is rather patchy after their first appearance, and we will not consider them in great detail. They did, however, produce a few notable forms among the early herbivores, which were abundant and successful in the Permian Period.

Procolophonids were relatively small animals 1 to 2 ft (30 to 60cm) in length, with a low-slung body and a short, triangular head. The teeth were chisel-shaped, and it is very tempting, given the solid, wedge-like head and powerful jaws, to suggest that they burrowed for roots and tubers.

The pareiasaurs are at the other end of the size range – up to the size of a modern hippopotamus. Sturdy, with strong legs, they had a back studded with small bony

One early radiation of reptiles in the Permian Period is represented by the pareiasaurs. These were very large, lumbering and heavily armored creatures, whose backs and heads were covered with bony plates. They were blunt-toothed, and therefore herbivores. It is possible that modern tortoises and turtles may be descended from the pareiasaurs.

plates, and a heavily bone-encrusted head. The teeth were blunt and leaf-shaped, which confirms that they were plant eaters. It seems obvious that pareiasaurs were clumsy, slow-moving animals. Their great size and thick skin would have protected them from smaller carnivores, but they may have been vulnerable to attack from equally large, predatory mammal-like reptiles, the dinocephalians.

The success of these herbivorous anapsids was, however, only relative. They were living in the shadow of what was without doubt the most important group of the time, the synapsids, which rose to dominance very quickly towards the close of the Carboniferous Period.

In the Triassic Period the first turtles and tortoises appeared, after which the anapsids produced very few new forms. Boxing in the animal with a bony shell was a successful strategy, but at the same time it was an evolutionary dead end.

SYNAPSIDS

From the Late Carboniferous through the Permian and Triassic Periods, the dominant land vertebrates were the synapsids or mammal-like reptiles.

Very much like modern reptiles, their fossils have been found in both relatively wet areas and drier zones, which suggests that they had reasonably non-porous skin. Curiously, the earliest known shelled egg has been found in the Lower Permian of Texas, and since the dominant animals of the time were these mammal-like reptiles, it seems likely that one of them was responsible for laying it – further proof of the existence of genuine reptiles at this time.

From their origins as relatively small animals such as *Archaeothyris* (16 to 20 ins/40 to 50cm long) the synapsids group soon produced animals the size of *Ophiacodon*, which reached lengths of 10ft (3m) and may have weighed as much as 450lb (200kg). These creatures, known as pelycosaurs, had very long bodies, strong, sprawling legs, and large heads. The majority

The pelycosaurs or sail-backed reptiles were long-bodied synapsids of the Early Permian, ranging up to 9ft (3m) in length. A few pelycosaurs had tail spines along their backs. Among them were the large predatory Dimetrodon *(how often have you seen this wrongly called a dinosaur?), seen here in the foreground. In the background is the equally large herbivorous* Edaphosaurus. *At present it is thought that the large "sail" was covered by a web of skin through which blood could be pumped so that it could act as a "solar panel" or "radiator" in order to control body temperature. The "sail" may also have acted as a means of recognition or, if it could change color, as an indicator of the animal's emotional state.*

were clearly predatory, since they had large stabbing fangs at the front of the mouth, with strong slashing teeth in the rest of the jaw. It has been suggested that some of these long-bodied animals were crocodile-like, inhabiting swampy areas and eating fish. However, there was also a significant number of purely land-based predators.

In the Early Permian there appeared one of the best known of all early predators. *Dimetrodon* ("two-sized tooth"), often mistakenly called a "dinosaur," reached 10ft (3m) long. It had very powerful jaws with curved teeth, serrated like a steak knife, for slicing through flesh, fronted by large stabbing teeth.

The distinctive tall "sail" running down *Dimetrodon*'s back has caused some dispute. Early ideas about its function ranged from that of an actual sail, the idea being that the animal used the wind to sail across the water, to that of a camouflage device which enabled the creature to lurk among swamp plants without being spotted by its prey. Nowadays it is generally accepted that these were land animals rather than early yachtsmen.

The sail has provided a very interesting insight into the way of life of these early reptiles. It is supported on bony rods which are greatly elongated extensions of its vertebrae, and seem to have been well supplied with blood. If covered in life by a webbing of skin, the sail may have acted as a solar panel to absorb the heat of the Sun, or as a radiator to throw out heat if the body became too hot. Calculations based on this assumption suggest that *Dimetrodon* may have been able to heat its body up from cold in the morning more rapidly than reptiles without sails.

If this is so, *Dimetrodon* would have had a distinct advantage in the evolutionary stakes. Reptiles, like all creatures without active control of their body temperature, become sluggish when cold. Small reptiles can warm up quite quickly in the morning by basking in sunlight. But the synapsids were large from the start, and therefore had a high ratio of mass to surface area. Although this means that they would not cool down very much during the night, they would lose enough heat to spoil their performance as predators. *Dimetrodon*, by warming up as fast as possible, would be able to outrun both its prey and its rivals. Later, it was the mammals' ability to control their body temperature precisely which led to their success.

It is strange that the sail idea was not copied by all early mammal-like reptiles. As far as is known, only *Edaphosaurus*, a large plant-eater contemporary with *Dimetrodon*, evolved a similar sail. This is more intricate, with cross-pieces – presumably increasing its surface area even further so that *Edaphosaurus* could heat or cool itself even more quickly than *Dimetrodon*.

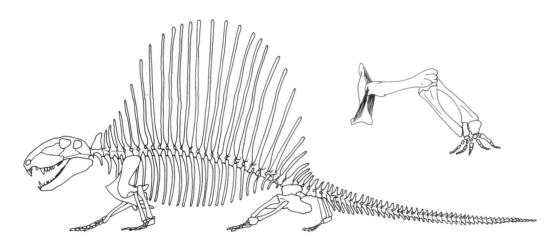

LEFT *The early mammal-like reptiles had a gait like that of a modern crocodile, with their legs held out from their sides. Thus sinuous backbone movements increased the stride length, while the strong back muscles powered the legs. The hip and leg detail indicates considerable rotation at the knee and ankle, while the toes had to be broad and long to give them a good purchase on the ground.*

Edaphosaurus and a similar, non-sail-backed form called *Casea* have large but very compact skulls. Unlike those of *Dimetrodon*, the teeth are very even in size – there are no large stabbing teeth at the front, for example. They are, in addition, chisel-shaped and much blunter – ideally suited for a diet of plants. Apart from the teeth on the edges of the jaws, the roof of the mouth was covered in small, pimple-like teeth which must have helped to crush and break up the plant food before it was swallowed.

The back of the skull in these synapsids has large openings for the attachment of strong jaw-closing muscles. In addition, the back of the jaw is expanded to increase the area for muscle attachment and the leverage of the muscles on the jaw (see the illustration on page 110).

The early mammal-like reptiles show a series of interesting changes in the way they moved on land. They had long, heavy bodies and long tails, and their legs sprawled out to the sides. This means that the belly was always held quite close to the ground when they walked. Seen from above, the legs swung in arcs to the sides of the body. In this arrangement the power exerted by the legs can be added to quite considerably by undulating the body or wriggling, which is achieved by bending the spine in time with the movement of the legs – a gait still to be seen in modern crocodiles and lizards. The tail was long and powerful because the main leg-moving muscles (retractors – the ones that pulled the leg backwards and propelled the animal forwards) were attached to its sides. Finally, these animals had broad feet and long toes, so that they could get a firm grip on the ground as they walked.

THERAPSIDS

From the Middle Permian Period through the Triassic Period a series of subtle changes came over the structure of the mammal-like reptiles. The rather typical long-

bodied, sprawling reptile that was represented by the pelycosaurs was gradually replaced by a different style of animal. These were known generally as therapsids, and they were much more varied in appearance.

Among the earliest of these were creatures such as *Anteosaurus*. Huge and very heavily built, with muscular jaws set on skulls 20 to 30 ins (50 to 80cm) long, for obvious reasons they are called dinocephalians ("terrible heads"). When they closed their jaws, their large front teeth interlocked to form a very effective slicing and cutting device, and it seems clear that the dinocephalians used these teeth to chop off from their prey pieces of flesh which they then swallowed whole. Their cheek teeth were quite small, and quite useless for serious chewing of food. Other dinocephalians such as *Moschops* (about to be assailed by *Anteosaurus*, below), adopted a plant-eating way of life, and possessed even-sized teeth which were better equipped for chipping off pieces of vegetation.

Dominant in southern Africa in the Middle Permian were huge, lumbering mammal-like reptiles such as the carnivorous Anteosaurus (LEFT), *and* (RIGHT) *its potential victim, the herbivorous* Moschops. *The anteosaur had large stabbing and cutting front teeth, but feeble cheek teeth, so it probably bit off pieces of flesh from its victim and then swallowed them whole.*

The bodies of these dinocephalians were very large but much more compact than those of the earlier pelycosaurs. The tail was shorter, while the body was more barrel-shaped and the legs were relatively longer. These external features suggest that a number of important changes were taking place.

First, the compactness of the body and its very large size – 10 ft (3m) or more in length, including the short tail – means that the skin area was very much reduced and as a result these creatures could keep their internal temperature relatively constant. Second, the fact that the legs were longer enabled them to hold the body higher from the ground. As a result the legs could swing more effectively under the body, giving the animal a better, faster stride and cutting down the need to wriggle the body from side to side when walking or running – this would be more difficult in a stocky, barrel-shaped animal anyway. The short tail also suggests that the tail muscles were now less important for moving the back legs. In addition, the toes were shorter and the feet narrower. This again fits with the idea that the legs were held more underneath the body than out to the sides, as they were in pelycosaurs.

The great size and heaviness of the head and the thickness of the bones over the eyes and brain have suggested to the American paleontologist Dr Herbert Barghusen that these animals indulged in head butting as part of their normal behavior – possibly comparable to social head butting in sheep, goats, and many antelope. Perhaps the dinocephalians lived in herds, and used head butting contests to maintain a hierarchy or establish mating rights.

Late Permian forms

The very heavily built dinocephalians were replaced in the fossil record by a range of mostly smaller and more agile carnivores and herbivores. *Lycaenops* ("wolf face") is typical of the carnivores. As the name suggests, it is very wolf-like in appearance, with quite long-striding legs and a wolf-like head and short tail. These were presumably fast-moving specialist killers. The very enlarged stabbing teeth near the front of the mouth are reminiscent of those of saber-toothed cats. These would have been important for slicing through the thick, scaly hides of their prey.

The prey of these saber-toothed therapsids was undoubtedly the very abundant therapsids known as dicynodonts that began to appear in Middle Permian times. They were so successful, in terms of numbers at least, that approximately 90 per cent of the fossil fauna that has been collected from rocks of Late Permian age consists of dicynodonts.

ABOVE *A rare and unexpected discovery has been made by a team of paleontologists from the South African Museum in Cape Town. These small, rounded objects appear to be the fossilized eggs of a Permian dicynodont.*

RIGHT *For a long time it was supposed that the large Early Triassic dicynodont* Lystrosaurus *was a lumbering, hippopotamus-like creature that wallowed in streams and waterholes. But recent work has suggested that it was a land-dwelling creature with a lifestyle not unlike that of a modern pig.*

Dicynodonts

These creatures are easily distinguished from other therapsids because they were highly modified for a diet of plants. Most were small to medium-sized, up to about 3 ft (1m) in length, though some of the later ones ranged up to hippo-sized. They had barrel-shaped bodies, stout but relatively short legs, short necks, and a large head that usually bears two large, downward-pointing tusks in the upper jaw. (The name of the group means "two dog teeth" – canine teeth – which should not be taken as suggesting that they were carnivores.) The remainder of the jaws was toothless and was covered in life by a tough, sharp, tortoise-like beak. The beak was a very effective cutter of plants, and the cut pieces were shredded between knife-like horny plates on the roof of the mouth. Large muscles on the side of the head moved the jaws very powerfully to and fro.

This system was obviously extremely effective, because these animals became incredibly abundant; it can safely be assumed that some formed herds, moving slowly and methodically across the Permian landscape. Their large numbers made them suitable prey for a wide range of carnivores, but even high levels of predation seem to have had little effect on their survival.

The majority of dicynodonts seem to have been surface browsers. A few have been identified as burrowers, perhaps specializing in feeding on roots and tubers; the wedge-like snout of *Cistecephalus* suggests that it adopted this mode of life. Some dicynodonts may have also nested in burrows. The Karoo Basin of South Africa has

revealed spiral burrows which were probably excavated by dicynodonts, and occasionally dicynodont fossils are discovered in nesting groups, as though they had been killed while asleep in their burrows. Eggs, possibly laid by dicynodonts, have also been collected from the Karoo.

Dicynodonts remained abundant in the Early Triassic: *Lystrosaurus* is common in the fossil record. But their numbers declined towards the close of the Triassic.

Cynodonts

From Late Permian times yet another group of carnivores appeared. These were the cynodonts ("dog teeth"). Smaller than the saber-toothed therapsids – generally less than 2 ft (60cm) long – these animals became more and more abundant in the Triassic Period. Their body proportions were similar to animals such as *Lycaenops*, but their heads were less modified – they did not depend for killing solely upon the huge stabbing teeth at the front of the mouth, but used a mixture of teeth along the length of the jaw, very reminiscent of the pattern seen in modern mammals.

At the front of the jaw on each side were small nipping teeth (incisors); behind these was a pair of large stabbing teeth (canines); while behind these were broader, sharp-edged cheek teeth that could be used for cutting and slicing up food before it was swallowed. Linked with the notion that these animals could chew their food before swallowing it was the fact that they had developed a bony palate in the roof of the mouth, which partitioned off the nasal passage from the mouth cavity. This feature enabled them to breathe and chew simultaneously without choking, and can be related to some important changes which were beginning to take place in the group as a whole.

Complicated muscles allowed the jaws to be moved very precisely so that chewing could take place. Being able to chew food before swallowing it speeds up the digestive process, which suggests that these animals needed to obtain their energy quickly. This necessity may have arisen because they used energy to create their own body heat to keep themselves warm. If this hypothesis is correct, it fits quite well with the idea that these animals were relatively small because they had developed a way of controlling their body temperature through internal heat production. Their predecessors in the Late Carboniferous and Early Permian had relied on being big, and therefore slow to gain or lose heat.

All this seems to make sense because they could continue breathing while engaged in chewing – the need to breathe quickly and regularly would not have been so great if they had been low-energy animals. Also there is evidence on the snouts of these creatures that they had sensitive whiskers. This is a vital piece of evidence because whiskers are specialized hairs, and if the animals had a hairy covering it would have contributed to keeping them warm by cutting down the rate at which body heat was lost through the skin to the environment – a problem for an animal that is relatively small and has a large surface area in relation to its body volume.

The picture which emerges from a consideration of the cynodonts is one of very mammal-like creatures. Modern mammals are characterized by having hair, by producing internal body heat (known as being endothermic), and by feeding their young on breast milk. Thus cynodonts may have been two-thirds of the way towards being true mammals.

Throughout the Triassic Period a variety of cynodonts appeared. Some were conventional carnivores, while others were smaller and more likely to have been insectivores, and yet others modified their cheek teeth to make them better able to crush food and no doubt became herbivores. It seems to have been these, perhaps more adaptable, herbivores that finally out-competed the phenomenally successful dicynodonts towards the end of the Triassic Period.

Some of the later mammal-like reptiles seem in many respects to resemble later mammals. The furry, whiskery image of Thrinaxodon *suggested here is almost that of a modern dog with pups. At present we cannot be entirely sure that this image is correct, but it does emphasize many of the important aspects of the mammal-like reptile story at the close of the Triassic Period.*

Since the discovery of a skeleton in the early 1960s in southern Africa, Megazostrodon *has been studied intensively because it seems to be a very early mammal. It lived in the earliest Jurassic, when the dinosaurs were just beginning to rise to dominance, and appears to have been a tiny, nocturnal insect-eater, not unlike a modern shrew.*

At this time the cynodonts became smaller and smaller, and apparently more and more mammal-like, until right at the close of the Triassic the earliest true mammals made their appearance in the form of tiny (4ins/10cm long) shrew-like insectivores such as *Megazostrodon,*

Eozostrodon, and *Morganucodon.* These tiny animals had teeth which were divided into incisors, canines, premolars, and molars (cheek teeth); they grew a single set of milk teeth, which suggests that they fed their young on breast milk; three middle ear bones to make their hearing more acute; and hair, suggested by the presence of whiskers. All these features can be traced back in one way or another to their cynodont forebears, and ultimately to those very reptile-like pelycosaurs of the Late Carboniferous Period.

The close of the Triassic Period draws a line under the evolution of the mammal-like reptiles. The first mammals did indeed evolve then, but instead of radiating and dominating the world they were supplanted by dinosaurs, which first appeared at this time and remained supreme on land for the next 160 million years. Only then could the real reign of the mammals begin. The next two chapters chart the rise of the other reptile groups, including the marine reptiles and the dinosaurs and their relatives, before we rejoin the mammals and the line which ultimately led to ourselves.

THE EVOLUTION OF EARS

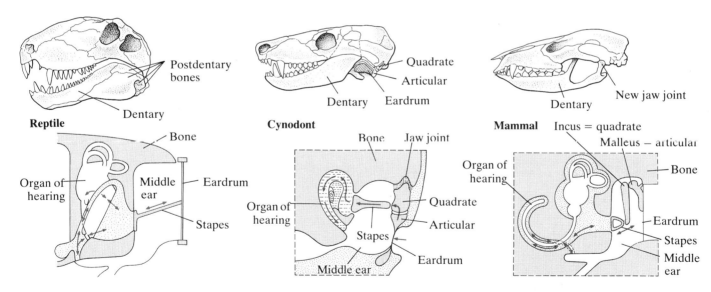

The reptile ear
In the early mammal-like reptile Dimetrodon *the large lower jaw consists of the dentary, which holds the teeth, and a group of postdentary bones running backward to the jaw joint. The ear lay behind the jaw. The eardrum was supported by a thin ear bone (the stapes), which passed sound vibrations to the sensitive part of the inner ear and organ of hearing.*

The cynodont ear
In Thrinaxodon *the dentary bone is much larger, and the postdentary bones are crowded to the back of the jaw around the joint. The eardrum is now located in a slot formed by the postdentary bones. Sounds are transmitted through these bones across the jaw joint formed by the quadrate and articular bones to the stapes, and then to the organ of hearing in the inner ear.*

The mammal ear
In Didelphis *a new jaw joint has formed between the dentary and the skull, replacing the joint found in reptiles between the quadrate and articular bones. The much-reduced postdentary bones still transfer sound vibrations in a chain of three bones: the malleus (articular), incus (quadrate), and stapes, none of which retains any jaw joint function.*

7

VARIATIONS ON A THEME

THE DOMINANCE OF
THE REPTILES

THE RISE OF the mammal-like reptiles during the Carboniferous, and their dominance on land during much of the succeeding Permian and Triassic, obscures the fact that many other types of reptile came into existence during this time. These included the ancestors of the major living reptile groups – the lizards, snakes, and crocodiles – as well as some very important groups, now extinct, which came to dominate the seas, air, and land during the Mesozoic Era (245–66mya): the marine reptiles (ichthyosaurs and plesiosaurs), the flying reptiles (pterosaurs), and the major land reptiles (dinosaurs).

The Triassic Period marks a major shift in the evolution of land vertebrates. It takes us from a period dominated by the synapsids or mammal-like reptiles, to one dominated by the diapsids or two-arched reptiles, and their descendants the euryapsids.

ABOVE *The porpoise-like head of the Jurassic ichthyosaur* Grendelius.

RIGHT *After gaining a firm toehold on land, reptiles diversified enormously. In the Cretaceous Period, for example, there were flying reptiles (pterosaurs) such as* Criorhynchus, *seen here snatching a fish from the jaws of* Elasmosaurus, *a giant plesiosaur.*

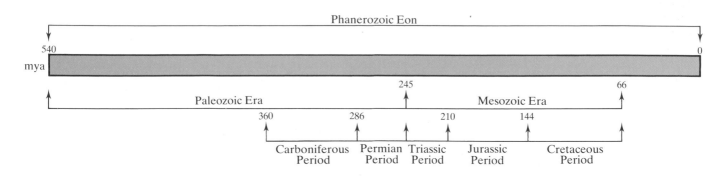

Phanerozoic Eon

540

mya

0

245

66

Paleozoic Era

Mesozoic Era

360   286   210   144

Carboniferous Period   Permian Period   Triassic Period   Jurassic Period   Cretaceous Period

Timescale of Earth history. *Reptiles show a striking rise in variety and abundance during the Permian and into the Mesozoic Era. The development of complete independence from water, made possible by the invention of the shelled egg, opened up a wide range of possibilities – including, paradoxically, a number of aquatic forms.*

DIAPSIDS

Living alongside the early mammal-like reptiles (pelycosaurs) in the Late Carboniferous Period were smaller, scuttling, lizard-like creatures such as *Petrolacosaurus*. To all intents and purposes this creature was much like other early reptiles, but it had two key differences. First, it had two openings at the back of its skull, which makes it a diapsid or two-arched reptile and therefore distinct from all the synapsid or mammal-like reptiles with their single skull opening. Second, it had unusually long legs and was presumably an extremely able runner. Lizard-like scampering forms have been extremely successful; animals of this general type have been around for over 300 million years, and are still extremely abundant in the tropical and subtropical regions of the world today.

Speed along the ground, or other ways of moving, seem to have been key features in the evolution of the two-arched reptiles. *Petrolacosaurus* no doubt used its speed to catch the insects and other small invertebrates which made up its diet. Unfortunately not much is known about the early history of the descendants of *Petrolacosaurus*: animals of this kind lived in upland areas where fossils were seldom preserved, and because they were small, light-boned creatures their remains would disappear all the more easily.

Mesosaurus and continental drift

One of the earliest reptiles to become fully aquatic was an important but puzzling little animal known as *Mesosaurus*. Its remains are extremely well preserved and come from South America and southern Africa. The body was quite elongated and the tail may well have had a small fin to aid in swimming; the legs were rather paddle-shaped, suggesting that the toes were webbed. The snout was slender and the jaws were lined with very fine, sharp teeth; it has been suggested that these animals fed

*The European green lizard (*Lacerta viridis*) is a modern representative of a style of reptiles that can be traced right back to the time of reptile origins in the Carboniferous. The overall similarity is so great that most paleontologists believe their style of life to have been identical.*

Mesosaurus is a puzzling little reptile from South America and southern Africa. The tail and feet suggest a capable swimmer, while the long snout and spiky teeth indicate a diet of small crustaceans or fish.

on small invertebrates floating among the plankton, which they engulfed and then strained out against their teeth before swallowing them whole. The relationships of *Mesosaurus* are a mystery. It is not obviously related to any of the known Permian groups, and although it appears to have a synapsid skull there is no resemblance in the rest of its skeleton to known mammal-like reptiles.

The reason for mentioning this enigmatic little creature is that it has an important place in the history of the understanding of the Earth and its processes. The fact that *Mesosaurus* was discovered in rocks of the same age and general characteristics in both South America and southern Africa prompted early speculation that these two continents had once been attached, even though they are now separated by thousands of miles of Southern Atlantic Ocean. To account for this extraordinary geographic distribution, strange ideas were tossed about concerning the existence of sunken continents or land bridges spanning the oceans. The problem was not resolved until the 1960s, following the establishment of sea-floor spreading and continental drift (see pages 11-12). The curious distribution of *Mesosaurus* fossils fitted very neatly with the idea that the continents of South America and Africa were in contact with one another during the Permian Period.

RETURN TO THE WATER

In Early Permian times another animal, again relatively small and scampering in build, is found alongside the large lumbering pelycosaurs such as *Dimetrodon* and *Edaphosaurus* in the red beds of Texas. Named *Araeoscelis*, it was very similar to *Petrolacosaurus* and is believed to have been quite a close relative. Its body is practically identical and the legs are just as long and

slender. There is, however, one key difference – in the arrangement of the bones in its head. This skull does not have two openings, but a single one high up on the side, which makes it a euryapsid according to the definitions on pages 111-12.

It seems most likely that *Araeoscelis* evolved from a diapsid similar to *Petrolacosaurus* by sealing up the lower skull opening. Perhaps this adaptation took place in order to reinforce the bones on the lower side of its head – it certainly appears to have quite large teeth and a deep, thickened lower jaw, a combination which indicates a diet requiring a lot of strength in teeth and jaws. Whatever the reasons for this reorganization, *Araeoscelis* became one of the earliest members of a group of reptiles which show a repeated tendency towards exploiting life in water.

BELOW *Animals such as the euryapsid (one skull window) reptile* Araeoscelis (BOTTOM) *were probably derived from reptiles such as* Petrolacosaurus (TOP), *the earliest known diapsid (two windows). It seems very likely that in* Araeoscleis *and similar types the single window was sealed over, for added strength.*

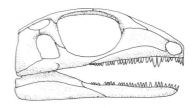

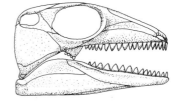

The remainder of the Permian and the Early Triassic reveal frustratingly little of euryapsids. However, from Middle Triassic times first nothosaurs, then placodonts, and later the much more familiar plesiosaurs and ichthyosaurs appeared in number and variety. This seems to have been the first really concerted effort by the reptiles to reinvade the waters. It is presumed that at least some of the early mammal-like reptiles (pelycosaurs) lived on fish in freshwater lakes; but none of them seems to have developed any other obvious swimming features such as paddles, flippers, or fins. Their only other water-oriented physical characteristics were the long body and the tail, which was presumably used for swimming.

In many ways reptiles seem very suited to life in the water. Their skins, being impermeable, protect them from the difficulties that some fish experience in coping with the differences between the composition of their own body fluids and that of fresh or salt water. In addition, reptiles breathe with lungs, rather than through gills, which means that no unprotected parts of the body such as thin gill membranes are exposed to fresh or salt

water. Lungs also provide ready-made adjustable buoyancy tanks which can aid swimming. The one drawback of life in water, as far as most reptiles are concerned, is the need to return to the land to lay eggs – witness the struggle of the large female green turtle at egg-laying time. Simply because shelled eggs are land eggs, they drown in water. A small number of reptiles were able to solve this problem.

Nothosaurs

Known mainly from the Middle Triassic of Europe, these are long-bodied creatures with well-developed limbs and long toes, which may well have been webbed. The neck is long and the head broad and low, with long, spiky teeth that were ideal for catching fish. Interestingly the nostrils, which would normally be positioned near the tip of the snout, are found on the top of it and some way back from the tip. Clearly this is an adaptation that would suit an animal that swam in water and from time to time came to the surface in order to breathe. Nothosaurs are a relatively short-lived group which did

BELOW *The slender, paddle-limbed* Ceresiosaurus *grew up to 13ft (4m) long. The finger bones exhibit hyperphalangy – extra bones to make the hands and feet more paddle-like.*

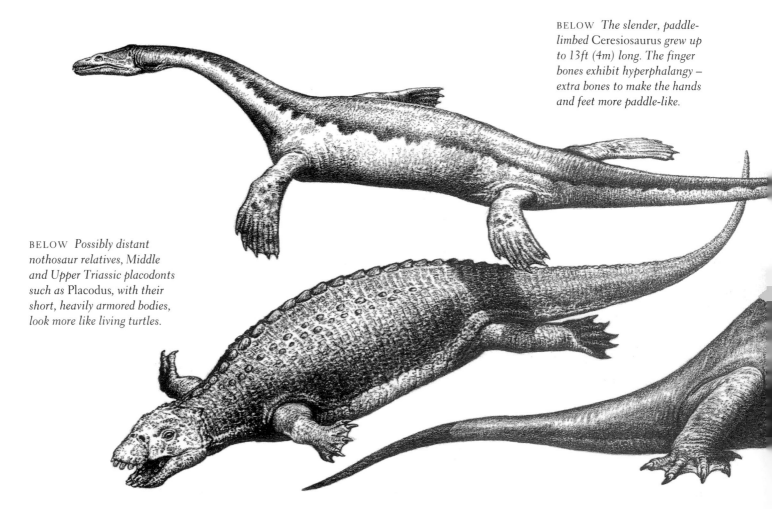

BELOW *Possibly distant nothosaur relatives, Middle and Upper Triassic placodonts such as* Placodus, *with their short, heavily armored bodies, look more like living turtles.*

not survive the end of the Triassic Period. They seem to have been replaced after that time by the plesiosaurs, which were more thoroughly aquatic.

Placodonts

Living alongside the nothosaurs was an equally short-lived group of bizarre reptiles called placodonts ("plate teeth"). Named on account of their cheek teeth, which are shaped like great flat crushing plates, these were superficially turtle-like creatures. Very sturdy, with a short neck and trunk compared to nothosaurs, they were up to 6ft (2m) long and some developed heavy, bony armor. Their legs were short, with broad, webbed feet, and they had a long tail which may have helped with swimming. The heads of these animals were remarkably strong. Some of them, such as *Placodus*, had front teeth shaped like pegs, while others such as *Henodus* had a toothless beak similar to that of a turtle. They would have used the beak to pluck molluscs from the sea floor before crushing them between their immense, flattened cheek teeth.

Like Ceresiosaurus, *the 10ft (3m) long* Nothosaurus *had a long neck, a trunk about the same length, short broad limbs, and webbed feet. It probably swam like an otter.*

Plesiosaurs

The plesiosaurs (literally "ribbon reptiles"), named for the long, almost ribbon-like backbone found in some, appeared in the Early Jurassic seas and lakes and were much more fully aquatic than either the nothosaurs or the placodonts. Their short, compact trunk, probably held very stiff in life, had a tight-knit breastplate formed of belly ribs (gastralia) which linked the shoulders and hips. These in turn were linked by ligaments to the arched spine. The tail was relatively short and does not appear to have aided swimming at all. In many plesiosaurs the neck tended to be very long and flexible, ending in a small head whose jaws were lined with strong, sharply pointed teeth. The limbs were fully modified into front and rear pairs of broad, tapering paddles with which these animals swam. The short, taut trunk allowed the paddles to generate thrust without causing the body to bend, which would have caused drag in the water by upsetting the smooth flow.

These creatures were presumably suited to a life spent paddling along in the surface waters. There they would have fed on fish and fast-moving invertebrates such as belemnites (squid-like cephalopods) and squid, perhaps catching their prey with darting movements of the head and whiplash movements of the neck – and perhaps even taking flying reptiles from time to time.

Alongside the rather elegantly long-necked variety of plesiosaurs was another type known as pliosaurs. These were on the whole larger and more compact creatures. Their bodies were again held stiff so that their paddles would have been used effectively. The tail was again not obviously used for swimming, but the neck was much shorter and the head considerably larger, containing huge stabbing teeth. Undoubtedly aggressive carnivores of the seas, they reached lengths in excess of 42ft (13m), with heads up to 6ft (2m) long. It seems quite probable that pliosaurs were cruising hunters not unlike modern sperm whales and killer whales.

One very interesting recent suggestion has emerged from studies carried out on the skull of the large pliosaur *Rhomaleosaurus*. It appears that the nostrils of this animal were arranged in such a way that it could swim along with its mouth slightly open. This would have enabled water to pass straight up into the scoop-shaped nostril openings in the roof of the mouth, through a channel where the smell sensors would have been located, and then out onto the snout through the nostril openings just in front of the eyes. This is exactly the reverse of what might have been expected: air normally passes from the external nostril through the nose to the nostril in the roof of the mouth and then on into the lungs.

Rhomaleosaurus was a powerfully built pliosaur 17ft (5m) or more in length, the approximate equivalent of a modern killer whale. Intriguingly, this animal appears to have located its prey partly by smell, just as sharks do today.

This arrangement would have allowed these predators to "smell" the water like a modern shark, rather than merely using the nostrils for breathing air in the normal manner. It may have greatly improved *Rhomaleosaurus*'s ability not only to find prey, but also to home in on and scavenge fresh kills by other animals – just as sharks do today. It would follow that *Rhomaleosaurus* breathed directly through its open mouth when it came up to the surface, and did not use its nostrils at all.

Exactly how plesiosaurs cruised around has been the subject of much discussion. No modern animal has four swimming paddles: turtles use only their front ones, and seals propel themselves by using their front flippers like paddles. So comparison of plesiosaurs with their modern counterparts in this context is not very useful.

They used to be visualized as rowing along, with the paddles moving back and forth. However, careful study of the shape of the paddles shows that they were built much more along the lines of a wing, and it is assumed that the paddles beat up and down like the wing of a bird, or indeed the paddle of a turtle.

The most powerful part of the paddle stroke was the downbeat, using the chest and inner leg muscles attached to the underside of the chest and pelvis. The upstroke may well have been essentially passive, pushed up by the water flow. If this theory is correct, it seems quite likely that the front and back flippers beat out of phase – that is to say, the front flippers beat downwards as the rear flippers moved passively upward, and vice versa. In this way forward propulsion would have been very even and regulated rather than jerky.

Others have suggested that plesiosaurs moved their back and front flippers up and down simultaneously, and that they linked this movement with an undulating, "porpoising" method of swimming. However, this seems unlikely given the extreme rigidity of the trunk in plesiosaurs: "porpoising" is possible only because whales, dolphins, and porpoises all have a very flexible back that can bend vertically as they swim.

Ichthyosaurs

These "fish lizards" were the supreme swimming reptiles. Early forms such as *Mixosaurus*, from the Lower and Middle Triassic of many parts of the world, had very strongly streamlined bodies: a long, thin snout lined with sharp teeth, a short neck, and a compact, smooth trunk. The front limbs were modified to form paddles, as were the smaller rear ones; the tail was long, deep, and topped with a fin. It is clear that this animal, unlike plesiosaurs which apparently depended on their paddles for locomotion, swam with side-to-side movements of the tail like a fish, possibly holding its hind fins against the sides of the body when swimming fast, and using them as fish-like fins to maneuver when chasing prey.

The early ichthyosaur Mixosaurus *has a classic reptilian elongate tail rather than the deep, fish-like tail seen in later ichthyosaurs. Its smooth, streamlined body could glide through the water with minimal friction and therefore minimal reduction of speed. The limbs were used not as paddles but as steering devices to assist with the capture of swift-moving prey.*

SWIMMERS OF THE MESOZOIC

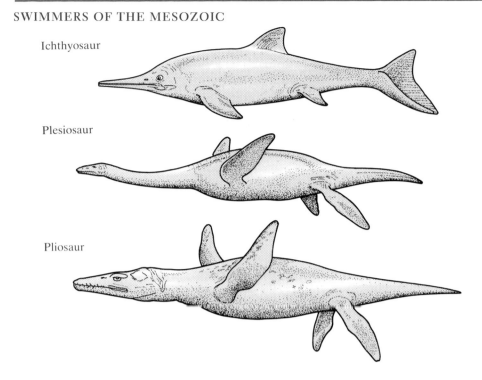

Ichthyosaur

Plesiosaur

Pliosaur

A very well-adapted, streamlined body has been achieved by the virtual loss of the neck. The deep tail fin beat from side to side to give swimming power, a fleshy dorsal fin aided stability, and the flippers served as steering devices.

These reptiles were less fish-like than ichthyosaurs, with a snake-like neck, and a short tail not obviously modified for sculling. Plesiosaurs may have employed "underwater flight," beating their paddles up and down in a flying stroke.

Attributes of ichthyosaurs and plesiosaurs combine here in a moderately streamlined body and fairly short neck. The paddles were clearly the main source of propulsion, probably giving pliosaurs endurance rather than sprinting power when chasing prey.

Later ichthyosaurs show a surprising range of body form. Some, such as *Shonisaurus* from the Late Triassic of Nevada, became enormous – up to 50 ft (15m) long – and would have looked rather different from *Mixosaurus*. The snout of *Shonisaurus* was very long and lined with conical teeth, while the body was quite stout, with long, heavy ribs; there were two pairs of long, tapering paddles both about 6 ft (2m) long. The tail was shaped much like that of *Mixosaurus*. It seems quite likely that this animal used underwater "flight" similar to that described for plesiosaurs – using the paddles like wings, and moving them up and down out of phase with one another. This method of locomotion would have been rather stately and may well have limited their food to the slower-moving, larger ammonites.

In Early Jurassic times some new types of ichthyosaur appear, including the giant *Temnodontosaurus* which reached lengths of 35 ft (10m) and may well have been a hunter of other ichthyosaurs. The tails of these new ichthyosaurs, including the classic *Ichthyosaurus* from the Early Jurassic of Britain, were strikingly downturned. Carbonized films showing the outline of the skin in these creatures reveal that the tail ended in a fish-like fin, with the tail bones curving down to lie along the leading edge of the bottom half of the fin. They also show that there was a fleshy dorsal fin in the middle of the back, which would have improved the creature's stability while swimming at speed. The deep, fish-like tail

suggests that these ichthyosaurs swam by using their tails rather than by flapping their paddles, and they may have been much faster, more aggressive hunters of active prey. The rear paddles are considerably smaller than the front ones, and all four paddles were probably used for steering and as diving planes.

In Late Jurassic and Early Cretaceous times ichthyosaur remains become increasingly rare, and the group as a whole seems to have undergone a rapid decline in abundance and variety during the Middle Jurassic. *Ophthalmosaurus* was a medium-sized, 10 to 13 ft (3 to 4m) long ichthyosaur well known from clay pits in eastern England, and notable for its enormous eyes – hence the name. Living alongside it was *Grendelius* (named after the monster Grendel in the Anglo-Saxon epic poem *Beowulf*), which is known only from a skull and has a relatively small eye.

By Late Cretaceous times ichthyosaurs are still found in the seas, but again their remains are rare, though widely distributed. *Platypterygius* is the principal type, discovered in North and South America, Europe, Russia, India, and Australia, and seems to have been a worldwide genus. The last traces of ichthyosaurs are found in rocks that date from about 25 million years before the close of the Cretaceous Period, so there is no question of linking the extinction of the ichthyosaurs with the fate of dinosaurs and all the other creatures that became extinct at the very end of the Cretaceous.

The wonderful state of preservation of many ichthyosaur skeletons from Lyme Regis in England and Holzmaden in Germany has provided some fascinating insights into the lifestyle of these creatures. Carbonized skin impressions have shown that the animals were extremely fish-like, with a streamlined body reminiscent of modern dolphins and swordfish, a fleshy dorsal fin, and in many cases a deep, very fish-like tail. Depth or narrowness indicate, respectively, whether the animal was a sprinter or a cruiser. This can be linked to the shape and arrangement of the paddles to define the likely swimming abilities of many ichthyosaurs: compare, for instance, a paddle-swimming slow cruiser such as *Shonisaurus* with the dolphin-like *Ophthalmosaurus*, *Ichthyosaurus*, and *Grendelius*.

Stomach contents and coprolites (fossilized droppings) are preserved with some ichthyosaurs, and these reveal the scales of bony fish and sharp curved hooklets from belemnites. Ichthyosaurs clearly preyed on small, very agile bony fish such as *Pholidophorus* as well as belemnites, whose bullet-like skeletons are found abundantly in rocks of this age.

More remarkable even than the preservation of stomach contents in some ichthyosaurs has been the discovery, in the abdomens of certain specimens, of embryo ichthyosaurs. Nor is this a particularly rare occurrence – at least 50 skeletons are now known to include partial or complete embryos.

The first discoveries of embryonic remains occurred in the 1840s in Britain and Germany, but the interpretations varied enormously. The British discovery, made by Channing Pearce, was heralded as evidence that ichthyosaurs gave birth to live young, while in Germany it was interpreted as evidence of cannibalism. The debate raged through the nineteenth century and into the twentieth. The German interpretation harks back to

LEFT *The huge Charmouth ichthyosaur, which has yet to be given a scientific name, is some 33ft (10m) long – about the same size as its contemporary* Temnodontosaurus. *A skeleton of this gigantic marine reptile was collected from sea cliffs near the town of Charmouth in Dorset in the southwest of England as recently as 1985, and is now on permanent display at Bristol City Museum. The Charmouth ichthyosaur may well have preyed upon other large marine reptiles and large, relatively slow-moving ammonites.*

BELOW *Another large ichthyosaur,* Grendelius, *was named after a literary monster – Grendel, from the Anglo-Saxon poem* Beowulf. *The skull of this creature was found in Jurassic clays in eastern England and is destined to go on display at the Sedgwick Museum in Cambridge, England. The remainder of the skeleton was never discovered, but it is reasonable to assume that it would have had normal ichthyosaur proportions, giving an overall length of some 13ft (4m).*

a very stereotyped way of thinking, which is simply that "reptiles lay eggs" and therefore could not possibly show evidence of potential live birth. It also points to a rather savage way of life, which perhaps fitted more conventionally with the general ideas that were prevalent at that time about life in the prehistoric world.

It seems quite logical that both scenarios are possible. However, it should be a simple matter to distinguish cannibalism from pregnancy. If the embryonic bones are very scattered then the embryo is likely to have been devoured, especially if it is mixed in with other obvious stomach contents such as belemnite hooks and fish scales. But if the embryo is intact and near the back of the abdomen (near the birth canal, or actually lodged in the birth canal as some are), then it is likely to be an embryo waiting to be born.

This artistic impression of an ichythosaur giving birth (LEFT) is based on some remarkable discoveries. Some skeletons contain the remains of young: if a female in the late stages of pregnancy died, spontaneous abortion may have occurred. The German fossil (BELOW) has babies inside and one being born.

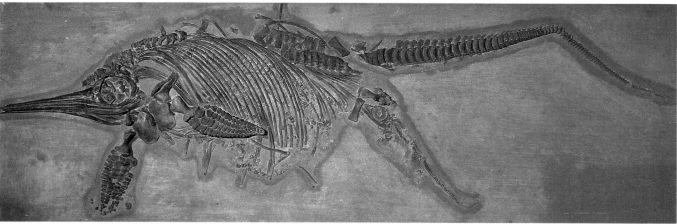

Numerous ichthyosaurs (mostly *Stenopterygius*) show embryos, some of which appear to be caught at the moment of birth. While it is theoretically possible that the mother died during the trauma of childbirth, it seems highly probable that the majority were females which died while pregnant; the subsequent early stages of decomposition of the carcass may have resulted in the expulsion of the embryo from the abdomen. This phenomenon of abortion after the death of the mother has been observed among stranded whales today.

It is quite unusual for paleontologists to be able to identify the sex of a fossil creature, but here there can be no doubt. This has allowed sexual differences to be examined in ichthyosaurs; but, frustratingly, very few ichthyosaurs show any obvious difference between males and females.

The eyes of ichthyosaurs are extremely large and contain enormous rings of bony plates called sclerotic ossicles. Similar plates are found in the eyes of birds and lizards and help to strengthen the eyeball, which was at first thought to be the function of the rings in ichthyosaurs. However, the rings also provide a tapered funnel into which the lens can be squeezed by the muscles that focus the eye. This changes the shape of the lens and helps it to focus on objects. It therefore seems highly likely that ichthyosaurs had extremely acute vision. As a result they probably inhabited the upper layers of the ocean, where light reaches, and hunted by sight rather

than by smell as appears to have been the case in pliosaurs (see pages 125-26) and is well known in sharks, or by ultrasound as used by whales and dolphins – both of which have relatively small eyes.

Lizard-like forms

Diapsid reptiles are relatively scarce in Permian times – since they were small and lived in drier upland areas, there are few fossil remains. Various Late Permian lizard-like forms are known which include paliguanids, practically identical to modern lizards. Contemporary with them were some highly specialized forms such as *Coelurosauravus*, which was described by Dr Susan Evans. It may well have been a tree dweller because it had enormously extended ribs which were no doubt used for gliding – a very early version of the modern flying lizard *Draco volans* from Southeast Asia.

Draco volans, *the flying lizard from southeast Asia, is not a true flier because it is not capable of powered flight. However, it has long, flexible ribs which it can hold out from the sides of its body to form a gliding membrane. These little insect eaters can leap from the branches of trees, spread their ribs, and glide long distances before landing on another tree. This method of moving about represents an enormous saving in energy, time, and risk when compared with the alternative: climbing down one tree trunk, across the forest floor, and up the next tree in search of its prey.*

Lizard-like forms reached their zenith in the Late Cretaceous Period; they included conventional lizards, early snakes, and various marine predators. During the Late Jurassic and Cretaceous, just at the time when the ichthyosaurs were declining in the seas, several groups of carnivorous lizard evolved. The early forms grew to about 3 ft (1m), but in the latter half of the Cretaceous Period one group, not much different from modern monitor lizards (the group to which the Komodo dragon belongs), took to the sea and became huge, predatory reptiles up to 50 ft (15m) in length.

Known as mosasaurs, because the first specimen was discovered in a chalk quarry near the River Meuse (Maas) in the Netherlands, they include *Clidastes*, *Plotosaurus*, *Mosasaurus*, and *Tylosaurus*. These animals were extremely elongated, seemingly with a fin on the end of the tail, and had modest-sized flippers for maneuvering. Their skulls were extremely large and their

jaws were lined with very large conical teeth. Along with the pliosaurs of the Late Cretaceous, these were the top carnivores of the seas.

ASCENT OF THE RULING REPTILES

The ancestors of the group known as archosaurs ("ruling reptiles"), which includes the crocodiles, pterosaurs, dinosaurs, and birds, also appeared in the Permian. They appear to be rather like lizards and their kin; however, there are some subtle differences. The trunks of the archosaur ancestors tend to be a little shorter and more compact, their legs are longer than is usual for lizards, and their necks are usually quite long. When moving, these animals must have relied more on swinging their legs than wriggling their bodies, and the body itself became increasingly rigid.

Early archosaurs

The first true archosaurs appeared in the Late Permian and Early Triassic. They can be differentiated from their immediate ancestors by a number of skeleton features. Perhaps the most distinctive is the appearance of a large opening on the side of the skull, just in front of the eye socket. This opening is known as the antorbital fenestra and seems, at least in the early forms, to be an area for the attachment of a large muscle which ran back beneath the eye socket and was attached to the back inside surface of the lower jaw. This muscle was used to snap the jaws together very sharply, and was probably an aid to feeding in a group which, to start with at least, appears to have been largely predatory.

Another frequent feature, particularly in early archosaurs, consists of rows of bony armor on the back (similar to, but less extensive than, those seen on the backs of modern crocodiles). Archosaurs usually display at least a paired row embedded in the skin on either side

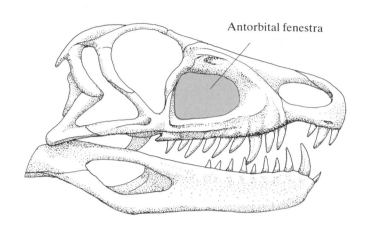

Antorbital fenestra

Important differences between the skull of a standard diapsid such as Petrolacosaurus (page 123) and an archosaur (ABOVE) include the antorbital fenestra, a large opening in front of the eye socket, and another opening on the side of the lower jaw. Archosaur teeth are also large and embedded in deep sockets. Euparkeria (BELOW) shows another classic archosaur trait: the row of bony plates or scutes along the sides of the backbone, as seen in modern crocodiles and alligators.

CROCODILES: MODERN EXAMPLES OF ARCHOSAUR LOCOMOTION

Crocodiles in water
BELOW *In water the body is buoyed up and the backbone is no longer in tension. The body can therefore be undulated in an eel-like manner when swimming, with the legs held close to the sides.*

Crocodiles on land
ABOVE *A walking crocodile uses its legs energetically because the body is held stiff and straight. The legs need to lift it clear of the ground so as to swing freely with each stride.*

of the spine, and sometimes there are further rows. At first they were believed to be simply armor for defense against other predators. However, their limited distribution renders this improbable – surely the back would have been covered in an all-over, mat-like arrangement if it was a defensive strategy?

Recent work by Dr Eberhard Frey has provided a neat alternative explanation. After studying the bony plates in the backs of crocodiles, it was realized that the bones were attached to the ribs and backbone by tough ligaments. This arrangement was designed to hold the spine very stiff when these animals were walking on land, and to prevent it from sagging excessively when the body was lifted clear of the ground. In water, where the weight of the body is buoyed up by displacement, the ligaments are relaxed and the spine is free to move from side to side in the normal swimming action of crocodiles. So the appearance of distinctive rows of bony armor in early archosaurs may well have been linked to holding the back stiff on land while the legs lifted the body clear of the ground as they walked.

In Late Permian and Early Triassic times some substantial archosaurs such as *Erythrosuchus* and *Archosaurus* appeared, which were heavy land animals. Another range of archosaurs took to the water and appear to have competed with both the large aquatic early tetrapods and the few mammal-like reptiles that ventured into the water around this time. These included forms such as *Proterosuchus* and *Rutiodon*, both of which were larger aquatic carnivores which closely resembled crocodiles.

The first crocodiles

Towards the close of the Triassic the very earliest true crocodiles appeared. Some of them were surprisingly compact and rather long-legged land predators; *Terrestrisuchus* is a typical example. Others, such as *Protosuchus* and *Notochampsa*, were more conventionally crocodile-shaped and may well have been at least partly aquatic, but it was not really until the next Period, the Jurassic, that the more conventionally long-bodied crocodiles first started to make their appearance, not only in rivers and lakes but also in the oceans as thoroughly marine predators.

The later archosaurs

The later Triassic saw the appearance of a variety of land-based archosaur types. They ranged from large and heavily built carnivores such as *Saurosuchus*, which were very mobile but totally quadrupedal (four-legged), to others such as *Ornithosuchus*, which combined a short trunk with a long tail to counterbalance the front part of the body, emphasizing the length and strength of the hind legs which thus bore the entire weight of the body. As a result *Ornithosuchus* became a very swift bipedal (two-footed) runner.

The stiff, short trunk and long, balancing tail of archosaurs seem to have made bipedal running a distinct and worthwhile possibility. Once this trait began to appear, toward the end of the Triassic Period, there was a minor burst of types. They included smaller carnivores such as *Lagosuchus*; some tiny, possibly insectivorous, creatures; and, most intriguing of all, small, possibly tree-dwelling insectivores, which may themselves have been close to the origin of the first genuine flying reptiles, the pterosaurs.

THE FLYING REPTILES

Several intriguing, tiny fossil archosaurs have been found in Late Triassic deposits in Europe and Asia. They hint at the origins of the first dedicated flying reptiles, the pterosaurs ("winged lizards").

Scleromochlus, found at Elgin in Scotland, is one among many of these small Late Triassic forms. It is known only from imperfect impressions of its bones in sandstone slabs. A reconstruction based on this material shows a small creature just over 8 ins (20 cm) in length. The very long, spindly back legs and light build suggested to early researchers that this was a tree-dwelling animal which might have possessed flaps of skin along the sides of the body. These appendages could have acted like a parachute to break its fall if it fell off branches while scrambling after prey – the modern flying squirrel has a similar arrangement.

It has been suggested that animals like this were intermediate between more conventional archosaurs and pterosaurs, but in truth the only thing that really links them is their small and lightly built skeleton. They are genuine small archosaurs, with the same limb and body proportions and no indication that their arms were increasing in length or starting to exhibit wing-like features.

Sharovipteryx, from Kirghizia in Central Asia, is another Late Triassic form which provides more positive evidence of flight, or at least of parachuting abilities. This extraordinary little animal is very well preserved. Its skeleton is slender and light and has similar proportions to that of *Scleromochlus*. But the fossil shows evidence that between the long, slender hind limbs and the tail *Sharovipteryx* possessed a genuine flight membrane, which lends support to the idea that at least some of these allegedly tree-dwelling reptiles were experimenting with flight.

Debatable origins

The origins of pterosaurs are, for the moment, the subject of some debate. On the one hand they seem to share some characteristics with early dinosaurs, particularly in the construction of the legs and hips. Some paleontologists in fact claim that animals such as *Lagosuchus* form a link between dinosaurs and pterosaurs. This is based upon the supposition that

Lagosuchus ("rabbit crocodile") was named because of its long, rabbit-like hind legs. This small 12–16 ins (30–40 cm) long animal was clearly a sharp-toothed, agile sprinter – a fierce hunter of small animals in the Late Triassic of Argentina. It represents one extreme of the radiation of archosaurs at this time.

Another small, lightly built archosaur of the Late Triassic Period was Sharovipteryx, *whose very well-preserved remains have been discovered in Kirghizia (Central Asia). The fossil reveals a broad membrane which spanned the space between the back legs and tail. It seems quite likely that this animal represents an early phase of experimentation with gliding membranes.*

early pterosaurs were able to run bipedally, in a similar way to dinosaurs. It is further related to the notion that pterosaurs took to the air by the extremely energy-consuming method of running along the ground and flapping their wings.

An alternative view is that pterosaurs evolved from diapsids earlier in the Triassic – ones that were not specifically like the ancestors of dinosaurs, and did not show any strong tendency towards bipedality, but simply pursued a tree-dwelling, insectivorous way of life. This, it is argued, allowed them to develop parachuting, gliding, and ultimately flying capabilities as an energy-saving by-product of this lifestyle.

The anatomy of pterosaurs

Pterosaurs had a very light, bony skeleton, and their bones were for the most part hollow and tubular. The skull was large relative to the size of the body, and supported on a well-developed series of neck bones. The trunk was quite short and compact to improve the anchorage for the wings, while the pelvis and hind limbs were relatively small and lightly built – particularly so when compared to the forelimbs and shoulders. The forelimbs were extraordinarily long, though most of the length was derived from the enormous exaggeration of the length of the fourth finger, which alone supported the flight membrane. Three short, clawed fingers were retained on the leading edge of the wing, and the shoulder girdle was strong and firmly connected to the breast-

bone and spine. The legs were quite long and slender, as were the feet.

Early pterosaurs (rhamphorhynchoids) possessed a long, bony tail, which was reinforced by thin bony splints and appears to have been tipped by a small, diamond-shaped vane – rather like the rudder on an airplane. The later pterosaurs (pterodactyloids) had very short tails.

The earliest pterosaurs

The first known pterosaurs were already well-developed flying reptiles. Examples from Europe include *Peteinosaurus*, *Eudimorphodon*, and *Preondactylus*. Specimens of *Eudimorphodon* and *Peteinosaurus* were discovered, both in a beautiful state of preservation, in rocks of Triassic age at a locality near the city of Bergamo in the Italian Alps. In general, their anatomy was as described above.

Peteinosaurus had a fairly conventional skull, large and high and similar in many respects to that of earlier archosaurs. Its teeth were also even-sized, simple, sharp cones. Its diet was most likely to have consisted of insects which it may have caught on the wing. This general lifestyle seems to accord well with the idea that earlier tree-dwelling archosaurs were insectivores which experimented with parachuting and/or gliding as a means not only of breaking their fall, but also of catching insects that would otherwise have been able to escape simply by flying away.

Eudimorphodon had remarkably specialized teeth: there were large fangs at the front and smaller, multi-spiked ones behind. This general configuration is similar to the arrangement of teeth in the mouths of fish-eating seals, and makes it very probable that this animal was an early fish-eating pterosaur.

Preondactylus seems to have had a similar lifestyle, and this is confirmed in a slightly bizarre way. Food pellets regurgitated by fish of the time contain the bones of *Preondactylus*, which strongly suggests that the latter was a fish eater which occasionally either crash-landed in the sea and fell prey to scavenging fish, or was actively preyed upon while hunting at sea level.

Jurassic and Cretaceous pterosaurs

Dimorphodon was a long-tailed, large-headed pterosaur whose remains were found in England. Its skull was similar in shape to that of *Peteinosaurus*, but its teeth were of two types: large, piercing ones at the front of the jaws and smaller, spiky ones behind. It may well have been a fish eater, judging by the shape of its teeth. Numerous Jurassic pterosaurs seem to have been fish eaters, the majority showing very elongate piercing front teeth which were probably used to spear and hold their prey as they skimmed over the wave tops.

Dorygnathus and *Rhamphorhynchus* are good examples of this type of pterosaur, and their style of feeding can be compared to that of the modern birds known as

In the Italian Alps of the Late Triassic two very early pterosaurs have been discovered: Peteinosaurus *(left foreground) and* Eudimorphodon *(right foreground, catching a fish). The latter has long spiky teeth at the front, and short multi-spiked teeth further back.*

skimmers. These birds have a long, blade-like bill which they lower into the water as they skim across the surface of a lake. The bill lances into the body of any fish unfortunate enough to be swimming near the surface, and the skimmer's head snaps downward as it lifts the fish clear of the water and flies off to its perch.

In the Late Jurassic modified types of pterosaur begin to make their appearance. They had one obvious distinguishing feature, a very short tail. *Pterodactylus* is a good early example of this kind of pterosaur. With a wingspan of about 16 ins (40cm) in some of the smaller species, these were small and presumably agile fliers. The long tail seen in all their predecessors would have provided considerable stability in flight, allowing them to cruise and swoop very effectively; however, they would have been less able to indulge in tight aerial turns and more elegant forms of aerobatic movement. The short-tailed *Pterodactylus* would by contrast have been an inherently unstable flier; much greater control would have been required of the animal to stop it tumbling from the

skies, but in compensation it would have been considerably more maneuverable. Its diet is not known, but it would seem likely that such small pterosaurs may have confined themselves to catching insects, a mode of life that would have required extreme agility in flight.

LEFT *The pterosaur* Pterodaustro *has a curious head, with very long, thin, bristle-like lower teeth. It was probably a filter-feeder, scooping up water and squeezing it out through the bristle teeth to trap small water creatures.*

Quetzalcoatlus ("feathered serpent," after one of the Aztec gods) is a celebrated pterosaur of the Cretaceous. When its remains were first discovered in Texas the paleontologists were astounded, because the wing bones seemed to be far too big. Yet when more material was collected the evidence. suggested that flying reptiles the size of gliders and light aircraft did indeed once live on Earth.

Many of these short-tailed Late Jurassic and Early Cretaceous pterosaurs had reduced numbers of teeth or lost them altogether. Others retained their teeth, but developed some very specialist methods of feeding. The Early Cretaceous *Criorhynchus* and *Tropheognathus* developed a large swollen rostrum (the tip of the snout) on the end of the jaws; this seems to have acted as a keel or cutwater when they were surface feeding on fish. In contrast the Early Cretaceous *Pterodaustro* from South America developed the most extraordinary long, curved jaws, the lower one equipped with fine, bristle-like teeth. It seems likely that these animals used their teeth to sieve small creatures such as shrimps out of the water. This arrangement is reminiscent of that of modern flamingoes, and suggests a similar lifestyle.

The giant flyers

In the Late Cretaceous some of the most remarkable of all pterosaurs appeared. *Pteranodon*, which achieved wingspans of up to 33 ft (10m), was a gigantic creature which appears to have fed upon fish, using its long, thin, toothless beak to scoop them out of the water and then storing them in a pelican-like pouch in the floor of its mouth before swallowing them. The heads of these pterosaurs show the development of a large crest, which appears to have balanced the aerodynamic drag caused by the long beak when it inclined its head downwards, and also acted as a rudder-like steering device.

The most remarkable of all pterosaurs, however, were the quetzals. *Quetzalcoatlus* from the Late Cretaceous of Texas seems to have reached wingspans in excess of 50 ft (15m), equivalent to the size of a modern light aircraft. These huge creatures have caused all kinds of problems to paleontologists.

First, they seem to exceed all expectations about the maximum size of flying animals – the first discovery of some of the wing bones of these creatures in recent years was greeted with utter astonishment. Second, their diet is a mystery. The bones of quetzals have been found in inland areas rather than in marine deposits, which suggests that they patrolled the skies above the plains of the Late Cretaceous.

This has provoked the idea that, rather like vultures of the present day, they may have been carrion feeders, perhaps picking over the remains of dinosaur carcasses. Whether it is realistic to imagine a creature with this huge wingspan scrabbling over a dinosaur carcass is debatable – it would seem to be very vulnerable to attack from a whole range of land-based predators. Quetzals also possess pointed, rather than sharply hooked, beaks, which seem poorly adapted for tearing at a carcass.

An alternative suggestion is that they lived on shellfish on the margins of inland waterways. However, they must have been incredibly ungainly creatures on land and quite unsuited for spending significant amounts of time there. They may in fact have been fish eaters like all the rest. Perhaps they were just larger versions of the more familiar *Pteranodon*-like pterosaurs – gigantic pterosaur equivalents of present-day albatrosses.

Bipedal or quadrupedal?

In recent years the anatomy and relationships of pterosaurs have been reinvestigated by a number of paleontologists. Detailed work on the skeleton of the early pterosaur *Dimorphodon* led Dr Kevin Padian to suggest that pterosaurs were bipedal – that they were capable of running on the ground, using their hind legs. Reconstructions of the creature running with its tail strung out behind, and its wings folded back along the sides of its body, are becoming increasingly familiar – but whether they actually did this in life is debatable.

In general terms the legs and feet of pterosaurs are rather frail-looking for continuous movement of this kind. The feet are not narrow, as they tend to be in runners, but broad, with the toes widely separated and of roughly equal length. This points to a flat-footed gait rather than one in which the animal was capable of standing high on its toes, as is usually the case for a runner.

Bipedal running in pterosaurs seems increasingly questionable. This does not mean that they could never stand bipedally – merely that they did not run habitually on their back legs. Indeed, it may well have been advantageous to be able to stand upright and spread their wings in order to take off from the ground.

The problem of structure and balance when standing on their hind legs is even more extreme in the larger, short-tailed pterosaurs. The absence of a tail to act as a rudder, the large size of the head and neck, and the general awkwardness of the huge wings – even when folded against the sides of the body – makes the idea that they could walk on their hind legs extremely unlikely.

It seems inevitable that pterosaurs would have walked on all fours, using the three hand claws to grip the ground, while the fourth finger, which supported the wing membrane, was folded back and upward in order to prevent the membrane from getting scuffed or torn. The legs, though partly drawn beneath the body, would tend to be splayed outward. Because of the great length of the forelimbs, the posture and general movement of pterosaurs on land was probably comparable to that of modern gorillas, though the wing membrane would have made them generally less fast-moving and agile.

Flight

The anatomy of the wings and shoulders of pterosaurs seems to show that the majority were very able flapping fliers, using a muscular mechanism very similar to that used by today's birds. This suggests that pterosaurs were highly energetic creatures – as birds and bats are – and therefore very unlike standard reptiles. This picture is reinforced by other recent discoveries.

Mammalian characteristics?

Fossil remains from Kazakhstan have confirmed something which has long been suspected in pterosaurs – they may have had a furry covering. A creature named

Could pterosaurs run? Analysis of the structure of the hips and hind limbs of the early pterosaur Dimorphodon *has led some paleontologists to suggest that they did not shuffle along the ground, as had been commonly supposed, but were capable of running on their back legs in a very bird-like manner. This intriguing possibility has, however, not yet been fully accepted. Considerable attention has now been focused on the detailed structure of pterosaur hip joints, feet, and toes, and on whether the wing membrane stretched down and attached to the lower leg.*

Sordes pilosus ("hairy devil") was described in 1971. The fine sediment surrounding the fragmentary skeleton included a distinct impression of fur covering most of the body areas, including the wings and tail.

A fur covering for insulation had long been expected by paleontologists because these animals would have been very susceptible to rapid cooling in the air, which might have rendered a conventional ectothermic reptile (one reliant on external heat) extremely sluggish. Furthermore, an insulated covering means that pterosaurs must have been able to generate their own body heat.

This makes pterosaurs comparable to modern mammals and birds, as high-energy, warm-blooded creatures – a combination that seems to stretch the definition of "reptile" to the very limit. But as we have already seen and will find again in later chapters, present-day definitions of the characteristics of groups of animals are often rather misleading – and the cause of much dispute and blinkered thinking among scientists.

Clearly pterosaurs would have to be well-coordinated creatures in order to fly, and as a result would have needed a complex brain. The brain cavity of pterosaurs certainly indicates that their brains were large, and large brains need an even temperature and a constant supply of oxygen and food in order to operate correctly. The only way that a large brain could function in a pterosaur was for the body to be insulated to prevent excessive temperature changes – and that seems proof enough. It seems likely, therefore, that all pterosaurs had some sort of furry covering.

In the case of the fish-eating forms the fur would have needed to be waterproof – waterlogging would have made it too heavy for the pterosaur to fly. This in turn implies that they may have preened their fur, and had some equivalent of an oil gland to maintain the condition of the fur and repel water.

At the close of the Cretaceous Period the pterosaurs, despite having produced the largest flying creatures that have ever lived, became extinct and were replaced by birds. But this did not happen as a dramatic switch from one group of flying vertebrates to another, with a sudden victory to the birds. Birds first appeared during the Jurassic Period, the earliest authenticated bird being *Archaeopteryx*, and the two groups shared the skies for the best part of 100 million years. The evolution and radiation of birds start with relatively small insect eaters, which in the Late Jurassic and Early Cretaceous appear to replace the small pterosaurs: by the close of the Cretaceous the only remaining pterosaurs were extremely large. The birds themselves were descended from the dinosaurs, whose origins we shall look at briefly here before discussing them in detail in Chapter 8.

ORIGINS OF THE DINOSAURS

During Middle Triassic times there existed a wide range of small, medium, and large archosaurs. The large forms tended to be heavy, quadrupedal carnivores, partly armored, and with large, powerful legs which could be swung beneath the body. This arrangement ensured that they had a good stride and could move relatively quickly and efficiently when in pursuit of prey; but when inactive they also had the option of allowing their legs to sprawl sideways from the body in a more typically reptilian posture. From the construction of their limbs it seems that they had what was in effect a "two-gear" system: a slow, sprawling mode and a fast, high-walk mode. Modern crocodiles do just this, and in some respects capture the essence of the way these Triassic archosaurs moved.

Some of the larger archosaurs such as *Saurosuchus* developed a more permanent upright stance of their legs, which meant that they were obliged to use them like pillars to support their body weight all the time – not just when they were in pursuit. They did this by twisting the hip bones outward so that the legs hung vertically downward. The new arrangement had two advantages: not only was the stride efficient, but the pillar-like legs were better positioned to support greater body weight. A large animal would now be most uncomfortable in a sprawling posture, in which its heavy body would be difficult to support.

The smaller archosaurs had similarly constructed limbs. But, as in the case of *Lagosuchus*, the hind limbs in particular became very much longer and were clearly adapted to being swung under the body – enabling a greater stride length which would have been particularly advantageous for running. It would appear that the earliest dinosaurs arose from these smaller bipedal archosaurs at some time toward the close of the Middle Triassic Period.

The importance of legs and hips

Dinosaurs are distinguished from archosaurs by the structure of their legs and hips. Unlike the archosaurs, dinosaurs had legs which could only move in a vertical plane beneath the body. Because of changes in the arrangement of their legs and hips, they could not adopt the sprawling posture of conventional reptiles.

In the hips the socket for the upper leg bone (femur) has now become very deep and has an overhanging lip along its top edge; its inner side has developed an opening or window at the point where the three bones which make up the hip meet. The lower hip bones (pubis and ischium) are much elongated and point downward between the legs. The femur has a head (the part of the bone which forms the hip joint) which is offset at right angles to the main shaft of the bone so that it can fit neatly into the hip socket. The knee joint is arranged so that the lower leg bones will only be able to swing backward and forward, just as in the case of the human knee. The ankle bones are similarly simplified so that the foot can only swing backward and forward, while the toes are tightly bunched to produce a narrow foot, the sole of which is constantly raised from the ground. As a result all dinosaurs walked on their toes, rather than on the entire length of the foot as humans do. All these changes are very clear and relatively easy to identify in the skeleton, provided that the essential parts of the hips or hind leg are preserved.

Dinosaur hips are also highly relevant to the form that their descendants would take. The two evolutionary strands, known as lizard-hipped or saurischian, and bird-hipped or ornithischian, are described in detail opposite and illustrated below.

EARLY DINOSAURS

The earliest known dinosaurs, often classified under the general grouping of "protodinosaurs," come from Argentina. They are found in rocks dated at about 225 million years old, and include four types: *Eoraptor*, *Herrerasaurus*, *Staurikosaurus*, and *Pisanosaurus*. All are relatively small, bipedal creatures, which are not too distant from the almost contemporary archosaurs such as *Lagosuchus*.

Carnivores

Eoraptor, *Herrerasaurus*, and *Staurikosaurus* were all meat eaters. In each of these creatures the head was relatively large, as were the eyes, and the jaws were lined with very sharp, knife-shaped teeth for slicing through flesh. The earliest dinosaurs were clearly sleek predators. The body was balanced at the hips, with a long, counterbalancing

DINOSAUR HIPS

Bird hips

RIGHT *In ornithischians the hip bones are arranged like those of modern birds. The upper hip bone (ilium) is rigidly connected to the backbone, while the ischium points back and down towards the tail. The pubis, which in reptiles points forward and down, in these dinosaurs lies alongside the ischium. Curiously, later ornithischians developed a forward-pointing area of pubis.*

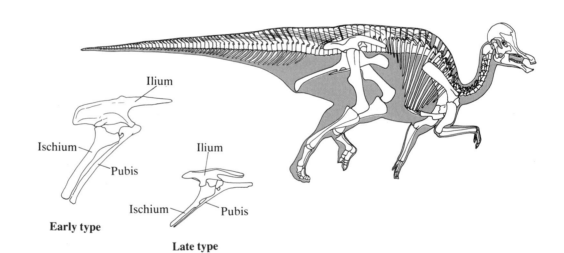

Ilium

Ischium — Pubis

Early type

Ilium

Ischium — Pubis

Late type

Ilium

Ischium — Pubis

Lizard hips
In this more conventional arrangement the ilium connects to the backbone, the ischium points down and back, while the pubis points forward and down as in most reptiles. Confusingly, the birds, which evolved from dinosaurs, are thought to have done so not from the ornithischian "bird-hipped" ones but from these saurischian "lizard-hipped". theropod types.

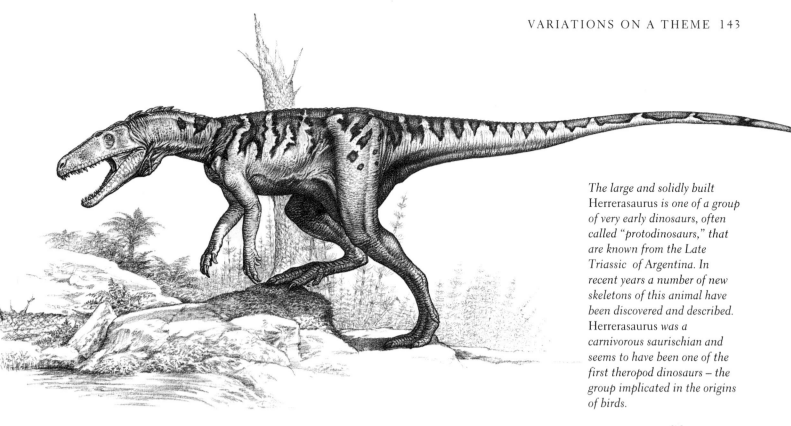

The large and solidly built Herrerasaurus *is one of a group of very early dinosaurs, often called "protodinosaurs," that are known from the Late Triassic of Argentina. In recent years a number of new skeletons of this animal have been discovered and described.* Herrerasaurus *was a carnivorous saurischian and seems to have been one of the first theropod dinosaurs – the group implicated in the origins of birds.*

tail, a relatively short trunk and a long, flexible neck. The arms were free to aid with the grasping of prey. This body form, once it was established, served predatory dinosaurs exceedingly well; dinosaurs of this general type lived on Earth for the next 160 million years.

Herbivores

Known only from a jaw with teeth, and parts of the spine, hips, and legs, *Pisanosaurus* is something of an enigma. The skeletal fragments indicate that this was a lightly built, long-legged animal with the limb structure of a dinosaur. The jaw is its most distinctive feature. It is quite short and deep, with a row of chisel-shaped teeth typical of a plant eater rather than a meat eater, and vaguely reminiscent of the jaw of the later herbivorous dinosaur *Heterodontosaurus* from South Africa. Further speculation on the part of paleontologists must await new fossil discoveries.

"Lizard hips" and "bird hips"

Saurischian ("lizard-hipped") dinosaurs include all the known carnivorous dinosaurs (theropods) and all the medium to very large herbivorous dinosaurs (sauropodomorphs). The hips of these dinosaurs are arranged in an entirely conventional manner, with all three bones radiating outward from the hip socket.

Ornithischian ("bird-hipped") dinosaurs include only herbivorous dinosaurs, and tend to be small to medium-sized creatures, distinguished not only by the shape of their hip bones but by their universal possession of a horny beak at the tip of their jaws. Their hip bones are different from those of saurischians because they are arranged in a pattern similar to that of living birds. The upper bone, known as the ilium, is in the normal position, though it frequently has a long, anterior prong. The two lower bones (the pubis and the ischium) lie together for much of their lengths and point backward and downward, so it appears that the pubis has swung backward to lie against the ischium.

Confusingly, during their later evolutionary history the ornithischians seem to have regrown a forwardly directed pubic bone by developing a small stub of bone near the front of the hip joint. In most fossil remains it is easy to discover that this has happened because a thin remnant of the original pubis remains alongside the ischium.

Why two types of hips?

There is no clear reason for this hard-and-fast distinction between the hips of saurischian and ornithischian dinosaurs. One notable theory that has been put forward by Dr Alan Charig contends that the differences reflect the way in which the muscles of the hips have been rearranged to cope with the way dinosaur legs work when they are close together.

From a mechanical point of view, it seems obvious that the lengthening of the bones of the pelvis is linked to the fact that the legs are moving vertically quite close together. The muscles attached to the lower pelvic bones which helped to swing the legs back and forth during the stride would not be so crowded against the upper leg bones, and would therefore be able to exert more force.

However, another problem outlined by Charig was that when the leg was swung forward it would have come perilously close to the pubis and the muscle which pulled the leg forward. This potential mechanical problem may have been overcome by the swinging of the pubis backward to lie against the ischium, and the migration of the pubis muscles up the front edge of the ilium to find a new position on the long anterior prong of the ilium.

This explanation seems to explain early ornithischian hips quite well. What it does not explain is why the pelvic arrangement of the saurischian dinosaurs persisted. Various ideas have been suggested, such as bipedality or quadrupedality with limited limb swings. But neither stands up to scrutiny. For the present, the jury is out.

THE PERMO-TRIASSIC WORLD

From the Late Triassic (225 mya) until the close of the Cretaceous Period (66 mya) the only significant land animals of any size were dinosaurs. I shall try to explain this overwhelming dominance in Chapter 8. But before moving on to that major topic I want to summarize some of the significant changes which had taken place on Earth during the time between the Late Carboniferous (330 mya) and the Late Triassic (just over 100 my later), so that we can put the changing populations of animals into a global context.

The majority of fossil deposits from Carboniferous times come from the tropical and subtropical zones of the world and are dominated by the coal swamps of these regions, which put a strong bias on the kinds of animals recovered. During Late Carboniferous and Early Permian times fossils were preserved in a wider range of environments. In tropical and subtropical regions at this time (the red bed deposits of Texas and central Russia) a mix of animals from drier uplands is found among a greater range of plant life. With the greater variety of plants, especially those which developed resistant seeds that were better able to survive in periodically dry areas, the vertebrates made the first major attempts to feed on them. The rise of a range of mammal-like reptile herbivores, starting with the early pelycosaurs such as *Edaphosaurus* and *Casea*, allows us to trace the changes in tooth shape, jaw action, and body form that took place during the Permian and Triassic Periods.

Much of our knowledge of the evolution of land animals during this timespan is derived from the extremely rich fossil beds of the Karoo Basin in South Africa. The complete sequence of sediments reveals a relatively cool temperate environment at first, following a period of Late Carboniferous glaciation – the southern continents were at this time positioned very close to the South Pole. In these conditions large, heavy-bodied, carnivorous mammal-like reptiles such as *Anteosaurus* predominated, alongside large, plant-eating pareiasaurs and small, possibly burrowing, procolophonids. The early mammal-like reptiles show a considerable change from the early long-bodied, very lizard-shaped pelycosaurs of the Late Carboniferous and Early Permian tropics. They may well have developed their barrel-shaped, compact bodies as a means of reducing their surface area to minimize heat loss through the skin, which seems to link with the notion that the sail-backed pelycosaurs were experimenting with body temperature control.

Through the Late Permian and Early Triassic, as the southern continents drifted north toward the tropical regions, the mammal-like reptiles became smaller and more varied in form. The dominant herbivores were the curious two-tusked dicynodonts, while a range of saber-toothed carnivores appeared. This change in variety and size perhaps reflects the general improvement in climate (reducing the need to have a large body mass to keep temperature changes to a sustainable minimum) and the greater variety of plant life, which evolved as a response to heavy predation by these early herbivores.

By Late Triassic times the climate had become increasingly hot and arid. In these conditions early dinosaurs began to appear. One of the most abundant was a large plant-eating saurischian, as much as 25 ft (7m) long, known as *Euskelosaurus*, but as conditions became drier and more desert-like it was replaced by a smaller and more lightly built herbivore known as *Massospondylus*, 6 to 9 ft (2 to 3m) long. Alongside this is evidence of some early ornithischian dinosaurs, *Lesothosaurus* and *Heterodontosaurus*. The very earliest mammals, such as *Megazostrodon*, are also found in these Late Triassic or earliest Jurassic times. But these mammals were extremely small shrew-like creatures no more than 4 ins (10cm) long, while the dinosaurs were 3 ft (1m) or more in length.

In the Late Carboniferous (ABOVE RIGHT), North America and Asia were separate and largely in the Northern Hemisphere. South America, Africa, Antarctica, and Australia were all joined. Southern Africa's polar position accounts for the extensive evidence of glaciations at this time. By Late Permian times (ABOVE CENTER) the southern continents had moved north, colliding with the northern ones. As they drifted away from the polar latitudes they came under the influence of milder climates. In the Triassic (RIGHT) the supercontinent Pangea continued to migrate north. The joining of the continents allowed previously separated animal groups to mingle: some of them achieved worldwide distribution.

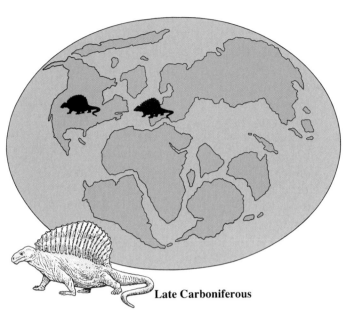

Edaphosaurus

Late Carboniferous

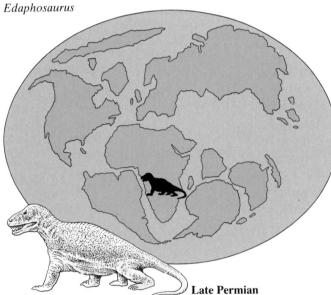

Anteosaurus

Late Permian

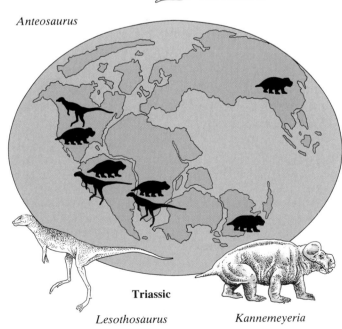

Lesothosaurus

Triassic

Kannemeyeria

CONTINENTS COLLIDE

During the Late Permian the large continental blocks, which had been separated by seas of varying size, gradually converged and joined together for the only time in the Earth's history to form a single enormous supercontinent named Pangea ("all Earth"). As a result the large mobile animals – vertebrates in particular – were able to migrate right across the supercontinent; this had a peculiar evolutionary consequence – fewer types of animal. Clearly, allowing animals to mingle in this way introduced competition between them. Thus the fossils on land at this time (Late Permian and Early Triassic) tend to look the same no matter where they are found. For example, the Early Triassic dicynodont *Lystrosaurus* is found in Africa, North America, China, and Antarctica, as are the therapsid *Thrinaxodon* and the little herbivore *Procolophon*. Such cosmopolitan species only make sense if the continents of the world were all together in one mass at this time.

A similar reduction in the range of species is seen in the seas. Estimates suggest that as many as 80 per cent of all sea creatures became extinct between the Early and Late Permian – a truly incredible period of extinction, far more dramatic than the event that marked the end of the dinosaurs at the close of the Cretaceous.

There are many explanations for the dramatic decline in the variety of fossil sea creatures in the Late Permian. It could of course be a false conclusion brought about by a lack of appropriate sedimentary deposits. However, the consequences of all the continents becoming "glued" together may indeed have been profound for sea creatures, most of which live on the continental shelf. First, joining the continents together removes a huge area of coastline. Second, the collision of the continents would have made the sea floor stop spreading for a time, while the huge undersea mountain ranges that formed along the spreading ridges on the ocean floors would have subsided. This in turn means that the volume of the ocean beds would have increased and sea levels would have dropped dramatically, perhaps by 300ft (100m) or more. Thus the sea would have retreated from the remaining continental shelf area as well. The effect on sea life would have been catastrophic.

Dramatic though these effects might have been in the sea and on the land, the most important change in land vertebrates was to take place at the close of the Triassic rather than the Permian. This was the switch from communities dominated by mammal-like reptiles to ones dominated by dinosaurs. Some of the mammal-like reptiles of the Triassic were surprisingly sophisticated, so their replacement by reptiles seems at first sight to be an unexpected mystery.

8

DINOSAURS AND BIRDS

AN UNEXPECTED STEP IN THE EVOLUTION OF LIFE

THE APPEARANCE of the first dinosaurs in the Late Triassic Period (225 mya) marks a major change in the history of vertebrate life on Earth. Until that time the evolution of the vertebrates had followed what appeared to be a steady and in some ways predictable course from the early tetrapods via the synapsids (mammal-like reptiles) towards the first true mammals. With the discovery of the fossilized remains of early mammals such as *Megazostrodon* in southern Africa, *Eozostrodon* in Europe, and *Sinoconodon* in China, all from about the same time in the Late Triassic or earliest Jurassic, it appeared that mammals had truly arrived. However, instead of eventually rising to dominance, for the next 160 million years they remained a relatively insignificant part of land-based life.

ABOVE *The feathers and flying lifestyle of* Archaeopteryx *mark it as an early bird, but it still has reptilian characteristics such as a long, bony tail.*

RIGHT *Dinosaurs had a definite impact during the Mesozoic. This scene shows the potential forest-clearing abilities of a herd of huge apatosaurs, flattening trees in the same way as the much smaller modern elephants.*

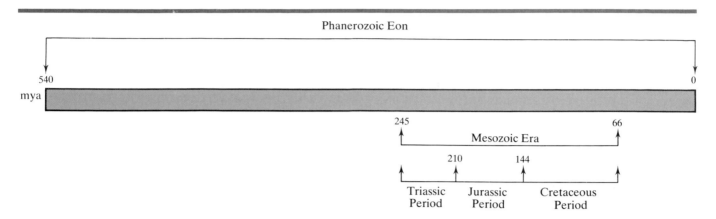

Phanerozoic Eon

540

mya

0

245   66

Mesozoic Era

210   144

Triassic   Jurassic   Cretaceous
Period   Period   Period

Timescale of Earth history. *Dinosaurs and birds both originated in the Mesozoic. The prelude to the rise of the dinosaurs was the extraordinary, unpredictable decline of the mammal-like reptiles,* *which late in the Triassic were replaced first by archosaurs and subsequently by true dinosaurs. Dinosaurs then dominated life on land for 160 million years.*

This waxing of the fortunes of mammal-like reptiles during the Permian and Early Triassic Periods, followed by their decline in abundance and variety before the appearance of the first mammals, and the sudden rise of dinosaurs in the Late Triassic, are among the least expected of events. For when we compare living reptiles and mammals today, the mammals seem to possess all the features to ensure success.

Mammals can generate body heat internally (they are said to be endothermic) and use subcutaneous fat, body hair, and sweat glands to control their body temperature very precisely. Such fine control ensures that they are not affected by climatic changes to the degree that reptiles are, and as a consequence are much more widely distributed across the world. The mammalian ability to control body temperature is linked to their relatively large brains and high intelligence. The brain is in effect a chemical machine and all chemical reactions are temperature-dependent. If the temperature of the brain can be maintained within strictly defined limits, its chemicals can work in regular and predictable ways and it can become a large and complex organ.

Reptiles, on the other hand, rely on external sources of heat (ultimately the Sun) and are said to be ecto-thermic, as a result of which they are largely restricted to the tropics and subtropical regions and are very scarce at higher latitudes. They can minimize temperature changes in the body by adopting particular behavior patterns in certain conditions – for example, they can bask in the Sun to raise their temperature to the desired level, and seek shade if they become too hot. However, this does not render them immune to temperature change. On cool, overcast days it may be impossible to bask, and therefore impossible for them to reach the optimum

temperature for body and brain activities. The animal may therefore be sluggish or unresponsive, even in a life-threatening situation such as the appearance of a predator. Because of their inability to control their body temperature well, the brains of reptiles can neither grow as large, nor become as advanced, as those of mammals.

These are the obvious differences which sum up what makes it so good to be a mammal, and why, if reptiles

Winners and losers: this is a simple representation of the changing fortunes of the mammal-like reptiles and earliest mammals (which fell into steady decline as the Triassic ended) and the archosaurs and dinosaurs (which became steadily more abundant through the Late Triassic and into the Jurassic).

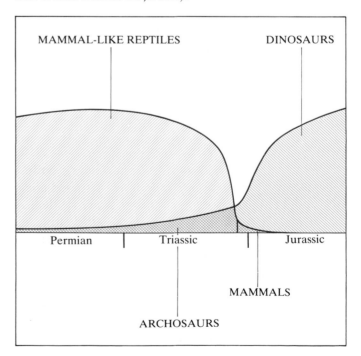

MAMMAL-LIKE REPTILES   DINOSAURS

Permian   Triassic   Jurassic

MAMMALS

ARCHOSAURS

and mammals were placed in a competitive situation, a bookmaker would firmly favor the mammal. Because mammals have far greater control over their body mechanisms, are effectively independent of the external environment, and are far more intelligent, they are more responsive to change and much more resourceful under conditions of stress.

We see this range of attributes around us all the time – not only in the human species, whose intelligence has had such a profound effect on the Earth, but also in an astonishing and bewildering variety of mammal species. Polar bears, for instance, survive in the frozen wastes of the Arctic, whales are beautifully adapted to life in the sea, and bats are capable of catching insects by echo location using ultrasonic squeaks.

Looking back through the fossil record, we can see that all this mammalian potential was available shortly after the appearance of the first mammals in the Late Triassic. Instead two factors – one of which is the qualities of the dinosaurs themselves, while the other remains a mystery – held this enormous biological potential in abeyance for 160 million years. The potential was finally released in a burst of evolutionary activity that took place only after another mysterious event had wiped out the dinosaurs at the end of the Cretaceous.

This entirely unexpected event adds spice to the history of life on Earth because it shows that life does not necessarily develop and progress in predictable ways. It also throws into question certain preconceived notions, such as the one that in some real way mammals are superior to reptiles. The fossil record seems to show us quite clearly that this is not necessarily so.

WHY DID DINOSAURS SUCCEED?

A number of theories have been put forward to explain how or why dinosaurs were successful at the expense of mammals at the end of the Triassic Period.

Leg posture

It has already been noted that dinosaurs have a posture unique among reptiles, in that the legs are tucked under the body in the form of pillars. This allows the legs to support the weight of the body very efficiently, and enables the animal to use long strides and thus to move very quickly over the ground.

While this shift in limb posture was taking place among the archosaurs, which were the dinosaurs' ancestors, the mammal-like reptiles were decreasing in size and beginning to experiment with limb design. Many of the mammal-like reptiles of the Late Permian and Early

Triassic began to develop longer legs positioned underneath the body. It is argued, however, that the archosaurs had perfected their limb posture first. Their greater agility and prowess as hunters allowed them to out-compete their fellow hunters among the mammal-like reptiles. Heavy predation of the herbivore members of the mammal-like reptiles also provided an opportunity for herbivorous archosaurs to evolve, and these were followed by some of the earliest herbivorous dinosaurs.

The rise of the dinosaurs can therefore be traced back to improvements in the limbs of Triassic archosaurs. Mammals, and their antecedents the mammal-like reptiles, did not achieve their own changes in time to prevent a takeover by the archosaurs. Once the later archosaurs and true dinosaurs had appeared they dominated the larger ecological niches, even though by this time some of the earliest true mammals had appeared and finally achieved a fully erect leg posture as well.

Dinosaurs as endotherms

A radical alternative to this idea was suggested by Dr Robert Bakker in the late 1960s. Assuming that mammals will always be superior to ordinary reptiles, and noting the rapid shift right at the end of the Triassic from mammal-like reptiles and mammals, Bakker proposed that the only logical explanation left was to assume that dinosaurs were not "ordinary" reptiles but "extraordinary" ones. They had to be endothermic, as mammals are today, and he put forward a number of intriguing arguments in favor of this suggestion.

○ Alone among reptiles, dinosaurs have upright legs. The only other groups that have erect limb postures are living birds and mammals – both of which are endothermic. It was therefore suggested that to be able to achieve an upright posture dinosaurs had to be endothermic in the first place.
○ This argument was refined a little later when it was noted that among erect endotherms again only dinosaurs, birds, and mammals had been able to achieve true bipedality. The degree of coordination necessary to adopt this posture suggested once again that dinosaurs had a complex brain – which implied that they were endothermic.
○ Another line of evidence brought in to support the notion that dinosaurs were endotherms came from counting skeletons in museums. It was found that those of predatory dinosaurs were much rarer than those of potential prey dinosaurs. This obvious imbalance is reflected in modern-day communities: predatory cats on the African plains, for instance, are few in number

compared to their prey animals. But when ancient reptile communities were examined a different pattern emerged, in which the numbers of predators and potential prey were more nearly equal. Nobody disputed that the ancient reptiles were ectothermic, so it appeared that ectothermic predators had relatively low food requirements and that quite high numbers of predators could live alongside their prey. Endotherms require far more food than ectotherms – much of what they eat is used by the body to produce heat, which explains why there are fewer predatory cats than their potential prey in modern Africa. The imbalance of predator and prey in dinosaur collections in museums therefore suggests that the predators may have been endothermic.

○ Examination of thin, polished slices of dinosaur bone under high-powered microscopes revealed the details of bone structure and blood supply. The overall structure, when compared to that of living mammal and reptile bones, resembled the former more than the latter. Mammal and dinosaur bones seemed more vascular (had more passages for blood vessels) than those of modern reptiles. The structure of bone is thought to reflect the activity level of the animal, and again the similarity between mammals and dinosaurs suggested high levels of activity – which made sense only if it was assumed that dinosaurs were endothermic.

○ Indications from the shapes of dinosaur skulls (some have elaborate crests, horns, or frills), large accumulations of footprints in some areas, and discoveries of apparent herds of dinosaurs in some locations, indicated that dinosaurs were involved in quite complicated behavior patterns – perhaps mating displays, herding or various forms of social signalling. All these seemed more comparable to the behavior patterns displayed by complex endotherms such as mammals and birds today.

○ Work on the skulls and brain size of dinosaurs tended to support the notion that some dinosaurs, particularly the carnivorous types, had quite large brains. A controlled, warm, endothermic body would have been needed to keep such a brain working properly.

○ Some plant-eating dinosaurs developed huge batteries of grinding teeth, which implies that they ate a great deal of food. Plant-eating mammals today, such as horses and elephants, have big grinding teeth. They need to eat a great deal of food to fuel their endothermic bodies; perhaps the same applied to these dinosaurs.

○ Circumstantial evidence points to dinosaurs having a fully divided and very large muscular heart – notably the fact that in the majority of dinosaurs the head is held above the normal level of the heart. The implications of this are explained in detail on pages 153-54. Again, it is only endothermic birds and mammals which possess a fully divided heart.

○ Finally, it is increasingly becoming recognized that birds and dinosaurs are very closely related. Some very bird-like dinosaurs have been discovered in recent years, and the earliest known bird, *Archaeopteryx*, is very dinosaur-like. Since birds are indisputably endothermic creatures, it follows that their ancestors may also have been endothermic.

A matter of luck?

In recent years it has become fashionable to look at the history of life on Earth as a series of incredibly improbable events, or accidents, rather than the more traditional view of it being a very slow unravelling of an extremely complex, but more or less continuous, thread. Stephen Jay Gould's bestselling book *Wonderful Life* portrayed this theme with considerable passion.

Attempts to gain a more precise view of the events of the Late Triassic have resulted in censuses being taken of the animals that lived in the interval between the first mammal-like reptiles' domination of the land and the appearance of dinosaurs in considerable range and variety. Depending upon how the data is interpreted, the success of dinosaurs in the long term may have been either a matter of gradual transition from mammal-like reptiles plus archosaurs to dinosaur-dominated communities, or a situation in which communities of mammal-like reptiles and archosaurs continued in harmony up to a specific moment, after which they were rapidly replaced by dinosaur-dominated ones.

The latter interpretation has formed the basis of an important argument which probes the very nature of any apparent succession of animal types in the fossil record and the degree to which it indicates evolutionary change in time. It is argued that the notion of major groups of animals competing with each other (by means of changes in their leg posture, say, or by virtue of their body temperature control) is misleading. Animals can be seen as competing as individuals in an ecosystem in the present day – that is one of the bases of modern ecology. But it seems much less likely that major groups (mammal-like reptiles and archosaurs) competed over a timespan measured in millions of years.

So relatively abrupt change, in this case from a world dominated by archosaurs and mammal-like reptiles to one dominated by dinosaurs, is favored. The sudden flip from one pattern to another is thought not to be driven by any form of competition, but to reflect some chance event that affected the Earth. Dinosaurs are seen in essence as simply lucky: they survived some ill-defined ecological catastrophe which claimed many other groups, notably the mammal-like reptiles and earlier archosaurs. No suitable cause has yet been identified for the supposed catastrophe that affected the Late Triassic world, although more recent discoveries are tending to blur the boundary of the so-called event. For the moment this view should be regarded as an important counterpoint to the more usual arguments concerning the rise of dinosaurs.

My own view of the origin and success of dinosaurs over other reptiles in the Late Triassic comes from a consideration of some of the factors mentioned above (in particular the way that mammals and reptiles work), and others (in particular the environmental conditions) which seem to challenge the assumption that mammals are superior to dinosaurs under all circumstances.

The geographical and fossil history of Africa in the Late Paleozoic and Early Mesozoic is encapsulated in these pictures of the modern world. In the Middle Permian, following the glaciation of the southern continents, the Karoo would have been tundra-like as in present-day Spitsbergen (TOP LEFT). By Late Permian times Africa had drifted north toward the equator and entered a relatively warmer cool-temperature climatic zone, represented here by a Swedish landscape (TOP RIGHT). The Middle Triassic saw the equivalent of a Mediterranean climate which was primarily warm and wet, such as in modern Majorca (BOTTOM LEFT). By Late Triassic/Early Jurassic times Africa had drifted into the equatorial desert zone, similar to present-day Saudi Arabia (BOTTOM RIGHT). Over tens of millions of years animals in Africa had to adapt to these steadily changing conditions.

RIGHT *Modern horsetails* (Equisetum palustre) *can be traced back to the Carboniferous, when they were substantial trees – browse fodder for both mammal-like reptiles and dinosaurs.*

BELOW *In the Late Paleozoic all the southern continents were dominated by* Glossopteris *("tongue wing"). For a long time it was thought to be a small, shrubby plant which formed the staple diet of browsing mammal-like reptiles, but nowadays the more widely held view is that it was much larger and tree-like, growing up to about 20ft (6m) tall.*

Environment

The rocks of the Karoo Basin of South Africa provide an almost unbroken sequence from the Late Carboniferous to the end of the Triassic, and provide an indication not only of the animals that lived through much of this time but also of the prevailing climate. Late Carboniferous–Early Permian times were dominated by glacial conditions, since the southern continents were still close to the South Pole. Mid-Permian conditions were a little warmer, with tundra dominating as the southern continents drifted northward. In the Late Permian cool, temperate conditions seem to have prevailed, and the first evidence of well-preserved, abundant, and quite large mammal-like reptiles is found in association with lowland coastal areas dominated by seed ferns (*Glossopteris*) and horsetails (*Equisetum*).

By Early and Middle Triassic times the climate was steadily improving and became predominantly warm–temperate, with lush vegetation supporting large numbers of mammal-like reptiles and smaller numbers of other types of reptile. These warm conditions become more and more prevalent as time passed and the continent drifted to lower and lower latitudes.

In Late Triassic times the climate was warm and dry. Short-lived streams supported narrow bands of vegetation and these in turn supported the populations of early dinosaurs, small mammal-like reptiles and early mammals. These conditions gave way finally to dry continental desert in the Early Jurassic, when dinosaurs seemed to predominate along with rare early mammals.

The rest of the Mesozoic Era (the combined Triassic, Jurassic, and Cretaceous Periods, which encompasses the time of the dinosaurs) was singularly warm and mild compared to the Earth today. There were no marked latitudinal climate bands such as we see today between the tropics and the polar regions, because there were neither northern nor southern polar ice caps.

REPTILES AND MAMMALS COMPARED

The most obvious difference between living mammals and reptiles is the way they control body temperature, which has already been explained in detail on page 148. To recapitulate briefly, mammals are endotherms, a condition which has some fixed requirements.

○ The external environment must be cooler than the mammal; otherwise it cannot easily lose heat and it risks overheating if it moves about at all (using muscles generates extra body heat).

○ A great deal of food must be available because 70 to 80 per cent of everything eaten by an endotherm is used to create heat.

○ Mammals have very little tolerance of changes in body temperature and rapidly exhibit signs of stress if it is raised by more than a few degrees, or fall into a potentially fatal state of torpor (hypothermia) if it drops significantly.

○ Losing heat by evaporative cooling – sweating or panting – means that liquid is lost to the environment, especially in warm conditions. Mammals therefore need constant access to fresh water.

Reptiles are ectotherms, and as a result have a very different strategy for life on land.

○ They live in areas that are relatively warm and are incapable of colonizing the cooler parts of the world.

○ They need only feed sparingly because they do not have to use food energy to create internal heat.

○ They lose very little water through the body, and therefore have no need to replace it. Indeed they conserve water in unexpected ways. Reptiles do not urinate as mammals do, but produce limey droppings similar to those of birds. Many also have salt glands, usually in the region of the eyes, nose, or mouth, which help to reduce water loss.

○ Reptiles can tolerate varying body temperatures.

There are certain environments where being a reptile may have some benefits, and one of these is a hot desert. For most land animals deserts are very challenging environments. Water is limited. So is food, because of the virtual absence of plants at the bottom of the food chain. Temperatures can range from extreme heat in the day to freezing at night. This combination of features runs counter to everything that seems essential to an endothermic mammal, and favors reptiles.

If this observation is applied to the time of dinosaur origins, it corresponds (in the Karoo at least) to a time of high temperatures and desert conditions. It is also the case that the earliest mammals were tiny – possibly nocturnal insectivores. Such creatures are best able to avoid the extremes of day- and night-time temperatures by living in burrows and emerging only when conditions are favorable; they also rely on food that is relatively abundant in the desert – insects. Like reptiles, insects with their waxy cuticles, ectothermy, and water conservation mechanisms are well adapted to desert-like conditions, which is why animals such as cockroaches survive so well in our modern centrally heated offices and homes.

I therefore see the success of dinosaurs as the triumph of reptile design over that of mammals at a unique time in Earth history. The story, however, is not quite as simple as that. As hinted at by Bakker, dinosaurs also appeared to do certain quite un-reptilian things which point to something unusual about the group as a whole.

Dinosaur hearts

Most dinosaurs adopted a posture in which the head and brain were higher than the heart. This implies that the heart had to be more powerful than that of typical reptiles, which have their head and heart at about the same level, because it would have to raise the blood pressure high enough to lift the blood to the level of the brain.

But having a heart capable of creating very high blood pressure poses a potential problem for other parts of the body, particularly the lungs with their delicate, thin-walled linings which can easily burst. To overcome this, it seems highly likely that the heart was divided down the middle, as it is in modern mammals and birds. This enables the blood to circulate at low pressure in the lungs and at much higher pressure elsewhere in the body.

In the undivided main pumping chamber of an amphibian heart (LEFT), oxygenated blood (pink) from the lungs mixes with deoxygenated (blue) returning from the body. Reptiles (CENTER) have a partly divided chamber, which reduces the mixing and gives them more energy. With the fully divided heart of mammals, birds, and probably dinosaurs (RIGHT), unmixed oxygen-rich blood circulating in the body provides high energy potential.

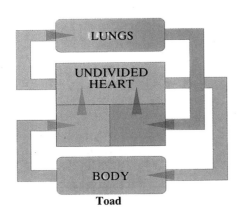

Toad

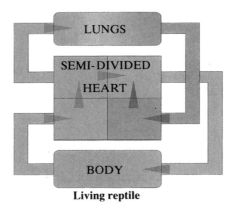

Living reptile

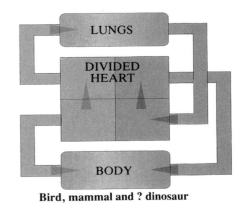

Bird, mammal and ? dinosaur

Troodon emphasizes some of the qualities of the dinosaurian reptile. The upright posture required a sophisticated brain to maintain balance. Its very long legs suggest an ability to run fast, and therefore high activity levels. It possessed raptorial claws on its feet, indicating a highly athletic killing technique. And finally it had a large brain, large forward-pointing eyes, and almost hand-like grasping claws. This was no ordinary reptile!

Having a divided heart with high pressure and low pressure circuits has a further benefit. Moving blood around the body at pressure and speed can facilitate rapid movement and sustained levels of activity that might have been impossible for conventional reptiles. Dinosaurs may well have had the benefits both of living economically as reptiles, and of being highly active.

Legs, posture, and intelligence

Being able to sustain high activity levels may also make sense of the legs and body posture of dinosaurs. Having an efficient heart and lungs allowed them to be active runners, especially in the case of the many bipedal types. The coordination of an active bipedal animal requires a sophisticated brain. This may well account for the relatively large brain of some of the apparently very agile, small predatory dinosaurs.

However, many of the claims concerning dinosaur intelligence, based on herding, nesting behavior, and social display – which were previously considered quite startling – have now been put in perspective. It would appear that for a long time we have had a very blinkered view of just how "intelligent" modern reptiles can be. For example, the zoologist Dr Hugh Cott has shown by observation of crocodile behavior in the wild (not in zoos, where they lie around and doze perpetually) that parental behavior and social interaction are very complex and well developed in these reptiles, and that dinosaur nesting behavior and social activities are not as remarkably bird- or mammal-like as was at first thought.

Growth and temperature control

Finally we come to the question of temperature control. Dinosaurs were on average large animals: none was less than 3 ft (1m) long, the majority were between 15 and 30 ft (5 and 10m) and a few were much larger. As explained earlier, one of the advantages (or in some cases disadvantages) of being large is that the surface area of the skin is small compared to total body volume. This means that the interior of the body is buffered against what might be happening outside.

A simple example is provided once again by crocodiles. If the body temperatures of baby crocodiles are measured over 24 hours they are found to fluctuate quite a lot, and tend to mirror quite closely the changes in external temperature. Adult crocodiles, in contrast, show far less marked temperature changes during the same period. The large size of the adult ensures that it is to some extent buffered against outside temperature changes.

In dinosaurs, it is possible to imagine a situation in which the average environmental temperatures were high, ensuring a high body temperature which would be perfect for high levels of activity. If there were occasional short periods of cold, then the sheer size of the dinosaurs would have allowed them to be buffered against such change and to remain active.

Baby dinosaurs would, however, be more vulnerable to temperature change – which presents the biggest problem to this whole area of theorizing. Work by Professor Armand de Ricqlès and Dr John Horner on the structure of the bone of baby dinosaurs has suggested that they were much like modern baby birds. They suggest that young dinosaurs had very warm bodies; they were to all intents and purposes endotherms (even though they lacked an essential insulating layer to keep the heat in) and grew very quickly to subadult size. However, as they grew larger their body chemistry gradually slowed down and they became more conventionally ectothermic, though they kept an even, warm body temperature because the climate was relatively constant and warm, and because their bodies were large and thermally buffered against short cold spells.

From these conditions it would appear that dinosaurs, though in many ways like conventional reptiles, had a number of unique attributes: they were large and had efficient legs and powerful hearts, they could move very quickly, they were well coordinated, and they had warm bodies. This remarkable combination of features existed at a time of warm climate worldwide.

Dinosaurs emerge as reptiles with a style of life which was perfectly suited to the Mesozoic world. Mammals, though they appeared in the Late Triassic, never really stood a chance in comparison.

Once dinosaurs had established themselves on land as small agile carnivores and herbivores they rapidly radiated into a number of distinctive types, no doubt filling an increasingly rich and varied set of ecological niches, and became noticeably abundant. Dinosaur fossils of certain types become quite easy to find in some Late Triassic rocks. Among the most abundant are the early predators, such as the theropod dinosaur *Coelophysis*, which has been found in large numbers in New Mexico. Equally the herbivores such as the prosauropod *Massospondylus* from South Africa and the European *Plateosaurus* are also found in considerable numbers.

EVOLUTION OF THE SAURISCHIANS

There were two major groups of saurischian dinosaurs: they comprised the carnivorous theropods and the herbivorous sauropodomorphs.

Early theropods

Once theropods appeared, their basic structure and design changed surprisingly little throughout their evolutionary history. *Eoraptor* from the early part of the Late Triassic is one of the earliest theropods, and defines theropod body design very neatly. The back legs were long and supported the whole weight of the body at the hip joint. The body was balanced by the long tail, which formed a cantilever against the relatively short and compact trunk, curved neck, and head. The arms, freed from weight support, were capable of grasping prey, and the claws were viciously hooked. The neck was moderately long and had a bird-like flexibility combined with strength. The skull was lightly built, the eyes were large – it clearly hunted by eyesight – and the teeth were compressed, curved blades, with saw-like edges for slicing through flesh.

Eoraptor ("dawn predator") is one of three very early dinosaurs that have been discovered in Argentina, in rocks in the foothills of the Andes that date back 225 million years. The long, strong hind limbs and lengthy, counterbalancing tail enabled this dinosaur to walk bipedally. The chest region is relatively short and compact, while the neck is long and flexible. Eoraptor *was clearly a predator: first, because its sharp, curved teeth were designed for cutting flesh, and second, because the short, powerful arms ended in sharply clawed hands for holding and disabling prey.*

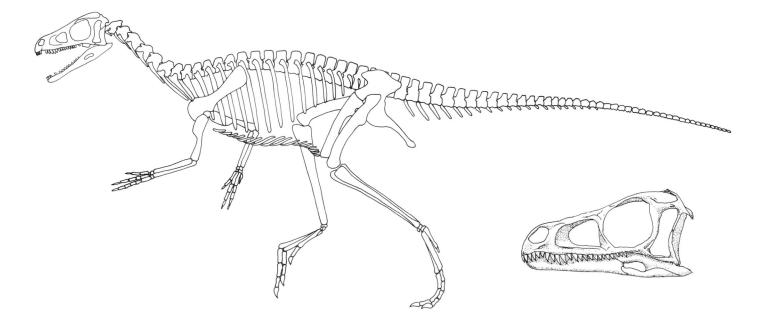

Two basic trends

Later Triassic and Early Jurassic theropods are built on similar lines to *Eoraptor*. However, two marked trends emerge. Some were large, heavy predators capable of tackling larger prey – these are distinguished by their large heads and jaws, short powerful necks, fairly short arms, and heavy, pillar-like legs. Smaller types, on the other hand, retained the features seen in the early forms, which were built for speed and agility.

Jurassic types

Theropods of the Early Jurassic are a little more varied than the very earliest types. The most common are *Coelophysis* and *Dilophosaurus*. *Coelophysis* ("hollow

face") was a medium-sized theropod (6ft/2m long) of slender build. It is of particular interest because it has been found in relatively large numbers in quarries in the southern United States; a closely related form called *Syntarsus* has been found in southern Africa.

The American finds include complete skeletons, which show that some of these creatures practiced cannibalism – they have traces of the bones of juveniles in the area where the stomach lies. It has been suggested that they might have been the remains of embryos, as with the ichthyosaurs (see pages 128-29), but here it seems that the skeletons are dismembered and partly digested, rather than intact and at the back of the abdomen where they might be expected if they were embryos awaiting birth.

Such observations require some explanation, because cannibalism does not seem a wise strategy for any species. Some present-day carnivores exhibit cannibalism – when a male lion takes over a new pride he immediately kills all the young cubs. This is interpreted by biologists as a means of ensuring that all the new cubs sired in the pride are his; it is a selfish act, but one that makes sense in terms of the survival of his genetic characteristics. *Coelophysis* might have been exhibiting the same kind of behavior. The large numbers of skeletons found in the

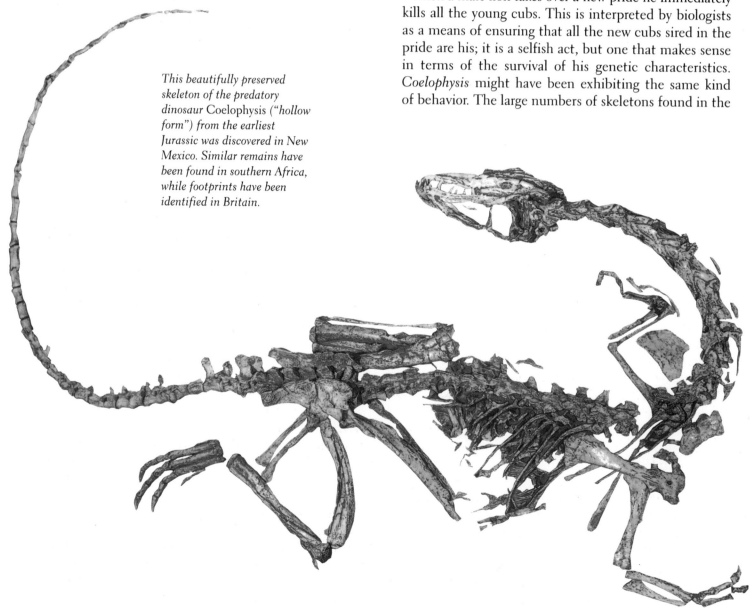

This beautifully preserved skeleton of the predatory dinosaur Coelophysis *("hollow form") from the earliest Jurassic was discovered in New Mexico. Similar remains have been found in southern Africa, while footprints have been identified in Britain.*

Like most predators, Coelophysis *may well have had a varied diet – being a fast-moving, agile creature it would probably have been attracted by anything that moved. Large insects were abundant during the Mesozoic, and may well have been considered fair game by young* Coelophysis.

same area of Arizona certainly suggest that this dinosaur was a pack animal rather than a lone hunter.

Dilophosaurus was a much larger theropod. Its body proportions were not much different from those of *Coelophysis*, but it had fin-like crests on its head. This very distinctive feature accounts for its name, which means "two-ridged reptile." Growing to lengths of about 13 to 16ft (4 to 5m), this dinosaur has been credited with being a scavenger, because of claims that it had relatively weak jaws and teeth.

Later in the Jurassic numerous theropods are known, ranging from the tiny *Compsognathus* (in life probably little more than 3ft/1m in length) to the large allosaurs, such as *Allosaurus* and *Ceratosaurus*.

Compsognathus took small prey such as lizards (the remains of one was actually found in its belly), for which its light build and nimble footwork were well adapted.

The heavily built forms were no doubt the major predators of the time. Long-striding on huge legs, and with very powerfully built necks and skulls, they would have been capable of pulling down large dinosaurs, especially if they hunted in groups. Again, large accumulations of the bones of these dinosaurs in some quarries in North America lend some credibility to this idea.

Dromaeosaurs

During Cretaceous times the general design of predatory dinosaurs began to vary more substantially from the basic "large" and "small" varieties recovered in the Triassic and Jurassic. Why this was so is not certain, but anatomically they certainly appear to be more varied and may well have been adopting strategies for dealing either with a wider range of prey, or with more varied techniques for catching and killing it.

Dromaeosaurs make their appearance in the Early Cretaceous, in the form of well-known dinosaurs such as *Deinonychus*. On the whole these were relatively small predators 9 to 13ft (3 to 4m) long, with moderate to large heads, large brains, large eyes, long grasping hands,

stiff tails, and extraordinary hind legs. The legs were powerfully built and the feet modified so that they walked on two of their four toes only. The first toe was quite short and resembled a dog's "dew claw," while the second toe was modified into a retractable, wickedly hooked, slashing claw – the source of the *Deinonychus* name, which means "terrible claw."

These were clearly highly intelligent, fast-moving predators able to run down prey and kill them with a combination of bites from their powerful jaws and vicious kicks from the hind feet. The discovery of a number of skeletons of this dinosaur close to the skeleton of the larger plant eater *Tenontosaurus* suggests that these animals may well have hunted in packs.

Deinonychus seems to have been the model for the creatures called "*Velociraptor*" in the film *Jurassic Park*. The real *Velociraptor* is a smaller form (6ft/2m long) of this type of dinosaur, whose remains have been found in Mongolia. *Velociraptor* is of special note because in the 1970s a Polish–Mongolian expedition recovered a complete skeleton of this dinosaur with its arms clasping the

While undoubtedly smaller than their prey, a pack of dromaeosaurs, such as these Deinonychus, *could have finished off the large ornithopod* Tenontosaurus. *A skeleton of the latter has been found with the skeletons of several* Deinonychus, *which may well have died in the fight. This strategy is exhibited today by Cape hunting dogs, which can exhaust and finally kill much larger wildebeest (see page 203).*

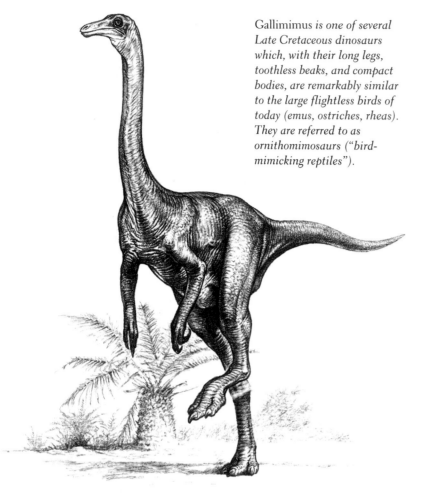

Gallimimus is one of several Late Cretaceous dinosaurs which, with their long legs, toothless beaks, and compact bodies, are remarkably similar to the large flightless birds of today (emus, ostriches, rheas). They are referred to as ornithomimosaurs ("bird-mimicking reptiles").

skeleton of another – the plant-eating *Protoceratops*. This seems to be an extremely rare example of dinosaur predation caught in the act.

Very recently a new and extremely large dromaeosaur has been found in Utah, and named *Utahraptor*. If correctly interpreted, this animal may have been up to 25 ft (8m) long and would have been capable of bringing down some of the very largest dinosaurs.

Ornithomimosaurs

Another group of theropods, the ornithomimosaurs ("bird mimics"), adopted a very different lifestyle. These dinosaurs developed extremely long, slender legs, clearly adapted for fast running; lost their teeth, and developed a sharp, bird-like, horn-covered beak; and had long, grasping hands which ended in claws rather than sharply hooked talons as in the case of dromaeosaurs. These creatures (*Gallimimus*, *Ornithomimus*, and *Dromiceiomimus* are typical examples) closely resembled large, living ground birds such as emus and ostriches, and are thought to have had a similar lifestyle. Feeding on a wide range of foodstuffs – small vertebrates, invertebrates, fruits, berries, and leaves – they avoided predators by being extremely nimble, fast runners.

Oviraptorosaurs

Another group of theropods which also lacked teeth and had bird-like beaks were the oviraptorosaurs. These dinosaurs were slender and fleet-footed, but had more raptorial hands, as well as curious snub-nosed faces and bizarre protuberances on their heads.

Oviraptor ("egg-snatcher") also comes from Mongolia and appears to have been a possible scavenger of eggs from the nests of other dinosaurs. Numerous egg fragments or nest sites, mainly those of the dinosaur *Protoceratops*, have been found in this part of the world. One explanation for the short, powerful beak of *Oviraptor* and the curious sharp ridges in the roof of its mouth is that it preyed on dinosaur eggs – either cracking them open directly, or putting them in its mouth and then cracking them so that the contents could be swallowed and the shell fragments spat out.

Tyrannosaurs

At the close of the Cretaceous Period some of the best known of all dinosaurs appeared, the tyrannosaurs. A distinct family of predatory dinosaurs, they are distinguished by their large size, solid skulls, and (to our eyes) ridiculously small arms and hands.

In essence the body form is little different from that of any other large theropod. Their long, powerful legs allowed these dinosaurs to move very swiftly, even if they could not run with the agility and nimbleness of their smaller relatives.

Tyrannosaurs relied on a devastating attacking technique. The huge head had jaws lined with relatively enormous, spear-like teeth; these animals very probably ran at their prey – other large dinosaurs – with the mouth wide open and took great bites from their sides, causing their victims to die very rapidly from shock and loss of blood. It seems very unlikely that tyrannosaurs would need to have indulged in prolonged battles to kill their prey, and they may well have retreated rapidly if their first lunge was not successful.

It has been suggested that tyrannosaurs may have been scavengers of kills made by other dinosaurs. This too is highly probable – lions will do exactly the same if it means they can get a free meal. However, in the same way that lions are not exclusively scavengers it does not seem likely that tyrannosaurs, built as killing machines, would have been exclusively scavengers either.

The short arms of tyrannosaurs seem redundant – almost an evolutionary afterthought. However, it does seem possible that they were equipped with powerful claws, which may well have been used as grapples to hook onto their prey while dismembering it.

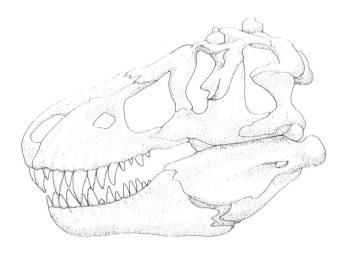

Tyrannosaurus, *the largest of all known predatory dinosaurs, had an enormous head. This skull* (ABOVE) *is nearly 4ft (1.3m) long and massively built. It is likely that tyrannosaurs rushed headlong at their prey with their mouths open* (BELOW). *The colossal impact and severe injury caused by the penetration of the long, sharp teeth would have caused almost instant death to the victim. Shown here are* (LEFT TO RIGHT) Daspletosaurus *and* Tyrannosaurus rex, *both from North America, and* Tarbosaurus bataar, *from Asia. To date, tyrannosaurs are known only from the Late Cretaceous of the Northern Hemisphere.*

Sauropodomorphs

In contrast to the fierce theropods, these were herbivores. The first sauropodomorphs appear in the Late Triassic. *Euskelosaurus* is one of the earliest known: found in South Africa, this was a heavily built creature between 20 and 26ft (6 and 8m) long. Quite unlike the early theropods, it seems to have been an essentially quadrupedal animal with a long neck and tail, and stout legs supporting a heavy trunk. Unfortunately, complete skeletons of this animal are unknown to date, so we do not have a complete picture of how it might have looked in life, although the first skull of *Euskelosaurus* has just been found by Dr Johan Welmann of Bloemfontein in South Africa. Slightly better preserved forms such as *Riojasaurus* are, however, known from South America.

A little later in the Triassic, and into the earliest Jurassic of South Africa, these early, very large forms are replaced by much more numerous and better preserved remains of *Massospondylus*. This was a smaller animal between 9 and 12ft (3 and 4m) long, slender, and very lightly built, and possibly better adapted to the hotter and drier climatic conditions of the time.

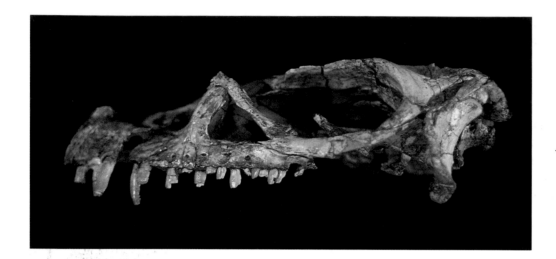

Remains of the Late Triassic/Early Jurassic sauropodomorph dinosaur Massospondylus carinatus *are frequently found in the Karoo of southern Africa. In this side view of a damaged skull the top has been pushed downward and the lower jaw is not shown, so the skull appears unnaturally flattened. These creatures represent a very successful early radiation of plant-eating dinosaurs and may well have been among the first browsers of high trees.*

The trunk was quite long compared with that of theropods, the belly was large to accommodate the bulky gut of a herbivore, and the neck was long. All these factors would tend to pitch the animal forward onto its front legs, but the long tail acted as a counterbalance. So although most of the weight was undoubtedly carried on the hind legs, the hand shows a curious combination of features which both allowed it to be used for grasping, and gave it the ability to spread the fingers on the ground for walking.

The heads of these animals were small compared to the overall body size. The teeth were small and slender, flattened from side to side and edged with coarse serrations which allowed these creatures to nip and rip at plant food, which they then swallowed in large chunks. Some well-preserved skeletons of *Massospondylus* show small, smoothly worn pebbles in the body cavity. These are most likely gastroliths (literally "stomach stones"), and were probably held in a muscular gizzard where they acted like grindstones to pound up tough plant fibers so that they could more easily be digested in their passage through the gut. The digestive system of many modern birds has a similar feature.

Compared with the theropods that were around at the time, these early sauropodomorphs were not particularly swift-moving or heavily defended creatures. They could have used the heavy claws on their hands and feet for defense if they reared up, and the long tail may have served as a whip, but this seems unlikely to have deterred a determined attacker. They were nevertheless extremely successful, judging by the number of fossils found in deposits of this age, and not just in South Africa – very similar animals are found in China, South and North America, and extensively across Europe.

From an evolutionary point of view it is curious that some of the earliest sauropodomorphs were large animals, and that the majority of slightly later forms tended to be smaller. This difference is most clear-cut in South

Africa, with a very sharp transition from *Euskelosaurus* in early rocks to *Massospondylus*. It may in part be dictated by climate, since large size is an appropriate adaptation for a reptile coping with slightly cooler climatic conditions; but it may also be a defense – larger animals have fewer natural enemies. This might have been an obvious strategy at a time when the earliest theropods were around, and still quite small, and there were still a number of larger, lumbering carnivorous archosaurs known as rauisuchians.

The general body form achieved by the small- to medium-sized early sauropodomorphs, despite its success in terms of numbers of fossils discovered, seems not to have lasted beyond the Early Jurassic. The rarer larger forms show much greater endurance and develop into some of the most spectacular land animals that have ever lived. In the Late Jurassic the dominant herbivorous dinosaurs were the descendants of these early forms, and include such spectacular creatures as *Diplodocus, Apatosaurus, Brachiosaurus, Mamenchisaurus,* and the giant of them all, if the few bones found so far are to be believed – *Seismosaurus*.

Footprint evidence suggests that herds of these gigantic dinosaurs moved across the Earth. Their effect on the ground was quite dramatic – in places it appears to have been churned up extensively simply as a result of the enormous pressure exerted by their feet. This churning can be measured several yards (or meters) beneath the surface and gives yet another measure of the incredible impact of these animals. Rocks that show evidence of this disturbance are said to exhibit "dinoturbation" – a word invented in recent years to acknowledge yet another effect of these creatures.

Imagining the impact on the ecosystem of a herd of such creatures is much more difficult – but some impression of the devastation that they must have caused is created in the illustration on pages 146-47. It is not unreasonable to suppose that dinosaurs such as these had a dramatic effect on the evolution of plants at this time – on the type of trees that grew, their defenses against this sort of attack, and the evolutionary opportunities that might have been created as a consequence of dinosaur herds clearing areas of land which might then be recolonized by new or opportunistic types of plants.

The main features of these dinosaurs are clearly derived from the earlier forms. The tail tends to be longer, and in some cases develops into a long, thin whip. The neck becomes longer – exaggerated to an apparently ridiculous degree in some. These two extraordinary structures are held together by a huge trunk supported on four extremely straight, pillar-like legs. On the end of the neck is a head built to entirely different specifications from the rest of the body – it appears tiny in comparison.

Grotesque though these animals seem at first sight, they are in fact a miracle of biological engineering. Despite the spine's immense length (at least 82 ft/25m in *Diplodocus* and in the region of 118 ft/36m in *Seismosaurus*), it shows clear evidence of design to save weight and maintain strength.

Instead of each vertebra being a solid disk of bone with various bony projections for muscle and rib attachments, it was "excavated" into an elaborately sculpted structure – the bone formed a series of spars to transmit all the stresses of weight support and movement. The body was also to a large measure self-supporting. The immense tail formed a huge cantilever which was connected by ligaments to the neck, so that the one supported the other. The back of the animal was arched as in a bridge to support the weight of the belly, and the legs were a set of pillars to support the entire structure like the piers of a suspension bridge.

RIGHT *Weighing somewhere in the region of 25–30 US tons (tonnes), the immense size of* Brachiosaurus *can only be appreciated by standing next to a real skeleton such as the mounted example in the Natural History Museum in Berlin, which dwarfs everything round about.*

Even allowing for the tremendous lightening of the skeleton made possible by hollowing out many of the bones, some of these animals must have weighed 33 US tons (30 tonnes) or more – well in excess of any land-based creature today. At first it was supposed that these animals were simply too heavy to walk on land, and they were often pictured wallowing in swamps. However, detailed study of skeletons shows a series of adaptations for life on land: the mechanical construction of the legs and feet closely resembles that of elephants, as do the ribs, spine, and indeed all aspects of the skeleton.

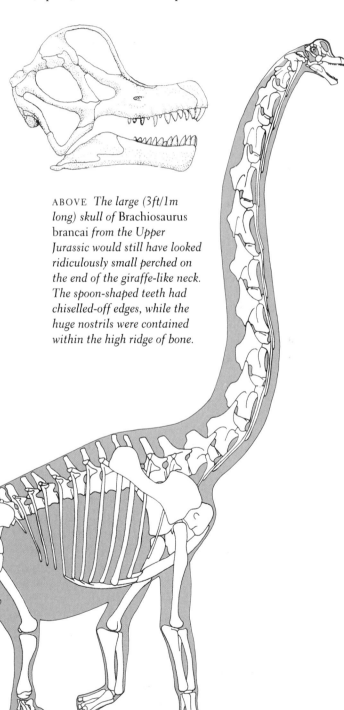

ABOVE *The large (3ft/1m long) skull of* Brachiosaurus brancai *from the Upper Jurassic would still have looked ridiculously small perched on the end of the giraffe-like neck. The spoon-shaped teeth had chiselled-off edges, while the huge nostrils were contained within the high ridge of bone.*

The size of these creatures may in fact be a simple consequence of their particular range of feeding adaptations. They appear to have been high browsers. Their teeth were rather simple and peg-like in most cases and found at the front of the mouth; they were designed for nipping or raking the foliage from trees, rather than for chewing. As in the case of the earlier sauropodomorphs, these dinosaurs seem to have had stone-laden gizzards which were used to grind up the toughest leaves. Their heads were simply devices for raking in large quantities of vegetation, which could then be thoroughly digested in the huge fermentation tanks formed by their stomachs.

Getting enough plant matter was the principal objective, which meant a good reach into the trees and thus an extremely long neck. The longer the neck, the longer the tail necessary to counterbalance it, and the stouter

In recent years there has been a spate of reports from North America of "the biggest ever dinosaur". On the left is Seismosaurus, *up to 120ft (36m) long and weighing some 50 US tons (tonnes).* Ultrasaurus (CENTER) *was a* Brachiosaurus-*like creature, and* Supersaurus (RIGHT) *resembled* Diplodocus.

the trunk and legs needed to be to support that neck. Obviously a very large head, which might have allowed these animals to feed more quickly, would become more and more difficult to support as the neck grew longer. It would be like trying to hold a large weight on the end of a very long pole – hence the relatively small head.

Some of these dinosaurs may well have increased their feeding range by rearing up on their hind legs. Others, such as the brachiosaurs, adopted the "giraffe" solution – they developed longer forelimbs and a sloping back so that they could reach higher into the trees without straining.

In Cretaceous times these huge sauropodomorphs became less abundant in some parts of the world; they are never found as frequently as they were in Jurassic rocks. Their body design also underwent a certain amount of "experimentation." Some Chinese dinosaurs appear to have developed a kind of rudimentary club at the end of the tail, perhaps as an alternative to the whiplash used in active defense. Others, such as the South American *Saltasaurus* and other Late Cretaceous titanosaurs, are known to have had armored bony plates embedded in the skin along their backs – perhaps as a simple form of passive defense.

In general, however, the sauropods of the Cretaceous are rather rare herbivores. The Cretaceous was really the high point of the herbivorous ornithischians.

EVOLUTION OF THE ORNITHISCHIANS

All ornithischians were plant eaters. They were, however, considerably more variable in appearance than the sauropodomorph saurischians. There were a number of distinctive groupings: lesothosaurs, ankylosaurs, stegosaurs, ornithopods, pachycephalosaurs, and ceratopians.

Lesothosaurs

Apart from the very early and rather poorly known form *Pisanosaurus*, the earliest ornithischians are represented by animals such as *Lesothosaurus*. This is the only adequately known version of this early range of dinosaurs, and its remains come from South Africa.

In body proportions it was not unlike a theropod, being bipedal with a long tail, short trunk, short front legs, slender neck, and small head. However, it had small grasping hands which did not end in hooked, raptorial claws, and the jaws were lined with small, distinctive, triangular teeth with coarse serrations down the edges.

Not more than about 3 ft (1m) in length, these were small, alert, sprinting animals, lightly built and highly agile. Probably feeders on succulent shoots and berries, rather than chewers of tough leaves and twigs, they would have been the approximate dinosaur equivalent of small antelopes of the African plains today. There was a small, pointed, horn-covered beak at the tip of the jaws, which aided in feeding – a distinctive character of all ornithischian dinosaurs. It also appears likely that these dinosaurs had small, fleshy cheeks which helped to hold the food in the mouth before it was swallowed – once again a feature which is found in all later ornithischians. It is likely that the later, more varied, types evolved from this early stock of small ornithischian dinosaurs.

Ankylosaurs

Very early in the history of the ornithischians a radically different type of animal evolved – one with well-developed armor plating in its skin. It gave rise to two types: the ankylosaurs and the stegosaurs. For defense against predators all seem to have relied on armor or spines, rather than on fleetness of foot.

One of the earliest armored dinosaurs known was *Scutellosaurus* from the Early Jurassic of Arizona. A relatively small animal between 6 and 12 ft (1 and 2m) long, it resembled the earlier *Lesothosaurus* in general body shape, though its legs were a little shorter, implying greater strength and less nimbleness. But, most distinctively, its back and sides were covered with rows of conical bony plates, and there is some evidence that the sides of its skull were also developing thickened bone.

The shift to larger, more heavily armored types seems to have been relatively rapid, because in the Early Jurassic of Britain the armored dinosaur *Scelidosaurus* is also found. This was a much heavier and more solid animal, 12 to 15 ft (3 to 4m) long, with more extensive armor and a bony reinforced skull. Being bulkier than *Scutellosaurus*, it was necessarily a quadruped and probably rather slower-moving, as suggested by its thicker limbs and broader feet.

Occasional remains of ankylosaurs are found from the Jurassic Period, but in the Cretaceous Period they become more numerous. One rather conservative line of ankylosaurs retained, with little modification, the body form that had been seen in animals such as *Scelidosaurus*. Called nodosaurids, they included *Sauropelta*, *Nodosaurus*, and *Edmontonia*.

The ankylosaurids, another group which appeared later in the Cretaceous and included *Euoplocephalus*, *Ankylosaurus*, and *Pinacosaurus*, modified this basic structure by adding to the armor plating around the head. Horns appeared on the upper and lower rear corners of the head; and, perhaps more usefully, a heavy, bony club on the end of the tail. This could be used against predatory dinosaurs, and was probably an extremely effective weapon: all predatory dinosaurs were bipedal, so a blow to the legs could relatively easily knock them over. For the larger tyrannosaur-sized predators such a fall could have been fatal if it broke one of their legs.

It is a curious fact that the snouts and beaks of nodosaurids are rather obviously narrower than those of ankylosaurids, and it seems quite likely that the two groups fed on different sorts of vegetation, which would enable them to coexist relatively easily. The teeth were also rather simple – not a great deal different from those of lesothosaurs.

Among ornithischians the ankylosaurs are striking, with their heavy skin armor providing protection against the teeth and claws of the large carnivorous dinosaurs. Edmontonia *from the Late Cretaceous of North America typifies the nodosaurid family of ankylosaurs, which lack the bony tail club of the rest.*

Stegosaurs

The stegosaurs are the other major group of armored dinosaurs, but appear to have pursued a slightly different strategy for the use of their body armor. The earliest types are known from the Middle Jurassic of China, and already differed from the earlier armored forms such as *Scelidosaurus* in that they seem to have developed only two rows of prominent spikes on either side of the spine. These spikes were sharply pointed in early forms, especially across the hips, on the shoulders, and along the tail, and it is not difficult to imagine that this arrangement was a major deterrent to most carnivores. In addition the relatively long tail, which was also covered in spikes, could be used as an offensive weapon when swung sideways at an attacker.

Stegosaurus is the classic stegosaur. A large animal ranging up to 23 to 26 ft (7 to 8m) in length, it had a long, low head, short front legs and long, pillar-like hind ones, and an imposing array of large alternating plates and spines along its back. The flat-sided plates are quite small in the neck region, but along the middle of the back and front of the tail they develop into huge diamond-shaped structures before tapering off towards the rear. The end of the tail is adorned with at least two pairs (four in some species) of very long, sharp spines.

The great disparity between the front and rear legs gave the animal a very low head when walking on all fours, which must have been ideal for feeding on low vegetation. However, it also seems quite feasible for these dinosaurs to have used their long tail as a counterbalance so that they could rear up to feed on higher foliage if they so desired. The front of the snout was narrow and adorned with a horny beak, and the teeth were numerous but not very different from those of either ankylosaurs or even the earliest ornithischians. Their teeth were designed essentially for simple cutting and tearing of plant tissues, with very little chewing taking place in the mouth.

The extremely large plates running down the back of *Stegosaurus* have been the subject of much debate. It was not certain at what angle the animal carried them. At first it was suggested that they had a defensive function and stuck straight upwards or were laid flat on the flanks of the animal as armor plating. In recent years their internal structure has been looked at more closely.

Stegosaurs: on top are the North American Stegosaurus *(LEFT) and the Asian* Tuojiangosaurus *(RIGHT). Foreground, left to right: the European* Dacentrurus, Lexovisaurus, *and* Kentrosaurus *from Africa. These three show spines projecting from the hips rather than the shoulder blades, as recent evidence suggests.*

It was discovered that the plates were honeycombed internally, rather than being solid and bony. There is also evidence of considerable blood supply, which suggests that they may have been involved in temperature control, as with the much older pelycosaurs *Dimetrodon* and *Edaphosaurus* (see page 113). Wind-tunnel experiments with models of these plates suggest that they are perfectly shaped for heat loss in a breeze – which is why they are diamond-shaped rather than simple rectangular blocks. Thus stegosaurs may well have used some or all of their plates as a means of losing heat if the body became too hot; alternatively they could have basked in the sunlight so that the plates acted as solar panels, absorbing heat and transferring it to the blood and the rest of the body.

The history of stegosaurs is very much limited to the Jurassic Period. There are no particularly reliable reports of stegosaurs in any deposits younger than the Early Cretaceous, and their history seems to be similar to that of the large sauropodomorphs which were also dominant during Jurassic times. Both groups were abundant in North America, Europe, Africa, and China.

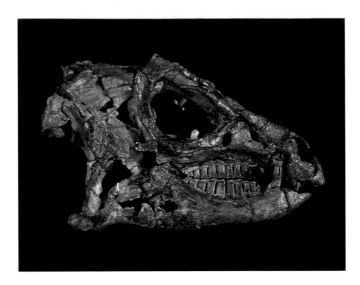

ABOVE *This well-preserved skull of the early ornithopod* Heterodontosaurus *illustrates some of the unusual features of this herbivore. The tip of the upper and lower jaw was covered by a small, horny beak. Immediately behind the beak there are large, sharp tusks, and behind these in turn is a set of blade-like cheek teeth which are sunken in from the side of the face. The channel in which the cheek teeth are set was covered in life by a fleshy cheek, which helped to hold* Heterodontosaurus's *food in its mouth while it was in the hitherto unknown process of being chewed.*

RIGHT *Recent work by Dr Tom Rich and his colleagues has revealed a fauna of small hyposilophodontid dinosaurs at a site now known as "Dinosaur Cove" in the Province of Victoria in southern Australia. On the left is* Leaellynasaura amicagraphica, *named after Tom Rich's daughter Leaellyn. To the right is* Fulgotherium australe (*there is also a slightly larger form known as* Atlascopcosaurus). *In the background is another animal, at present unnamed: although it is at present known only from a single thigh bone, the bone is clearly that of a larger hypsilophodontid.*

Ornithopods

The name of this group means "bird feet," referring to their distinctive three-toed footprints. Some of the earliest ornithopods lived alongside the lesothosaurs. *Heterodontosaurus* from the very latest Triassic/Early Jurassic of South Africa was only 3 ft (1m) in length and similarly proportioned to *Lesothosaurus*. The main differences seem to lie in the arms and hands – *Heterodontosaurus* had hands which were large, heavily clawed, and reminiscent of those of the early sauropodomorphs – and in the detailed structure of the head.

The jaws and teeth of *Heterodontosaurus* were highly distinctive. The front of the jaws was tipped with a beak, but immediately behind this was a pair of large tusk-like

teeth, and behind these in turn was a row of cheek teeth arranged in columns and shaped so that they wore down to produce a chisel-like cutting blade. The jaws were heavy, with powerful muscles capable of clamping them tightly together, allowing *Heterodontosaurus* to chew its food – something which none of the animals considered so far had been able to do.

Heterodontosaurs, of which there seem to have been quite a few types, were mobile and agile dinosaurs which, thanks to their tusks and taloned hands, may have been quite able to defend themselves against small contemporary theropods such as *Syntarsus*. Their running speed may well have allowed them to evade any of the larger predators of the time.

In later Jurassic and Early Cretaceous times ornithopods were found in steadily rising numbers. A variety of small forms included *Hypsilophodon*, 6 ft (2m) long, a very agile, fast-running dinosaur from the Early Cretaceous of England. Although otherwise similar to *Heterodontosaurus*, this animal did not have the large tusks in the jaws, a feature which seems to have existed only among the very early forms. Relatively large numbers of this dinosaur were discovered in a small deposit in Britain, which suggests that they may well have lived in small herds.

Living alongside animals such as *Hypsilophodon* were larger creatures such as *Iguanodon*, which reached

lengths of 33 ft (10m). Much more heavily built animals, these differ mainly in size and structure of the head, which is much longer-snouted, with larger jaws and more numerous teeth to process larger quantities of food. It is also noticeable that *Iguanodon*, which would have been far less nimble than *Hypsilophodon*, had a defensive weapon – a thumb claw modified into a very large conical spine which could cause considerable damage at close quarters. There is also evidence that the animals spent some of their time on all fours – the hands had hooves rather than claws on the ends of the middle three fingers. The little finger was modified to enable it to grasp foliage.

Large numbers of *Iguanodon* have been discovered in several places across Europe. This suggests that they were very abundant animals of the Early Cretaceous Period, representative of the rise to dominance of the ornithischian herbivores in the Cretaceous.

Hadrosaurs

In the Late Cretaceous a group of animals very closely related to *Iguanodon* made their appearance. These were the hadrosaurs or "duckbilled dinosaurs." The remains of thousands of them have been found in parts of North America and Asia. Not very different from *Iguanodon* in overall shape, duckbills were notable for the loss of the large thumb spike so characteristic of the latter, and retained only four fingers on their hands. The head was very elongated; some, such as *Anatotitan*, had a very broad, duck-like beak at the front. Behind the beak was a thick battery of small teeth to grind up vegetation before it was swallowed.

The comparison with ducks is understandable but unfortunate, because it builds a mental picture of large, water-dwelling, dabbling creatures. As a result hadrosaurs are frequently pictured in or around water, although in fact they dwelt mostly on plains or in scrubby bush. Hadrosaurs were the approximate dinosaur equivalents of the wildebeest, zebra or buffalo of the present day or recent past.

The duck-like beak – actually more comparable to the beak of a tortoise – was sharp and tough for cutting off lengths of foliage very efficiently. Immediately behind the beak there was a small gap or diastema before the food met the teeth – in fact cutting blades composed of thousands of teeth. The teeth grew in vertical rows, each cemented to its neighbor to form a very powerful "megatooth." Because the teeth grew continuously they were constantly replacing themselves, despite the fact that they were worn down quickly by the abrasive plant food. The jaw muscles in these dinosaurs were extremely powerful and provided a very effective grinding system.

In recent years hadrosaurs have provided many new insights into the general biology of dinosaurs. Some hadrosaurs had crests on their heads. *Parasaurolophus*, for instance, had a distinctive tubular crest which communicated with its throat and, when the animal uttered a cry, would have acted as a resonator. Presumably these dinosaurs trumpeted to one another as part of their social behavior.

Other insights have come from the work of Dr John Horner in Montana, following the discovery of nesting sites of the dinosaur *Maiasaura*. The way in which these dinosaurs nested in colonies, and revisited the same nesting area year after year, is reminiscent of the breeding behavior of birds. Their construction of complex nest mounds, and the way they cared for their hatchlings during their early stages of growth, takes us

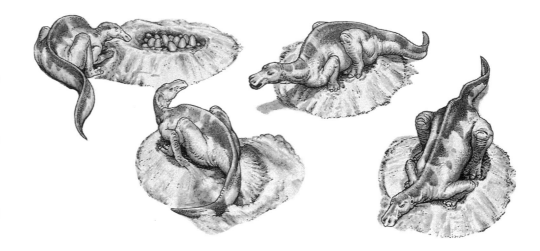

LEFT *This imaginary scene depicts various pachycephalosaurs and hadrosaurs. Clockwise from top left: spiky-headed pachycephalosaur* Stygimoloch, Pachycephalosaurus, *short-crested hadrosaur* Saurolophus *(sitting), tubular-crested hadrosaur* Parasaurolophus, *crestless hadrosaur* Edmontosaurus, *and crested hadrosaurs* Corythosaurus *and (foreground)* Lambeosaurus.

ABOVE *Nesting sites belonging to the dinosaur* Maiasaura *("good mother reptile") have been discovered by Dr John Horner in Montana in the northwestern United States. It seems that the same site was visited year after year, similar to the breeding behavior of birds such as swallows. On the right, a female is digging out a nest mound. Of the two* Maiasaura *next to her, one is asleep while the other takes up an aggressive posture to defend her nest from possible rivals or predators. The fourth female (top left) is covering her newly laid eggs with a layer of sand. On the same site Dr Horner also found remains of quite large young, indicating that they stayed in the care of their parents for some time. This sophisticated behavior pattern is like that of crocodiles, which herd their hatchlings together in pools to protect them from predators until they are able to look after themselves.*

rare as fossils, and only found in the Late Cretaceous Period, these animals appear to be bipedal runners built broadly along the lines of earlier ornithopods. Their skulls, however, are strangely modified: in many, the roof of the head is greatly thickened.

Rather than indicating great brain power, the doming of the skull was a result of considerable thickening of the bones. Mechanical analysis of the skull suggests that this was associated with an ability to withstand head butting. The stresses created by butting seem to be transmitted via bony tracts that lead to the neck joint and onward down the spine, which is appropriately stiffened. A parallel has been drawn between pachycephalosaurs and living mountain goats, sheep, and many antelopes that indulge in head butting as part of their social life in herds.

As far as we can tell from the fossil evidence, these were relatively rare animals in most communities. However, whether they were genuinely rare as living animals, or merely lived in upland areas where fossilization is very unlikely to occur, is a moot point at present.

There may be some distant relationship between pachycephalosaurs and the last great group of ornithischians to be considered, the ceratopian dinosaurs. Most of the similarities are to be found in the structure of the skulls, which are highly modified in both groups. These resemblances may be fortuitous rather than a sign of true kinship. Only more research and new discoveries will clarify this matter.

away from the popular stereotypes of dinosaurs either perpetually battling with one another (*T. rex* vs. *Triceratops*), or, like *Diplodocus*, wallowing idly in a swamp, waiting for extinction.

Pachycephalosaurs

Another very distinctive group of ornithischians was the "thick-headed dinosaurs" or pachycephalosaurs. Rather

Ceratopians

The last major group of dinosaurs to develop were the ceratopians ("horned faces"). They first appeared in the Mid-Cretaceous in the form of animals such as *Psittacosaurus* from Mongolia and China. These creatures were bipedal runners, along similar lines to the earlier small ornithopods. The main difference lay in the skull, which was deep and very narrow at the front. The beak was also modified into a rather hooked parrot-like form.

The rhinoceros-like ceratopians had horns and frills which seem to have been signaling devices. Triceratops (LEFT), with its three large horns, solid frill, and sharp, parrot-shaped beak, is one of the best known of all dinosaurs. Pachyrhinosaurus (CENTER) has a broad, knobbly pad on its nose and a more decorated frill, while Styracosaurus (RIGHT) has a single large nose horn and a frill decorated by very long, decorative spines.

These relatively small animals, 3 to 6 ft (1 to 2m) long, lived alongside another slightly larger type of ceratopian known as *Protoceratops*, 6 to 9 ft (2 to 3m) long. This had some similarity in the skull and body, but its skull was considerably larger and adorned with a large frill covering the neck; it had short, blunt horns on the nose and over the eyes. It was quadrupedal, a posture which must have been dictated largely by the size of the head, which would have tended to pitch the animal forward.

A variety of small ceratopians similar to *Protoceratops* are known from North America and Asia in the early part of the Late Cretaceous, but these were very rapidly replaced by rhinoceros-sized or even larger animals which appeared in great number and variety during the closing stages of the Mesozoic Era. One of the best-known examples is the very late form *Triceratops*, which grew to between 25 and 33 ft (8 and 10m) in length, and had a relatively short and very heavy frill and three very long horns – one on the nose and one above each eye.

Naturally it has been suggested that the horns and frills of these dinosaurs developed to deter predators. Clearly the horns may have been used as weapons of defense against the contemporary tyrannosaurs, and the frills would have protected the neck area. But other ceratopians had wider, fancier, and less robust frills and smaller horns which would have been much less effective in a defensive role.

Comparisons are now drawn between the horns of ceratopians and those of modern antelopes, which play an important role in establishing the social structure of herds. Horns are used as visual signals between individuals, or if necessary (especially at mating time) for wrestling matches as tests of strength between males. It is now thought that ceratopians may well have used their horns and frills in similar ways. Horns could have been used both as signals and for head wrestling, and the frills may have been brightly colored and used in display.

The curious parrot-like beak of ceratopians was backed by jaws lined with hundreds of teeth arranged as scissor-like cutting blades. These were clearly highly adapted herbivores feeding alongside the hadrosaurs on particular kinds of Late Cretaceous plant life. As with hadrosaurs, there is convincing evidence that ceratopians lived in large and socially complex herds. Bone beds have been discovered which seem to indicate that these dinosaurs were occasionally caught in flash floods while migrating across open country – hundreds or even thousands perishing at a time.

DINOSAUR HISTORY: A SUMMARY

This chapter has so far revealed something of the enormous range and variety of dinosaurs across the 160 million years or more of their existence. It may be helpful now to summarize the history of the various types, in order to place it more clearly in a geological time frame and to point the way to a discussion of their dramatic extinction.

Origins

Dinosaurs seem to have arisen at some time in the latter half of the Middle Triassic Period, the first types being small, bipedal carnivores. These resembled the many species of small theropod which persisted for a long time afterwards. From this early stock evolved small and large carnivores (6 to 23 ft/2 to 7m long) which replaced the medium and large archosaurs of the time.

By Late Triassic times early plant-eating forms had evolved. The first of these were a herbivorous offshoot from the theropod line and are now recognized as early sauropodomorphs; these very rapidly radiated as medium and large (up to 32 ft/10m long) herbivores of the Late Triassic. A second herbivore group, the ornithischians, may have evolved from some very early sauropodomorphs. Their evolution began with a reorganization of the hip bones. This enabled the (necessarily enlarged) herbivore abdomen to hang between the legs, so that the body could be more effectively balanced at the hips and the animal could be a bipedal, highly mobile form of small to medium size (3 to 9 ft/1 to 3m long), in contrast to the mainly quadrupedal sauropodomorphs of the time.

The discovery of "bone beds" – dense accumulations of dinosaur bones – in certain regions of North America, particularly Alberta in Canada, has prompted considerable interest in the possible causes. One celebrated example consists of a series of bone beds, each of which contains the bones of a single species only. This suggests that these dinosaurs lived in herds. If so, like all herd dwellers they would have needed to migrate from time to time when they had used up the available food in the area of land they were currently occupying. Migratory herds such as the Centrosaurus shown here are always susceptible to natural disasters, and it seems likely that these bone beds are evidence of disasters such as flash floods which would have drowned part of the herd, washing their remains downriver to form a future bone bed.

During this period the world consisted of a single land mass known as Pangea. Consequently dinosaurs of these types are now found in most regions with only slight variations.

Radiations

The dominant dinosaurs of the Jurassic Period were the larger theropods, from the early *Dilophosaurus* to the top carnivores of the Late Jurassic such as *Ceratosaurus*, *Allosaurus*, and *Yangchuanosaurus*. Small carnivores are not so well preserved at this time, and their evolutionary history is less well known apart from the well-preserved skeleton of *Compsognathus* from the Late Jurassic of Germany. This little skeleton is curious enough to make it probable that, when more fossil evidence is uncovered and analyzed, small Jurassic theropods will prove to be an extremely interesting group. At least some of them are likely to be close to the ancestry of birds.

Among herbivores the sauropodomorphs are by far the most important types in range, variety, and number. So far they have been found in all the continents except Antarctica, but who knows what the future may bring? The gradual break-up of Pangea began during the Early Jurassic. As a result, populations of sauropodomorphs drifted apart and evolved in isolation. This accounts for the distinctive nature of the animal life of China and South America at this time when compared to the rather more similar fauna shared by North America, Europe, and Africa, which were still adjacent to each other. In comparison, the dinosaurs of the Late Triassic and earliest Jurassic seem much more cosmopolitan.

The sauropodomorphs of the Late Jurassic were also spectacularly large animals, far surpassing anything that has walked on Earth either before or since. Their effect on the plant kingdom at this time, through forest clearance, large-scale destruction, and "dinoturbation," would have been drastic.

The other herbivorous group, the ornithischians, were relatively rare in most communities during the Jurassic Period. Among the armored dinosaurs stegosaurs were around in some numbers, though they did not dominate the ecology. Ornithopods were also present in small numbers, but again their presence was marginal compared to that of the sauropodomorphs.

The Early Cretaceous marks the beginning of a major shift among the herbivorous dinosaur communities. The gigantic sauropodomorphs became less abundant almost everywhere, except perhaps for South America, and were replaced by small- to medium-sized ornithopods. In Late Cretaceous times the pachycephalosaurs appeared, though not in great numbers. At this time, too, the ceratopians arrived. Right at the end of the Cretaceous they became extremely abundant, rivalling the ornithopod hadrosaurs in number and variety.

The Cretaceous Period also marks an evolutionary shift among the theropods, with a much less clear-cut breakdown into "large" and "small" forms, and much greater variety. The Early Cretaceous saw the appearance of some bizarre theropods such as the high-spined forms (*Spinosaurus*, *Acrocanthosaurus*, *Becklespinax*), and *Baryonyx*, a difficult creature to classify – its body resembles that of a large-clawed theropod, but its head has more in common with that of a fish-eating crocodile.

The Early Cretaceous is also the time when the aggressive dromeosaurs made their appearance in North America, Europe, and Asia. South America produced its own very curious large carnivore: *Carnotaurus*, a bull-horned predator distantly related to *Coelophysis* and *Dilophosaurus* and with extremely short forearms which seemed in many ways to be anticipating the development of the North American and Asian tyrannosaurs at the end of the Cretaceous.

Seen from the front, the skull of the theropod dinosaur Carnotaurus sastrei *clearly displays the extraordinary bull-like horns which project from the upper side of the head.*

In Late Cretaceous times the variety of theropods increased, with lightly built, toothless forms emerging, as well as a variety of small, highly agile predatory types such as troodontids, elmisaurids, and avimimids. There were also some extraordinarily puzzling forms such as the segnosaurs, which seem to fit nowhere; the deinocheirids, known only from a huge pair of arms; and therizinosaurs, known only from arms ending in the most enormous claws.

Amid this bewildering variety emerged the ultimate carnivores of the age of dinosaurs, the tyrannosaurs (*Tyrannosaurus*, *Daspletosaurus*, *Albertosaurus*, *Nanotyrannus*, and *Tarbosaurus*). It seems at least possible that the range and variety of carnivorous dinosaurs in the Cretaceous simply reflected the enormous quantity of ornithischian prey available. Perhaps this is too simplistic to constitute a complete explanation, but there is little doubt that the variety of prey in the Cretaceous was far greater than in Jurassic times.

DINOSAUR–PLANT EVOLUTION?

The reign of the dinosaurs coincides with some dramatic changes in plant life. At the outset of the reign of dinosaurs, plant communities were divided into stable conifer-based forests, with abundant maidenhair trees (ginkgos), cycads, horsetails, tree ferns, and seed ferns around watercourses. The ground-cover plants were mainly ferns of various kinds.

During Jurassic times the conifers began to evolve into greater variety. This was presumably a response to the activities of the new sauropodomorph dinosaurs, which were the first substantial vertebrates to prey heavily on trees. Some trees, such as the araucarias (monkey puzzles), produced extremely tough leaves to resist the attentions of these creatures, and the development of conifer needles and probably a range of chemical defenses may also have been adaptations to avoid predation. Unfortunately the dinosaurs were able to fight back, using fermenting chambers in their gut to detoxify the plant chemicals, and a range of tooth structures to improve the way in which they dealt with the tough needles of conifers.

The devastation left in the wake of herds of large sauropodomorphs is hard to imagine, though the scene depicted on pages 146-47 is an attempt to evoke their ecological effect on plant communities. The response of the plants is interesting. Into the areas of forest pulverized by sauropodomorphs came new "experimental" plants – ones that were able to reproduce rapidly and gain a foothold in what had been up until that moment an extremely stable forest ecosystem. It is just possible that such opportunities resulted in the evolution of the first flowering plants. These are noted for their rapid speed of germination from seed, and it may be no coincidence that they first arose in Early Cretaceous times.

EXTINCTIONS

The extinction of the dinosaurs at the close of the Cretaceous Period 66 million years ago followed a period of complete domination on land which had lasted 160 million years – an impressive span of time by any reckoning. The close of the Cretaceous, however, marks the extinction not only of dinosaurs but also of a variety of other creatures. The scope of these extinctions is not as great as those of the Permo–Triassic (see page 145), but the notoriety of dinosaurs has given extra interest to the later event.

Theories about dinosaur extinction were first proposed in the nineteenth century, and although several hundred have been put forward none has gained widespread acceptance. A number of questions are raised. What was the precise timing of the event – was it instantaneous, or was it spread over a longer period of time? What was the exact pattern of extinction among all the groups concerned? And what were the factors that permitted some groups to survive the event apparently unscathed?

Sudden death or slow decline?

Fossils from both marine and land-based deposits of the Cretaceous Period show that it ended quite abruptly. Unfortunately it is not possible from this evidence to confirm the timing with an accuracy better than 1–2 million years. Radiometric dating gives equally uncertain timings, ranging from about 500,000 to 5 million years. A technique known as magnetic reversal analysis reduces the extinction event to a period not greater than 300,000 years, but this is still far too imprecise to enable paleontologists to say whether we are talking about an instantaneous extinction or one spread across many thousands, tens of thousands or hundreds of thousands of years.

Winners and losers

The animals that perished included all dinosaurs and pterosaurs, several early bird groups, several groups of marsupial mammals, plesiosaurs (marine crocodiles and ichthyosaurs seem already to have become extinct in the Mid-Cretaceous), and mosasaurs, as well as all the remaining ammonites and belemnites among the cephalopods, some common molluscs known as rudist bivalves, several groups of plankton (notably the ones with chalky skeletons), and some groups of bony fish. Groups that survived included lizards, snakes and most crocodiles, turtles, amphibians, placental mammals, most plant groups, and gastropod and bivalve molluscs.

No common theme emerges from consideration of these groups, so we cannot pinpoint any particular factor which might have caused the extinction. The "pattern" looks like a random assortment of survivors and victims.

Extinction theories

Early theories began with Professor Richard Owen's notion of 1842 that the composition of the atmosphere changed at the close of the dinosaur era, with a drop in the level of carbon dioxide and a corresponding rise in the level of oxygen. This greater "invigoration" of the air did not suit the giant Mesozoic reptiles, but favored the more "vigorous" mammals and birds.

Other ideas that have emerged since that time include "racial senescence" – the idea that the dinosaurs as a group had lived long enough and were showing signs of genetic exhaustion. They were exhibiting features such as gigantism, an inability to adapt to changes in the environment, excessive hormone production, and slipped discs.

Other theories include "little green men"; competition with mammals, which ate their eggs; the evolution of caterpillars, which ate the herbivores' food; the rise of chemical defenses in plants, resulting in the dinosaurs dying of constipation or diarrhea; the effects of UV or cosmic rays; volcanic activity; geomagnetic reversals; climate change; the sea flooding the land (as suggested earlier for the Permo–Triassic extinction) or withdrawing from previously flooded areas; and intense mountain-building episodes. At best, most of these are whimsical.

At present there are only three theories that are argued about with any conviction: the extraterrestrial catastrophe model proposed by Luiz Alvarez in 1980, the ecological succession model proposed by Leigh Van Valen in 1984, and the intense vulcanism model. Alvarez found evidence to suggest that a huge meteorite had crashed into the Earth, causing – among other disasters – several extremely cold months or years because of dust in the atmosphere. Van Valen's theory was that the dinosaurs had been the victims of a gradual deterioration in climate which favored mammals. The vulcanism model comes from observations in rocks of Late Cretaceous age in India. These suggest that there were gigantic volcanic eruptions that spewed millions of cubic kilometers of lava onto the Earth's surface. The environmental impact may well have caused many extinctions.

Today we are no closer to a final explanation, and evidence is still balanced among the three theories. That a change in the fauna was taking place cannot be doubted. That something dramatic happened is also quite clear from the fossil evidence at the end of the Cretaceous Period. But why should so many unrelated groups choose this time to become extinct?

It is very tempting to suggest that a number of groups, already on the wane for ecological reasons, were pushed into oblivion by either a final meteorite impact or vulcanism, so that all three theories play a part in the extinction event. But until more data is available no positive judgment can be made.

THE ORIGIN OF BIRDS

Since the 1860s the evolution of birds has been debated with considerable interest. The first bird feather was discovered in very fine-grained limestone rocks of Upper Jurassic age in southern Germany in 1860; and in 1861 the first skeleton of the animal which possessed such feathers was discovered in the same quarry. The creature, which measured about 1 ft (30cm) in length, was named *Archaeopteryx* ("ancient feather").

When first described by Professor Richard Owen in 1863 on the basis of the first skeleton, which was purchased from the quarry by the British Museum, it was identified as an ancestral bird; no thought was given to its position in the evolution of the group as it was already considered to be fully bird-like. Since then, however, this fossil has been the focus of heated debate.

At present the skeleton of *Archaeopteryx* is considered to be similar in almost all respects to a small theropod dinosaur. Very interestingly, one skeleton of *Archaeopteryx* was preserved with only the faintest indication of feathers around its body. For many years this specimen was stored in a museum in Eichstätt in southern Germany and labeled *Compsognathus* – remains of this small theropod dinosaur had also been discovered in these fine-grained limestones. If nothing else, this confusion demonstrates the similarity between small theropod dinosaurs and *Archaeopteryx*. The Eichstätt skeleton remained misidentified for 20 years until the leading expert, Professor John Ostrom of Yale University, noticed the error.

Archaeopteryx lithographica ("ancient feather from lithographic limestone") is a remarkable fossil. Its remains are preserved on slabs of fine-grained lithographic limestone, and as a consequence the softer tissues, including the feathers, have been preserved as an impression where they were pressed into the limey mud into which the animal was buried. In addition to the feathers (which link Archaeopteryx to birds) it also has claws on its wings, teeth in its jaws, and a long bony tail – all of which are known as classic reptilian features.

In the fine details of its anatomy *Archaeopteryx* shows a strong resemblance to dromaeosaurs such as *Velociraptor* and *Deinonychus*. This places the origin of birds very close to the dinosaur group as a whole, and to theropods in particular. It also poses a rather obvious question: did dinosaurs all die out at the close of the Cretaceous Period? The answer may well be an emphatic no. It seems that one group, the theropods, survived, heavily disguised as birds. This is an intriguing possibility for a number of reasons. Some paleontologists have argued that possibly some theropods were feathered, as birds are today. But from a practical point of view, it may mean that birds provide us with an opportunity to study aspects of the behavior and activity patterns of theropods.

Learning to fly

The suggestion that birds may have evolved from small, running predators has also provoked much debate about the origin of flight. Some experts have suggested that flight originated in animals that ran along the ground and flapped their arms (or wings) in order to gain lift for take-off. If this were true, it would have been an incredibly energy-consuming method of evolving flight.

With some ingenuity a flapping method of moving the arms has been proposed as a method of insect catching. It is suggested that "protobirds" – the ancestors of *Archaeopteryx* – used the short feathers fringing their arms to trap insects, and flapped their arms and leaped

FROM DROMAEOSAUR TO BIRD?

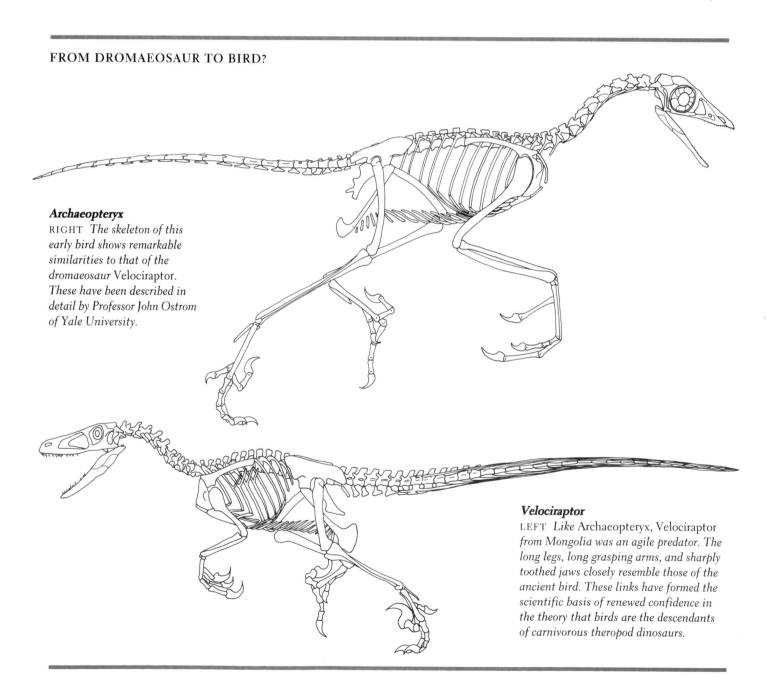

Archaeopteryx
RIGHT *The skeleton of this early bird shows remarkable similarities to that of the dromaeosaur* Velociraptor. *These have been described in detail by Professor John Ostrom of Yale University.*

Velociraptor
LEFT *Like* Archaeopteryx, Velociraptor *from Mongolia was an agile predator. The long legs, long grasping arms, and sharply toothed jaws closely resemble those of the ancient bird. These links have formed the scientific basis of renewed confidence in the theory that birds are the descendants of carnivorous theropod dinosaurs.*

at their quarry. If the feathers produced any lift during the leap, enabling the animal to travel further, there would be an evolutionary reason for the arms to enlarge and become genuine wings.

Intriguing though this argument is, it strikes me as less probable than the more traditional view, which has the advantage of being much less demanding of energy in its early, and presumably most critical, stages. This idea envisages the protobird as a small tree climber, feeding on insects. Parachuting and simple gliding mechanisms, such as fringing feathers, would have been useful to break the fall of an animal moving in the trees and occasionally falling. They may also have allowed these insectivores freedom to leap in pursuit of prey, and to use a controlled landing as a means of catching prey and surviving an otherwise fatal fall. The stages between parachuting, paragliding, gliding, and finally full flapping flight can then be much more comfortably evolved without the need for an enormous, energy-draining leap at any of the intervening stages.

Feathers preserved around the skeleton of Archaeopteryx *suggest that it was capable of flight. But the structure of the flight feathers is such that it would not have been capable of extremely energetic flight or of techniques such as hovering.*

While *Archaeopteryx* seems to have been a relatively modest flier with limited flapping abilities, it was succeeded by more conventional short-tailed birds in the Early Cretaceous of China. Some birds, including rather gull-like forms such as *Ichthyornis*, and early flightless forms such as *Hesperornis*, are known from the Late Cretaceous, but unfortunately birds have incredibly fragile skeletons and so in general their fossil record is extremely patchy.

Curiously, birds, for all their fragility, feature strongly, albeit briefly, in the next chapter. They make a dramatic appearance at the beginning of the Tertiary Period, immediately following the extinction of the dinosaurs – and they appear not as delicate little creatures, but as large and fearsome predators.

9

THE TERTIARY WORLD

TOWARD OUR MODERN PLANET:
THE RISE OF MAMMALS

THE WORLD OF the Tertiary Period was one of turmoil and change, both geographically and environmentally. The movements of great land masses had a radical effect not only on the distribution of animal communities throughout this time, but also on worldwide climate patterns. During these 64 million years the elements of the world that we now recognize as familiar developed. After the extinctions at the end of the Cretaceous, mammals diversified to an astonishing degree. Ranging from whales larger than the largest dinosaur to bats lighter than some butterflies, and diversifying into a bewildering range of herbivores, carnivores, and insectivores on land, the mammals represent the ultimate in adaptability. For sheer scope and versatility in terms of bodily form and environmental range of tolerance within a single group, they are unsurpassed in the history of life on Earth.

The first mammals in the Americas.
Hesperocyon (ABOVE) is an early member of the
dog family, which seems to have originated
in North America in the Oligocene.
Some of the most spectacular deposits of
fossil mammals can be found in
present-day Los Angeles, at the La Brea
tar pits (RIGHT).

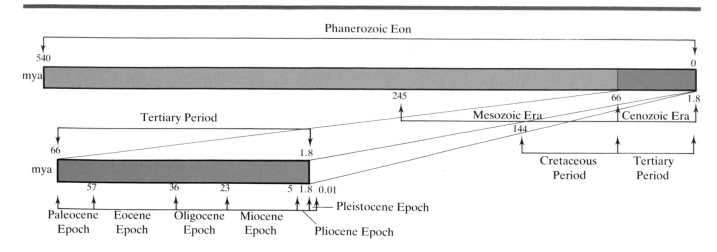

Timescale of Earth history. *After being small and inconspicuous for a long time mammals finally asserted themselves in the Tertiary Period, following the mass extinctions at the end of the Cretaceous.*

Their rise and diversification along a path taking many unexpected twists and turns, can be traced in the fossil record which was laid down throughout the Tertiary.

SURVIVORS FROM THE CRETACEOUS

During the Mesozoic Era the land was dominated by dinosaurs. But other groups coexisted with them: lizards, snakes, crocodiles, mammals, and to some extent birds. These latter were extremely important because, following the demise of the dinosaurs, terrestrial ecosystems were quite suddenly stripped of all the top herbivores and carnivores. From an evolutionary point of view, any survivors of the Cretaceous extinctions were handed a wonderful opportunity to evolve into the ecological niches that had been vacated by dinosaurs. The story of the Early Tertiary Period is just that – a time of rapid evolution and adjustment among the various surviving groups.

The majority of non-dinosaurian reptiles – which consisted of lizards (excluding the giant marine mosasaurs), snakes, turtles, and smaller crocodiles – survived the extinction with no discernible sudden change in the fossil record. But despite the fact that they were now offered an opportunity to capitalize on the demise of the dinosaurs, they did not take it. The animals that really prospered after the close of the Cretaceous Period were mammals and birds. Until then the mammals had been literally dwarfed by the dinosaurs. For the most part they were confined to the role of small, probably nocturnal insectivores, though there were also a few slightly larger rodent-like creatures called multituberculates to be found during this time. The birds, which were either relatively small flying forms such as *Ichthyornis* or aquatic fishers such as *Hesperornis*, were equally dwarfed by the pterosaurs.

Mammals and birds share a number of features. Most notably, they are highly intelligent and resourceful animals, with the ability to learn from their experiences and also to manipulate conditions to make them more favorable. They are frequently cooperative, gathering in flocks or herds, which in some ways have the characteristics of "super-organisms." And, of course, they are endothermic – they generate their own body heat (see page 148). This makes them independent of external environmental conditions and opens up a wide range of cooler habitats closed to ectotherms such as reptiles. Whether mammals and birds are able to exploit such conditions depends ultimately on their resourcefulness in finding sufficient food to fuel their energy-hungry bodies, and this is where their great intelligence is critical to survival.

DIFFERENCES BETWEEN BIRDS AND MAMMALS

Despite their physiological similarities, birds and mammals come from very different stocks. Birds appear to share their ancestry with carnivorous dinosaurs, whose ancestors can be traced back to the Late Carboniferous Period (see *Petrolacosaurus*, page 122). Mammals trace their ancestry back through the mammal-like reptiles of the Permo–Triassic, and ultimately to forms such as *Archaeothyris* (see page 111), also of the Late Carboniferous. So both groups diverged very close to the time of origin of the reptiles. These differences can be seen today in subtle ways.

Insulation

The fur and feathers of the two groups are clearly different solutions to the same problem of creating an insulating covering to the skin. In some ways hair and feathers are similar – both are made of a substance called keratin, and both grow in a similar way – but their structure is very different. It seems likely that they evolved from reptilian scales (which are also made of keratin) at different times and within very different lineages of reptiles.

Skin

The scaly skin of the legs and feet of birds is tough and impermeable and contains no glands; clearly it harks back to their dinosaur origins. In contrast the skin of most mammals is soft, pliable, porous, and multilayered; it also contains sebaceous (oil) glands and sometimes sweat glands too.

Hearing

The ears are very different in the two groups. Mammal ears usually have a fleshy outer flap for collecting and amplifying sounds, and combine this with a unique middle-ear structure containing three tiny bones (see page 119). The sound vibrations collected by the outer ear are focused onto the tympanic membrane (eardrum) and transmitted and amplified by these little bones to the sensors of the inner ear. The incredible sensitivity of this system reaches its supreme expression in the development of ultrasonic echo location systems for hunting, as seen in modern bats and toothed whales.

Birds, in contrast, retain a reptilian ear. They have no fleshy sound-collecting part, just a simple hole on the side of the head which is normally covered by a thin layer of feathers. (The "ear tufts" of owls are simply feathers, and purely ornamental.) There is only a single bone transmitting sound from the tympanum to the

Insulation and other functional features are provided for in different ways in different types of creature. In the cat (ABOVE), fur is critical to maintaining a constant internal body temperature. Heightened sensitivity and responsiveness are indicated by the largeness of the ears, the eyes, and the head in general (which in turn encloses a large brain).

LEFT *The bald eagle* (Haliaetus leucocephalus) *is insulated by feathers. Again, the large head and enormous eyes mark it as a marvellously adept predator. The scaly, glandless skin covering the feet and legs is clearly shown.*

inner ear, so the degree of sharpness and amplification is a little lower in birds than in mammals. Nor have any birds developed the sophisticated ultrasound systems of bats, for example – though oil birds do use a clicking sound as an elementary form of sonar for maneuvering in dark caves and at dusk.

Breathing

The lungs of birds and mammals differ enormously in structure. Mammals have what is termed a "tidal" breathing system: air is drawn straight into the lungs, which are large and spongy, and then pushed out again. The whole system is driven by air pressure: expanding the chest by raising the rib cage and lowering the diaphragm lowers the air pressure in the lungs and draws air in; lowering the ribs and raising the diaphragm increases the air pressure in the lungs and forces air back out again. While fresh air is in the lungs, respiration takes place. A disadvantage of this system is that some air is always left in the lungs. This residual air is stale – low in oxygen – which means that mammalian respiration is not very efficient.

Birds, by comparison, have small lungs which are positioned between bellows-like air sacs, so that the air passes in one direction through a system of fine tubes from one air sac to the other. In terms of efficiency, this arrangement is vastly superior to the lung system of mammals, since it does not leave any stale air behind in the gas exchange part of the lung. Lung systems with air sacs are also seen in some modern reptiles, which demonstrates their distant kinship with birds. The high efficiency of the lung system of birds is directly related to their extremely energetic way of life as flapping fliers.

Reproduction

Finally, the reproductive systems of mammals and birds are very different. Birds retain the basic reptilian scheme, laying shelled eggs in nests, and indulging in elaborate behavior patterns to ensure that the young hatch and are reared to fledgling status.

Mammals show a very interesting shift away from the laying of eggs. A couple of primitive mammals, the echidna and the duckbilled platypus, have retained the egg-laying habit. The female echidna lays an egg which she then pushes into a depression on her belly. After a few days the egg hatches and the young animal is nourished on milk produced by glands on the sides of the depression. Platypuses burrow into river banks and construct nests in which they lay a clutch of two or three eggs, which the mother incubates until they hatch. Here, too, the hatchlings are placed in a recess on the

EFFICIENT AND INEFFICIENT BREATHING SYSTEMS

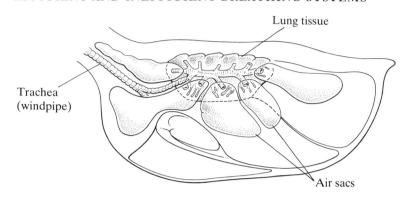

Bird

Bird lungs
The lungs of birds operate between bellows-like air sacs which force a stream of air through the tubular respiratory part of the lung in the center. This arrangement results in very efficient gas exchange and means that there is no residue of stale air in the lungs to reduce the large quantities of energy needed for flying.

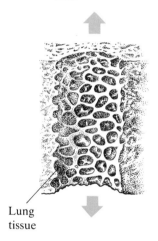

mother's belly where they are fed on milk. Milk is a key factor in the life history of mammals, because through it the mother provides a sustaining source of food for rapid growth of the young.

Apart from these two extraordinary examples, all mammals give birth to live young which are then suckled on milk produced by the mother. Milk is produced by mammary glands – hence the origin of the name mammal. There are, however, two fundamentally different ways in which the young may be reared, and this allows us to distinguish two major types of mammal today: the marsupials and the placentals.

The Australian echidna (Tachyglossus aculeatus), a primitive mammal, lays shelled eggs which are held in a recess on the mother's belly. After hatching, the young lap milk from the sides of the recess and grow rapidly. This baby, seen in a burrow, is more mature but still lacks the hardened spines characteristic of the adult. Note the long snout – these animals eat termites, which they collect on their long, sticky tongues. The front legs have long, powerful claws which help them to burrow into the sun-hardened walls of termite mounds.

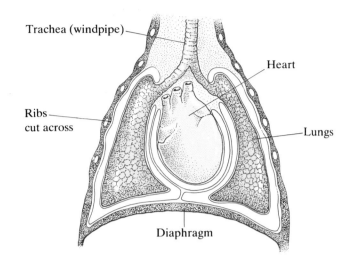

Trachea (windpipe)

Heart

Ribs
cut across

Lungs

Diaphragm

Mammal

Lung
tissue

Mammal lungs
*The lungs of mammals operate
in a "tidal" system. The
ribcage expands and contracts
and the diaphragm moves up
and down. This changes the
pressure inside the lungs,
forcing air in and out in a
repeated cycle. It is a less
efficient system than that of
birds because some stale air is
always left behind.*

MARSUPIALS

Today marsupials are confined mostly to Australasia, with one family (the opossums) in South and North America. They give birth to their young at an extremely early stage of their development. The tiny neonate, or newborn animal, crawls through its mother's fur to a special pouch known as the marsupium, where it becomes permanently attached to a nipple and feeds on a highly nutritious milk which allows it to grow very quickly.

When the neonate has grown larger it detaches itself from the nipple but still continues to live in the marsupium, taking milk at regular intervals from another nipple, which dispenses a less concentrated product. Gradually, however, it begins to venture out of the marsupium to forage, returning less and less frequently to take milk.

In this way the young animal spends a long period in contact with the parent, and learns how to survive under the protection and tutelage of the adult. The adult mammal invests a lot of time in its young, and in ensuring their survival to reproductive age.

In some marsupials the rearing of young reaches a remarkable degree of adaptation to their environment. Kangaroos are an excellent example. Living in extremely dry regions, the kangaroo is able to be opportunistic and take advantage of any improved conditions very rapidly. A female kangaroo is pregnant most of the time, but is able to hold the neonate in a form of suspended animation until she is ready to give birth – when conditions are suitable.

In good conditions female kangaroos may have one neonate suspended in their reproductive system (waiting in line), another neonate on a teat taking concentrated milk, and an older juvenile using the pouch occasionally and taking milk from the other nipple – a remarkable piece of physiological engineering. If conditions deteriorate the female behaves in what appears to us to be a ruthless manner, and jettisons the neonate from the pouch. In so doing she is sacrificing her young to ensure her own survival, knowing that she still has a young neonate waiting in her reproductive system to replace the abandoned animal should conditions improve.

Marsupials, so often pictured as nature's curiosities and "second-class" mammals, are in some cases supremely well adapted to their habitats in ways that are beyond the means of placental mammals. The pouch does, however, limit the marsupials' ability to invade water. Severe droughts in the Australian outback in recent years have emphasized the survival qualities of the kangaroo, for instance, because the domestic species introduced by humans, notably cattle and sheep, have done very badly in these conditions.

PLACENTALS

More widespread than marsupials, placentals have been able to take to the air and the open sea. They have a more precise reproductive mechanism than marsupials.

The development of a full placenta to nourish the fetus means that it stays attached and grows for a much longer time in the mother's uterus before emerging. The precarious early existence of a marsupial is avoided. On the other hand, the mother has to take on a much more permanent commitment to the growing fetus. In many ways this can be regarded as a "parasite" taking its nutrition from the mother – at the expense of the mother in some instances.

When the young placental mammal is born it is still highly dependent on its mother, especially for food. During this time its constant contact with its parents offers training in survival. This equips the maturing mammal with the resources necessary to succeed in a competitive world.

CHANGES IN CLIMATE

Greater intelligence, in-built periods of training for life, control over body temperature, and overall durability may well have been the reasons why mammals and birds were so successful during the Tertiary Period. The close of the Mesozoic Era marked the beginning of a change to much more variable climatic regimes throughout the world – culminating in the present conditions, which are dominated by the ice-capped North and South Poles and the very sharp differences in climate between the polar regions and the equator. It seems, judging from the plant record of the Late Mesozoic, that progressively more extreme seasonal conditions were affecting much of the world at this time. Unpredictable weather and distinct seasons require animals to exhibit greater durability if they are to survive.

MIGRATION AND EVOLUTION

While the earliest mammals, such as *Eozostrodon*, appeared in Late Triassic times, it was not until the Late Cretaceous that the first identifiable marsupial and placental mammals appear in the fossil record. *Alphadon* and *Vincelestes* are marsupials found abundantly in North and South America in Late Cretaceous times, while *Zalambdalestes* is an incredibly well-preserved Late Cretaceous placental from Mongolia. Placental remains, though much less perfect than the Mongolian specimens, are also known from North and South America.

Until the extinctions in the Late Cretaceous, the marsupials were as abundant as placentals; but far more of them were lost during the Cretaceous–Tertiary boundary event. Discoveries made so far suggest that marsupials originated in North America. From here they spread to found colonies in South America and Australia.

The curiously split distribution of living marsupials has provoked considerable speculation about how they could have ended up in this pattern. Did the Australian ones get there by hopping across the islands of Southeast Asia? Were there land bridges that allowed marsupials to reach certain parts of the world? All manner of hypotheses abounded until the 1960s. But then the theory of continental drift was accepted, and it was realized that the geography of the world has changed over time.

According to the fossil record, the Late Cretaceous and Early Tertiary marsupials of the Americas belonged to several families. In the Tertiary Period members of the didelphid family (which includes today's opossums) spread from North America into Europe, Africa, and Asia; their fossils are found in these areas until the Miocene Epoch, after which they become extinct. The members of the opossum family in North America also became extinct in Miocene times, but much more recently opossums have reinvaded Mexico and the United States from South America.

Current theories suggest that marsupials originated in the Americas in the Cretaceous and from there spread across other continents. Australia's separation from Antarctica in the Early Tertiary left marsupials to evolve more or less in isolation, while South America developed a mixed marsupial and placental fauna.

Zalambdalestes

Thylacinus cynocephalus is a tragic case of human-induced extinction. In the wild, it was probably wiped out by the various placental dogs introduced by human settlers; the last member of the species (RIGHT) died in a Tasmanian zoo in 1936. This marvelous creature typified the process of evolution and the phenomenon of convergence. Despite being a marsupial, as a carnivore it had evolved into a body form (ABOVE) outwardly almost identical to that of a placental carnivore such as the wolf.

The fossil record of marsupials in Australia is very sparse, and only a few fragmentary fossils date back as far as the Oligocene. The positioning of the continents in Late Cretaceous and Early Tertiary times would have allowed marsupials to spread into Australia via Antarctica on land, because these continents were still connected at this time. This theory has now been partly confirmed with the discovery of Eocene marsupials in Antarctica.

The isolation of early placental mammals with marsupials in South America, and the almost complete isolation of Australia with its mainly marsupial fauna, allowed a remarkable set of biological experiments to take place. For a considerable part of the Tertiary Period groups of mammals evolved entirely alone on their particular continents. Studying the fossils of Tertiary mammals gives a fascinating insight into the biological potential of mammals as a whole, and also the process of evolution.

AUSTRALIAN MAMMALS

The marsupials of Australia are more varied than those found on any other continent, but paleontologists know very little about their history. While the earliest marsupial remains date back to the Oligocene Epoch, by far the best part of the fossil record dates only from as recently as the Pliocene and the Pleistocene – the last 5 million years of life on Earth.

Native marsupials

Cave deposits from Australia have revealed giant kangaroos (*Procoptodon*). These were grazers with short and exceptionally deep faces, indicating that they had very strong jaw muscles which enabled them to feed on tough grasses and leaves. There were also giant wombats (*Diprotodon*) – herbivores the size of a hippopotamus. These animals were preyed upon by the marsupial "lion" (*Thylacoleo*) and the more lightly built marsupial "wolf" (*Thylacinus*). The marsupial lion was powerfully built and had exceptionally large incisor teeth, which it must have used instead of the more usual canines for stabbing, and very long, blade-like cheek teeth for slicing up the flesh of its victims.

Wombats, kangaroos, and marsupial lions are very distinctive and there is nothing quite like them elsewhere. This confirms that evolution of faunas in isolation – as appears to be the case in Australia – can produce its own very individual animal types. However, the marsupial wolf or thylacine – of which the last, very sadly, died in captivity in a zoo in the 1930s – demonstrates very clearly the process known as convergent evolution. From very different stocks, the marsupial carnivores and placental carnivores produced animals almost identical in physical form, the true wolf and the thylacine. Both are quite long-legged and long-bodied animals; their proportions are uncannily similar; and their skulls are so similar that they are used as a classic "spot-the-difference" examination question for zoology students.

Unlike carnivores, the plains-dwelling medium-sized herbivorous marsupials and placentals are radically different. Marsupials produced kangaroos (RIGHT), which are fast-moving, bounding grazers and browsers. Their equivalent in placentals (ABOVE) might be this sable antelope – also a browser, also fast, but a galloper rather than a bounder.

Australia also produced marsupial versions of the mole, anteater, climbing insectivores, and leaf eaters. The nearest it was able to produce to the large hoofed grazers and browsers of the rest of the world were wombats and kangaroos. There is not much physical resemblance between wombats (which look like bears) or kangaroos and grazers such as horses or antelopes, but in terms of their ecological role, and also in size, they are the nearest equivalent. The fundamental difference is the kangaroo's use of bipedal hopping rather than quadrupedal galloping. This probably placed constraints on the maximum size to which kangaroos could grow – *Procoptodon* may well represent the maximum size for a purely hopping animal.

Why marsupials failed to produce a creature closer to a horse or antelope is a mystery. One obvious limitation that could have affected marsupials as a whole may have its origins in their method of reproduction. Giving birth to a very immature neonate, as marsupials do, requires the premature development of the forelimbs, because they are used by the neonate to climb from the birth canal into the pouch. The necessary arrangement, at this stage of life, of a broad five-fingered hand and powerful arm and shoulder will not be readily modified later into the type of slender limb with reduced toes that is characteristic of an animal such as a horse. Marsupials may simply never have had the potential to develop the

RIGHT A newly born (neonate) opossum (Didelphis virginiana), is seen firmly attached to a nipple inside the marsupium or belly pouch of the female. The front legs are well developed compared to the hind ones, and have a broad hand with five fingers at the end of a powerful arm and shoulder. These features enable the young opossum to crawl from the birth canal to the marsupium and attach itself. This arrangement allows the neonate to feed on its mother's milk from an early stage, and avoids the need for the adult to develop a complex placenta/ uterus structure. The long time spent with the adult enables the young marsupial to learn survival techniques. However, it may be jettisoned by the mother if environmental conditions are unfavorable. This apparent drawback is in fact a positive feature, for new young are quickly produced as soon as conditions improve.

equivalent of the horse. The giant wombat was at least a quadruped, but far from agile.

Bipedal bounding rather than running, as large ground birds do, is also something of a puzzle. It may have something to do with having a pouch mounted on the belly between the legs. Recent measurements of the energy consumption of animals at speed have shown that the kangaroo is more energy-efficient than any other animal. So, once acquired, this gait was an advantage – but only within a limited size range: the effect of a very large dinosaur, for instance, attempting to hop does not bear thinking about!

PLACENTAL IMMIGRANTS

For most of its history the Australian fauna was not exposed to placental mammals. Bats had access to the continent, and a few rodents island-hopped to Australia once it had drifted close to Southeast Asia. But the first placentals in any great numbers arrived a mere 40,000 to 60,000 years ago, when the Aborigines brought in the dingo. Only 200 years ago these were joined by the Europeans' domestic and farmyard animals (cats, dogs, rabbits, sheep, cattle) and the vermin that arrived as

The pig-sized capybara (Hydrochoerus) *is the largest living rodent. Other members of this characteristic South American family include common domestic pets such as guinea pigs and chinchillas, and the notorious bank-burrowing coypu.*

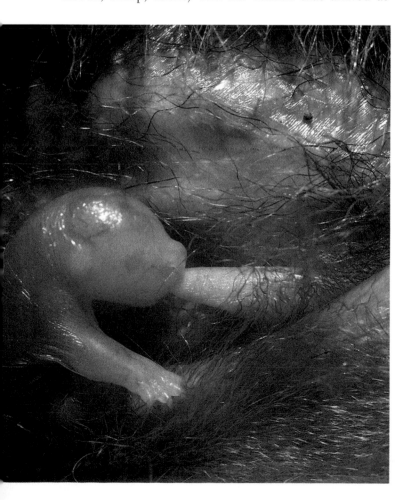

stowaways aboard ships. Human expansion, hunting, and cultivation of the land have created bridgeheads from which the placental population has been able to expand at the expense of the native marsupials, causing large-scale extinctions of the indigenous fauna. Looked at in historical terms, Australia will be interpreted by paleontologists of the future as having undergone a mass extinction of marsupial mammals.

SOUTH AMERICAN MAMMALS

The history of South America is rather different from that of Australia because it inherited a mixed population of marsupials and placentals at the time when it became isolated from the rest of the world. The early mammals of North and South America were shared until the Cretaceous Period, when the two continents separated. For much of the succeeding Tertiary, South America remained a continent-sized island, separated from all other land masses. As with Australia, its isolation resulted in the evolution of its own native fauna.

South America had its own distinctive families of carnivorous and insectivorous marsupials, some of which mimicked saber-toothed cats, bears and dogs, and small shrew-like creatures. The herbivores were mostly placentals and included various medium to large rodents ranging up to the size of small deer (the capybara is a living example), as well as other kinds of placentals which mimicked horses and hippos. There were also several types which were entirely peculiar to South America, notably the edentates, which include the armadillos, the tree sloths, and the giant extinct ground sloths; these are described in detail overleaf.

The carnivorous marsupials started out as rather short-legged, dog-shaped creatures known as borhyaenids, of which *Prothylacinus* is a good example. From these early forms evolved the impressive saber-toothed carnivores of South America such as *Thylacosmilus*, which looks remarkably similar to the true saber-toothed cats which evolved on the northern continents. The huge, scimitar-like canines were used as stabbing teeth, and the blades were protected by a flange on the lower edge of the front of the lower jaw.

Opossums were abundant omnivores, and many smaller, very shrew-like insect-eating creatures evolved which had long, scalpel-like front teeth, together with sharp, spiky cheek teeth for cracking open insect cuticles.

One interesting small marsupial herbivore known as *Argyrolagus* had the appearance of a small kangaroo, with long back legs, and possessed crushing teeth. It is not known whether it also bounded like a kangaroo.

Edentates

Some of the most distinctive South American animals were the edentates – this name means "toothless," which is a little confusing because most of them have teeth. The point is that they have lost their front teeth, while the cheek ones are rather reduced.

The armadillo (Dasypus) is a member of the distinctive South American family known as edentates. Some of its extinct relatives, called glyptodonts, had armored shells which some have claimed were large enough for humans to shelter inside.

Among the edentates were armadillos, which first appeared in the Paleocene and are characterized by an armored bony ring around the tail, together with armor plates over the back and on top of the head. The majority resembled modern armadillos, but during the more recent Pliocene and Pleistocene Epoch some very large armadillos appeared which are known as glyptodonts. Some were almost as heavy as a modern hippopotamus.

These were in many respects the mammalian equivalents of the ankylosaurian dinosaurs which were alive in the Late Cretaceous. The huge, dome-like carapace (shell), built of small polygonal nodules of bone, would have been proof against the marsupial saber-tooths of the time. Indeed some of the glyptodonts, such as *Doedicurus*, had an armored tail which ended in a viciously spiked club, a weapon of defense similar to that possessed by the ankylosaurs.

The skulls of glyptodonts were very deep, and housed extremely powerful muscles which allowed these animals to grind up abrasive grasses. Their cheek teeth had open roots, which means that they grew continuously to compensate for the speed at which they must have worn down in life.

Sloths were another group of edentates, represented today only by the tree sloths. The earliest members of this group are found in Eocene times, and seem to have been partly tree-climbing leaf eaters. From the Miocene onwards sloths appear to have pursued two radically different styles: either as purely tree-dwelling animals, or as much larger ground-dwelling tree browsers known as ground sloths.

Some of the latter were truly massive animals. *Megatherium*, for instance, measured up to 23 ft (7m) in length – this was nearly all body, for the tail was extremely short and stumpy: it was used as a prop when the animals reared up to reach high branches. The arms of these animals were extremely powerful, and ended in massive hands with huge claws which would have been used to break or pull down branches from trees; the creature may also have toppled smaller trees. Its hind legs were short and extremely powerful to support its great bulk in the rearing position, and the feet were peculiarly twisted, so that the creature must have walked with a shuffling gait. The hind feet also had a single, very large hooked claw, whose function is uncertain.

These animals were clearly bulky, rather ungainly, and potentially easy prey. However, their arms and large claws were extremely dangerous weapons of defense and they had a particularly thick skin. Samples of ground sloth skin found in caves in southern South America show that it was also toughened by tiny nodules of bone, which may have helped to protect the sloths against carnivores.

Tree-browsing ground sloths such as Hapalops (LEFT) *died out a few thousand years ago. It is still possible to collect skin fragments and droppings in caves in isolated parts of South America. One of the largest examples of these animals was* Megatherium, *which could be 20ft (6m) long. Modern sloths* (ABOVE) *are their relatives, but are entirely tree-dwelling, living in the rainforest canopy. It is likely that their extinct forebears were equally ponderous in their movements.*

Despite their apparent ungainliness, ground sloths appear to have been very successful in their time, spreading widely into North America when these continents became reconnected in the Pliocene via the Panamanian isthmus. They finally died out less than 10,000 years ago.

Hoofed animals

The modern hoofed animals of South America bear many resemblances to hoofed animals such as horses, pigs, rhinoceroses, and antelope in the rest of the world; yet clearly the two populations evolved very much in isolation. It is surprising how often these animals came to look similar to one another – an interesting example of what is known as convergent evolution.

One of the most striking examples of prehistoric hoofed animals in South America were the litopterns, which ranged from rabbit to camel size. Some, such as *Diadiaphorus*, were extremely horse-like, with long legs and toes that have been modified by loss or shortening

to a single hoof which touched the ground. However, unlike horses, litopterns had large nostrils which were positioned quite high up and toward the back of the snout. This feature is quite often associated with animals that have some sort of fleshy trunk, such as tapirs and elephants; so the litopterns may, as a group, have looked rather different from horses.

The notoungulates were the largest of the hoofed South American animals. Some were about beaver-sized, but others, such as *Toxodon* from the Pleistocene of Patagonia, were as large as hippos.

Newcomers from the north

The unique South American fauna was added to at intervals by the apparently random arrival of animals from the north. Bats flew in; others may have arrived on rafts of vegetation, or even by swimming. Primates (monkeys, which evolved into the marmosets and all the distinctive prehensile-tailed monkeys of South America) and rodents (guinea pigs and their relatives) appeared in the Oligocene. Bats are found from the Miocene, though their remains are so rare that it is impossible to tell whether they might have arrived earlier.

THE GREAT FAUNAL INTERCHANGE

Looking at the fauna of South America today it is clear that the majority of the very distinctive earlier animals have gone. None of the hoofed animals remains, the carnivorous marsupials are no longer around, and the glyptodonts and ground sloths are missing. These extinctions seem to have taken place from the Late Pliocene (about 3 mya) onward and coincide with the development of a permanent land bridge between South and North America. At this time North American animals such as raccoons, rabbits, dogs, horses, pumas, deer, and the elephant-like mastodonts ventured south, while several South American forms moved north: opossums, armadillos, glyptodonts, ground sloths, monkeys, and porcupines.

It has often been claimed that the main extinctions, those of the South American hoofed animals and edentates, took place because the northern species were in some mysterious way "superior" – better competitors.

At various times during the Tertiary Period North and South America were connected by a land bridge, which enabled animal groups either to intermingle or to evolve in isolation. The two continents became permanently connected in the Late Pliocene, about 3 million years ago.

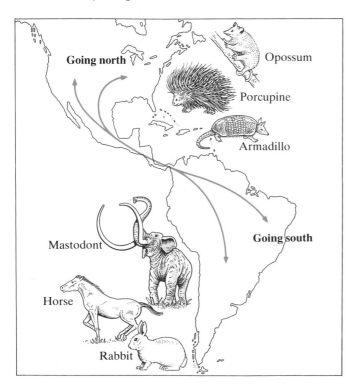

But the fossil record does not seem to support this notion. Both edentates and notoungulates were on the wane when the interchange began in the Late Pliocene. And, even after that time, the speed at which the remaining species became extinct was similar to the speed at which the invading mastodonts and horses went extinct in the same place. Also, in many cases there were simply no northern equivalents of ground sloths, glyptodonts, and toxodonts for competition to have taken place. Equally, the opossums seem to have thrived in North America, and today have become a notable pest and urban scavenger in many cities in Canada and the United States.

In general terms the interchange of animals seems to have been relatively equal. It appears unequal only because some of the really dramatic mammals (the large ungulates and unusual edentates in particular) were in decline and became extinct early in the Pleistocene. But this does not seem to have been a consequence of interference from more sophisticated northern species.

THE REST OF THE WORLD

The first Epoch of the Tertiary Period is known as the Paleocene; it lasted from 66 mya until about 57 mya, and marks the time of the adaptive radiation of the mammals – in other words, they were able to exploit the ecological riches left by the extinctions and to produce many different varieties. What was seen in South America and Australia was repeated in different ways in the main northern continents; but their faunas seem to have been more uniform in type, probably because most of these land areas were in contact for some time during the Tertiary Period.

The types of animals found in fossil deposits of this age include a range of relatively small mammals, many of which were not greatly different from those which lived alongside the dinosaurs: small insectivores of various sizes, such as *Stilpnodon*; many multituberculates and some of the earliest rodents, such as *Paramys*; and some very early primates, including *Plesiadapis* – these were browsers that lived in trees. There also appeared, in Late Paleocene times, the first of the great waves of herbivorous mammals, which ranged from badger-sized up to the size of a pig; some examples are *Titanoides*, *Pantolambda*, and *Ectoganus*.

The most curious aspect of this early radiation of mammals is that there were no particularly large herbivores; the largest were rhino-sized creatures such as *Uintatherium*, but they did not make their appearance until the very latest Paleocene. *Uintatherium* had peculiar paired knobs on its head, which may have been sheathed

BIZARRE FLESH-EATERS OF THE TERTIARY

Carnivores on the hoof
During the Late Tertiary a variety of curious-looking carnivores appeared. They seem to represent a cross between a typical hoofed or ungulate plant eater and a more conventional carnivore. The body and legs are sturdy but adapted for speed, yet the toes appear hooved rather than clawed.

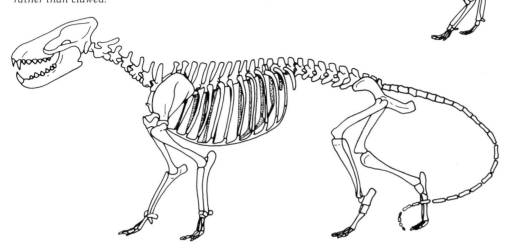

Mesonyx and Oxyaena
One group of these animals was named mesonychids after the wolf-sized Mesonyx *(LEFT), which had pointed cheek teeth adapted for cutting meat, like those of a dog.* Oxyaena *(ABOVE) belonged to the creodont group, whose members ranged from the size of a stoat to that of a bear.* Oxyaena *was cat-like in form.*

in horn and certainly gave it a slightly bizarre appearance. In addition it had large, blade-like incisor teeth which fitted against wing-like pieces on the sides of the lower jaw.

How these animals lived is a mystery because, although modern rhinoceroses have horns, they lack enlarged canines, whereas the only equivalent modern herbivores with enlarged incisors are very small deer – muntjac and musk deer – which use them for slashing bark and, more importantly, for dominance contests within herds. Other uintatheres found in Europe and Asia do not have an enlarged or knobbly head.

All these early herbivores were either rooters or browsers. The grasses that dominate parts of the world today (the African savannah, for instance, or the Central Asian steppes), and tend to dictate the types of animals found in such areas, had not yet evolved.

No large mammalian carnivores are found at this time. Several types of carnivorous mammal did appear, but these were generally small mongoose- to cat-sized animals known as creodonts (*Tritemnodon, Oxyaena, Sinopa*), or hoofed animals (mesonychids) such as *Mesonyx*, which were wolf-sized and had quite large stabbing teeth, together with pointed cheek teeth which could have been used for cutting flesh. It may seem surprising that a hoofed animal should be a carnivore, but there is no reason why it should not.

KILLER BIRDS

The ecological niche occupied by today's large carnivores was taken during this time by some uncommonly large ground-dwelling birds, of which *Diatryma* of the Late Paleocene and Early Eocene of North America and Europe is one of the best known. *Diatryma* had a huge head, with a very deep, powerful beak capable of crushing the bones of its prey.

These birds stood 9ft (nearly 3m) high, and had extremely powerful legs which, like those of their ancestors the theropod dinosaurs, would have been used to outrun and overpower their prey. Their short wings and stumpy tail may well have been used for balancing while attacking their prey.

Despite their great size, these birds would have been light and very swift animals with enormous endurance. The skeletons of all birds are designed for lightness – they have hollow bones and an extensive air-sac system (see page 184) throughout much of their bodies. With their size and speed advantages *Diatryma* and its like would easily have outpaced the competition at that time, so their early success as carnivores is not so surprising. It seems quite likely that they would have been able to leap at their prey, taloned feet outstretched, as the first stage of attack, before delivering a bone-crushing bite to the victim's neck.

Mammals were challenged for a while in the Early Tertiary by giant ground-dwelling predatory birds, of which Diatryma *is a well-known example. In North America it would have been a fast-moving, devastating predator of mammals such as the early horse* Hyracotherium. *The huge beak ended in wickedly curved tips used for killing and dismembering prey.*

The Paleocene was a remarkable time, dominated as it was by these huge predatory birds – and if evolution had taken a slightly different course the world might still be dominated by these large dinosaur descendants. Although the giant birds such as *Diatryma* died out in much of the world after the Eocene, following the appearance of the first large predatory mammals, they remained dominant in South America. Here, in the form of animals such as *Phororacos* and *Andalgalornis*, they

continued as the top predators through to the Miocene, presumably feasting on the horse-like litopterns and other hoofed mammals of the time.

THE MAMMALS ESTABLISH THEMSELVES

From the Eocene Epoch (57 to 36 mya) onward the mammals became major players in life on Earth. Not only did they become firmly established in all the principal land ecosystems, but they also did something which had been beyond the means of the dinosaurs: they reinvaded the seas and took to the air. During this period North America, Europe, and Asia were in continuous land contact, the climate was relatively mild, and the mammals seem to have prospered.

Bats

The chance discovery of the fossilized skeleton of a bat, *Icaronycteris*, in Early Eocene rocks in North America shows that the evolution of the group had proceeded apace during the Paleocene – perhaps even during the Late Cretaceous. This early form was an insectivore, judging by the shape of its spiky teeth, and very similar in most respects to modern insectivorous bats, probably flying at dusk and using an elementary form of sonic clicks to aid the location of prey in failing light.

The history of bats is fascinating and frustrating. Their early appearance as fully formed creatures implies a considerable period of evolution, but since they are such light, fragile animals the chances of fossil remains being uncovered are very slight. Nevertheless the fossil record, despite its slimness, shows that by the end of the Eocene the first horseshoe bats had appeared – which suggests that full ultrasonic echo location of prey evolved very rapidly in the group as well.

Herbivores

Among the other groups of mammals the herbivores, which for much of the Paleocene were mostly small creatures, increased in size and variety. The plant-eating uintatheres were well established and ranged up to 13 ft (4m) in length. Other herbivores included *Coryphodon*, a pantodont which grew up to 9 ft (3m) long, and may well have been a tapir-like creature of dense woodlands. The early browsing ancestor of our modern horses, *Hyracotherium*, was an alert animal about the size of a

---

ULTRASONICS – "RADAR" FOR BATS

Fossil bats

ABOVE *Despite their incredible fragility, bat skeletons are known in the fossil record. This is the skeleton of the Eocene bat* Palaeochiropteryx *from Europe. Just as in the case of* Icaronycteris, *the earliest known bat whose remains were found in North America, these animals appear to have been flying insectivores. They may well have used high-frequency click sounds to detect and home in on their prey in the poor light conditions of dusk, the ideal time for hunting for insects.*

Modern bats

BELOW *The greater horseshoe bat* (Rhinolophus) *is shown in flight in the vicinity of a potential prey item. These bats are able to emit extremely high-frequency squeaks (ultrasonic calls) from their noses. The echoes from such squeaks bounce off objects around them and are picked up by the huge and highly sensitive ears. By this mechanism they are able to create a "sound picture" of their surroundings which is similar to the* images created on TV screens by man-made radar systems. This bat has located a moth in an ultrasonic sweep and is closing in for the kill. Amazingly, certain moths have developed counter-measures. Some have special ears on their abdomens and take evasive action when they hear a bat's chirps, while others produce blasts of sound in order to "jam" the bat's sensitive detection system and make their enemy temporarily "blind."

terrier, with four hoofed toes on its front legs and three at the rear. They appear to have been small, scampering animals of the forest, very different from modern horses. The arrival of hoofed animals in the Eocene was a major event in terms of the later evolution of plant-eating mammals, for they have become among the most numerous of living mammalian herbivores.

Odd- and even-toed ungulates

All modern hoofed mammals or ungulates are divided into forms with an odd or even number of toes. The odd-toed forms (known as perissodactyls) include horses, tapirs, and rhinoceroses; they are distinguished by the fact that most of the weight of the animal is borne on the middle toe of the foot – either a single enlarged hoof as in the horse, or a central toe and one on either side as in the tapir and rhinoceros.

UNGULATES: ODD AND EVEN TOES

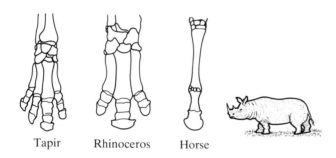

Tapir   Rhinoceros   Horse

Perissodactyls – odd toes
ABOVE *These include the ancient and modern tapir (here, the fifth toe is just disappearing), horse, and rhinoceros. The weight tends to pass through the single or middle toe.*

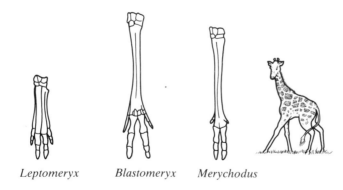

Leptomeryx   Blastomeryx   Merychodus

Artiodactyls – even toes
ABOVE *Most hoofed animals today (cattle, deer, giraffes, and so on) are artiodactyls and support their weight on the middle pair of toes. Fossil forms include those illustrated.*

The even-toed forms (known as artiodactyls) include the great majority of hoofed animals, such as sheep, deer, cattle, pigs, hippopotamuses, camels, and giraffes. Their feet are arranged so that at least two of the middle toes bear equal weight. In the smaller and lighter forms this may mean that the foot is simply cloven, as in sheep and goats; alternatively the side toes may also be visible, though smaller, as in cattle; while in very heavy artiodactyls such as hippopotamuses there are four toes to bear the animal's weight.

Both groups of ungulates include heavy and lightly built forms, and even though their legs and feet are arranged differently they share many adaptations. Heavy hippopotamuses and rhinoceroses have short leg bones. Lighter, faster animals such as deer and horses have longer, lower leg bones. The only part of a horse's leg that touches the ground is the equivalent of a human middle fingernail or third toenail.

Such mechanical adaptations are very common in evolution – similar ones are seen in dinosaurs. The feet and lower legs are short and broad to support the weight of heavy animals; while in light, fast-moving animals the emphasis is on length of stride, so the lower parts of the leg are as long as possible and the feet are very light to enable them to be moved fast. Reducing the number of toes to the minimum of a single hoof, or a pair of small cloven hooves, keeps the weight of the foot to a minimum and is ideal for a fast runner. If we compare this scenario to human athletics it is obvious that sprinting is far easier in light running shoes than in heavy walking boots – considerable effort is needed to swing the boot to and fro.

Odd- and even-toed ungulates were roughly equal in number and variety in the early Triassic. However, from the Oligocene Epoch onwards the artiodactyls (even-toed) gradually rose to dominance, making up about 90 per cent of living ungulate communities.

Early carnivores

Among carnivorous mammals, the various groups which appeared in the Paleocene continued to prosper. During the early part of the Eocene the large predatory birds still dominated. Then in Late Eocene and Early Oligocene times the first of the really large land predators are found. The dog-like mesonychids produced animals such as *Andrewsarchus*, a gigantic predator or scavenger whose remains have been discovered in Mongolia. Only its skull has been found so far, so the shape of its body is a mystery. On the basis that it was related to the earlier *Mesonyx* a rather bear-like appearance has been attributed to it, and it may indeed have had habits similar to those of modern bears.

LEFT *Modern sperm whales, members of the odontocete or toothed whale group, are superbly adapted for ocean life. Their massive bulk is buoyed up by the water and their bodies are streamlined to reduce the energy expended in swimming. They prey on giant squid at great depths, for which purpose they use a sonar-type system like that of bats, centered on a facial organ called the melon.*

RIGHT Pakicetus, *from the Early Eocene of Pakistan, is one of the earliest known whales. Relatively small and possibly sealion-like in character and habits, it was probably an aggressive, entirely aquatic predator. The triangular teeth at the rear of the jaws have saw edges, indicating an ability to cut meat which is not found in modern toothed whales. Another difference from their modern counterparts is found in the ear region. In these early whales it was not modified for detecting ultrasonic sounds and had more of a resemblance to that of modern seals, which is adapted for airborne sounds.*

Whales

Modern whales include the largest animals that have ever lived. The blue whale can reach a length of 100 ft (30m), which may have been exceeded only by the sauropodomorph dinosaur *Seismosaurus*, and a weight of 145 US tons (130 tonnes), which is well above that of any land animal including dinosaurs. Whales are carnivores, feeding on squid, fish, or shoals of planktonic organisms such as krill.

Apart from their need to return to the surface to breathe, whales are completely adapted to life in the sea. Their body form is streamlined to minimize energy loss through friction as they move through the water, powered by their horizontal tail fluke. The hind limbs are absent and the front limbs are modified into flippers which are used for steering and to control roll. Their bodies are coated by a thick layer of blubber which conserves heat, and they have no sweat glands. Their senses are very specialized: smell and vision are rather poor, but touch and hearing are acute; whales' brains are large and extremely complex. The more research that is done on whale behavior and communication, the more complex do they appear.

Living whales are divided into two groups: toothed whales (odontocetes), which include the sperm whales, killer whales, dolphins, and porpoises, and the whale-bone whales (mysticetes), which comprise the baleen whales. (The baleen is a kind of curtain which hangs down from the roof of the whale's mouth and traps krill and other food.) There was once a third group, the archeocetes ("ancient whales"), now entirely extinct.

The earliest known whale is *Pakicetus*, from Early Eocene rocks in Pakistan. Only part of a skull has been discovered, and it is far from certain what the animal looked like. Its teeth resemble those of mesonychids, which suggests that these large, bear-like carnivores of the Early Tertiary may be its ancestors.

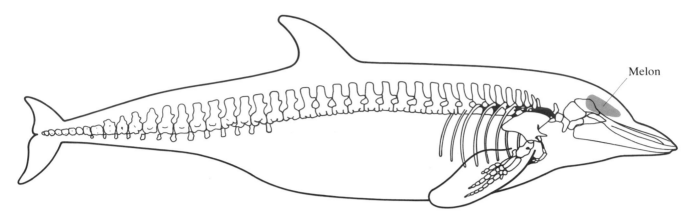

Melon

By the Miocene, as this example of a porpoise (Kentriodon) of that age shows, the modifications to the skull and body form of toothed whales or odontocetes were essentially complete. In particular the skull was fully modified, the bones of the snout having become long and slender so as form a broad trough which accommodated the area of fatty tissue known as the melon or spermaceti organ. This organ had a number of functions: it was used for navigation, for communication between individuals, and as a lens which could focus ultrasonic squeaks on potential prey in order to stun or kill it.

Whale remains from the Middle Eocene have been found in Africa and North America, and by the Late Eocene different kinds of whales were apparently quite widespread around the world. They range from *Protocetus*, a relatively small whale which reached lengths of 6 to 9ft (2 to 3m) and had a long snout armed with simple pointed teeth adapted for catching fish; through medium-sized whales such as *Zygorhiza*, which reached lengths of 23ft (7m) or so and seems to have resembled a porpoise; to the huge forms such as *Basilosaurus*, a 65ft (20m) long creature with pointed teeth in the snout and very large slicing teeth behind. These early whales did not have ears that were capable of detecting ultrasound in the way that modern toothed whales can, and probably relied on their eyesight when they were hunting.

Toothed whales (odontocetes) seem to have arisen in the Late Eocene. Most were porpoise-sized, though some – the sperm whales – grew much larger.

Miocene toothed whales include forms reminiscent of the ichthyosaurs. The 6ft (2m) long *Eurhinodelphis* from the Pacific Ocean was a long-snouted porpoise with an upper jaw which was longer than the lower one. Its similarity to *Eurhinosaurus* or *Excalibosaurus* of the Jurassic is unmistakable, and yet another wonderful example of the way in which different animals may adopt the same solution for a particular way of life.

By Miocene times odontocete skulls had been modified: the facial area was dished to accommodate a large fatty structure called the "melon," which acts as a lens to focus the ultrasonic signals which these creatures use

for echo location – to communicate, to find prey, and to avoid obstacles. The ear was also modified to be sensitive to high-frequency sound, so that an acoustic picture of the creature's environment could be assembled in its brain to supplant the hitherto predominant visual picture. Modern toothed whales such as dolphins are acutely aware of the shape, texture, and density of objects in the water through ultrasound alone; and as a further refinement of this system, it has been suggested that the narrowly focused beam of ultrasound that they are able to emit when homing in on prey may be used as an acoustic weapon to stun and immobilize their prey before it is eaten.

The whalebone whales (mysticetes) may well have arisen in Oligocene times by way of forms such as *Mauicetus* from New Zealand. This animal was already toothless and may well have possessed baleen plates; it is not possible to be certain because these plates are made of horn (keratin) and would not be expected to fossilize. The appearance of mysticete whales correlates well with the development of a full circum-Antarctic current: when Antarctica finally separated from South America the sea could move right round the whole continent. This, along with climatic cooling, may have led to a rise in the quantity of plankton, which abound in icy waters. Baleen whales may well have been able to capitalize on this rich new source of food.

THE CONTINENTS DRIFT ON

During the Oligocene Epoch, which lasted from 36 to 23mya, the geography of the world continued to change. Europe separated from North America. In the Southern Hemisphere an ice cap formed on Antarctica, and this began to affect vegetation on a global scale. The dense forests which had formerly covered many of the lowland areas were replaced by more open woodland conditions with clearings, creating evolutionary possibilities for running herbivores and carnivores. The ice cap also locked up a large quantity of the Earth's water, causing sea levels to drop. As a result the shallow sea which had separated Europe from Asia disappeared, and animals were free to migrate between the two areas.

At this time the true rodents, or gnawing animals, make their appearance in the fossil record in some numbers, and seem to be replacing the multituberculates, which right through the reign of the dinosaurs had occupied that ecological niche. Early species of rats, mice, voles, hamsters, and beavers have been identified in Oligocene sediments.

The large browsers included an extraordinary horned form known as *Arsinoitherium* (after Arsinoë, wife of Ptolemy, King of Egypt, the country in which it was found). The size of a rhinoceros (though some remains suggest something as large as a modern elephant), these animals are found across southern Europe and in Africa. They seem to have been the broad equivalent of the uintatheres (see page 195). Unfortunately their remains are rather rare and scattered, and how, or on what, they lived is a mystery.

Odd-toed ungulates

The perissodactyls, which had developed into quite a varied group in Eocene times, now underwent a number of changes. The early horse *Hyracotherium* died out in Europe and Asia, but various types of later horse appeared in North America. *Mesohippus* was about the size of a greyhound (slightly larger than *Hyracotherium*) and had slightly slimmer feet, having lost one of its front toes. But these were still far from the plains runners that horses are today, and their teeth show that they were still leaf browsers.

Titanotheres also became notable at this time. Starting off as rather small, pig-like creatures in the Eocene, by Oligocene times they had developed into animals such as *Brontotherium* ("thunder beast"). Standing 6ft (2m) high at the shoulder, these massive animals again resembled the uintatheres. The snout was adorned with a pair of large, divergent, curved horns, giving them a vaguely rhinoceros-like look. It may be

BELOW *This extraordinary-looking animal, discovered in Egypt and named* Arsinotherium *after a Pharaoh's wife, bears a vague similarity to a modern rhinoceros because it is heavily built, about the same size, and has horns on its face. But this similarity is deceptive. Remains of these animals have been found in rocks of Oligocene age and represent an early radiation of hoofed mammals into creatures of a larger body size. In ecological terms, however, they may well have been the broad equivalent of the black rhinoceros of today – large herbivorous browsers of the Oligocene plains.*

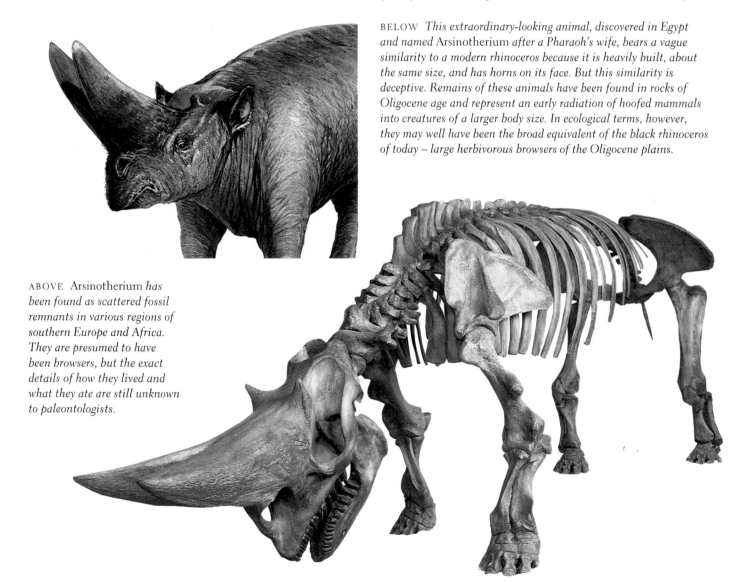

ABOVE *Arsinotherium has been found as scattered fossil remnants in various regions of southern Europe and Africa. They are presumed to have been browsers, but the exact details of how they lived and what they ate are still unknown to paleontologists.*

LEFT *The massive* Indricotherium *was by far the largest member of the rhinoceros family, measuring up to 13ft (4m) at the shoulder, and probably weighed 15 US tons (tonnes). In general terms these animals were equivalent to large sauropod dinosaurs, the main difference being that dinosaurs had huge tails and necks.*

that the titanotheres replaced the uintatheres, but if they did their success seems to have been relatively short-lived, because this group did not survive beyond the close of the Oligocene.

Rhinoceroses seem to have arisen from small, tapir-like Eocene animals such as *Hyrachus*. They make their appearance in Oligocene times in a most dramatic way, producing some of the largest land-living mammals known, which rivalled the big sauropodomorph dinosaurs in body size. These were very tall, hornless rhinoceroses (indricotheres), for example the 16ft (5m) tall *Indricotherium* from Central Asia and China. Sauropodomorph dinosaurs such as *Apatosaurus* always appear larger than other animals because of their enormously long necks and tails; however, if the necks and tails are discounted, the main bulk of the animal is not a great deal larger than that of these huge mammals. The tall, pillar-like legs and long necks, reminiscent of those of giraffes, must have given the indricotheres the ability to forage on tall trees.

While these kinds of rhinoceros prospered in Eurasia, none has been found in North America. The North American rhinoceroses, such as *Hyracodon*, were smaller, rather long-legged, running creatures which looked very similar to early horses. In the well-watered areas lived larger, barrel-bodied types with rather short legs and eyes perched near the tops of their heads, which look for all the world like early equivalents of the familiar modern hippopotamus.

Even-toed ungulates

The artiodactyls were well represented in Oligocene times. There were still many rooting and browsing types, including a variety of pig-like animals. Entelodonts are often called "giant pigs," though they are not closely related; they were very abundant in Oligocene times. They grew to about the size of modern cattle, and had large heads with grotesquely enlarged cheek bones; their legs were surprisingly long for the size of the animal, and it would appear that they were fast runners. Other groups included oreodonts, a variety of abundant, and again rather pig-like, creatures, as well as various ancestors of modern camels, giraffes, and deer.

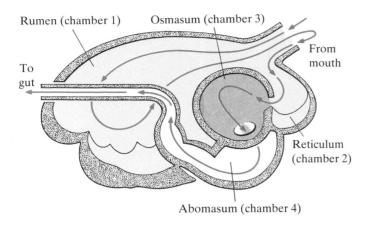

In ruminants, digestion of tough plant food starts in the rumen. Regurgitation allows further chewing, before the food returns to complete its digestive journey in the rest of the gut.

At this time the earliest ruminants appeared; as with modern forms such as cattle, they were frequently horned. The stomach of a ruminant is a complex organ divided into four compartments. The rumen, the largest portion, receives the food as soon as it has been swallowed. Here it is mixed with micro-organisms and digestive juices and churned around for some time, so that the process of digestion and bacterial fermentation can begin. The stomach then forces a portion of the semi-digested broth back up into the mouth, where it is chewed again ("chewing the cud" in cattle). This process allows the ruminant to break up tough plant material even further. The food then goes down to the rumen for the second time.

The rumen has at its far end a fine filter called the reticulum, which delays the progress of the food through the stomach until it has been broken into small enough fragments to pass to the omasum. Here fluids are removed from the food before it is passed to the final chamber, the abomasum, which is the equivalent of the stomach of most non-ruminant mammals. Here the food is broken down by acid, and then the materials are passed into the intestine for further digestion and absorption of its nutritious substances. The incredibly thorough process of digestion allowed by this complex apparatus ensures that most of the nutrients in the plant food are absorbed.

CARNIVORES

The carnivorous mammals of the Oligocene show a major change in the fortunes of various groups. The huge bear- and dog-like mesonychids disappeared and were replaced by recognizable ancestors of modern dogs and cats.

The dog family

Some of the earliest members of the canid family (foxes, jackals, wolves, and dogs) are found in the Oligocene of North America, where the group as a whole seems to have had its origins. The earliest forms were rather like mongooses and from the very outset were highly successful creatures, noted particularly for their adaptability and stamina.

Their teeth consist of stabbing canines and slicing cheek teeth (carnassials), with flatter crushing teeth behind, allowing them to be omnivorous or even vegetarian if necessary. Their vision is excellent: their forward-pointing eyes give them good depth of vision, while their long snouts house very sensitive organs of smell. The long legs and slender feet enable them to run fast and with great endurance, giving them a huge range. Highly intelligent and very social animals, mostly living in packs, they use their numbers to advantage both for cooperative hunting and for rearing their young.

Hesperocyon is one of the extremely successful dog-like carnivores. The combination of long legs, lithe body, forward-pointing eyes, and long jaws marks this animal as an unmistakable dog relative, and its habits would probably have been similar to those of modern canines. It was most likely a pack animal with a complex social structure. Hunting in packs was highly beneficial: cooperation enabled them to bring down very large prey which individuals would not have dared to tackle alone.

PREDATORS OF THE SAVANNAH

The large cats: biters and stabbers

The lion-sized, heavily built saber-toothed cat Smilodon *may well have preyed on mammals as big as elephants. The preposterously enlarged canine teeth would have stabbed into the thick hide of their prey and severed the neck arteries. Large neck muscles which ran down to the chest allowed the head to be operated almost like a chopper. Modern biting cats such as the cheetah, however, have shorter canines and powerful jaw-closing muscles which enable them to suffocate their prey.*

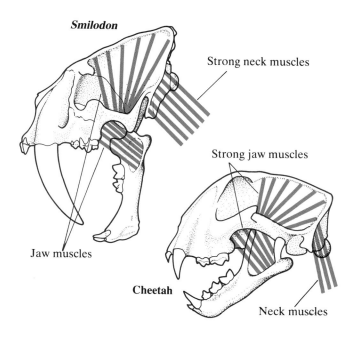

Smilodon

Strong neck muscles

Jaw muscles

Strong jaw muscles

Cheetah

Neck muscles

The cat family

The members of the felid family represent the ultimate in carnivore evolution – fast, highly intelligent, well equipped with claws and teeth, often large, and extremely ferocious. People usually think first of the more spectacular large cats; however, in terms of the history of the group the small felids about the size of the modern domestic cat are more important. From a very early stage they have been the primary hunters of the abundant small rodents. Their range as native animals is worldwide, apart from Australasia, where humans have introduced them in recent times.

In the fossil record most attention tends to be given to the saber-toothed cats, even though saber-like canines evolved in a number of groups of mammalian carnivores. In the Oligocene Period, *Hoplophoneus* and *Dinictis* were 3 to 5 ft (1 to 1.5m) long saber-toothed cats in North America.

THE RISE OF THE GRASSLANDS

The Miocene (23 to 5 mya) and Pliocene Epochs (5 to 2 mya) continued the dramatic explosion of Tertiary mammal life. The ice-capped South Pole continued to expand and influence the climate, which became steadily cooler during the Oligocene and Miocene.

The more temperate climate favored open countryside rather than dense forest, and it was at this time that the grasses evolved. Huge areas on all the major continents developed grasslands – nowadays, according to where they are in the world, called savannah, prairie, steppe, pampas, or outback. The grasslands seem to have provided ideal conditions for mammals to evolve, since these regions were able to support far greater numbers than would an equivalent area of forest.

BELOW *A cheetah at full speed is a fantastic sight. The bodies of these animals, with their long, slender legs and flexible backbone, are superbly adapted for bursts of high-speed activity at up to 60mph (100kph). But every ounce of energy is used up in the chase, and unless the cheetah catches its prey quickly it soon tires and has to look elsewhere for its next meal.*

At this time, too, Africa, which had long been separated from the other northern and southern continents, finally collided with southern Europe. The impact caused the land to buckle and rise up to form the Alps. At roughly the same time India collided with southern Asia, which led to the formation of the Himalayas. Interchange of mammals between Europe, Africa, and India was now possible. In the Pliocene, North and South America also became linked by the Isthmus of Panama.

Life on the open plains is very challenging in many ways, and this tended to be a spur to evolution. Grasses are tough, and difficult to chew and digest, so that the teeth and jaws and digestive systems of herbivorous mammals needed modification. Their cheek teeth in particular became very complex at this time. Folded layers of enamel, cement, and dentine created an effective and long-lasting rasping or grinding surface for pounding up tough grass stems before they were swallowed. Powerful jaw muscles developed at the same time.

Living in flat, open spaces also means that animals are more conspicuous. Most of the really successful herbivores became fast runners, while the carnivores that preyed upon them employed a variety of pursuit strategies: fast sprinting (felids and canids), endurance running (canids), cooperative hunting (felids and canids), and stealth (felids).

Odd-toed ungulates

Although perissodactyls were abundant early in the Tertiary Period, by Miocene times they were represented only by horses, rhinoceroses, tapirs, and the strange, clawed chalicotheres. These creatures first appeared as small forms in the Eocene and were still around in the Miocene. At that date they included animals such as *Moropus*, a large creature with a horse-like head, very long front legs which ended in large curved claws rather than hooves, and a sloping back. These animals have no obvious equivalent today, though they may have lived somewhat like the giant ground sloths of the Americas. Their teeth allowed them to chew tough leaves, and it seems likely that their very powerful front legs were used to pull down branches from trees in wooded areas, and also to root in the ground for tubers. The last of the chalicotheres seems to have lived quite recently in geological terms – within the last 2 million years – in Africa.

Moving in groups provides a degree of protection on the open plain for prey animals such as wildebeest (TOP). But when one individual animal, often sickly or juvenile, is singled out and harassed to exhaustion by a pack of Cape hunting dogs (ABOVE), even its formidable horns are no help.

The rhinoceros group became very important in Oligocene times, but declined in importance during the later Miocene and disappeared from North America. However, its members continued to flourish in Europe and Asia, giving rise in the latter continent to the two modern species, the Indian and Javan rhinos. Once the continents had become linked, rhinoceroses also crossed to Africa. Here they gave rise to the two African species alive today: the black rhinoceros with its long, pointed upper lip, which is adapted to browse on leaves, and the white (a mistranslation of the Afrikaans word meaning "wide") rhinoceros, which has a broad, flattened lip for feeding on grass. The tapirs, confined to heavily wooded areas of Southeast Asia in the present day, are very little changed from the earliest forms known.

The horse group benefited enormously from the changes in climate and plants that occurred in the Middle Tertiary, and as a result produced a wide range of browsing and grazing forms. In the Miocene Epoch horses, which were at first confined to North America, were able to migrate across the Bering Strait to Asia and Europe, where they are represented by *Anchitherium*. In North America in later Miocene times a new type of horse appeared – one which took advantage of the

Many horse-like creatures appeared in the Miocene and radiated with the development of the grasslands. The legs of Merychippus *(*BELOW*) are long and slender, with hooved toes. The head is large and the snout long to provide room for the powerful grinding teeth necessary to chew tough grasses.*

spread of the grasslands. This animal, named *Merychippus*, stood about 3 ft (1m) tall at the shoulder, considerably larger than earlier horses. It had much reduced side toes on its feet, so that it was effectively single-hoofed; it also had high-crowned teeth, which were better able to cope with a diet of tough grasses.

Larger horses with longer legs, capable of running at speed, yet feeding on grass, needed a long neck compared to those which fed on taller plants. The long neck and heavy head of *Merychippus* were supported by an elastic ligament with stretched across the tips of the neck spines from the shoulder region to the back of the head. Reaching down to feed stretched this ligament, so that the head sprang easily back into the normal upright running posture without any effort on the part of the animal.

Fast running was essential in the Miocene to escape the larger felids and dogs. The legs of *Merychippus* show a distinct trend of shortening the upper bones and elongating the lower ones. This arrangement allows the main leg-moving muscles to be concentrated at the top of the leg, leaving the lower leg as mostly sinew, bone, and skin. A small movement of the muscles at the top of the leg causes a large movement of the foot, which consequently moves extremely fast.

Horses that were similar to *Merychippus* lived on into the Pliocene, alongside other three-toed horses such as *Hipparion*, which was quite widespread in Asia and Europe until about 2 million years ago. In North America the Pliocene saw the appearance of *Pliohippus*,

The horse can be traced throughout the Tertiary in the Americas, yet unexpectedly it then became extinct in that part of the world. It was not until the Spanish "conquistadores" arrived in the early 1500s that the horse was reintroduced.

which was even more like a modern horse. It stood about 4 ft (1.3 m) tall at the shoulder, and now had a single hoof with much reduced side toes which would not have been visible in the living animal. Right at the end of the Pliocene a derivative of *Pliohippus* appeared in South America, but this form did not last very long.

The close of the Pliocene, about 5 million years ago, saw the rise in North America of the first modern horses belonging to the genus *Equus* – basically a larger, longer-legged version of *Pliohippus*. The new genus was extremely successful, spreading widely into Europe, Asia, and finally into Africa and India in the succeeding Pleistocene Epoch. Within the last 15,000 years – very recently, in geological terms – the horse died out in North America (its evolutionary home) as well as South America, and it was not until the Spaniards invaded the latter in the sixteenth century that it was reintroduced to the American continent.

Even-toed ungulates

The artiodactyls were at their most successful in the Miocene Epoch, rising to become the dominant plant eaters. The pigs and their close relatives, the peccaries of the Americas, were extremely numerous; many developed very large canines which could be used for rooting, or as defensive weapons. Their other teeth were adapted for crushing, rather than grinding, and this seems to have allowed them to have very catholic tastes ranging from carrion in some rare examples to leaf eating at the other extreme. The huge entelodonts reached their largest in the form of 10 ft (3 m) long *Dinohyus* of the Early Miocene. Anthracotheres were water-loving, pig-like animals of the Miocene and Pliocene, with barrel-shaped bodies and rather short legs. They may well have filled the ecological niche of the modern hippopotamus, which seems to have replaced the anthracotheres in the Late Pliocene.

Camels spread during the Miocene, mainly in North America; they reached South America across the isthmus in Pliocene times, resulting in the evolution of the llama, alpaca, vicuña, and guanaco. Until the Miocene camels had ranged from rabbit- to sheep-sized. However, with the spread of grasslands they became larger and developed notably longer necks, and greatly increased the length of their legs.

With very long-legged animals the normal stride pattern is one in which the front and back legs on each side move out of phase (the front leg moves back as the back leg moves forward, and so on). Clearly in long-legged forms this might lead to the front leg hitting the back leg, since the one would overlap the other. To avoid this situation camels move with a pacing gait, in which the legs on each side move in phase together (which is why camels are so uncomfortable to ride on). Fossil trackways from the Miocene show that the early camel *Protolabis* adopted just this gait when walking. The combination of long neck and legs led to quite close similarities between some camels (*Aepycamelus*) and modern giraffes.

Some close relatives of the camels were the protoceratids, an unusual group of animals about the size of deer, which they superficially resembled. They are instantly distinguishable by their amazing sets of horns, which grew on the tip of the snout as well as on the back of the head; examples include *Syndoceras* and *Synthetoceras*, both of which appeared during the Miocene. These elaborate horns no doubt served a function during fights for dominance within herds, and during the rutting season. The symmetry of the horns suggests that they may not only have been used for posture and display, but also for head-pushing contests with horns locked together.

Another major group of even-toed ungulates was the pecorans (literally "cattle," but also including other ruminants such as deer and giraffes). All groups have paired horns on their heads, ranging from the small ossicones of giraffes to the impressive antlers of deer and the sharp horns of antelopes and cattle.

Deer and giraffes appear to have their origins in Early Miocene times. One of the first of this group was *Blastomeryx* from North America, a relatively small,

HORNS AND ANTLERS

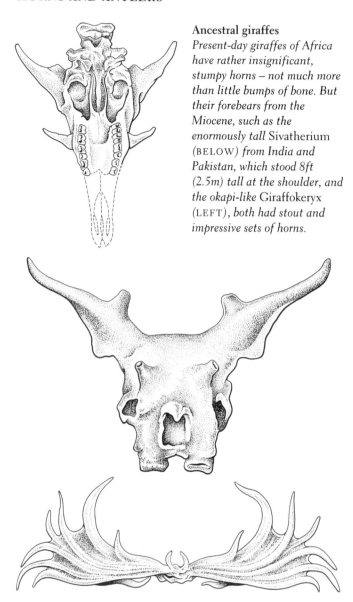

Ancestral giraffes
Present-day giraffes of Africa have rather insignificant, stumpy horns – not much more than little bumps of bone. But their forebears from the Miocene, such as the enormously tall Sivatherium *(*BELOW*) from India and Pakistan, which stood 8ft (2.5m) tall at the shoulder, and the okapi-like* Giraffokeryx *(*LEFT*), both had stout and impressive sets of horns.*

The "Irish Elk"
ABOVE *Some antlers, such as those of* Megaloceros *(the "Irish Elk") were the product of sexual selection in favor of the males with the most visually impressive displays.*

Early bovoids
RIGHT *Bovoids such as cattle, antelopes, and goats can trace their origins back to forms such as* Eotragus *in the Miocene, with a simple pair of short, backwardly pointing horns.*

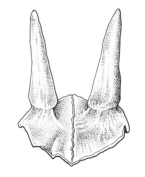

hornless creature with well-developed canine tusks. Despite this early appearance it was only in the Pleistocene that deer spread across from Asia to North America, where they evolved into the American elk and moose.

True deer evolved in Europe and Asia in Miocene times and developed an impressive array of antlers; these are the primary means of distinguishing the different species. The antlers grow from bony stumps each year and are then shed. Every year the antler may add an additional tine (spike) until the full complement of the species has been attained. Large spreads of antlers would appear to be an inconvenience for forest-dwelling animals, as many of these are. However, these structures are sexually selected: males compete for females during the rutting season on the basis of either simple antler display or head-pushing contests of strength. This requirement overrides the biological "sensible" strategy, which would be to keep the antlers to a modest size. Extremes of sexual selection were reached in the Pleistocene with the appearance of the giant deer *Megaloceros*, mistakenly called the "Irish Elk," which had an antler span of up to 10ft (3m).

Giraffes also appear in the Miocene, this time in India, in the form of *Giraffokeryx*, which looked similar to a modern okapi. One giraffe line persisted in India, producing a giant horned form named *Sivatherium* which stood 8ft (2.5m) tall at the shoulder. Giraffes never reached the Americas, where their place seems to have been taken by early camels, and died out in the Pleistocene in all areas except Africa.

Finally there are the bovoids, probably the most efficient grass eaters of all. In the Miocene they produced the groups that are today recognized as cattle, horse antelopes (waterbuck, hartebeest, wildebeest, oryx), true antelopes, duikers, sheep, and goats, and the exclusively North American pronghorn.

All bovoids have simple, unbranched horns made up of a bony core covered in a horny sheath. Although the horns may vary in shape they are very effective weapons of defense; they are also important as signaling devices between individuals.

The evolution of bovoids began in the Early Miocene with the appearance of *Eotragus*, a short-horned form which has been found in Africa, Europe, and Mongolia. By the end of the Miocene – no more than 15 to 20 million years – over 70 genera had appeared, so that in the Pliocene large herds were roaming the grasslands of Europe, Asia, and Africa. It was only in the Pleistocene that bovoids were able to migrate from Asia, probably island-hopping across the Bering Strait, into North America; here they founded populations of bison, musk ox, bighorn sheep, and mountain goat.

Elephants and their relatives

Modern elephants, of which there are now only two living species, the African and the Indian, are but a poor remnant of what was formerly a very diverse and abundant group. The early evolution of the group appears to have taken place in Africa. *Moeritherium* from the Late Eocene–Early Oligocene of Africa has a deep skull, and its upper and lower second incisors are enlarged into mini-tusks. The animal has the proportions of a long-bodied pig, and it may well have lived an amphibious life rather like a small hippopotamus.

The large, deep skull and tusk-like front teeth suggest that Moeritherium *from the Late Eocene of Africa was probably an early representative of the stock from which modern elephants derive. Its habits are not known, but it is often envisaged as a kind of hippopotamus living in or around areas of water.*

Related to *Moeritherium* were the deinotheres, an extraordinary group of elephant-like animals. They appeared in the Miocene of Africa and Eurasia and persisted until the Pleistocene of Africa. Though elephant-like in body form, including a trunk, they show a number of differences. There were no tusks in the upper jaw, but there was a single pair of huge, downward-curving tusks in the lower jaw. It appears that the tusks may have been used as levers, either for removing bark or for digging. The massive teeth were ridged and presumably used for crushing plant food. Deinotheres were most abundant in Late Miocene times; the largest of all was *Deinotherium giganteum*, which may have stood as high as 13 ft (4m) at the shoulder.

Some more conventional earlier elephants known as mastodonts are represented by creatures such as *Phiomia*, an Oligocene form from North Africa. These had large heads; nostrils which had migrated back over

Among some of the more outlandish-looking of the elephants known from the Tertiary are the shovel tuskers, with their peculiar flattened lower tusks. Platybelodon *was from Asia, while the similar* Ambelodon, *shown here, was an American example. It seems likely that the lower tusks were used quite literally as shovels while feeding, to lift vegetation from boggy areas.*

the snout, indicating the presence of a trunk; and moderately large upper and lower tusks. Larger early elephants from Miocene times include *Gomphotherium*, an early mastodont found widely in Africa, southern Europe, and Pakistan. Reaching the size of modern Indian elephants, they had both upper and lower tusks up to 6ft (2m) long. The neck was very short and powerful to support the heavy head and tusks, and the trunk must of necessity have been fully formed if the animals were to be able to browse effectively. Their teeth are massive and contain groups of large, rounded mounds for crushing their food; this is the origin of the name "mastodont," literally "breast tooth."

By Late Miocene times mastodonts had migrated into America, and very similar creatures are found in Mongolia (*Platybelodon*) and North America (*Ambelodon*). The lower tusks in these forms were flattened and may have been used as shovels for scooping up aquatic vegetation or perhaps for rooting with. Until the Pleistocene mastodonts survived in North America in the form of *Mammut*, a very long-tusked form, and spread into South America, where they were represented

by *Cuvieronius*, which has been found in Andean sediments.

The true elephants and mammoths arose in the Pliocene from animals not unlike the mastodont *Gomphotherium*. At an early stage these forms lost their lower jaw tusks (a condition seen in some of the later mastodonts such as *Mammut* and *Cuvieronius*) and developed a different way of moving their jaws and using their teeth. Instead of having rows of knobbly teeth and using complex side-to-side movements of the jaws as in the case of mastodonts, true elephants and mammoths swing the lower jaw forward and back. And rather than having lumpy teeth, they developed huge cheek teeth which emerge from the gum one at a time, as if on a conveyor belt. The teeth are arranged as a series of crosswise plates of enamel, dentine, and cement which act, as they wear down, like a pair of gigantic files between which the vegetation is shredded before being swallowed.

Three lines of elephant evolved in the Miocene. One led to the modern African elephant (*Loxodonta*) and was confined to Africa. The second gave rise to *Elephas maximus*, the Indian elephant, which first appeared in Africa and then spread across Europe into what is now mainland Asia and Japan. The third lineage, the most specialized of all, comprised the mammoths. They appeared in Africa and then spread into Europe and Asia before migrating into North America in the Early Pleistocene. It was in the Pleistocene that they reached their peak of abundance.

Carnivores

The carnivores of the Pliocene included numerous felids and canids, which preyed upon the hugely varied hoofed herbivores. The most impressive of these were the saber-toothed cats. *Machairodus* was an extremely widespread form, whose remains have been found in Europe, Asia, Africa, and North America. *Homotherium*, a highly specialized saber-toothed cat, appeared in Late Pliocene times and has been referred to as a scimitar-toothed cat because its canines are shorter than those of most saber-tooths, but extremely sharp. Most unusually, its front legs were very long while its hind ones were extremely stocky and rather bear-like.

It has been suggested that these cats were specially adapted to prey upon the abundant mammoth population of these times – not least because a cave in Texas has revealed the remains of cubs and adults alongside the bones of young mammoths. From the Oligocene onwards the main line of biting cats is found alongside the saber-tooths; they include cats such as *Nimravus*, with the size and build of a cheetah. *Metailurus* of the Miocene and Early Pliocene continued this trend, and modern cats seem to be derived from cats of this general type in the Early Pliocene.

Hyenas appeared in the Late Pliocene and spread across Europe to Asia and into Africa, where they now survive. An early hyena built on the lines of a fast-running cat invaded North America, but did not survive long. Today they survive as very effective pack-hunting scavengers and predators, overlapping with the African hunting dogs which fill a similar niche.

Canids included raccoons, which appeared in Late Oligocene or Early Miocene times, as did the bears. Modern dogs were established in Europe and Africa by the end of the Pliocene Epoch.

Another interesting group which appears to be directly descended from the canids as a whole consists of the seals, sea lions, and walruses. It was in Miocene times that these carnivores seem to have reinvaded the seas. One of the earliest forms was *Allodesmus*, which shows many similarities to seals. It has flippers, a very reduced tail, large eyes, and rather simple spiky teeth – a modification associated with a diet of slippery fish. The first true seals, sea lions, and walruses have been found in Late Miocene sediments.

BRIDGING THE TERTIARY AND THE QUATERNARY

In biological terms the Early Tertiary world was almost a vacuum, following the sudden disappearance of a huge range of reptiles that had dominated the land, sea, and air for the previous 160 million years. No wonder mammalian evolution, held back for so long, erupted like champagne from a suddenly uncorked bottle.

There is one group which has not been given much consideration at all during this review of the Tertiary world: the primates, our ancestors. I shall deal with human ancestry in the next chapter, along with the events that have occurred during the last 2 million years in the most recent geological Period, the Quaternary or "Fourth Age" of life on Earth.

Some early offshoots of the carnivore line ventured into the seas. Allodesmus of the Miocene resembled a modern sea lion and may have had a similar way of life. Watching sea lions today, especially in zoos, reveals their close similarities to dogs: their barking call has a familiar timbre, and their facial expressions suggest an undoubted, if remote, kinship.

10

INTO THE
FOURTH AGE

THE RISE OF PRIMATES AND
OUR EARLY FOREBEARS

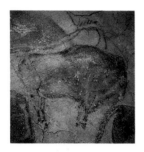

THE QUATERNARY or Fourth Age comprises the last 2 million years of life on Earth and starts with the Pleistocene Epoch, which continued until about 10,000 years ago. Paleontologists cannot agree about the precise dating of the Pleistocene Epoch: some say it began 1.6 million years ago, others 2 million years ago. After the Pleistocene comes the Recent or Holocene Epoch, as it is more properly named, which charts the last 10,000 years of life on Earth. The Holocene is usually the province of archeologists rather than paleontologists, and will not be considered in any great detail in this book. However, the rise of the human species is an evolutionary topic of great importance which I shall be considering, together with its implications for life on Earth, in this chapter.

ABOVE *The cave paintings of the early humans known as Cro-Magnons often depicted hunting scenes. Did these pictures of abundant game express reality, or what the hunters were hoping for?*

RIGHT *Discoveries in the Rift Valley of Africa enable a picture of human prehistory to be pieced together. One of the most interesting groups were the australopithecines, such as this band of* Australopithecus africanus *who clearly combine human and ape characteristics.*

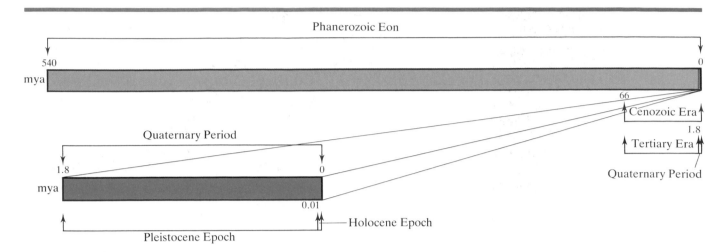

Timescale of Earth history. *The pace of vertebrate evolution quickens in the latter half of the Tertiary and into the Quaternary – from the Late Pliocene there are more tangible traces of human ancestry. Other important events include the Ice Ages and their considerable effect on animal and plant life. The most recent of these Ice Ages ended around 10,000 years ago.*

THE ICE AGES

The Pleistocene Epoch was marked by at least four major Ice Ages, during which ice sheets spread southward and covered much of northern Europe, Asia, and North America. Ice, in the form of large glaciers, also accumulated in the high mountains south of the ice sheets – the Alps, the Carpathians, and the Himalayas. The cumulative effect was radically to alter the climate of the entire world.

Between the Ice Ages there were periods of warmer weather known as interglacials, during which animals were able to migrate northward. For example, there are sequences of fossil remains of elephants, rhinoceroses, lions, hyenas, and hippopotamuses at intervals across the last 700,000 years in cave and cliff deposits in England. These suggest that the climate must at times have been warm and subtropical.

The most recent Ice Age ended about 10,000 years ago. At this time, the mammal life of several continents underwent major change. In North America three-fourths of the large mammals became extinct: they included all the mammoths and mastodonts, all the horses, tapirs, camels, deer, peccaries, ground sloths, and glyptodonts, and many of the large predators such as the saber-toothed cats. Similar extinctions affected South America, which lost four-fifths of its fauna: many edentates (except for the tree sloths and armadillos), a number of rodents, and all the carnivores, peccaries, camels, deer, horses, and mastodonts. Similarly in Australia many species perished, including many of the marsupial carnivores, diprotodonts, echidnas, and kangaroos.

The past million years have seen a succession of Ice Ages, when ice sheets spread south from the North Pole and outward from the mountains on the northern continents. These Ice Ages were separated by warmer periods, known as interglacials, when the ice retreated. The chart below shows the timescale of these events, and significant changes in animal life.

Years ago	Main faunal changes	Climate Warmer	Colder
10,000–130,000	Extinction of mammoth, woolly rhino, spotted hyena Disappearance of hippo-dominated fauna Arrival of hippo-dominated fauna		
130,000–1,000,000	Disappearance of many species		

Europe, Asia, and Africa suffered relatively less. The woolly mammoths, giant deer, and woolly rhinoceroses died out; but many others, such as hyenas, lions, horses, and hippopotamuses, disappeared only from Europe and concentrated their home ranges further south.

What caused the extinctions?

Was it rapid climatic changes following the retreat of the ice sheets that caused this marked drop-off in species – or was it another reason? The alternative scenario is that it was the spread of human populations across the world at this time that exerted pressure on the large mammals – they were wiped out by hunting.

At present the arguments are balanced. Those who favor human expansion point to the coincident spread of human populations and the pattern of extinctions; it is also curious that the extinctions should affect the large mammals alone. In addition it seems odd that this particular interglacial period should have caused extinctions among mammals, when several similar periods of warming had occurred without widespread extinctions.

On the other hand human populations entered continents before the major extinctions occurred, especially in Australia and possibly in North America; and it is curious that many species that were probably not hunted disappeared as well. The truth may of course be a compromise between these two viewpoints – climatically induced extinctions for some animals, and human hunting and destabilization of ecosystems for others. But to understand the situation fully one must discover something about humans and their evolutionary history.

EVOLUTION OF THE PRIMATES

Modern humans (*Homo sapiens sapiens*) belong to the mammal group known as primates. There are about 200 living species of primates, which range from small lemurs and bush-babies to the great apes such as the orang-utan and gorilla. They are essentially arboreal (tree dwellers), and are characterized by a set of features which are essential for this style of life: agility, intelligence, and parental care of the young.

Agility

A lightly built skeleton is essential for life in trees. The arms and legs must also be capable of a large range of movement. Many mammals have only a limited range of movement in their front and hind limbs – the ungulates, for example, are adapted to swinging their limbs back and forth in a vertical plane and cannot splay them out-

ward to any great extent. Primates, including humans, have a huge range of movement in their arms and legs. They also have grasping hands and feet in which the thumb or big toe is enlarged; this enlarged digit can be swiveled to "oppose" the other digits in order to hold firmly onto branches. An improved sense of touch is conferred by having fingers and toes which end not in claws, as in most mammals, but in flattened nails, leaving the underside of the digit free to develop into a sensitive pad.

Intelligence

Primates tend to have larger brains in relation to body size than most mammals, and correspondingly greater intelligence. Being able to cope with the precarious life in trees requires excellent coordination, and this is made possible by the large brain. The eyes are also large and on the front of the face, as was the case with the carnivorous mammals; but in most primates the eyes look in exactly the same direction and the face tends to be flattened. Overlapping of the two fields of vision allows for stereoscopic vision and good depth perception, which is absolutely essential for judging distances for leaping between branches. This brings together agility, sensitivity, awareness of the three-dimensional world, and coordination.

Parental care

The nurturing of young is an important part of primate societies. Primates mostly have a small number of infants at any one time – usually only one, or at most two. Gestation times are long, and after birth there is an extended period of parental care which gives the young primate time to learn life skills and social behavior. Primates have clearly adopted a strategy that requires a heavy investment of time and energy in their offspring, giving them the best possible chance of survival in the world. This seems to have paid off, in that the majority are quite long-lived.

Many of the traits mentioned above will seem very familiar, but they are by no means unique to humans. On the whole we have inherited our traits from our primate forebears and then elaborated some of them, particularly our parental care of the young, which takes longer than with any other mammal. But we rely less on agility than our arboreal ancestors.

Fossils of early primates

The fossil record of early primates is rather patchy. It has been claimed, on the basis of isolated cheek teeth, that the first primates appeared in the Late Cretaceous and

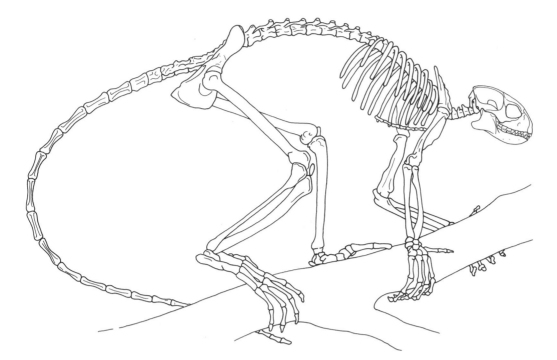

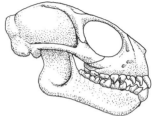

Two Eocene primates. Smilodectes (LEFT), *with its long, balancing tail and grasping hands and feet, seems close to the origin of modern lemurs. The forwardly pointing eyes were essential for stereoscopic vision. Tetonius* (BELOW) *has a shorter snout, fewer teeth, and larger eyes. It may well be an ancestor of the modern tarsiers, galagos (bushbabies), and lorises.*

belonged to a small, rather squirrel-like group of animals known as plesiadapiforms (named after *Plesiadapis* from the Early Eocene of Europe). These animals had large eyes on the side of the head, quite a long snout, and sharp claws on front and hind feet.

A considerable range of relatively small primate-like tree climbers is found in Eocene deposits: all show the combination of long hind limbs, grasping hands and feet, and a long tail which would have enabled them to move through the trees with some alacrity. One group in the Eocene includes animals such as *Smilodectes* and *Tetonius*, which show many more convincing primate characters in the skull. The brain is much enlarged; the snout is much shorter and less dog-like; and the eyes are very large and point forward so that the creatures would have had excellent stereoscopic vision.

These animals are thought to be related to living primates such as the lemurs of Madagascar, the lorises and galagos (bush-babies) of Africa and Asia, many of which are rather squirrel-like in appearance and habits. They are classified not as true monkeys, but as prosimians ("pre-monkeys"). Although these animals have excellent vision and are very agile climbers, they retain some of the features associated with other kinds of mammal. These include a preference for scent marking of territories using urine or special scent glands; therefore their sense of smell is still extremely acute compared with that of the majority of anthropoids.

The ring-tailed lemur (Lemur catta) belongs to a special group of primates unique to the island of Madagascar, which became separated from mainland Africa in the Early Tertiary. The result is a "snapshot" of early primate evolution.

RIGHT Ateles geoffroyi, *the spider monkey from Panama, displays the classic features of New World monkeys. A very adept tree climber, it has long limbs and fingers for climbing and grasping branches, together with a long, flexible and highly muscular tail which amounts to a fifth limb.*

BELOW RIGHT *This short-tailed macaque from southern China is a member of the widest-ranging group of Old World monkeys. Their origins seem to have been in Mediterranean Europe, from where they have gradually spread eastward across Asia as far as northernmost Japan.*

Monkeys

The true monkeys are known as anthropoids ("man-like"). In the present day they are divided neatly into two types: the New World monkeys of South America and the Old World monkeys of Africa and Asia.

New World monkeys have rather widely spaced nostrils, and many possess prehensile tails. They range in size from small marmosets through the acrobatic spider monkeys to the large howler monkeys.

Their origins can be traced back to the Oligocene, when the first traces of this group are found in South America. It has been supposed that the ancestors of modern New World anthropoids – some intermediate form which was neither directly New World nor Old World – managed to migrate to South America by taking a perilous trip on a raft of vegetation washed out to sea at some time in the Eocene, when the African and South American continents were appreciably closer than they are now.

All these New World monkeys are very adept tree climbers, a function for which they are highly specialized. They inhabit the dense South American jungles, feeding on leaves and fruit from the trees. Marmosets retain the habit of scent marking their territories. However, the majority of these monkeys have abandoned their acute sense of smell (this corresponds with the shortening of the snout) and vision is their primary sense.

Old World monkeys are widely spread across Asia and Africa, and include the macaques, baboons, and mandrills. They are distinguished from New World monkeys by their narrower noses and closely spaced nostrils, as well as much shorter or absent tails.

Aegyptopithecus from the Lower Oligocene of Egypt differs from other ancient Old World monkeys in its relatively large brain and fruit eater's teeth.

Early Old World anthropoids have forwardly pointing eyes and include monkeys that still retain a distinct muzzle, such as *Aegyptopithecus* from the Lower Oligocene of Egypt. These appear to have lived in swampy, well-forested areas and are likely to have been agile tree-dwelling creatures feeding mainly on fruits rather than leaves. The skeletons of these creatures are not well known, but what evidence there is suggests a branch runner similar in most respects to a macaque. The skulls are interesting because they appear to show sexual dimorphism (a clear distinction between males and females) – the males have much larger canine teeth.

In comparison to the South American monkeys, the Old World equivalents of the present day are not as highly specialized for a tree-living existence. The baboons in particular are well adapted to foraging in relatively open ground, and indeed the majority of Old World monkeys seem quite prepared to make forays from the forest. Pronounced sexual dimorphism can be observed in troops of baboons and mandrills, the males being much larger, heavier, and more aggressive than the females.

The great apes

The members of the third major group of anthropoids are commonly known as apes; these are separated first geographically, and then into small and large forms. The gibbons and orang-utan are confined to Southeast Asia, while the African line is represented by the chimpanzee and gorilla. In addition to these anthropoids there is another group – humans, whose origin seems to be associated with life in Africa, but who have now achieved worldwide distribution. The origins of anthropoid apes can be traced back to the Miocene, at which time some

primate fossils have been discovered which seem to be ancestral to all later anthropoids.

The earliest well-known ape is *Proconsul* from the Early Miocene (about 17 mya). About the size of a baboon, it appears to have been sexually dimorphic and has been interpreted as a branch-running arboreal quadruped. There are, however, many similarities to modern chimpanzees in its arm and shoulder anatomy, so it may have been capable of swinging underneath the branches of trees (brachiating). In comparison with forms such as *Aegyptopithecus* the snout is much shallower and the braincase considerably larger.

Toward the end of the Miocene Epoch the mainly African distribution of these *Proconsul*-like apes was increased by the connection between Africa and Asia across the Arabian peninsula, and they appear to have migrated into both Europe and Asia. Two slightly different sorts of ape evolved at this time: a Euro-African version (the ancestors of modern chimps, gorillas, and humans); and an Asian version based on *Ramapithecus*, which gave rise to the gibbons and the orang-utan.

RIGHT *The orang-utan is the largest of the Asian great apes. Large-brained, highly intelligent, and "wise-eyed", they are similar in size and feeding habits to the African gorilla.*

BELOW *The beautifully preserved skull of the Miocene ape* Proconsul africanus, *discovered in Kenya. This baboon-sized fruit eater had features seen in various modern monkeys.*

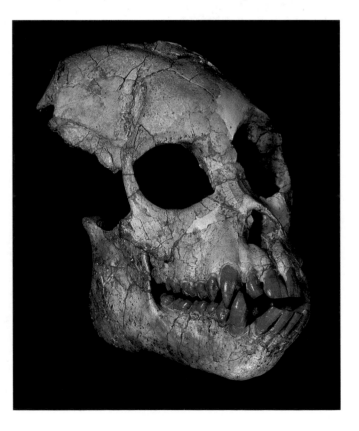

The Asian version of these apes also gave rise to the largest ape that has ever lived. *Gigantopithecus*, whose remains, mostly in the form of large teeth (originally collected as "dragon's teeth" in Chinese markets), come from the Pliocene of India and the Pleistocene of China, may have been 8 ft (2.5m) tall, and may have reached a weight of nearly 670 lb (300kg). This huge animal appears to have been a leaf eater, and must have roamed the forest floors of Southeast Asia, since it would have been far too large and ungainly to have survived in the trees. It has been speculated that the mythology of the Himalayan Yeti may be associated with this gigantic ape.

The last of the fossil record of African apes is represented by *Kenyapithecus*, which comes from the Middle Miocene (about 16 mya) and may represent a form very close to the common ancestry of modern African apes and humans. At this point in the history of the anthropoid apes there is a most frustrating gap in the fossil record: nothing is preserved between about 14 and 4 mya. The great African apes, the gorilla (*Gorilla*) and the chimpanzee (*Pan*), have no fossil record at all, and therefore might have diverged from humans at any time during that 10 million year gap. But while the fossil record remains mute on the subject of human ancestry from the other apes, human ingenuity has not.

Evidence from DNA

The techniques of modern molecular biology have been applied to the problem of human origins. Comparative analysis of the DNA of humans, chimpanzees, gorillas, and the other great apes has shown that human DNA is closest to that of the chimpanzee. Further tests on a variety of proteins such as hemoglobin and myoglobin have also indicated the same general pattern, with the chimpanzee being our closest relative; the gorilla is a little more distant, followed by the orang-utan and the gibbon. The degree of similarity has been used to chart the approximate times of divergence of these different species. The consensus is that humans diverged from chimpanzees between 7 and 5 million years ago, and that the African and Asian apes have been separate for at least 9 million years.

Gigantopithecus remains originally came to light through the study of "dragon's teeth," sold in Chinese markets. The teeth and jaws of this large Pleistocene ape have been found widely across Asia from India to China. Its jaws indicate that it was possibly even larger than the gorilla, and that it fed on leaves and possibly grasses. Its remains have been found in association with a wide range of mammals such as tapirs (bottom left), muntjac (bottom right), mouse deer (above the muntjac), giant pandas and gibbons, as well as the elephant Stegodon, seen here in the background.

BIPEDAL WALKING

Humans

The upright stance adopted by apes and humans has resulted in significant changes to their bodies. Discrepancies between the two relate to their differing lifestyles. Humans, except for a short period as babies, always walk upright. Their backbone has therefore developed an S-shaped curve so that the weight of the rib cage and shoulders is borne by the hips. The human foot and toes have become long and flat for ease of walking and balancing, while the long leg bones and the complex knee and ankle joints enable long, swinging strides to be taken. The pelvis is short and broad so that it can support the guts.

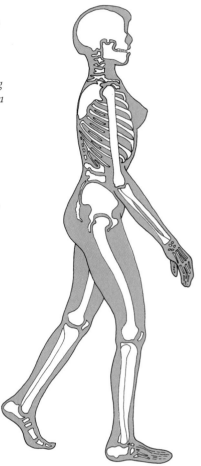

Apes

The smoothly curved back of apes pitches them forward to support the body when moving on all fours. Their feet, with curved toes and an inwardly twisting big toe, resemble human hands and are used for grasping, as are the bandy legs. The guts hang from the forward-tilted pelvis, whose length also helps to support the back when apes walk on all fours.

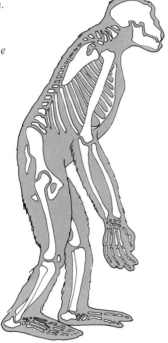

The first hominids

Humans belong to a family of apes known as the Hominidae. This includes a number of fossil forms that can be traced back over the past 4 million years. Two key characteristics separate hominids from other apes: their large brain and their complete bipedalism.

Bipedalism in this sense is taken to mean not just walking on the hind legs, as with a kangaroo or a bipedal dinosaur, but to have a fully upright stance with the spine vertical. This has led to profound anatomical changes in the body. The foot becomes a long, flat structure, with straight, flat toes, giving sufficient length to make balancing easy. In comparison, apes have a foot which is adapted for grasping: the toes are curved and the big toe is able to twist inward so that it can oppose the other toes – their feet are like our hands.

The leg bones are long and straight, providing humans with a long stride, and the range of movement of the knee and ankle joints is adapted so that the leg can swing back and forth efficiently. Apes have shorter legs which are more bent – they appear bandy in front view. Clearly, their legs are as much for grasping branches as for walking on.

The pelvis of humans is short but broad, and acts like a basin to support the guts. That of apes is rather long and forwardly tilted, and was more an area from which the lower gut could hang; the extra length of the pelvis also helps to support the back when these animals rest and move on all fours (known as "knuckle-walking"), as they do in the wild.

The backbone of humans has an S-shaped curve to ensure that the weight of the rib cage and shoulders passes downward through the center of gravity, rather than being in front of it. Apes, on the other hand, naturally pitch forward because their back is smoothly curved – which is the best shape to support the body when moving on all fours.

Finally the human head, since it is perched on top of the vertebral column rather than at the front, is modified so that the joint lies underneath and the head is more or less balanced. Again apes, since they are tilted forward, tend to have the joint between the head and neck at the rear of the skull, and the neck vertebrae usually have long projections (known as spines) to support the large muscles necessary to hold the head up.

Evidence for the evolution of upright bipedalism comes from an unexpected source – footprints. A remarkable trackway, discovered on a layer of volcanic ash in Tanzania by the paleontologist Mary Leakey, has been very precisely dated at 3.75 million years old. Some of the oldest known hominid skeletons, of similar date, have also been discovered in the same part of Africa. When upright bipedalism arose is difficult to tell – the fossil record of hominids does not go back beyond 4 million years. However, if the molecular evidence is to be believed (see page 219), fossil hominids may have originated in the region of 5 and 7 million years ago.

It is also a puzzle why it should have been necessary for hominids to become upright bipeds. This may well have been tied to the changing environment of the Late Miocene. At this time the dense tropical conditions

An expedition led by Mary Leakey to Laetoli in Tanzania in 1978 discovered this remarkable set of tracks, preserved in a layer of fine volcanic ash. These human-like footprints of two adults and a child walking together are about 3.6 million years old, and prove that upright, free-striding walking had been achieved by that date. Australopithecus afarensis *is the only hominid known to exist at that time. The footprints at the top are those of* Hipparion, *an extinct, three-toed horse.*

which covered most of Africa began to retreat to the western part of Central Africa, leaving the East as more open savannah country. The classic forest-dwelling apes retreated with the forests, eventually giving rise to the modern gorillas and chimpanzees. The more open areas were taken over by the ancestors of baboons. These previously arboreal monkeys developed a more quadrupedal gait and adopted the lifestyle of a generalist omnivore and scavenger (though some, such as the gelada baboons, became committed herbivores and feed exclusively on grasses), living in social groups and adopting the behavior patterns of many plains-living animals.

But some apes also remained in the open. The strategy of these hominids was to become long-striding upright walkers. The long and efficient stride ensured that these apes were able to travel over great distances with little difficulty, and also gave them a high vantage point from which to spot predators or potential prey. Carrying the body upright brought other advantages, too: most notably it released the hands, which could then be used in a variety of ways for carrying infants, food, and weapons.

The large brain seems to have developed after the postural changes in the body had occurred. The earliest known upright hominids (dating back 3.6 million years) had brains which were broadly in the size range of those of modern apes; judging by the shape of the fossil skulls, the shape of the face was also similar. During the intervening time hominids with slightly larger brain capacities developed, and about 1.6 million years ago members of the genus *Homo* appear. Their brain capacities seem to be on the lower edge of the normal range of those of modern humans.

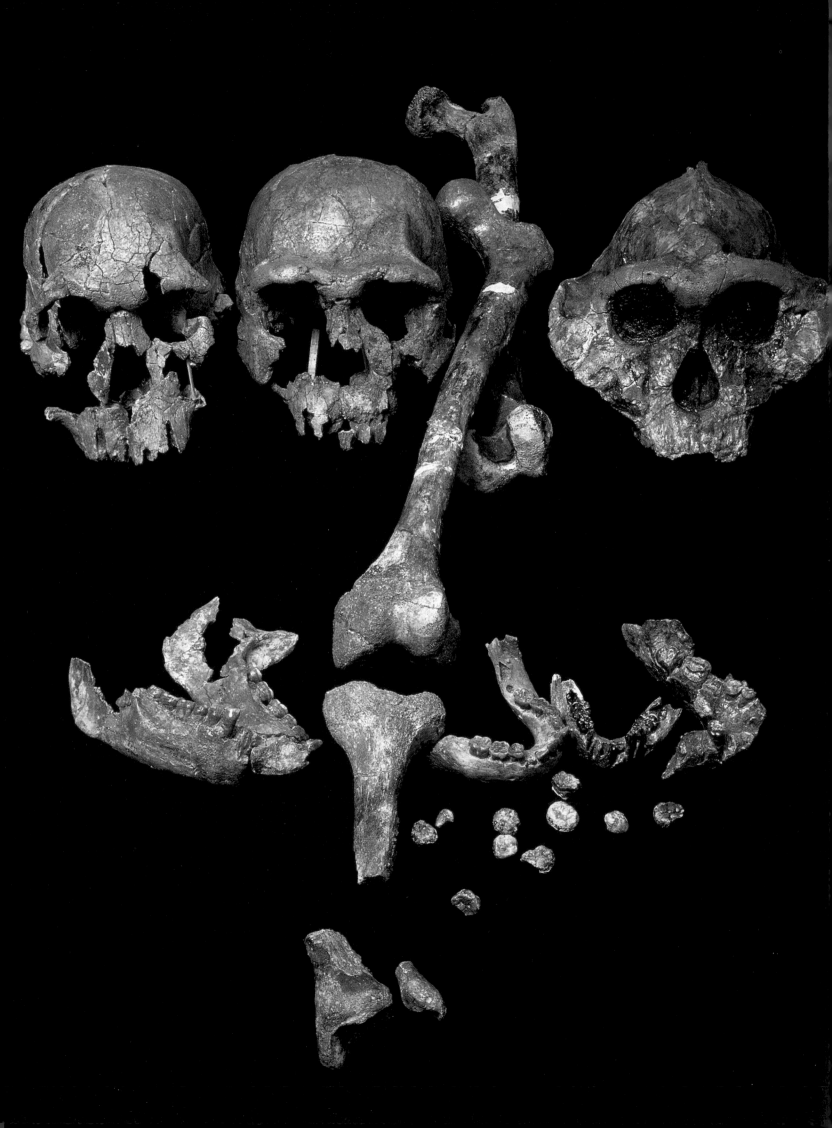

LEFT *Expeditions to East Turkana in Kenya in the 1970s and 1980s, led by Richard Leakey following aerial reconnaissance, were extremely successful in unearthing a remarkable array of hominid skulls and bones.*

One of the most celebrated early discoveries was "1470 man" (left), the first moderately complete skull of a creature suspected to exist by Richard's father Louis – this was the relatively large-brained "handy man", Homo habilis. In addition, important remains of Homo erectus (center) and Australopithecus robustus (right) were excavated in geological strata of a similar age. These discoveries have all been dated at about 1.5 million years old, and provided proof that the human lineage was not, as had often been portrayed in textbooks on the evolution of the human race, a simple matter of one species succeeding another in a straightforward sequence.

The story was clearly far more complex, with several species existing contemporaneously, though separated ecologically, within this region of Africa in the pleistocene. Brain size (an indicator of intelligence)is one of the probable factors which explain why some species survived while others died out, but the whole subject is still the subject of considerable research by paleontologists.

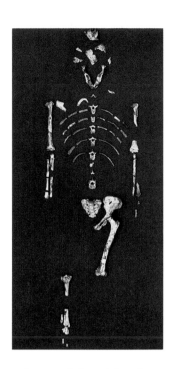

LEFT *Australopithecus afarensis is the scientific name of the skeleton affectionately known as "Lucy." The name was coined because the Beatles' pop song "Lucy in the Sky with Diamonds" was playing repeatedly on the radio in the early 1970s, when the remains were being examined and reassembled at the base camp of Don Johansen's expedition at Hadar in Ethiopia. This, the first reasonably complete hominid from rocks over 3 million years old, indicated that a fully erect bipedal posture had already been achieved. It was confirmed by Mary Leakey's discovery of the hominid tracks at Laetoli.*

The development of the brain brought with it a number of related changes in the shape of the skull. The upper part of the braincase mushroomed on top of the spinal cord, so that the area of the skull that contained the brain grew larger at both back and front. At the front, this produced the forehead, while the rest of the face gradually came to lie beneath the front part of the brain. In this way the projecting muzzle, characteristic of the faces of apes, became lost in hominids.

The jaws became lighter and shorter, and the rows of teeth became arc-shaped. The cheek teeth became squared off and grew a coating of thick enamel to resist the abrasive effects of a diet of tough plants; associated with this adaptation the canine tooth, which is still prominent and pointed in apes, became equal in size to the others in the tooth row, and was now shaped more like an incisor. The reduction in size of the canines meant that the teeth of hominids did not become locked together at the front when the jaws were closed; thus the jaws could be moved from side to side in a very effective grinding motion, which was ideal for feeding on tough plants and seeds.

Finds in East Africa

All the really early hominids are found in East Africa, in a strip dominated along its western edge by the East African Rift Valley, which runs from Ethiopia in the north to South Africa. Since the 1950s considerable work has been done by paleontologists in this part of the world; the result is a fascinating range of fossil hominids that are beginning to fill the gaps in the story of the middle phases of human origins.

Some of the oldest hominid fossils were found in the early 1970s in Hadar, Ethiopia, by a team from the United States led by Dr Donald Johanson. They discovered the partial skeleton of a hominid, a young female which they affectionately called "Lucy." More formally, she has been named *Australopithecus afarensis* ("southern ape from Afar" – the Afar triangle being the general area from which the fossils were first discovered).

"Lucy" is a little over 3 ft (1m) tall, with a rather ape-like face and a brain size of about 24 cubic ins (400cm³) – similar to that of a small chimpanzee. She exhibits a number of decidedly ape-like features, including quite large canine teeth, relatively short legs, and curved toe bones. But she also shows a number of distinctly hominid features, including an arc-shaped row of teeth, and leg bones and a pelvis which are fully adapted for upright walking.

"Lucy" is dated at about 3 million years old, but other specimens from Laetoli in Tanzania are dated very accurately to 3.75 million years. These include not only bones, but the famous trackway, discovered by Dr Mary Leakey (see page 221), which proves that fully bipedal hominids were walking around at this time.

In many ways "Lucy" is an enigma. She seems to represent an animal that was essentially human from the neck downwards, but retained a rather ape-like head.

Between 3 and 1 million years ago, several different kinds of australopithecine lived in East Africa. One of the first to be collected was *Australopithecus africanus*, known more familiarly as the Taung Child. The beautifully preserved skull of this infant australopithecine was recovered from a lime quarry at Taung in the early years of the twentieth century.

In 1925 the paleontologist Professor Raymond Dart described this specimen as an early hominid, rather than as an ape. It is hard now to imagine the controversy this stirred up; all the authorities of the time concluded that Dart was in error and this was in fact a genuine ape that had nothing to do with human origins. It was another 12 years before his very far-sighted comments were proved to be correct through the discovery by Dr Robert Broom of a further, this time adult, specimen from a limestone cave at Sterkfontein in South Africa.

At least three types of *Australopithecus* are known from Africa at this time. There is a lightly built species, the one first discovered by Raymond Dart. These stood about 4ft (1.3m) tall and may have weighed 90lb (40kg), with a brain capacity of about 30 cubic ins (500cm³) and a rather shorter muzzle than the earlier *Australopithecus afarensis*. The canine teeth are shorter, but the cheek teeth are still very much larger than those of later *Homo* specimens. More extreme examples of *Australopithecus* include a species known as *Australopithecus robustus* ("robust southern ape") from South Africa, and *Australopithecus boisei* from East Africa (better known as "Nutcracker Man"). Both of these are massively built animals in comparison with *Australopithecus africanus*, reaching heights of about 5ft 6ins (1.7m) and weighing about 155lb (70kg). The brain capacity of these animals was slightly larger than the *africanus* specimens, at about 33 cubic ins (550cm³).

These southern apes have very heavily built skulls. The jaws are very strong, there are extremely prominent brow ridges, and there is a clear "sagittal crest" – a ridge of bone where the jaw muscles on each side join up – running down the midline of the skull above the braincase. The combination of these features indicates the presence of huge jaw-closing muscles, which would have given these animals a tremendously powerful bite. The teeth confirm this notion, being extremely large and covered in very thick enamel for durability. The southern apes were clearly highly specialized herbivores, probably eating tough grain and seeds as their main diet.

Various types of australopithecine can therefore be imagined as coexisting in Africa, simply because they fed on different things. Perhaps the robust species fed on tough grasses, roots, and berries, while the lighter species had a more mixed diet, including eggs, lizards, and other meat items when they could be obtained.

That, at least, is the image created by looking in general terms at the teeth and jaw mechanism. However, when Dr Alan Walker of Johns Hopkins University in Baltimore subjected the teeth of the robust species of *Australopithecus* to examination under a scanning electron microscope, something unexpected emerged. The worn surfaces of the teeth exhibit a pattern of dents and scratches left by food which is very similar to the marks seen on the teeth of modern chimpanzees. This suggests that their diets may have been broadly similar. Chimps have a high content of berries and soft fruit in their diet, but may also feed on meat, sap, eggs, ants, and termites.

It may be, therefore, that the robust australopithecines had similar broad tastes in food. Perhaps different kinds preferred different environments – one species favoring open savannah, while the other was happier in moister woodland. For the moment we do not really know whether species of *Australopithecus* were ecologically separate; all we have are their skeletal remains.

The first true humans

Some fragmentary remains, including a lower jaw, parts of the braincase, and hand and foot bones, were found in Olduvai Gorge in Kenya in 1961 by Jonathan Leakey, son of the famous anthropologist Louis Leakey. Then a nearly complete skull was discovered in 1972 by Richard Leakey, another son of Louis, near Lake Turkana in Kenya. These remains may very well be those of the oldest known members of our own genus *Homo*, and are dated at between 2.5 and 1.5 million years old.

Unpromising though they might look, these simple stone shapes represent the kind of every day tools that habilines (Homo habilis) may well have fashioned. It has been suggested that stones may have been used to crack bones in order to extract nutritious marrow from animals killed by lions or leopards – one element in the scavenging way of life led by these early hominids. Not until the time of the more sophisticated Neanderthal man would stones be selected, cut, and shaped to perform different specific tasks.

In comparison to the known australopithecines these are lighter and more slenderly built creatures. The brain capacity was greater, ranging up to 48 cubic ins (800cm³). The hands seem to have been very similar to human hands and apparently capable of making simple stone tools. The creature was therefore named *Homo habilis*, "handy man."

This early human stood about 4ft (1.3m) tall, approximately the same size as its contemporary *Australopithecus africanus*, but had a very large brain for its size – almost comparable to that of humans of equivalent height.

The remains of habilines – hominids of the *Homo habilis* type – are found in rocks in East Africa which include simple early stone scrapers and hand-held axes, which they may well have made. Experiments have been made to try to recreate these tools from chunks of flint, in an effort to distinguish between naturally shattered pieces of rock and those which show definite evidence of manufacture by humanoid hands.

Australopithecus versus *Homo?*

It is clear from the East African discoveries that at least three hominids lived in this area in the Late Pliocene and Early Pleistocene. It is not certain how these similar apes coexisted. As mentioned above, there may have been some form of ecological separation that allowed all three to live side by side without significant competition. It is tempting to suggest that they were divided by feeding preferences, with the robust australopithecines being specialist herbivores, while the lighter australopithecines were omnivorous and early *Homo* was primarily a predator – using weapons to kill and dismember game animals, possibly including australopithecines.

At present there is no way of substantiating these suggestions, and very intense paleontological work is being undertaken in the Rift Valley of Africa to try to disentangle this fascinating topic and pin down the real nature of our early forebears. Were they early aggressive predators? Or were they more peaceable forms living on mixed diets and feeding more opportunistically?

When did *Homo* evolve?

In addition to the problem of the coexistence of early hominids in the same general area of Africa, there is another question to be answered. What was the precise nature of the evolutionary relationships between the australopithecines and early species of *Homo*?

The discovery of *Australopithecus afarensis* was seen by some, particularly by the Leakeys working in Kenya, as pushing back the origins of the earliest humans considerably. They argued that this early ape seemed to be very much an australopithecine, rather than an early ancestor of both *Australopithecus* and *Homo*. They therefore proposed that *Australopithecus afarensis* lived alongside an as yet undiscovered early member of the genus *Homo*.

The alternative view was put forward by Donald Johanson and his colleagues, who had collected the remains of "Lucy." They held that this specimen reveals *Australopithecus afarensis* as being close to the early common ancestor of the two groups – the later australopithecines and the early members of the genus *Homo*. I favor the view that "Lucy" is an early australopithecine. Both groups of hominid had developed a fully upright posture, so there is no evidence from this quarter. However, all the skull characteristics of "Lucy" are more primitive than those of *Australopithecus africanus*.

Homo erectus

A new hominid appeared for the first time in Africa about 1.6 million years ago. An almost complete skeleton of this version of an early human, known as *Homo erectus*, was collected by Richard Leakey at Lake Turkana in 1984.

From the shape of its pelvis it appears to be a male, and from the state of eruption of the teeth he seems to have been about 12 years of age. He stood about 5ft 3ins (1.6m) tall and had a brain capacity of about 52 cubic ins (850cm³). The skull is more primitive than that of modern humans (*Homo sapiens*): there are prominent eyebrow ridges, the forehead slopes backward quite markedly, the jaw is rather heavy, and there is no chin (the chin is a very characteristic human feature). The remainder of the skeleton is little different from that of a modern human. For that reason, when the first discovery of a creature of this kind was made in the 1890s in Java, this skeleton of "Java Man" was given the name *Pithecanthropus erectus* – which means literally "upright ape man."

Other remains of *Homo erectus* are found widely across Africa, and have been dated at between 1.6 million and 200,000 years old. From about 1 million years ago (in the Middle Pleistocene) *Homo erectus* begins to be found in other parts of the world. It reached China ("Peking Man") and Java by 800,000 years ago and Europe by 500,000 years ago.

The "Peking Man" cave site at Choukoutien is remarkable because it includes a large number of specimens of *Homo erectus* dating from between 600,000 and 200,000 years ago. During this time there seems to be a steady increase in brain capacity from about 55 cubic ins (900cm³) to about 67 cubic ins (1100cm³).

The cave also provided evidence of some major cultural changes made by this species of human. They include the development of the use of fire, of the use of a more or less permanent habitation – a "home" – and of some elements of early tribal life. Elsewhere, *Homo erectus* remains appear to be associated with stone tools and weapons which show a much greater precision than those produced by *Homo habilis*. These tools are associated with a culture which is referred to as Paleolithic ("Old Stone Age") or Archeulian, and indicate that *Homo erectus* hunted in a cooperative way.

Neanderthal Man

The very first remains of Neanderthal Man were discovered by men quarrying lime in a cave in the Neander valley in Germany, not far from Düsseldorf, in February 1857. This was a propitious time for the remains of an early fossil human to be discovered, just over two years before the publication of Charles Darwin's *Origin of Species*.

The origin of humans and the relationship between humans and the great apes were hotly disputed subjects at the time. One side, the "progressionists," was prepared to accept an ancestry linked to that of apes, while their opponents simply could not accept such a proposition and required humans to be the subject of special Creation – if not by God himself, then at least by some God-inspired process.

The infuriating aspect of the discovery, however, was the fact that it could not be reliably dated. The interpreters of the material split into two distinct camps: those who believed that the anatomical features were consistent with it being an ancestor of humans, and those who considered it more likely to be a modern and somewhat deformed human who had died recently.

The remains included the top of the skull, limb bones, and the pelvis, all from one individual. The bones were unusually thick and heavy, and the limb bones appeared somewhat bent in comparison to those of modern humans. In the absence of clear-cut dating, the speculations which surrounded this discovery might seem hilarious today.

One quite serious theory was put forward in 1864 by F. Mayer, a Professor of Anatomy at the University of Bonn. He was convinced that the remains belonged to an anatomically modern human, but one who had suffered from rickets as a child. However, as the learned professor was to point out, bent legs may also develop through prolonged horse riding. As a result he concluded that, since the Cossack army had camped near the Neander valley in 1814, this was probably the skeleton of a deserter who had hidden there and died. But as Professor Thomas Huxley – a decided "progressionist"

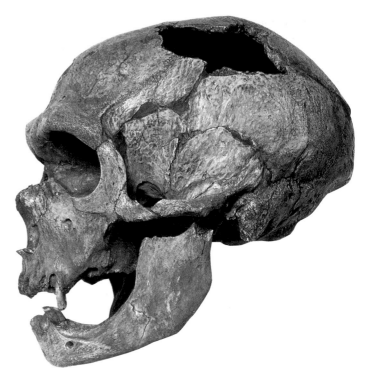

An intelligent human
ABOVE *The skull of* Homo sapiens neanderthalensis *was discovered in caves at La Chapelle aux Saints in southern France in 1908. Well-preserved specimens such as this testify to the undoubted intelligence of these early humans – their brain capacity tends to be slightly larger than that of modern humans. Nevertheless the large jaws and beetle brows of Neanderthals have given rise to the totally unjustified perception that they were dull and stupid "ape men."*

and strong advocate of Darwin's theory of evolution – pointed out, it was a mystery how the crippled and dying Cossack had scaled a 65 ft (20m) precipice, and then removed all his clothing and equipment before burying himself after he had died!

In that same year Professor William King of Queen's College, Galway, reviewed the Neander material. He concluded that this must have been an ancestor of humans – a simple creature whose "thoughts and desires . . . never soared beyond those of the brute." To distance it from *Homo sapiens* he decided to call it *Homo neanderthalensis*. In this way he distinguished an early form of human – it was no doubt rather a controversial suggestion at the time, but one that has often been adopted since then, as new discoveries have been made.

The remains were deeply puzzling, for the skull indicated two very contradictory facts. First, there were quite

The art of toolmaking
Compared to the simple tools of habilines, those of Neanderthals were far more varied and sophisticated. Stones of the right type were chosen and then chipped and fashioned to suit their intended purpose. Shown here are a pointed borer, a hand-held scraper, and a chopper; other typical tools included hand axes and anvils. All these indicate patience and considerable craft, genuine hallmarks of human intelligence.

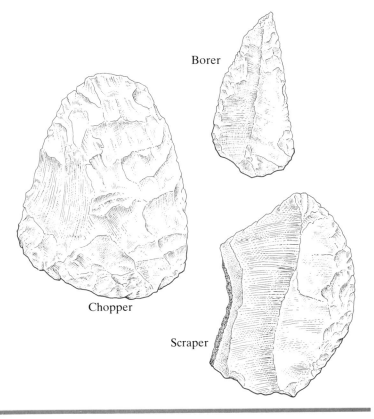

Borer

Chopper

Scraper

pronounced eyebrow ridges. This feature had been categorically stated to be an ape character by the great anatomist of the time, Professor Richard Owen – who, incidentally, considered that humans had been specially created. Second, it had a large brain capacity (79 cubic ins/1300cm^3) – equal to, or slightly larger than, that of some living humans. This point was noted by Professor Huxley. Large brain size has always been a very consistent measure of the relationship of primates with humans ever since Huxley made this observation on the Neander specimen.

Since the 1860s a number of better preserved Neanderthal specimens have been discovered, including much more complete skulls. Not only are the brow ridges very prominent, but the teeth are larger and the jaws heavier. Indeed, the whole of the skeletal frame is more robust than that of modern *Homo sapiens*. Today,

these features are regarded as no more than variants, perhaps equivalent to a special race of human beings, and a distinction is drawn between modern humans and Neanderthals by dividing the two into subspecies: modern humans as *Homo sapiens sapiens* and Neanderthals as *Homo sapiens neanderthalensis*. In effect, modern humans are represented by a variety of types of which Neanderthals represent one extreme.

Compared with the distribution of *Homo erectus*, that of Neanderthals is restricted to Europe and the Middle East in sites dated between 100,000 and 35,000 years ago. The most abundant remains come from northern and central Europe and are often associated with the Ice Ages. The stocky build (reminiscent of the Inuit or Eskimo race) would have been much better adapted to withstand periods of intense and persistent cold than the more slender build of modern humans.

Neanderthals seem to have been culturally advanced, making complex tools (various scrapers and borers have been found) and weapons (arrowheads) from a variety of materials (wood, bone, and stone) associated with the Middle Paleolithic or "Mousterian" tool culture. Artifacts of this kind are preserved in cave sites, particularly in southwestern France in the area of the Dordogne, and reveal aspects of Neanderthal culture which are reminiscent of some tribal customs today – including burial with gifts and food for the afterlife.

The Neanderthals apparently disappeared about 35,000 years ago, before the last great Ice Age which ended about 10,000 years ago. The cause of their extinction is a mystery. It is possible that they died out during a warm interglacial phase. Competition with contemporary populations of modern humans is another scenario. Alternatively, as a result of interbreeding with modern humans, their genes may simply have become dispersed in a common gene pool.

Modern humans

The most ancient representatives of anatomically modern humans may be between 300,000 and 150,000 years old. The problem lies in the interpretation of some of the earlier finds, which are on the borderline between anatomical *Homo erectus* and *Homo sapiens sapiens*.

The earliest undisputedly modern human skulls have been identified in Africa as between 120,000 and 100,000 years old, and therefore overlap in time with the remains of the Neanderthals. It seems quite likely that *Homo sapiens sapiens* evolved in Africa about 150,000 years ago, and that the Neanderthals therefore constitute a relatively short-lived and highly specialized race of humans which were especially adapted to the intermittent cold periods of the Late Pleistocene.

Following the disappearance of the Neanderthals in Europe, modern humans migrated into Europe and onward into Russia about 40,000 to 35,000 years ago. The earliest forms are known as Cro-Magnon Man, after the area in France where their remains were first discovered. Their tools were more sophisticated than those of the Neanderthals, and in addition they left a remarkable record of their life and times in their cave paintings, of which the most famous are at Lascaux in France.

At about the same time there are records of modern humans in Australia. The time when humans entered North America is much disputed; the first human artifacts date back about 12,000 years, though in theory humans could have island-hopped across the Bering Strait to Alaska much earlier than this.

The Cro-Magnon humans created wonderful cave paintings, notably at Lascaux in France and Altamira in Spain. Given their subject matter – deer, bison, and other animals feature frequently – perhaps these caves had ritual significance: places to be visited to bring good fortune in an imminent hunt.

According to the fossil record, anatomically modern humans arose in Africa between 150,000 and 100,000 years ago. About 40,000 years ago they spread rapidly to populate the modern world. This very recent ancestry, in geological terms, is supported by molecular biological studies of the degree of similarity between widely spread human populations today. All human populations are extremely similar genetically, even though distinct racial types can be identified. The greatest degree of variation is actually to be found in Africa, where the species has been longest established, so the biochemical evidence and that from the fossil record seem to be in accord.

The hunter-gatherer culture

The evidence left behind at sites of habitation points to a simple hunter-gatherer style of life. These people would have relied on a combination of hunting, plant gathering, and occasional opportunistic scavenging of carrion. This technically undemanding way of life appears to have been practiced since well before the

advent of modern humans, for perhaps 2 million years. Much of the activity would have been centered on a home base, and it would seem logical that there was some form of social organization among early hominid populations. Unfortunately the fossil record does not reveal any useful information on this matter.

Since the early 1960s detailed investigations have been carried out on the nature of modern hunter-gatherer groups such as the !Kung San (formerly called Bushmen) of southwestern Africa. When first viewed by European explorers these people were thought to be pitiable, a condition summarized in the words of the seventeenth-century philosopher Thomas Hobbes: "No arts; no letters; no society and which is worst of all, continual fear and danger of violent death; and the life of man, solitary, poor, nasty, brutish and short."

This view, imbued with a European sense of cultural superiority, demonstrates a woeful lack of understanding of the relationship between human groups such as the !Kung in their natural environment. Researchers living with these people discovered that in the wet summer

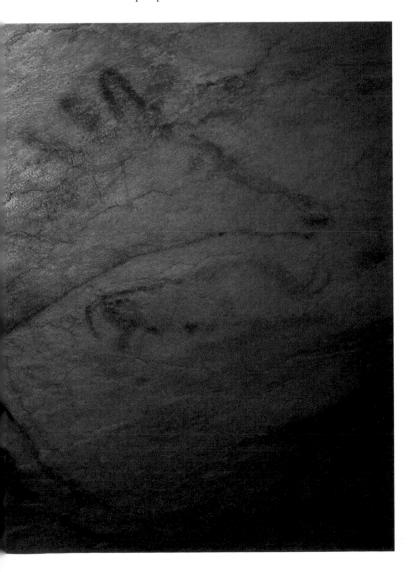

months they tend to hunt and gather in small bands of about six families (30 individuals in all – an apparently magical number associated with many hunter-gatherer groups around the world, and probably representing an optimum number for this sort of activity). These small bands tend to move to new camps every few weeks, so that they never have to travel too far in search of food – again an efficient strategy for foraging.

In the winter months, when it is dry, the parties tend to congregate near larger permanent waterholes and indulge in considerable socializing: dancing, story-telling, exchanging gifts, arranging marriages, and so on. It emerges, therefore, that the hunting parties are really part of a larger social colony, which draws together at specific times of the year for intense social contact.

Larger social units such as this present their own logistical problems. Foraging for food tends to take progressively longer as time goes on and nearby resources are exhausted, and high-density living eventually provokes some conflict. As soon as the rains return the parties disperse, but these are not the same ones that came together at the beginning of the dry season. The social gathering allows for reordering into different groups.

While apes may live in social groups, these too are relatively small – usually 30 or fewer – and they never indulge in the kind of mass social activities displayed by equivalent human hunter-gatherer communities. How wrong Hobbes' view of these people now seems. The only item they might seem to lack is "letters," but these they carry around in their heads in their songs, dances, and stories which form a rich cultural heritage.

The division of labor within the hunter-gatherer society is reasonably clear-cut. The men are the hunters – they have the advantage of speed and strength for such activities. The women are the gatherers of plants (hunting would probably be difficult with noisy children in tow), and contribute two-thirds of the !Kung diet.

Curiously, the gathering of plants takes considerably less time in the average week than hunting: about 44 hours of work are put in by the men and about 40 hours by women – but this excludes child rearing, so on average the women still work longer than the men. Despite this inequality of effort, the women apparently do not feel exploited, because they have economic prestige and political power in their society. The structure of !Kung society does not seem so uncivilized when compared to the status of women in some of the so-called "civilized" parts of the world today.

Equally, the ethical nature of hunting among the !Kung is a remarkable example of sharing from which capitalist societies might learn. Once the prey has been killed, the hunter initiates a complex process of sharing the raw meat. This ritual is dictated by kinship and

The tribal peoples of Namibia such as the Kung San exhibit many of the characteristics which may have been established by early hominid communities of hunter-gatherers. Their ability to make weapons such as bows and arrows for killing at a distance (RIGHT) enables them to bring down large prey which an unarmed human would find impossible to overcome. Their skills in tracking their prey are unsurpassed and relate to their intimate relationship with the African environment. The butchering and sharing of the kill from such hunting expeditions appear to be highly ritualized, and are vital in helping to bind together the social structure of the group.

OPPOSITE ABOVE *Social gatherings allow for ritual bonding within the tribe, and for intense periods of social exchange of information (stories, and facts about their environment) at set times of the year.*

OPPOSITE BELOW *The women appear to have few problems regarding their social status in this type of society. They perform a vital role, not only in rearing young, which makes them less able to participate in hunting expeditions, but also in more local gathering of food. Indeed, their food-gathering ability may be, on balance, more important than the hunting of game by the men.*

obligation, which pervades the entire social group and is the foundation of their society. Infants in all societies have a capacity to share and also to be selfish; it is the sharing characteristic that is nurtured within this type of society, and molds the behavior of the adults.

Although we have no real way of knowing the truth, it is very possible that such stable bands of egalitarian hunter-gatherers, with their periodic communal celebrations, may have been the stuff of which modern humans were made.

The development of settled societies

Not until the Neolithic (New Stone Age), between 20,000 and 10,000 years ago, do settlements that were inhabited by humans show evidence of permanent social groups larger than about 30 individuals. At this time agriculture began to establish itself. The ability of humans to manipulate ecosystems started at this point. Cultivation produced areas artificially planted with crops, and selective breeding of plants began to produce

evolutionary anomalies. These are reflected in many of the domesticated breeds of plants which we now take so much for granted and tend to think of as natural, such as wheat and barley.

Stable communities which were able to subsist on crops began a process of civilization which resulted in an increasingly rapid development of biological manipulation and technology. First, to improve the agricultural techniques simple tools were invented. Animals were domesticated and harnessed to work the land and to provide food and clothing. Concentrations of human social groups also produced greater complexity of interaction, and the development of specialist skills within the overall community – skills which could then be "sold" in exchange for the necessities of life.

The establishment of fixed communities would have started with small villages, but eventually led to towns and cities. Ultimately nation-states began to emerge. From that moment human populations have risen steeply worldwide, and technological advances have occurred with breathtaking speed on a geological scale of time. In the space of 10,000 years (the tiniest blip in the history of life on Earth, which has so far lasted close to 4 billion years) humans have risen to dominate the planet to an unparalleled degree. How the Earth will be able to sustain the overwhelming rise of the human population is something that must concern us all.

THE END OF EVOLUTION?

Paramount among all these social and cultural changes was the opportunity for teaching and learning, which is such an inherent part of the human social condition (as it was, and still is, among hunter-gatherer communities). The transfer of skills has transformed the biological process which led to the appearance of the first human communities from one based strictly upon the evolutionary principle of the survival of the fittest, as expounded by Charles Darwin, to one far more akin to the discredited theory proposed by Lamarck, the inheritance of acquired characteristics.

The reason for suggesting this is simply that, once human settlements began to develop, their environments ceased to be natural in a strict sense. Humans began to disrupt local ecosystems and have done so increasingly over time, to the point where large-scale changes such as rising extinction rates, global warming, and holes in the ozone layer are taking place as a direct consequence of human interference with the mechanisms of the Earth.

Humans have taken the biological principle of homeostasis – independence from the environment – a stage further. They have developed systems which have allowed them, despite their physical limitations, to inhabit most parts of the surface of the Earth. Human dwellings and clothing insulate their occupants from a possibly hostile environment, and are paid for by extracting the mineral resources of the Earth. Medical technology and social welfare schemes ensure that people live longer and that even the weak survive for far longer than they would have done in the wild.

Humans have thus been able, by virtue of their great intelligence and technological innovations, to avoid the unpleasant side effects of the evolutionary process (the survival of the fittest) that led to their appearance in the first place. The evolution of humans – especially those in the richer nations – might therefore be considered to have ceased. Genetically, the human species is becoming increasingly homogeneous, aided by the migration of human populations around the world and intermarriage between racial types. It has been argued quite recently that greater homogeneity among human populations

will actually limit our potential to evolve new species in the future – the more alike we all are, the less chance there will be of some novel genetic variant, a potential new species, becoming established in a local population and forming the basis for the rise of a new (and better?) species of human.

Humans have an unparalleled position in the world today. Technological advances have meant that we now have the ability to destroy our planet by a nuclear holocaust. Equally, we have the capacity to use technology to minimize the impact of the human population on our planet. The last two centuries have witnessed the Industrial Revolution. This watershed in human existence, though of enormous benefit in social and technological terms, has led to attitudes which perpetuate the selfish exploitation of the Earth's resources and the large-scale pollution which this generates.

Rising awareness among technologically advanced countries of the global effects of industrialization, population growth, and pollution has led to increasingly vigorous campaigns by organizations such as Greenpeace and Friends of the Earth, which are beginning to influence politicians. However, while the world is still divided between rich, industrially competent states and the remainder, whose priorities are speedy industrialization of their impoverished economies and provision of basic food supplies to their rapidly growing populations, there is little chance of a consensus being reached.

Yet, for all this gloom and despair, it would seem that we humans are, intellectually and technologically, more than capable of solving many of our problems. All it needs is a concerted effort on the part of nations: our advanced societies have much to learn from the sharing and cooperation which underpinned the society of our simple hunter-gatherer ancestors. Let us hope and trust that we can still live up to the name which the Swedish scientist Linnaeus gave us over two centuries ago: *Homo sapiens* – "the wise man."

The abilities of the human race are without doubt phenomenal. No other species on Earth has the intellectual power, the dexterity, and the manufacturing ability. But where is all this remarkable ability taking us? These refugees from the war in Ethiopia in the 1980s present us with a vision that seems to sum up the despair that can often assail us as the media offer up the latest instance of human inhumanity around the world. Yet each human in this picture has so much to offer. Each man, woman, and child is a miracle of biological engineering, the product of a fantastic evolutionary story that stretches back hundreds of millions of years over the history of life on Earth. Let's not waste this fantastic heritage, but put it to good use – to enrich and develop our lives and those of the species who happen to share our planet, and to plow back something into the Earth from which we came.

CHRONOLOGY OF LIFE

EON	ERA	PERIOD	Significant geological/ climatic changes	Main developments in plant and animal life
			Formation of Earth about 4,500 mya	No life
Archean 3,800–2,500 mya	Precambrian to 540 mya		Date of earliest known rocks 3,800 mya	Single-celled organisms (oldest known fossils 3,500 my old)
Proterozoic 2,500–540 mya				Earliest fossil animals and plants in latest Precambrian (600–550 mya)
Phanerozoic 540 mya–present	Paleozoic ("ancient life") 540–245 mya	Cambrian 540–505 mya		In earliest Cambrian, first animals with hard skeletons, e.g. molluscs

In Mid-Cambrian, Burgess Shale creatures including *Pikaia*, earliest chordate (group that includes humans)

First stage of rise in numbers and diversity of marine creatures, followed by their extinction |
| | | Ordovician 505–440 mya | More stable climate worldwide | Second stage of rise in numbers and diversity of marine creatures (new range), e.g. jawless fish

In Late Ordovician, first land-based plants, leading to first ecosystems around watercourses |
| | | Silurian 440–407 mya | | In Late Silurian, first fish with jaws and fins

First land animals associated with new water-based ecosystems (invertebrates) |
| | | Devonian 407–360 mya | Warm, swampy environments | In Early Devonian, first bony ray-finned and lobe-finned fish

In Late Devonian, first four-footed vertebrates (tetrapods) on land (fish fins evolve into limbs) |
| | | Carboniferous 360–286 mya | Warm and swampy in Early Carboniferous

In Late Carboniferous, glaciations in southern continents (southern Africa, Antarctica), at this time clustered close to S. Pole. Likely result is shift to more seasonal conditions and stronger latitudinal climatic zoning. | Carboniferous coal swamps (tree-dominated forests)

Amphibians (near water)

First reptiles (on land) develop from early tetrapods

From Late Carboniferous, mammal-like reptiles start to be dominant on land (and remain so until end of Triassic) |
| | | Permian 286–245 mya | Southern continents start to drift north toward tropics, eventually sliding together to produce Pangea | Mammal-like reptiles, archosaurs and first gliding reptiles, dominant on land

Mass extinction of marine creatures |
| | Mesozoic ("Age of Reptiles") 245–66 mya | Triassic 245–210 mya | Warm, wet climate worldwide, becoming hotter and drier toward end of Triassic | At end of Triassic, first dinosaurs, first true mammals, and disappearance of mammal-like reptiles

Lush forest growth |

EON	ERA	PERIOD	Significant geological/ climatic changes	Main developments in plant and animal life
Phanerozoic 540 mya–present (cont.)	Mesozoic 245–66 mya (cont.)	Jurassic 210–144 mya	Southern continents separate from northern ones Tropical climate (warm and wet)	Dinosaurs dominant First birds Lush forest growth
		Cretaceous 144–66 mya	Africa and S. America separate from each other; N. America separates from Europe Major transgressions of sea onto land Worldwide cooling in Mid-Cretaceous	First marsupial mammals appear in S. and N. America; first placental mammals appear in northern hemisphere First flowering plants in Late Cretaceous (possible result of forest destruction) Dinosaurs become extinct at end of Cretaceous
	Cenozoic ("Age of Mammals") 66 mya–present	Tertiary 66–1.8 mya		Diversification of mammals; many faunas develop in isolation because continents now separated
		Paleocene Epoch 66–57 mya		The rise of giant, predatory land birds
		Eocene Epoch 57–36 mya		First horses, whales, and bats
		Oligocene Epoch 36–23 mya	Europe separates from N . America	First mammal fossils found in Australia
		Miocene Epoch 23–5 mya	Formation of Antarctic ice-cap lowers sea levels and creates land bridge between Europe and Asia. Climate grows steadily colder and encourages development of grasslands. Africa, Europe, and southern Asia join up and allow interchange of mammals	First ape (*Proconsul*)
		Pliocene Epoch 5–2 mya	N. and S. America join permanently	First evidence of upright bipedalism (3.75 mya) and first known upright hominids (3.6 mya)
		Quaternary 1.8 mya–present Pleistocene Epoch 2 mya–10,000 years ago	Ice Ages with subtropical interglacial spells	First members of genus *Homo* (1.6 mya) Massive extinctions after last Ice Age on brink of Holocene Neanderthal man (first tool-maker) about 100,000–35,000 years ago Cro-Magnon man (more sophisticated tools, cave paintings) 40,000–35,000 years ago First permanent communities and beginnings of agriculture: end of hunter-gatherer lifestyle (Neolithic/New Stone Age 20,000–10,000 years ago)
		Holocene Epoch 10,000 years ago–present		Growth of human civilization Rise of technology

FURTHER READING

1 The Origin of the Universe

Cattermole, P & Moore, P: *The Story of the Earth.* Cambridge University Press: Cambridge, 1985.
Well-written, popular book on the formation of the Earth.

Darwin, C: *The Origin of Species.* JM Dent (Everyman's University Library): London, 1975.
A modern facsimile of Darwin's epoch-making book, with commentary by a modern evolutionary biologist.

Gribbin, J: *Stephen Hawking: a Life in Science.* Penguin: London, 1992.
An excellent introduction to Hawking's *A Brief History of Time.* The best way to approach Hawking is to read this book first.

Hawking, SW: *A Brief History of Time: From Big Bang to Black Holes.* Bantam Books: London, 1991.
Difficult, but mind-bending fun to read. Ideas about the origin of the Universe from one of the world's leading cosmologists.

Maynard Smith, J: *The Theory of Evolution.* Penguin Books: London, 1975.

Patterson, C: *Evolution.* British Museum, Natural History: London, 1978.
One of the best guides to the process of evolution. Written with the lay-person in mind.

Pellant, C (ed): *Earthscope.* Salamander Books: London, 1985.
Dense, well-illustrated guide to the structure of the Earth.

Smith, DG (ed): *The Cambridge Encyclopedia of Earth Sciences.* Cambridge University Press: Cambridge, 1982.
The ultimate book on the Earth – clearly something into which to dip, not to be read from cover to cover. Quite scholarly in places.

Stanley, SM: *The New Evolutionary Timetable: Fossils, Genes and the Origin of Species.* Basic Books Inc: New York, 1981.
A semi-popular book explaining the paleobiological contribution to the evolution debate.

Van Andel, TJ: *New Views of an Old Planet: Continental Drift and the History of the Earth.* Cambridge University Press: Cambridge, 1985.
A refreshing look at the Earth, the processes that affect it and how organisms fit into the general scheme of things.

2 Beginnings of Life

Bernal, JD: *The Physical Basis of Life.* Routledge & Kegan Paul: London, 1951.

Cairns-Smith, AG: *Seven Clues to the Origin of Life: A Scientific Detective Story.* Cambridge University Press: Cambridge, 1985.
A very interesting alternative view concerning the origins of organic molecules which are seen as being stabilized by clay minerals. An iconoclastic approach – maybe he's right!

Fox, SW & Dose, K: *Molecular Evolution and the Origin of Life.* Marcel Dekker: New York, 1972.
Detailed explanation of some of Sidney Fox's work.

Haldane, JBS: "The Origin of Life", *The Rationalist Annual,* 1929: 148, pp. 3-10.

Margulis, L: *The Origin of Eukaryotic Cells.* Yale University Press: New Haven, 1970.
Early book explaining her endosymbiotic theory for the origin of eukaryotes.

Margulis, L: *Symbiosis in Cell Evolution.* WH Freeman: San Francisco, 1981.

Oparin, AI: *The Origin of Life.* Macmillan: New York, 1938.
Translation of this Russian scientist's ideas which proved remarkably similar to those put forward by the British scientist and philosopher JBS Haldane.

Oparin, AI (ed): *The Origin of Life on the Earth.* Pergamon Press: Oxford, 1959.

Orgel, LE: *The Origins of Life.* Chapman & Hall: London, 1973.
A classic book on the subject.

Schopf, JW (ed): *Earth's Earliest Biosphere, its Origin and Evolution.* Princeton University Press: Princeton, 1983.
A scholarly review of the origins of the organic world and ecosystems.

Schopf, JM (ed): *Major Events in the History of Life.* Jones & Bartlett: Boston, 1992.
A scholarly collection on the origins of life and some of the major events involved, written by some of the leading scientists of the moment.

Urey, HC: *The Planets.* Yale University Press: New Haven, 1952.

3 The Strange Cambrian World

Chen Jun-yuan, Hou Zian-guang & Lu Hao-zhi: *The Chengjian Fauna – Oldest Soft-bodied Fauna on Earth.* National Geographic Research and Exploration: 1989.
The material includes that which scuppered ideas about *Hallucigenia* walking about on stilts.

Conway Morris, S: "The Middle Cambrian Metazoan *Wiwaxia corrugata* (Matthew) from the Burgess Shale, British Columbia, Canada", *Philosophical Transactions of the Royal Society*, 1985: B.307, pp. 507-86.
Scientific articles about the strange Cambrian animals.

Conway Morris, S & Peel, JS: "Articulated Haldieriids from the Lower Cambrian of Northern Greenland", *Nature*, 1990: 345, pp. 802-805.

Glaessner, MF: *The Dawn of Animal Life*. Cambridge University Press: Cambridge, 1984.
The classic view of the fauna of Ediacara.

Gould, SJ: *Wonderful Life: The Burgess Shale and the Nature of History*. Hutchinson Radius: London, 1990.
A racy piece of writing by a serious scientist with a journalistic style, this is a review of the animals and an overview of some of the scientists who studied them. They may not have appreciated all his comments and asides, but this book has thrown a great deal of light on the people working on Cambrian faunas.

Jefferies, RPS: *The Ancestry of Vertebrates*. British Museum, Natural History: London, 1986.
The ultimate book on our ancestry via echinoderms, by the leading proponent of this view.

Seilacher, A: "Vendozoa: Organismic Construction in the Proterozoic Biosphere", *Lethaia*, 1989: 22, pp. 229-39.
A very different view of Ediacaran organisms.

Sprigg, RC: "On the 1946 Discovery of the Precambrian Ediacaran Fossil Fauna of South Australia", *Earth Science History*, 1988: 7, pp. 46-51.
Comments from the man who discovered the Ediacara site.

Wade, M: "Preservation of Soft-bodied Animals in Precambrian Sandstones at Ediacara, South Australia", *Lethaia*, 1968: 1, pp. 238-67.

Whittington, HB: *The Burgess Shale*. Yale University Press: New Haven, 1985.
An atlas of the Burgess Shale fauna.

Whittington HB & Briggs DEG: "The Largest Cambrian Animal, *Anomalocaris*, Burgess Shale, British Columbia", *Philosophical Transactions of the Royal Society*, 1985: B.309, pp. 569-609.
A scientific review of the most remarkable Burgess Shale animal.

4 The Teeming Seas

Barnes, RD: *Invertebrate Zoology* (5th edition). Saunders College Publishing: New York, 1987.
The ultimate guide to how invertebrates live and work as animals.

Black, RM: *Elements of Palaeontology*. Cambridge University Press: Cambridge, 1970.

Carroll, RL: *Vertebrate Paleontology and Evolution*. WH Freeman: New York, 1988.
Very scholarly, the most detailed book on vertebrate paleontology in print today.

Clarkson, ENK: *Invertebrate Palaeontology and Evolution* (2nd edition). Unwin Hyman: London, 1986.
A valuable compendium on invertebrate fossils and their evolution. A guide to what you really ought to know.

Lambert, D: *The Cambridge Field Guide to Prehistoric Life*. Cambridge University Press: Cambridge, 1985.
Simple guide to vertebrate and invertebrate fossils.

Moy-Thomas, JA & Miles, RS: *Palaeozoic Fishes*. Chapman & Hall: London, 1971.
Scholarly book on ancient fishes.

Murray, JW (ed): *Atlas in Invertebrate Macrofossils*. Longman: London, 1985.
A useful guide to the identification of fossil invertebrates.

Nield, EW & Tucker, VCT: *Palaeontology: An Introduction*. Pergamon: London, 1985.

Romer, AS: *The Vertebrate Story* (5th edition). University of Chicago Press: Chicago, 1959.
This book on vertebrate evolution seems rather old-fashioned today, but was written in popular style by one of the best (now dead) vertebrate palaeontologists of the century and a very dear man.

Sepkoski, JJ: "A Kinetic Model of Phanerozoic Taxonomic Diversity. I. Analysis of Marine Orders", *Paleobiology*, 1978: 4, pp. 223-51.

Sepkoski, JJ: "A Kinetic Model of Phanerozoic Taxonomic Diversity. II. Early Phanerozoic Families and Multiple Equilibria", *Paleobiology*, 1979: 5, pp. 221-51.

Stahl, BJ: *Vertebrate History: Problems in Evolution*. McGraw-Hill: New York, 1974.
Student text on vertebrate evolution. A little dated, but a nice, thoughtful approach.

Valentine, JW: *Evolutionary Paleoecology of the Marine Biosphere*. Prentice Hall: New York, 1973.
Some very interesting ideas.

5 Gaining the Land

Alexander, R McN: *The Chordates* (2nd edition). Cambridge University Press: Cambridge, 1981.
A textbook on how vertebrates work, with a little bit about their history.

Carroll, RL: *Vertebrate Paleontology and Evolution*. WH Freeman: New York, 1988.

Coates MI & Clack JA: "Polydactyly in the Earliest Known Tetrapod Limbs", *Nature*, 1990: 347, pp. 66-9.
The scientific description of those amazing feet!

Goin, CJ & Goin, OB: "Further Comments on the Origin of the Tetrapods", *Evolution*, 1956: 10, pp. 440-41.

Inger, RF: "Ecological Aspects of the Origin of the Tetrapods", *Evolution*, 1957: 11, pp. 373-76.

Little, C: *The Colonisation of Land: Origins and Adaptations of Terrestrial Animals*. Cambridge University Press: Cambridge, 1983.

Panchen, AL (ed): *The Terrestrial Environment and the Origin of Land Vertebrates*. Academic Press: London, 1980.
Scholarly textbook on the evolution of life on land.

Radinsky, LB: *The Evolution of Vertebrate Design*. University of Chicago Press: Chicago, 1987.
Interesting, design-orientated book on vertebrates by a paleontologist who died far too young.

Romer, AS: "Tetrapod Limbs and Early Tetrapod Life", *Evolution*, 1958: 12, pp. 365-69.

Stahl, BJ: *Vertebrate History: Problems in Evolution*. McGraw-Hill: New York, 1974.

Stewart, WN & Rothwell GW: *Palaeobotany and the Evolution of Plants* (2nd edition). Cambridge University Press: Cambridge, 1993.
Scholarly textbook on the fossil history of plants. All you might ever want to know – and more!

6 Conquering the Land

Allin, EF: "The Evolution of the Mammalian Ear", *Journal of Morphology*, 1975: 147, pp. 403-37.
The scientific article which tried to solve the problem of how mammals evolved their hearing system.

Carroll, RL: *Vertebrate Paleontology and Evolution*. WH Freeman: New York, 1988.

Kemp, TS: *Mammal-like Reptiles and the Evolution of Mammals*. Academic Press: London, 1983.
Scholarly book on the origins of mammals – probably the book to read if you are really interested.

Kermack, DM & Kermack, KA: *The Evolution of Mammalian Characters*. Croon Helm: London, 1984.

King, GM: *Dicynodonts: A Study in Palaeobiology*. Chapman & Hall: London, 1990.
Detailed look at one particular group of rather odd, but very abundant mammal-like reptiles.

Pough, FH, Heiser, JB, & McFarland, WN: *Vertebrate Life* (3rd edition). Macmillan: New York, 1989.
Textbook on the vertebrates, both living and fossil. Very nice comprehensive approach to the subject.

7 Variations on a Theme

Carroll, RL: *Vertebrate Paleontology and Evolution*. WH Freeman: New York, 1988.

Frey, E, Reif, WE & Westphal, F (eds): "Aspects of the Biomechanics of Crocodilian Terrestrial Locomotion", *Third Symposium on Mesozoic Terrestrial Ecosystems*. Attempto: Tubingen, 1984.
How archosaur backs work.

McGowan, C: *Dinosaurs, Spitfires and Sea Dragons*. Harvard University Press: Cambridge Mass., 1991.
Popular book looking at the way dinosaurs, marine reptiles and pterosaurs worked as living animals.

Weishampel, DB, Dodson, P & Osmolska, H (eds): *The Dinosauria*. University of California Press: Berkeley, 1990.
The ultimate book on dinosaurs. Rather scholarly, no nice color pictures, but huge numbers of facts and details.

Wellnhofer, P: *The Illustrated Encyclopedia of Pterosaurs*. Salamander Books: London, 1991.
The complete guide to pterosaurs, beautifully illustrated.

8 Dinosaurs and Birds

Alvarez, L: "Mass Extinctions caused by Large Bolide Impacts", *Physics Today*, 1987: July, pp. 24-33.

Bakker, RT: *The Dinosaur Heresies*. William Morrow: New York, 1986.
Rather strongly biased, this is Bakker's view of the world of dinosaurs. It is powerful and beguiling, but not altogether as scientifically well founded as it sounds.

Benton, MJ: *On the Trail of the Dinosaurs*. Kingfisher: London, 1989.
Good book about dinosaurs and how they are studied.

Czwekas, SJ & Olson EC: *Dinosaurs Past and Present* (Volumes 1 & 2). Natural History Museum of Los Angeles County: Los Angeles, 1987.
Art meets science in the dinosaur world – an interesting pair of volumes.

Feduccia, A: *The Age of Birds*. Harvard University Press: Cambridge Mass., 1980.
Covers much of what we know about fossil birds.

Hecht, MK, Ostrom, JH, Viohl, G, & Wellnhofer, P (eds): *The Beginnings of Birds*. Freunde des Jura-Museums: Eichstätt, 1985.
Dinosaurs and birds examined in great detail.

Horner, JR & Gorman, J: *Digging Dinosaurs*. Workman: New York, 1988.

Horner, JR & Lessom, D: *The Complete T. Rex*. Souvenir Press: London, 1993.

Lambert, D: *The Ultimate Dinosaur Book*. Dorling Kindersley: London, 1993.

Norman, DB: *The Illustrated Encyclopedia of Dinosaurs*. Salamander Books: London, 1985.
Detailed and well-illustrated book on dinosaurs, but rather out of date nowadays.

Norman, DB: *Dinosaur!* Boxtree: London, 1991.
Popular book on dinosaurs written for a wide audience.

Officer, CB, Hallam, A, Drake, CL & Devine, JD: "Late Cretaceous and Paroxysmal Cretaceous/Tertiary Extinctions", *Nature*, 1987: 326, pp. 143-49.

Ostrom, JH: "Archaeopteryx and the Origin of Birds", *Biological Journal of the Linnean Society*, 1976: 8, pp. 91-182.
The article which revived the debate about dinosaurs and the origin of birds.

Paul, GS: *Predatory Dinosaurs of the World.* Simon & Schuster: New York, 1988.
Interesting artwork. Best treated as an illustrated guide to theropods.

Raup, DM: *The Nemesis Affair: A Story of the Death of Dinosaurs and the Ways of Science.* WW Norton: New York, 1987.
Racy whodunnit about the extinction of dinosaurs written by a scientist who is firmly convinced that meteorites have periodically bombarded the Earth.

Russell, DA: *An Odyssey in Time: The Dinosaurs of North America.* University of Toronto Press: Toronto, 1989.
An idiosyncratic look at dinosaurs and the evolution of life by a slightly eccentric, but delightful paleontologist.

Sloan, RE, Rigby, JR, Van Valen, LM, & Gabriel, D: "Gradual Dinosaur Extinction and the Simultaneous Ungulate Radiation in the Hell Creek Formation", *Science*, 1986: 232, pp. 629-33.

Weishampel, DB, Dodson, P, & Osmolska, H (eds): *The Dinosauria.* The University of California Press: Berkeley, 1990.

9 The Tertiary World

Carroll, RL: *Vertebrate Paleontology and Evolution.* WH Freeman: New York, 1988.

Halstead, LB: *The Evolution of the Mammals.* Eurobook Limited: London, 1978.
Rather old but nevertheless well-written and popular book about mammal evolution by another paleontologist who died far too young.

Kurten, B: *The Age of Mammals.* Weidenfeld & Nicolson: London, 1971.

Kurten, B & Anderson, E: *Pleistocene Mammals of North America.* Columbia University Press: New York, 1980.

Macdonald, D: *The Velvet Claw.* BBC Books: London, 1992.
An illustrated history of predatory mammals.

Rich, PV & Thompson, EM (eds): *The Fossil Vertebrate Record of Australia.* Monash University Press: Clayton, Australia, 1982.

Savage, RJG & Long, MR: *Mammal Evolution: An Illustrated Guide.* British Museum, Natural History: London, 1986.
Authoritative guide to mammal evolution. Nicely illustrated.

Simpson, GG: *Splendid Isolation: The Curious History of South American Mammals.* Yale University Press: New Haven, 1980.
A review of the history of South America by the man who knew it all.

Spinar, ZV: *Life Before Man.* Thames & Hudson: London, 1973.
Some marvellous illustrations of fossil animals by a superb artist of his day (Burian).

Walker, EP: *Mammals of the World.* (3rd edition, 2 volumes). Johns Hopkins University Press: Baltimore, 1975.

10 Into the Fourth Age

Gribbin, J & Cherfas, J: *The Monkey Puzzle.* Bodley Head: London, 1982.
Popular account of human origins.

Johanson, DC & Edey, MA: *Lucy: The Beginnings of Humankind.* Granada: London, 1981.
A very easy-to-read "best seller" on the discovery of the famous hominid "Lucy".

Leakey, REF: *The Making of Mankind.* Michael Joseph: London, 1981.
The book of the TV series. Some beautiful pictures and a nicely written account.

Lewin, R: *Human Evolution: An Illustrated Introduction.* Blackwells: Oxford, 1984.
Very readable account of human origins.

Oakley, KP: *Man the Tool-Maker* (6th edition). British Museum, Natural History: London, 1972.
Small, rather scholarly book on toolmaking.

Reader, J: *Missing Links: The Hunt for Earliest Man* (2nd edition). Pelican Books: London, 1988.
A nicely written account of the trials and tribulations of the people who have searched for human origins.

Stringer, CB & Gamble, C: *Solving the Puzzle of Human Origins: In Search of Neanderthals.* Thames and Hudson: London, 1993.

Sutcliffe, AJ: *On the Track of Ice Age Mammals.* British Museum, Natural History: London, 1985.
The best review of life and times during the Ice Ages. Perhaps a little scholarly, but it is all there and fascinating.

Tattersall, I: *Man's Ancestors: An Introduction to Primate and Human Evolution.* John Murray: London, 1970.

INDEX

ACKNOWLEDGMENTS

Picture and Artwork Credits

The publisher would like to thank the artists, museum archives, private individuals and picture agencies who have generously provided the pictures and artwork in this book, and by courtesy of whom they are reproduced. Credits are by page number.

1-11 Lineart 32 middle right, 46-47 bottom, 51 top left, 52 left, 58 bottom, 59 top, 59 bottom (after Lemche and Wingstrand), 62 bottom, 72, 83 bottom (after Andrews and Westoll, 1970), 94 (Radinsky, 1987), 119 bottom, 145, 148 bottom, 184-185 top, 186, 192, 201 top, 206, 212 bottom, 227; **Doug Allan/Oxford Scientific Films** 214 bottom; **Altamira, Spain/Bridgeman Art Library** 210, 228-229; **Kathie Atkinson/Oxford Scientific Films** 33, 52 top right, 85; **Peter Atkinson/Planet Earth Pictures** 79; **Gary Bell/Planet Earth Pictures** 78; From: **Florentine Codex, Biblioteca Laurenzeana, Florence** 205; **Denise Blagden** 106-107 (microsaurs after Carroll and Gaskell, 1978), 114 top right (leg detail after Jenkins, 1971), 142, 155 left, 163 main picture, 178, 193 (L to R after: Scott, 1888; Osborn, 1895), 214 top (after Simon, 1964), 220 (L to R after: Napier, 1979; Clark, 1971); **Tony Bomford/Oxford Scientific Films** 77 bottom; **Michael Botham/Robert Harding Picture Library** 151 top right; **Dr Tony Brain/Science Photo Library** 20-21; **Dr Derek Briggs, University of Bristol** 17 middle right; **Dr L. Carlo/Science Photo Library** 22; **Chartwell Illustrators** 24 top, 32 top, 58 top, 61 top (after Naef, from Shrock and Twenhofel), 64, 68 both, 69, 73, 77 top, 80 (from top: after Traquair, Moy-Thomas and Bradley Dyne, Lehman), 86, 102 top, 103, 110 bottom left (after Carroll), 111 bottom right, 122 top, 138 top, 148 top, 182, 196, 197 top, 198 (after Kellogg), 202 left, 212 top; **© Dr Mike Coates** 96 top, 97, 109, 212 top; **Photograph by Dr John C. W. Cope** 35 top, 36 inset; **Stephen Dalton/Oxford Scientific Films** 195 right; **Phil Dotson/Photo Researchers/Oxford Scientific Films** 188 top right; **John Downes/Planet Earth Pictures** 231 bottom; **Fredrik Ehrenstrom/Oxford Scientific Films** 96 bottom; **M. E. England/Ardea London Ltd** 133 left; **Dr Fred Espenak/Science Photo Library** 12 bottom; **Mary Evans Picture Library** 18, 27; **Jean-Paul Ferrero/Ardea London Ltd** 131; **Field Museum of Natural History, Chicago Neg# 75400C5/G** 98; **Michael Fogdon/Oxford Scientific Films** 133 right; **Jeff Foot/Survival Anglia** 183 left; **David Fox/Oxford Scientific Films** 19; **Simon Fraser/Science Photo Library** 13; **Clive Freeman/The Royal Institution/Science Photo Library** 20; **© Duncan Friend** 41; **François Gohier/Ardea London Ltd** 17 middle, 215 top; **Don Hadden/Ardea London Ltd** 188-189; **David A. Hardy/Science Photo Library** 10 top left, 10-11, 12 middle; **Hans Christian Heap/Planet Earth Pictures** 151 bottom right; **© Hunterian Museum, Glasgow** 76 bottom; **©. Institute of Human Origins, Berkeley, CA, USA** photograph by Institute of Human Origins 223; **Rodger Jackman/Oxford Scientific Films** 51 bottom right; **Carol Jopp/Robert Harding Picture Library** 230-231, 231 top; **Antony Joyce/Planet Earth Pictures** 91; **Jean Michel Labat/Ardea London Ltd** 183 right; **Martin Land/Science Photo Library** 64 left; **Zig Leszczynski/Animals Animals/Oxford Scientific Films** 122 bottom; **Kenneth Lucas/Planet Earth Pictures** 71 left, 188 top left; **John Lythgoe/Planet Earth Pictures** 152 right; **Alastair MacEwen/Oxford Scientific Films** 29; **Patrick Matthews/Robert Harding Picture Library** 151 bottom left; **Mark Mattlock/Planet Earth Pictures** 102 bottom; **Tom McHugh/Photo Researchers/Oxford Scientific Films** 81; **M L Design** 14, 153; **P. Morris/Ardea London Ltd** 35 bottom left, 152 left, 177, 195 left; **Leighton Moses** 28; **NASA/Science Photo Library** 24 bottom; **© National Geographic Society, USA** 117, 218-219; **Natural History Museum, London** 7, 54 top and bottom, 130 middle, 187 right, 199 main picture, 209, 216 bottom; **Natural History Museum, London/M. Long** 119 top, 187 left, 199 inset, 208, 209; **Natural History Museum, London/John Sibbick** 136-137, 138-139; **NIBSC/Science Photo Library** 23; **David Nicholls** 110-111, 123 bottom (after Riesz, 1981), 132 top (after Walker, 1964), 155 right, 161 top, 163 inset, 214 inset (after Szalay, 1976); **Dr David Norman** 6, 15, 17 middle left, 42, 116, 162, 168 top, 174; **#73.1235, Museum of Northern Arizona,** photograph by Marc Gaede 156, **Claude Nuridsany and Marie Pernnon/Scientific Photo Library** 55; **M. Ogilvie/Planet Earth Pictures** 151 top left; **John E. Paling/Oxford Scientific Films** 71 right; **D. Parer and E. Parer-Cook/Ardea London Ltd** 185; **Peter Parks/Oxford Scientific Films** 51 bottom left, 57, 63; **Michael Pits/Survival Anglia** 215 bottom; **K. Puttock/Planet Earth Pictures** 87; **Dr Morley Read/Science Photo Library** 45; **John Reader/Science Photo Library** 221, 222, 224, 226; **Alan Root/Survival Anglia** 81; **Royal Observatory/Science Photo Library** 9; **Sebastiao Salgado/Magnum Photos Ltd** 233; **Peter Scoones/Planet Earth Pictures** 52 bottom right, 82 bottom; **Jonathan Scott/Planet Earth Pictures** 203 top and bottom; **Dr Paul Selden, University of Manchester** 92; **© John Sibbick** 17 top, and bottom left, 30-31, 31, 34, 35 middle and bottom right, 36 main picture, 39, 40, 44, 46-47 top, 48, 50, 56-57, 66, 67, 74, 76 top, 84-85, 88 top, 100, 100-101, 104, 105, 108 main picture (1990), 108 inset, 112 (1990), 114-115, 118 (1990), 120, 120-121, 123 top, 124-125, 126 top, 126 bottom (with Chartwell Illustrators), 127 (with Chartwell Illustrators), 128, 128-129, 130 top (with Chartwell Illustrators), 132 bottom (1990), 134, 135, 140, 143, 146, 146-147, 154 (1992), 157, 158-159, 160, 161 bottom, 164-165, 166, 167, 168-169, 170-171, 171 top, 172 top, 172-173, 179, 180, 180-181, 191 left, 194, 197 bottom, 200, 201 bottom, 202-203, 204, 207, 210-211, 216 top; **John Sibbick with Leighton Moses** 25 top and bottom, 37; **Dr Peter W. Skelton, The Open University** photograph by Richard Carlton 62 top, 194; **John Stamford/Science Photo Library** 8-9; **Sinclair Stammers/Scientific Photo Library** 61 bottom, 65, 82 top; **UPI/Bettman** 26; **Herwarth Voigtmann/Planet Earth Pictures** 53; **J. Waters/Planet Earth Pictures** 189 top right; **Wendy Webb** 88 bottom (after Edwards, 1986), 89 (L to R after: Eggert, 1974; Kidston and Lang, 1920; Taylor, 1988; Edwards, 1980); **Wardene Weisser/Ardea London Ltd** 217; **Norbert Wu/Planet Earth Pictures** 51 top right, 190, 191 right.

Author's Acknowledgments

I would like to thank Sarah Mahaffy for wanting me to write this book and for having the faith that I would complete it. Elaine Collins struggled valiantly with early editorial phases of the project, while Esther Jagger saw the editorial work and coordination of the book through to completion – with a little help from Pizza Express! Kit Johnson has once again created a beautifully-designed book, whose layout and setting will, I am sure, add much to the reader's enjoyment and understanding. John Sibbick has, as usual, been a pleasure to work with; it seems many years since I was a struggling student in London and he was a struggling artist, but I think that deep down we still feel the same about prehistoric animals – that they are fun! Denise Blagden and David Nicholls again managed to turn out their excellent line artwork in next to no time. And finally thanks to all the editorial and production staff at Boxtree for their help and support throughout this project.